The Poet as Mirror

The Poet as Mirror

Human Nature, God and Jesus
in Twentieth-Century Literature

Karl-Josef Kuschel

SCM PRESS

Translated with great pleasure by John Bowden
for Karl-Josef Kuschel,
to celebrate his fiftieth birthday,
from the German *Im Spiegel der Dichter.
Mensch, Gott und Jesus in der Literatur
des 20. Jahrhunderts,*
published 1997 by Patmos Verlag,
Düsseldorf.

0 334 02738 1

First published 1999 by
SCM Press
9–17 St Albans Place London N1 0NX

SCM Press is a division of
SCM-Canterbury Press Ltd

Typeset by Regent Typesetting, London
and printed in Great Britain by
Biddles Limited, Guildford and King's Lynn

Dedicated to the Theological Faculty of the University of Lund
in gratitude for the award of an honorary doctorate

Contents

Prologue

A time comes when one knows more precisely than before why one is doing what one is doing. A time comes when in the process of questioning and doubt convictions have formed which one does not give up as easily as before. A time comes when despite all seeking and further exploration, despite all questions and further questions, structures of thought have developed which one finds to be of greater firmness, more stable solidity. The test of experience has provided good reasons for them. When such a time comes, it is a good thing to give an account and present things in order. That is what I shall do here.

1. Ways of thought

Here I shall be talking about poets and other writers who have stirred my heart and mind since I began to think theologically. They are not the foundation of my faith, but they have often stimulated it. For me, experiences in life have often been reading experiences. Thought has come from specific images, theory from the senses. Moreover, in my career, time and again I have found that it was not so much sermons, catechisms and theological treatises as the poets, novelists and playwrights who disclosed to me a bit of truth in truthfulness. They disturbed my self-satisfaction, my contentment with the plausibility I had gained for the moment, my satisfaction with the answers that I had found. Poetic texts cast their spell on me with their beauty, compelled me with the rhythm of their language, enthused me with their imagery. At the same time they brought me recalcitrant memories of what had not been reconciled. They confirmed my determination always also to mistrust my own perceptions and to make my role as a Christian, a theologian and a citizen the subject of criticism. Through poetic texts I learned to see, and at the same time unlearned an over-hasty praise of creation and a zealous and obsequious trust in officials and institutions. I learned that particularly as a theologian one has to escape role-expectations if one is trying to maintain self-respect before oneself and one's Creator. Through poetic texts I learned that in the name of God one can and must resist full-blown assertiveness, be faithful to one's own thought – and also faithful to one's own doubts.

In this book, for the first time I am attempting a style of my own. I am trying to make an analysis orientated on problems and at the same time to relate a bit of biography. My own life story and the story of my experiences is an essential element in my way of doing theology. I do not want to bracket off my own experiences here in a pseudo-objectivistic way, yet I do want to remain orientated on problems of substance. I want to speak as objectively as possible without being excessively personal and without professional jargon. And I want to speak about the great themes of faith: the riddle of human nature; God, the abyss; the faces of Jesus.

Am I 'functionalizing' literature in so doing? Yes, and why not? I am doing so in the way in which all readers 'functionalize' a good text when they make it 'their' text, in other words when they discover that this text says to them the bit of truth in truthfulness which they need. But functionalizing does not mean either doing violence to or commandeering. Doing violence to texts means interpreting them contrary to their meaning, and commandeering them means misusing them for offers of meaning which lie outside them. Both would be the death of any creative, fruitful dealing with literature.

'Functionalizing' (if this ugly word has to be used) means simply conceding that some literary texts have become indispensable to me over what is now quite a long life and period of reading. They have become 'my' texts. My theological thought has often been sparked off by them; they have forced questions on me that I had not allowed to arise out of naivety or for the sake of convenience, or had suppressed; they expanded the horizons of my thought and sent me on unfamiliar ways. Or they simply overwhelmed me by the compelling power of their language. They got into my blood and my brain. I learned many of them by heart; in this way they became a part of my memory, a part of my spiritual home. Yes, I confess that the texts I want to talk about on the following pages are 'my' texts, because I do not want my theological thought to be below their level.[1]

If this enterprise is to be found a place in theoretical scholarship, then it must be ssen as being closer to aesthetic reception than to aesthetic production.[2] As is well known, as a first theory of literary criticism, the aesthetics of reception as this is understood by Hans Robert Jauss and Wolfgang Iser gives the reader or the interpreter an influence on the results of reception or interpretation. For this theory, the reader is a constitutive element in the interpretation of texts. This necessarily presupposes that a literary text will be understood in different ways by different readers, and will show variant meanings. That means that the reader gains some freedom. The literary text is not simply a self-contained composition, the meaning of which can be understood only rightly or wrongly, but an entity with many levels, in which the event of communication with the reader also plays an important role. Text and context stand in a reciprocal relationship, without the context being allowed to manipulate the meaning of the text arbitrarily or the text 'in itself' becoming the only criterion of truth. So there is no necessary contradiction between the autonomy and the function of a work of art, between truth 'in itself' and truth 'for me'.

The emphasis on the subjectivity of the 'for me' is also important because this book does not claim to present *the* picture of human nature, *the* picture of God or *the* picture of Jesus in twentieth-century literature, or even to speak for *the* Christian theology. It contains a quite deliberate selection and a perspective which has been consciously chosen. It has not been possible to discuss here all the literary texts which are personally important to me or all the themes of literature which are relevant to anthropology, theology and christology. For that, many poets from Benn to Bernhard, from Horvarth to Handke, would have had to be mentioned. So the selection of texts has been determined by my own experience: these are examples. By means of these texts and themes (there could be, and later must be, others) I want to demonstrate why this literature is indispensable to me personally for present-day talk of human nature, God and Jesus.[3]

2. Mephisto's cunning warning

My confrontation with the writers and poets over this question began at a very early stage, in 1967. It was my last year at school in my home town of Oberhausen in the Rühr. One day my German teacher, whom I greatly admired, began to go round the class with the usual question what we intended to study after our matriculation. His reaction to my answer, 'theology', penetrated so deeply into my soul that it is still vivid to me. After my answer, which was not unexpected for him, this man quite spontaneously quoted to the whole class (which embarrassed me a great deal) verses from Goethe's *Faust*. They were meant in a very friendly way:

> To tell the truth about this branch of learning,
> it's hard to keep from taking the wrong course,
> and there's a lot of latent poison in it,
> that hardly differs from the medicines it offers.[4]

As is well known, Goethe put these words into the mouth of his Mephistopheles – with a deeper intent. They come from a witty dialogue between the devil and a naïve pupil who does not know which faculty to join. So – naïve as I too was as a pupil – I was to heed the warning that theology is a 'branch of learning' which manifestly more than other branches can put people on the 'wrong course'. It is more dangerous than much that it is comparable. There is a 'poison' in it which is more dangerous than many others because at first one doesn't perceive it at all. So is theology an enterprise which seems tantamount to a means of healing the sick?

Only later did I understand that these four lines from Goethe anticipate in a nutshell the whole of the modern critique of religion. Feuerbach with his projection theory, Marx with his consolation theory and Freud with his illusion theory merely reinforce what is already suggested in nucleus here. So I was warned when I began to study theology, and to the present day this warning has stamped my way of doing theology.

Over the course of time I have become certain that theology in particular needs a potential intrinsically to mistrust itself. This intrinsic mistrust is to derive not from rational scepticism but from an awe of the incomprehensibility of God himself. For it is precisely here that the danger of any theology lies: in the production of superficial certainties, of over-hasty meaning and consolation. The enigmatic nature of God is covered over with so-called 'offers of meaning'. For fear of 'being made uncertain' many people are afraid of confronting themselves and others with the often disturbing truth of God which frequently runs contrary to what we call our own human 'meaning' . As if 'God' were the way of soothing our human question of meaning and not the disturbing truth about human beings which gives us clear sight. That is what probably Goethe had in view: theology functions all too quickly as 'medicine' without people having previously made a ruthless diagnosis of their illness or having been confronted with the truth of God. Talk of God is all too easily misused to suppress the abysses of our own existence, the contradictions of evolution and the absurdities of history. Theology is then confused with professional consolation, with the production of meaning for difficult times, with a soothing therapy for pains of the soul. In short, theology degenerates into becoming the tranquillizer for a middle-class society.

3. The protest of the 'outsider' against the priest

In my experience, no one has more movingly related how one can reject over-hasty certainties and consolations for the sake of one's own dignity and God's than the Frenchman Albert Camus, for example in his text *The Outsider*, which I encountered at an early stage of my study. From my first reading on I was deeply impressed by the fact that the 'hero' of this narrative, Meursault, who is condemned to death after a trial of which he cannot make sense, rejects any comfort in the death cell from the representatives of religion. Hardly any other scene in literature has remained so vivid to me: when the priest visits the prisoner in his cell to talk with him about his imminent death, his sins and God's righteousness, Meursault asks to be excused any religious consolation and attacks the priest for his innocent assurance and certainty of faith:

> I'd taken him by the neckband of his cassock, and, in a sort of ecstasy of joy and rage, I poured out on him all the thoughts that had been simmering in my brain. He seemed so cocksure, you see. And yet none of his certainties was worth one strand of a woman's hair. Living as he did, like a corpse, he couldn't even be sure of being alive. It might look as if my hands were empty. Actually, I was sure of myself, sure about everything, far surer than he; sure of my present life and of the death that was coming. That, no doubt, was all I had; but at least that certainty was something I could get my teeth into – just as it had got its teeth into me . . . Nothing, nothing had the least importance, and I knew quite well why. He, too, knew why. From the dark horizon of my future a sort of slow, persistent breeze had been blowing towards me, all my life long, from the years that were to come. And on its way that breeze had levelled out all the ideas that people tried to foist on me in the equally unreal years I then was living through.[5]

Since I had grown up religiously naïve, this scene was at first a tremendous provocation to me. Someone rejects the comfort of religion? What could lie behind that? An atheist's lack of suspicion? A blasphemer's arrogance? The depression of someone in despair? Only slowly did I come to understand that these categories critical of atheism, which had been instilled in me, failed in the face of this text. For here a person is not refusing religious comfort out of despair, a lack of suspicion or arrogance, but out of a sense of his own dignity, his own pride. Here someone is demonstrating self-confidence – precisely when faced with absurdity. This is not complained about, but quite soberly accepted. Indeed, in this text the scheme that was familiar to me is turned completely around: it is the believing priest who, in the eyes of the man condemned to death, exists 'like a dead man'. And it is the unbeliever who, in the face of his death, lives almost with the certainty of the believer. From the 'depths of the future' there comes a 'dark breath' which makes everything a matter of indifference! And 'future' here does not mean transcendence, but death. Without really wanting to, each time I read this story I found myself on the side of the 'outsider' against the priest. Why?

I gradually came to understand that this text was right in rejecting a belief which all too easily sets out with a hope in a transcendent meaning. I understood above all that the outsider was the more truthful person, someone who had quite soberly come to terms with the brutality and chaos in life. This person had inexorably conceded that in principle people must now live without comfort; indeed it is part of their dignity and their pride, far from any hybris, to refuse the comfort of religion, which is always only consolation. It is more truthful, but harsher and more cruel, finally to bury religious hopes as self-deception.

And yet, despite all the sympathy that I feel for this Meursault, who is so bold as an outsider to the world, in the end I did not understand him. During his whole absurd life had a dark breath risen up to him from the depths of his future? However beautifully poetic this image is, it cannot settle my questions about this life. I have often asked myself why Meursault never goes on the offensive and says why his life is absurd. Why, in the face of a death sentence the reason for which he cannot see and which merely reinforces the absurdity of his existence, doesn't he rebel against this death? Why can he sit so quietly in his cell, aggressive only towards his religious comforter? Why not the same aggressiveness towards the absurdity of his own life? Why no 'revolt' of the kind that Camus could personally inscribe on the banner of his philosophical programme? So why does Meursault not put the order of this world in question? Why this leaden indifference at the end?

I told myself: if you speak of God, you will never display a naïve certainty like Camus' priest. But for other reasons than those of Camus' hero. You will not do so for *God's* sake. For I became aware that belief in God means being always and unavoidably subject to tribulation. Nothing is a matter of indifference any more. 'God' – that is the *question* of the order of this world and the meaning of this life. It is an open question, sometimes a burning wound. After all, it is precisely the experiences of absurdities in one's own life and in the history of this world that provoke the primal question what this life and this history are all about: who bears ultimate responsibility for their meaning and order? Later I found in the Jewish writer Elie Wiesel, who will be discussed at length later in this book, a similar basic notion: 'It is true that the tragedy of the believer is greater than that of the unbeliever. It is no problem not to believe; that's that. But to believe and nevertheless to have questions to which there are no answers, that is a problem.'[6]

So particularly someone who is as sober and free of illusion as Camus' Meursault can never simply be content with the world, 'absurd' as it often seems. Such a person doubts. And those who doubt, believe. *Dubito ergo credo, credo ergo dubito.* I understood that particularly doubt in creation involves faith, and faith in God entails doubt. Doubt and faith are not enemies, but brothers. They come from the same origin, because the world, grotesque as it is, raise questions which no religion, no philosophical theory and no political system have yet solved. Therefore even a philosophy of absurdity in the style of Camus can be a consolation, no longer to rebel against the order of the world but to accept it as 'absurd'. Even the philosophy of absurdity can be a false certainty, 'medicine' for depression. However, for me, belief in God means not having finished with the fact of the 'world' and the facts *in* this world. There is more to the world than meets the eye.

4. Being able to write like Flaubert

I concede that as a theologian I need the language of the poets as much as my daily bread. One does not need to read the most recent demographic surveys to know how remote traditional religious language has become from the reality of life. The departure from a faith conceived of in dogmatic terms is essentially also the expression of a crisis in the traditional language of the church and religion. Such language has often survived, but its metaphors have become hollow. Images often derive from worlds of language that have been submerged, and any naïve transmission of them produces precisely what it tries to prevent: the decay of religious language. Linguistic critics have long since noticed that the 'production'

of religious language has not kept up with the great processes of upheaval
in society and culture, say from a feudal to a democratic-pluralist society;
from an agricultural, small-town society to an industrial society with its
big cities; from a society with a monolithic structure to a multicultural
and multireligous society. In religious language, a particular order of the
church and society has become frozen, and if it is transferred to changed
social conditions, it must often seem comical or ridiculous.

It is in fact a remarkable phenomenon that feudal society was tremendously productive in forming language. Talk of God as king, ruler,
almighty father, gracious judge, was the expression of a relationship
between God and human beings dominated by the scheme of above–
below, independent–dependent, command–obedience. By contrast, the
democratic pluralist society has not yet been able to articulate its
understanding of the world in religious terms in such a way as to have
established itself at the level of the religious consciousness. Democratic
titles are hardly viable in religion: God as president, chairman, general
secretary, sounds ludicrous. But we have got used to talk of Jesus as
brother. That is an achievement of the nineteenth century and arose in
middle-class circles. How frozen everything is, is shown by the dispute
over the feminist critique of language. Many people still find calling God
'mother' unimaginable.

These are only spotlights which are meant to illuminate how the crisis
of religious language cannot be blamed on the religious consumers, but is
intrinsic to the historical process of the formation of religious language.
Any self-critical theology is aware of this dilemma today. It consists in the
fact that theology has constantly to be communicated, yet can only fail in
the process: it cannot be loyal to the normative documents which point to
a particular picture of the world and linguistic profile, while confronting
new worlds of experience into which the old language has to be translated.
Here theology has often enough fallen victim to linguistic sclerosis.

No one has seen that more acutely or described it more self-critically
than the Catholic theologian Fridolin Stier, whom many people discovered only after his death in 1981 through his two volumes of 'Notes,
Meditations and Reflections'.[7] I am among their number. In these books
I found a style of theological thought which had arisen from listening
to the language of the poets. Here a theologian – without diluting the
content of his message in any way – had consistently listened to the poets
and learned from their critique of language and sensitivity to it. So I find
Stier's books models of their kind. Here is an entry dated 13 November
1968 from Stier's 'Perhaps Somewhere It's Day':

After reading theological treatises: torture! This language is bombastic, and really suffers from swellings. It needs the scalpel of the linguistic surgeon or radiation, at least a slimming pill or a diuretic . . .
pathology;
language which suffers from swollen feet, lipomas,
oedemas, watery swellings of the linguistic cells,
from constipation, labouring over the expression, arthrosis, stiff, unbending movement of thought . . .

In somatic medicine there is the knife and medication, but in linguistic medicine, which needs them . . .? To compel the spirit of clarity to expression, to sharpen the sense of linguistic form, not to allow professional terminology to degenerate into esoteric double Dutch . . .

Theologians need to write like Flaubert, who spent whole days looking for the one appropriate word. When Guy de Maupassant showed him his first novels, Flaubert gave them back teeming with red marks and deletions.[8]

This anecdote about Gustave Flaubert as a merciless linguistic surgeon can be supplemented with another. For in fact linguistic criticism is at the service of the appropriate word. So the language of theologians, too, must be free of any superfluous chatter, verbosity and bathos, and aim at precision. The morality of doing theology should lie precisely here: in being responsible for every word which comes from one's mouth or gets put down on paper. Every act of writing should be a moral act. And this morality which is intrinsic to writing as responsibility to the word is expressed very vividly in another anecdote which the poet Gottfried Benn told of the French politician Clémenceau in his essay 'Ageing as a Problem of Artists':

Recently I read the following story about Clémenceau. He had engaged a new private secretary and in the first few days was instructing him in his tasks. Some letters, said Clémenceau, you will have to write by yourself. Listen: 'A sentence consists of a noun and a verb: if you want to use an adjective, ask me first.'[9]

Fridolin Stier's theology changed as a result of this linguistic sensitivity. It took on its distinctive profile by a constant re-examination of what in this world is taken for granted, checking it by ever new questions. What marks out Stier's style of theological thought is the basic attitude of amazement about what has previously been affirmed so uncritically, a

refusal to be content with stereotyped formulae, a mistrust of falling
in love with plausibility once it has been achieved. Even what is most
familiar to him as a theologian becomes alien in the course of his notes;
his theological prose is a prose which interrupts itself and which has
built-in hesitations.

> Theology is said to be 'talking of God'. What does 'talking of' mean?
> If we talk 'of' something – the record we have just heard, the wedding
> in a neighbour's house to which we've been, the next elections in which
> we shall take part, we speak of love, we speak of death – this some-
> thing is always a given for those who speak – something that is there,
> that has happened, been seen, experienced, always something real. But
> what are we talking of when we say that we are talking of God?[10]

Retreats from a triumphalistic theology, a theology that covers everything, measures everything, discusses everything – that is the procedure
of Stier's self-questioning. Farewell to a theology of surveying – that is
the underlying tenor of all these notes and reflections. Farewell to a loud,
self-confident and unassailed display of faith: that is what this theologian
fights for page after page. And instead of this, the withdrawal of talk of
God into the questioning, the modesty and humility of someone who
does not have his God but is on the way to him. Instead of this, there is
programmatically a 'theology in the forecourt', which deliberately puts
itself in the great tradition of 'negative theology'.[11]

> Theology in the forecourt – that is my theology; that is what I would
> call it if there were a name for it. Here, in the forecourt, to be precise,
> in the forecourt of the pagans, I have pitched my tent for departure. A
> great hearsay brings me news of the sanctuary through the air, I hear
> psalms ringing out in the distance; it is night . . . The forecourt is large;
> anyone who wants to get into the sanctuary must go through here . . .[12]

Here Stier consciously makes use of literary forms in order to articulate
his theology. He makes use of a complicated mixed form of diary, a
collection of aphorisms, a poetic sketchbook, a breviary of meditations
and a journal of work. The variety and openness of the forms reflects
open, experimental thought. Theology becomes theo-poetry in which the
theology goes over into poetry and the poetry is tied back to the theology.
In this way the reader is drawn into an interplay which brings clarity of
vision.

The Protestant theologian Dorothee Sölle has rightly said that the word 'poetry' is more appropriate for the theological reception of texts than the word 'literature'. The term 'literature' can in fact embrace the whole span from advertisement text to hermetic poetry, and in this way becomes blurred. Therefore the word 'poetry' does more justice to the theological interest in literature, since it contains the word *poiein*, which as we know means create, make, renew. And theological interest in texts is focussed on that alone: on appropriate shape, vivid composition, complete form. To quote Dorothee Sölle:

> Too much falls under literature which has not the least to do with *poiein*, create, make, renew. Franz Kafka says, 'A book must be like an axe for splitting the ice of the soul'; this image contains the criterion for poetry with which we can distinguish Dante from the illustrated magazine. The language which we mostly use is unsuitable for splitting the ice in us. We do not reach one another, the words do not touch us in the depths, the soul becomes rigid. We are looking for a language which splits this ever thicker ice of the soul.[13]

5. Transcendence: the encounter with the great work of art

This statement about the function of language and thus of great poetry already indicates that the texts of the poets are more than providers of catchwords for the spirit of a particular time, more than thematic illustrations aimed at homiletics, catechesis and religious education. Any theologian who investigates literature only for its content will get it wrong. And anyone who gets literature wrong has not understood anything about it and has succumbed to the theological disease of 'contentism'. The literary work no longer makes an impact with its own power of form and beauty in the sense intended by Franz Kafka, but degenerates into a reservoir of themes.

But literature can break up given realities only because it depicts a reality of its own – in concentrated form. Like any work of art, great poetry is a reality of its own kind, an intermediate world between the empirical world (which is interpreted with the help of the sciences) and the metaphysical-religious world (on which philosophy and theology reflect). In other words, any great work of art is a world in itself, mysterious in the making, inexhaustible in significance, incalculable in effect. In this way the great work of art becomes an analogy to that reality which theologians denote with the unusable word 'God' . . .

George Steiner in his book *Real Presences* (1989) deserves credit for having reintroduced this basic notion into discussion of literary criticism.[14] This book has sparked off a controversy[15] because in it, at the highest philosophical level, Steiner has confronted his own discipline with the thesis:

> All good art and literature begin in immanence. But they do not stop there. Which is to say, very plainly, that it is the enterprise and privilege of the aesthetic to quicken into lit presence the continuum between temporality and eternity, between matter and spirit, between man and 'the other'. It is in this common and exact sense that *poiesis* opens on to, is underwritten by, the religious and the metaphysical. The questions: 'What is poetry, music, art?', 'How can they not be?', 'How do they act upon us and how do we interpret their action?', are, ultimately, theological questions.[16]

This thesis is also a provocation for Christian theology, which especially in its ecclesiastical and orthodox manifestations always finds it difficult to give the aesthetic an appropriate theological place. The Protestant theologian Karl Barth is an example. In his early 'dialectical phase' between around 1919 and 1933, Barth saw the task of theology – following Kierkegaard's critique of aesthetics – above all as a criticism of culture from the perspective of the revelation of God. Over against the aestheticism and cultural optimism of nineteenth-century liberal theology (Schleiermacher, Ritschl and von Harnack), which all too harmoniously identified Christianity and culture, human aesthetic experience and the revelation of God, Barth emphasized the radical difference between revelation and culture, the word of God and the products of human art. If culture were understood – as Barth put it in 1926 in a programmatic article on 'The Church and Culture' – as the idea of the final goal and embodiment of the norms by which human action should be guided, then the church 'could only speak negatively and polemically on the significance of culture'. Both entities would then 'exist not only on different levels, but on mutually exclusive levels, as truth and error'.[17]

Barth was convinced that a work of art as such can never embody the quality of revelation, can never be a 'real presence' of the divine. For human beings there is revelation only in Jesus Christ, who in turn is accessible to them only through the foundation document of revelation, holy scripture. No work of human culture can assume this function. On the contrary, for Barth, 'culture' (and in particular including works of literature) simply shows the split in human beings. For since human beings are 'confronted only with themselves before God', they stand before the rift which goes through their existence, and before the *question* of a synthesis.

> Whatever deserves the name culture has in some fashion originated
> from this rift and this problem. Culture implies lack and consciousness
> of lack. It means seeking through men and failing to find the unity of
> God. Inexorably the mirror of our dual existence which the Word
> of God holds before us shows both the urgency and the frightfulness
> of the problem of culture.[18]

For Barth in this phase of his life there was no room for a 'theology of culture', for a theological quality of aesthetic experience – in contrast to his great contemporaries Rudolf Bultmann and Paul Tillich on the Protestant side or Hans Urs von Balthasar and Romano Guardini on the Catholic side.[19]

Certainly Barth did not stop at this radical dissociation of culture and revelation. Thus after a programmatic shift in his theology (from 'dialectic' to 'analogy') he was ready to accord art at least the function of parable. His prime example here was the music of Wolfgang Amadeus Mozart – by no means just the religious programme music (for example the masses and the *Requiem*), but all Mozart's music. The style and character of all Mozart's compositions were theologically relevant for Barth. For he thought that he had recognized that all Mozart's music comes from a 'height' where 'everything is known and from where the right and left hand of existence, happiness and pain, good and evil, life and death, have all been perceived in their reality as well as in their limitation'. Mozart, he said, turned into music 'real life in its two-sidedness, but in spite of this against the background of God's good creation and therefore always with a right turn, never with a left turn'.[20] In this, Mozart's music is 'beautiful, comforting, moving'. [21] Indeed, as a 'Protestant Christian and theologian' Barth could see Mozart's music as something like a 'parable' of the kingdom of heaven.[22]

On the basis of this function of art as parable, the later Karl Barth could now also deal with literature in quite a different way, as is shown by his moving correspondence with the writer Carl Zuckmayer from the last two years of his life, between 1966 and 1968, 'Late Friendship'. Here too the point of comparison was similar to that with Mozart. Barth saw the special feature of Zuckmayer's stories as being 'the never-failing mercy in which human darkness, perversity and wretchedness is seen by the narrator'.[23] Mephistopheles is 'absent'.[24] With Zuckmayer, the 'grace of God which surrounds everything and everyone gently but imperceptibly' governs and characterizes even the 'most trivial, most bizarre, indeed the craziest scenes and situations'.[25] And after this insight Barth makes the remarkable comment:

And among the best is that you yourself are evidently hardly aware how much in your, as one says, purely 'secular' writing you have in fact exercised and still exercise a priestly ministry: to an extent which can be said of only a few professional priests, preachers, theologians and so on of the Catholic or Protestant confessions.[26]

So is the writer in fact a priest in his own way because in the end he too puts the human in the perspective of mercy? Barth must have felt this concession to be so bold that in the next letter he immediately protects his remarks against misunderstandings:

Now I wrote to you last time that I understand your literary activity to be one in *priestly* service. And you were somewhat surprised by this understanding, but clearly agreed with it. God in the bark of every tree – all right, I will also go along with that. But God in the bark of every tree is God the Creator (I have attempted to understand and praise him as such in no less than four part-volumes of my *Dogmatics,* but I shall not burden either your bookshelves or you yourself with them). But the *priestly* ministry is about God the *reconciler* of the creation which has fallen away from him, indeed which fights against him. He is certainly one and the same, but it is now the God who is true, acts and saves in Jesus Christ alone. Thus *worship* is due to him and to him alone as such: in his living word attested by Holy Scripture, or for you as a Catholic especially in his presence in the eucharistic sacrifice – but God in the bark of a tree only inclusively, indirectly, in a mediated form. You remark that the theologian in me has shown his teeth in this excursus. He had to do that for the sake of honesty and asks the writer for forgiveness, but also for understanding and perhaps for his reflections.[27]

We can sense that here a theologian is afraid of his own courage to give too much theological weight to the aesthetic possibilities of human beings. The mistrust remains. God's presence in the word of Holy Scripture or in the 'eucharistic' sacrifice is theologically no problem. But in the 'bark of a tree' or in a work of art – 'only inclusively, indirectly, in a mediated form'!

Perhaps only now can we see how provocative George Steiner's book is. For Steiner does not think of limiting God's presence only to 'Holy Scripture' or even to the 'eucharistic sacrifice', or claiming it only indirectly in a work of art. For him, 'God's presence' in any great, serious work of art is evidently a direct one. And this 'presence' does not depend on the tendency of this work of art or the conception of its content, but solely on its aesthetic quality. Steiner puts all the emphasis here: human beings can experience transcendence in the encounter with a great work of art. And in order to understand that, we must have understood how Steiner defines a work of art and what value art has in the overall context of other spheres of reality.

A first step is that, contrary to the current tendency to ignore the religious dimension in great documents of the history of art, Steiner recalls that, say, literature from Homer and the *Oresteia* to the novels of Dostoievsky and Kafka is inconceivable without 'a transcendental dimension'.[28] This dimension 'informs art from the caves at Lascaux to Rembrandt and to Kandinsky'.[29] Statistically, according to Steiner, 'Western painting, sculpture and much of what is incarnate in architecture have, until the Enlightenment, been religious and, more specifically, Scriptural, both in motivation and representational content'. Tragedy in particular 'is god-haunted from Aeschylus to Claudel': 'It posits man unhoused at those crossroads where the mystery of his condition is made naked to the ambiguous intercessions of menace and grace.'[30] The same is true of the model novel. Here too 'the great exemplars continue to ask, aloud or beneath their breath (as in Proust), the one question ineradicable in man: Is there or is there not God? Is there or is there not meaning to being?'[31]

But in recalling this, Steiner wants to do more than to do justice to history. As a second step he wants to go beyond the fact that the 'God-hauntedness' of great artists, the primal religious questions of great art, are rooted in the 'mystery' of human existence: in an existence of pain and death. As long as human beings lived dispassionately and reconciled with themselves and God in a state of paradise, there was 'presumably no need of books or of art'.[32] Things changed only with the awareness of death. A high seriousness of questioning arises, and this seriousness is 'finally, religious':

> The *Oresteia*, *King Lear*, Dostoievsky's *The Devils* no less than the art of Giotto or the Passions of Bach, inquire into, dramatize the relations of man and woman to the existence of the gods or God . . . After the Book of Job and Euripides' *Bacchae*, there had to be, if man was to bear his being, the means of dialogue with God which are spelt out in our poetics, music, art.[33]

But Steiner uses this recollection of religious statements in modern art or the religious self-understanding of great modern artists only to reinforce a figure of argument which proves to be much more fundamental. The focal point of Steiner's thrust – a third stage – is reached where he claims that all great art has the character of transcendence.

To explain this, Steiner makes it clear that the work of art has a reality entirely of its own, to which the rules of scientific verification and falsification do not apply. For Steiner, the whole understanding of art depends on the fact that art escapes all academic theories of interpretation which seek to understand it. A great work of art is inexhaustible in its meanings and thus ultimately incomprehensible. A scientific theory must satisfy the criteria of verifiability or falsifiability and the laws of predictable application. But that does not apply to the products of art. Aristotle's *Poetics of Tragedy* or Sophocles' *Oedipus Rex* are not falsified by Shakespeare's *Hamlet* or Büchner's *Woyzeck*. No poetological theory can predict the composition of Kafka's parables, of Chopin's Nocturnes or of Joyce's *Finnegan's Wake*. No, according to Steiner, in aesthetic discourse no analysis, no doctrine, no programme of an interpretative critical nature is superseded or obliterated by any later construction – in complete contrast to the natural sciences. The Copernican theory of the cosmos finally falsified the Ptolemaic theory. In chemistry Lavoisier's theory of phlogiston has proved untenable. But is what Aristotle had to say about mimesis and pathos superseded by Lessing or Bergson? Is Rembrandt's painting obliterated by Kandinsky?

It follows from this that in the sphere of art other laws apply, the laws of freedom, of non-determinability and complementarity. 'Art' represents a reality which ultimately stems from freedom, only exists in freedom and requires free encounter and appropriation. Therefore, for Steiner, the artists themselves are the best interpreters of art, because they alone have experienced what it means to sustain freedom, to shape reality and thus make the creative 'leap from nothingness' to form. Art is the sphere where there are no presuppositions, where nothing can be grounded or comprehended, and in this way can also avoid all exploitation by ideology and commerce.

That means that the encounter of men and women with a great work of art must have a quite distinctive character. What really happens when a person becomes free from the 'dominance of the secondary and the parasitic',[34] and is directly exposed to the experience of a great work of art? This is what Steiner seeks to illuminate. He makes this clearest by means of music. For the effect of music in particular is not 'rationally explicable'. What 'shows', 'manifests' itself to the hearer in music cannot be fully grasped by the means of reason or brought under scientific laws. Therefore music can also be the best model for what Steiner attempts to define by 'real presence'. Music 'brings to our daily lives an immediate encounter with a logic of sense other than that or reason'.[35] 'Music has celebrated the mystery of intuitions of transcendence'[36] from the songs of Orpheus to Beethoven's *Missa Solemnis*, from Schubert's late piano sonatas to Schoenberg's *Moses and Aron* and Messiaen's *Quatuor pour la fin du temps*. No, according to Steiner, music is 'plainly uncircumscribed by the world as the latter is an object of scientific determination and practical harnessing'.[37] What men and women experience in the encounter with a musical work of art also far exceeds 'any specific religious motive or occasion'. Therefore music continues to be 'the unwritten theology of those who lack or reject any formal creed. Or to put it reciprocally: for any human beings, religion has been the music which they believe in. In the ecstasies of Pop and of Rock, the overlap is strident.'[38]

These, then, are the decisive key words: no great work of art can be embraced by any scientific theory about its origin, significance and effect; it is a reality in itself, incommensurable, inexpressible, incomprehensible. Thus the encounter with the work of art is an encounter with a distinctive reality in which men and women become not manufacturers of products, but recipients: hearing, seeing, reading. In the act of dedication art becomes the 'making formal of epiphany';[39] 'there is a "shining through" which human beings with their scientific technological or purposive reason cannot grasp. Poetry, art and music therefore relate men and women 'most directly to that in being which is not ours'.[40]

6. Easter Saturday existences

These theses of Steiner's need careful theological criticism. Thus investigation of the concept of transcendence is indispensable. What do men and women really experience in encounter with a work of art? God himself, as he reveals himself through a work of art? Or do men and women experience in an encounter with a great work of art above all their own capacity to transcend themselves in the way understood by Gottfried Benn (giving form to the banal) or Ernst Bloch (surpassing oneself and going beyond one's limits). And is it not each time the recipient who has the experience of transcendence in a great work of art because he or she already presupposes transcendence *a priori* – according to the formula

'You get out what you put in?' But Steiner claims a mechanism of 'open-ing oneself' to the work of art which does not exist in reality. A work of art does not open itself up automatically, but only to a specific recipient who already brings along specific presuppositions. The work of art 'opens' itself only when those who receive it open themselves and interpret what they perceive with their senses as the revelation of 'God' or a pointer to 'transcendence'. There is too little reflection in Steiner on this role of the different recipients of art.

Granted, Steiner is extremely convincing wherever he keeps to a phenomenology of encounter between the individual and the work of art, in other words where he sketches out a differentiated hermeneutic of encounter. Indeed, Steiner is nowhere more impressive than where he gives a specific account of the experience of the homeless instability and alienation of our human condition; where he speaks of the impossibility for human beings to be reconciled with death; where he vehemently objects to locating literature and art 'beyond good and evil', tearing apart aesthetics and ethics. But talk of God? Why should the incursion of 'the other', the presence of 'the other' in the work of art, be an experience of God? Not every experience of mystery as a result of a work of art is itself an experience of God. At any rate there is no compulsion towards that, not even an encounter with a work of art the content of which possibly had precisely the opposite intention.

All these questions show that it is erroneous to call all serious art an *opus metaphysicum* and thus completely to leave aside the self-understanding of the artist or what the content of the work of art actually conveys. For in that case Steiner would have to say that all the art which is anti-metaphysical in content, from Brecht's *Hauspostille* through the poems of Gottfried Benn and the prose of Wolfgang Hildes-heimer to the dramas of Peter Weiss and the poetry of Günter Kunert is either not to be taken seriously or is to be labelled 'metaphysical'. In the latter case, this would extend the concept of metaphysics so that it became random, and nurture the suspicion that here all art (including non-metaphysical or anti-metaphysical art) was being commandeered for metaphysics. This would damage rather than help the dialogue between literature and theology.

On the other hand, theologians have to be told that there is no going back to a disqualification or ignoring of the aesthetic on the basis of a theology of revelation, since even its greatest representative (Karl Barth) conceded that art could function as a parable of the reality of God; indeed, he was ready to accord literature even a 'priestly office'. Already for theologians like Paul Tillich and Romano Guardini, a work of art was by no means of religious significance only if it used religious material or illustrated a religious message. Both had recognized that the dimension of the religious could shine through the style and form of a work of art. Already in the 1920s Paul Tillich had written:

> It is in fact possible to see the direct revelation of an absolute reality in relative things in a still life by Cézanne, an animal picture by Marc, a landscape by Schmidt-Rottluff, an erotic picture by Nolde. The content of the world, experienced in the religious ecstasy of the artist, shines through things: they have become 'holy' objects.[41]

And Romano Guardini saw the 'nature of the work of art' among other things in its projection of what was not yet there. Certainly art cannot say 'how it is to be; nevertheless it gives a mysteriously comforting guarantee that it will come. It opens up as it were behind every work of art. Something arises. One does not know either what it is or where, but deep down one feels the promise.'[42] Thus, like Steiner, both theologians affirm that art has a partial character of revelation or foreshadowing.

Therefore in theological terms the great work of art is to be defined as an illumination of the mystery of human nature, as an illumination of the mystery of the truth about human beings. In this truth, in fact something of the truth which God is in fullness can shine out 'as a foretaste'. Thus art is a special, incomparable human work in which as in no other human work 'more' than the human being can shine out, deeper truths than human truths can break forth, greater things can be intimated than human beings are in a position to comprehend. Thus the work is no more, but also no less, than the place of the true-seeming, the partial truth of which needs to be transcended, i.e. to be confirmed, criticized and surpassed, by the perfect truth which is the incomprehensible God himself.

Thus as a human work, a work of art remains in suspension in a way which cannot be done away with.[43] It can make a claim to show forth truth, i.e. bring it to light. But since – theologically speaking – this truth in the work of art is only partial and the whole truth is guaranteed only by God, the work of art can only be the place of the seeming-true, and thus contains only the possibility of truth, which like all human projects can be subject to self-deception. For the ultimate verification of human products as signals of the truth lies with God himself. In this sense, like all human works, the work of art remains in suspension between the light of truth and the delusion of truth.[44]

Works of art as places of the seeming true are symbolic illuminations of the mystery of human nature – that is my theological definition. For its part, Christian faith illuminates the human condition, the human mystery, in the light of the word of God, attested in holy scripture. Both the artist and the theologian meet in the struggle for an ultimate depth and truth of human nature, the theologian with an appeal to the content of the foundation document of revelation, the artist with a reference to the form of his work of art. George Steiner has coined the term 'Easter Saturday existence' for this basic situation of great art. I would also like to adopt it for the theologian, who in my understanding is similarly not someone who has arrived but a seeker, a doubter before God, sometimes one who despairs with God. This is what Steiner says:

There is one particular day in Western history about which nether historical record or myth nor scripture make report. It is a Saturday and it has become the longest of days. We know of that Good Friday which Christianity holds to have been that of the Cross. But the non-Christian, the atheist, knows of it as well. This is to say that he knows of the injustice, of the interminable suffering, of the waste, of the brute enigma of ending, which so largely make up not only the historical dimension of the human condition, but the everyday fabric of our personal lives. We know, ineluctably, of the pain, of the failure of love, of the solitude which are our history and private fate. We know also about Sunday. To the Christian, that day signifies an intimation, both assured and precarious, both evident and beyond comprehension, of resurrection, of a justice and a love that have conquered death.

If we are non-Christians or non-believers we know of that Sunday in precisely analogous terms. We conceive of it as the day of liberation from inhumanity and servitude. We look to resolutions, be they therapeutic or political, be they social or messianic. The lineaments of that Sunday carry the name of hope.[45]

Thus all great art and all great theology arises from this tension: the knowledge of pain and death and at the same time of the hope of new life, liberation from inhumanity and alienation. Everything comes about in this sphere of the 'between' – between Good Friday and Easter Day. Everything arises in the tension between the recollections of cruelty which cannot be suppressed and the hope of a fulfilment which can only be guessed at.

7. What is inter-cultural theology?

Sensitivity to language and awareness of the transcendental character of the great work of art make up the cultural competence of theology. Cultural competence is the expression of a truly intercultural theology. By contrast, in contemporary theology interculturality is understood in one-sidedly ethnic terms. The term, which originally derives from more recent theology of mission (and is still imprisoned within these limits), denotes the rooting of the universal Christian message in the different cultures of the continents of this earth. The inculturation of Christianity is understood as a process of the acceptance and transformation of the various cultures of peoples and nations which cannot be concluded in history – as a counter-concept to the way in which, over the centuries, missions have made Christianity with an exclusively Western stamp a foreign body within non-Western cultures. The accommodation, indigenization and contextualization of the gospel are parallel concepts. This kind of inculturation is deliberately focussed on the development of new Christianities which differ from Western culture. An authentically African, Asian, Latin American Christianity is called for in which the Christian message is expressed and lived out anew in the language of the particular cultures. This kind of inculturation is indispensable, and the intercultural, contextual theology which has meanwhile come into being in Asia, Latin America and Africa is of the utmost significance for the capacity of Christianity to survive spiritually in the third millennium.[46]

However, it is time to overcome the one-sidedness of this ethnic concept of culture and emphasize that dimension of the cultural which has always been bound up with the concept of culture: the aesthetic, artistic dimension. Here I am aware that I am taking up a concept of culture which was used by the great cultural analyst, Wolf Lepenies, in his book *The Three Cultures* (1985). In it he attempted to locate his discipline, sociology, as a third culture between the culture of literature and the culture of science. The interculturality of theology therefore also shows itself by its aesthetic competence. And aesthetic competence is the capacity for a critical perception of the world of the arts and a discussion of the cultural and aesthetic phenomena of a largely post-Christian secular environment. Indeed it is quite clear that there has been no stopping the advance of the aestheticizing of the world in which we live, above all those of us who live in the industrialized countries. Not only do the media of pictures and print prepare reality for millions of people in an aesthetic way, but in the face of this presentation the observers also necessarily develop an aesthetic sense of life. Products of the history of art, old and new, are providing meaning and orientation for an increasing number of people. Whereas the museums attract an international public of millions – especially for special exhibitions – institutions like the churches, which used to provide orientation, are increasingly losing significance. Those who diagnose culture say with some justification that our culture is becoming a museum, and in so doing they confirm a long-cherished expectation: in a post-Christian culture, for millions of people the museums have replaced the churches; the artists the priests; the objects the altars. Theatre and film premieres are often regarded as the only events that can transcend a banal everyday reality.

Moreover, sociologists of culture like Gerhard Schulze describe our present reality as an 'experience society' and speak of an 'aestheticizing of everyday life' that has been taking place in Germany since the end of the Second World War. What they mean is that whereas in the post-war period up to 1968, in many German families the sole concern was for survival, and a modest provision of offers of experience (the cinema, the theatre concerts, radio) was experienced against the background of complete deprivation, today millions of people have an experience which is no longer just survival. After modest beginnings in the post-war period, the 1960s produced a first 'enormous thrust towards aestheticizing'. Equipped with ever greater potential in the quest for experience (time, money, mobility, equipment), consumers discovered that the whole of everyday life could be treated aesthetically. In other words, the public won for themselves unlimited listening to music, travelling, buying clothes, eating and drinking, sex, dancing, going out at night. And in the 1980s this wealth of experience increased even more rapidly. German society became a complete 'experience society', in which a market of experience did not satisfy real need but a dependence which people had created for themselves. According to Schulze, in the 1980s the situation was:

> The experience market has developed into a dominant sphere of everyday life. It brings together a tremendous capacity for production, a potential for investigation, political energy, intellectual activity and time for living. For a long time the public and those who offer experience have been played off against one another. Producers routinely manipulate the unwritten rules for marketing experience, increasingly resorting to techniques of suggestion. The experience market is still a growth industry. The growth path of intensification (increased depth

of experience, refinement, heightening of quality) has taken the place of the growth path of expansion which was previously dominant (expansion of the spectrum of production, expansion of the sales of particular kinds of products, expansion of turnover).[47]

This process of an increase in the aestheticizing of the world in which we live is matched by a process of the decrease of aesthetic competence in the sphere of the church and theology. Excessively preoccupied with the functionalizing of art for church purposes; still largely imprisoned in a traditional normative concept of beauty; still allergic to new, often provocative styles in pictorial art, film and contemporary literature, churchgoing Christians are losing contact with their living cultural environment. The cultural programmes offered by church academies do not make much difference here, since they reach only a fragment of the church clientele. Such well-meant programmes often work against the interests of their committed practitioners, like the famous fig leaf, which shows up the nakedness all the more unsparingly.

The most visible sign of this cultural-aesthetic loss of competence is the fact that there is virtually no education for aesthetic competence in the training of priests and theologians. Happily, this fact has also been self-critically conceded by the German Catholic Conference of Bishops in a statement on 'Art and Culture in Theological Training'. First of all a pronouncement is made (and unfortunately so far it is no more than a pronouncement):

The arts should represent integrated elements in the study of theology. This applies particularly to the graphic arts, architecture, literature and music, which have a tremendous importance in the tradition and life of the church . . . Theologians, catechists and teachers of religion must be put in a position to deal responsibly with artistic questions and decisions. Here exercises and studies are called for in the following fields:

- A discussion of lines of development in the history of particular arts;
- Insight into current conceptions and questions and their origin;
- Grappling with the foundations of the history of art and the philosophy of aesthetics.
- A heightening of the capacity for perception; a development of a sense of the methodological problems associated with this;
- Investigations into the particular setting of the arts in the life of church and theology and the specific conditions for their reception.[48]

So two things are bound up with cultural competence: gaining know-ledge and a capacity for criticism; gaining experience and criteria for 'discerning the spirits'. A false aestheticizing of religion or a sacralizing of art is to be avoided. Religious and aesthetic experience, theological and aesthetic reception remain fundamentally different. Neither can simply be replaced by the other. Both spheres of perception, experience and reflection remain with their autonomy and independence intact. And yet there are productive tensions between religious and aesthetic experience: religious experiences can be the starting point and object of artistic reali-zation, and aesthetic experiences can suggest the dimension of religious experience, provoke it positively or deny it radically. This book sets out to describe the tension between affirmation and criticism, between prophetic gestures and protesting refusal. It develops basic themes of an intercultural theology; it is an attempt to build a bridge from the world of poetry to the world of theology and vice versa. By way of anticipation I shall use a specific example to explain what this bridge-building looks like in the sphere of graphic art. I am referring to the picture on the cover of this book.

8. An uncanny 'head of Christ'

I have chosen this picture by the painter Herbert Falken deliberately. Hardly any of the many pictures of Christ in twentieth-century art has touched me more deeply. The painter lives in a village called Langen-broich near Düren, west of Cologne, where he has his studio. Not far away, in Stolbert-Schevenhütte, he is also active as a Catholic priest. For many years Falken had a friendship with Heinrich Böll, who was his neighbour in Langenbroich in his last years. Falken looked after Böll when he was dying, buried him and dedicated a cycle under the title 'Lazarus' to his dead friend.

On Good Friday 1995 I visited Herbert Falken in his church and his studio. He had agreed to take part in a series of lectures for my faculty the next summer term. I was to be his dialogue partner. He let me choose eight pictures from his oeuvre, which by now was extensive,[49] and we both commented on them.[50] I was struck by a unique 'Head of Christ', a picture from 1981, which for me represents the climax so far of Falken's artistic and theological grappling with the subject of Christ. Much from the history of art and from the history of his own painting has come together here and now been quite independently transformed, inimitable in style and evocative power.

- From the history of the iconography of Christ there is the image of the shroud with the face of the suffering Christ: *Ecce homo.*
- There is the tradition of Russian icons: with the concentration on the face at the centre of the picture and the distinctive contrast between light and dark, which makes it seem as if the face comes to the observer from the depth of space.
- There is the personal artistic grappling with the self-portrait, the penetration of the depths of human nature by means of the face and the eyes.

Here the contrast between precision and a lack of contour is established with great virtuosity. Only the eyes, nose and mouth emerge sharply from the lack of form, drawing the observer even more strongly under the spell of this face. And one is fascinated above all by the confused lines on the head of the figure. They suggest waving, unruly hair, which reinforces the uncanny impression given by this appearance. Here we encounter someone who seems to have unprecedented powers. But the tangled lines could also indicate convolutions in the brain which have become visible, because the brain seems to be growing from the skull. In that case the garish white convolutions would be like glowing, shining rays of energy, which further strengthens the impression that this figure emanates a superhuman energy. So here we encounter a figure which seems to belong in this world and at the same time in another world; which enters the visible and still has contact with the world of the invisible.

I know no other picture of Christ in which a painter has succeeded in making the mystery of this Christ optically visible on so many levels: the mystery of the two worlds to whom he belongs. It is the world of the divine and the world of the human. This figure seems strangely tangible, yet intangible: earthly in appearance, and yet evidently impossible to reduce to the earthly; emanating energy without crushing the earthly; uncanny in its emergence from the dark and yet not going beyond human bounds; with penetrating eyes which nevertheless do not appear cold and merciless. This is a face which one cannot have too much of and which contains more than can be expressed in words; a face the mystery of which seems to be unfathomable: comprehensible and yet incomprehensible, appearing yet withdrawing, present in the world and yet in an enigmatic way not of this world. One comes under the spell of this face, and this can spark off a process of self-knowledge. Rilke's verse from his poem 'An Archaic Torso of Apollo' can be associated with this: 'There is no place which does not see you. You must change your life.'

This picture combines the two things about which George Steiner talks: the mystery of a work of art which escapes finally being put into words, and the mystery of a figure like Jesus, who does not fit into any scheme and who cannot finally be grasped by any theory. In addition there is the mystery of the double existence of a person who as an artist is a theologian and as a theologian is an artist. This is what Falken said about this double existence in our Tübingen dialogue lectures:

> I lead a double life, I am a priest and a painter.
> As a theologian I have to think, as a painter I have eyes in my head. Is that right? So has the theologian to be blind and has the painter to work without a brain? Certainly not. There is a logic of the eyes and a seeing of the brain.
>
> Perhaps I'm crazy: the human brain and Christ's crown of thorns show similar interweavings.
> Does HIS crown of thorns perhaps slip down into MY brain through the skull?
>
> Often the theologian in me hinders the painter in me.
> His thought causes pains in the head, stabs from the brain into the eyes. Conversely, the painter's gaze gets lost in the convolutions of the crown of thorns, as if these were beginning to think and make sense.
>
> The theologian and the painter in me provoke one another, but they also help one another to make leaps. The theologian learns to see from the painter before he begins to think. And the painter should learn to think from the theologian, so that he keeps what he paints under control. Is that right? Not completely! The painter in me doesn't allow his painting to be dictated by the theologian within me. And conversely the theologian? The theologian in me picks up visual aids from the painter in me before he begins to think and to preach.
> The theologian in me and the painter in me are brothers. We are I myself. The one cannot live without the other. We need each other.
>
> My brain is my crown of thorns, that's what I have . . . called pictures.
> I have a labyrinth in my head. My eyes often enough celebrate passion and resurrection in my skull.[51]

This book, too, is written in awareness of this double existence which is an invitation to new ways of thinking, ways of thinking of faith in dialogue with the poets.

A. The Riddle of Human Nature

We all live and die in a riddle,
and if you like, you can call the sense of that religious.
It is a somewhat demanding word,
but the awareness of hopeless uncertainty
is tantamount to a kind of piety.

Thomas Mann

I. Terror about oneself and the world

Why is creation as it is? Why are human beings as they are and not otherwise? I remember that it was not the quest for God which led me to study theology; from earliest childhood I was familiar with 'my God', who only later became questionable to me. It was the enigma of human beings: myself with all my contradictions, which I did not find resolved with other human beings either. Human beings are well-meaning but weak; full of good intentions but failures; wanting good but doing evil. Who are we? Often our self-awareness is fragile and our sense of value susceptible to interference. If we look critically in the mirror and begin to be honest with ourselves, what do we find?

1. The conversation with the Glass Man: Kurt Tucholsky

For a long time I looked for a text which expresses this experience. I found it in Kurt Tucholsky. It is entitled 'The Man at the Mirror', and it was published in *Weltbühne* on 10 January 1928.[1]

The look in the mirror

What does 'the man' see first of all when he looks in the mirror? He sees himself again as 'Glass Man'. He sees himself as a counterpart, and because he sees himself again as another person, he can enter into dialogue with himself: I and the Glass Man. What have the two to say to each other? Kurt Tucholsky makes use of this mirror split, and the result is an exciting conversation between the man and his *alter ego* in glass:

Suddenly your gaze is caught in the mirror
and remains there.
You see:

The naked, shaven cheeks,
– 'cheeks': that's good for other people,
the gently curving mouth, the smooth upper lip,
the tie sits – no, it doesn't,
oops!

Now you're impeccable.
Hair, nose, neck, collar, shoulders are a well-composed picture –
your gaze affirms your deeply.

You rest content,
you see the silky shell of the ear-lobes,
imperceptibly you straighten yourself up –
you are so content with yourself,
and feel the healthy marrow of your life.

So the first look at the mirror brings confirmation: an impeccable look, an immaculate appearance, important for its effect on others. In the mirror the man sees first of all his well 'composed' pose which he can affirm with pleasure and self-satisfaction. But then:

And the flies have sat on the mirror,
or a chemical process has speckled the quicksilver
little blind pupils are sitting on it . . .

Now turn the inner rangefinder of the eyes round again:
On the right temple
– but only if one looks more closely –
there are a few small wrinkles,
trenches in the skin –
no, they aren't yet wrinkles,
but one day they will form at this place.

The man has for the first time seen something to disturb him. To begin with, only fly-specks on the immaculate glass, but then, the sharper the perception becomes, possible wrinkles on the skin, signs which will disturb the immaculate surface and make the 'healthy marrow' of life seem a little bit different. Anxiety about old age creeps up:

Then you're an old man;
then people say, 'Old Caspar – ';

then a girl to whom you whisper something will be gently teased –
'With the old man..?', her friends say.
Old man.
How you look at each other:
the glass man and you!
Never
never will another person ever look at you like this,
without a touch of irony.
You can't see yourself at all in the mirror.
Tat twam asi – ?

Your face is smooth, washed clean and massaged.
Time has lapped over it.
You've fabricated your face, the rubbish tip of your feelings,
laughed it together,
kissed, kept silent, suffered, sighed: lived together –
look, there are some slight marks under your left eye.

Make your mirror face.
Nothing of what has happened in recent years
Is visible on you.
Everything is visible on you.

Fakirs should sometimes hypnotize themselves.
If you look at yourself in the mirror for a long time, the encyclopedia
says,
you fall into a trance . . .
you look at the man in the mirror,
who sees as you see –
you see, as he sees, as you . . .
Tear your gaze away! Wake up.

What does the look in the mirror produce; what must the man hear from
the Glass Man?

Who are you, Glass Man?

One thing above all: time will not pass even you by without leaving a trace; in the long run the immaculate appearance is only a game; the perfection is only pretence. Already manifestations of old age are perceptible; already one perceives little marks on oneself. The face in the mirror proves to be an artificial face, a façade which has been set up deliberately. You want to paint over it – your feelings and everything that belongs to life: lies and laughter, kisses and silence, suffering and silence. Although you want to keep it hidden, everything is visible. Look and mirror look, man and Glass Man – they get wise to each other. But the man is not yet ready to concede the self-deception:

> Like this, with arm propped up, it would make a good photograph for
> the illustrated papers;
> the poet looks seriously at the subscribers,
> demanding respect and even given a cursory glance;
> unapproachable, very assured,
> as if hewn from frozen lard – a finished product.
> In the two glittering points which are fixed in the centre of your eyes,
> life shines.
> Really we're quite beautiful, like — ?
> You look at yourself as men look at themselves in the barber's shop
> when, hair cut, they get up:
> 'Thank God, it's all there, and here we are, on parade – '
> They give themselves a long look in the mirror.
> Company inspection, made by Corporal Eye –
> they can't tear themselves away,
> then they pull down their waistcoats –
> and with new strength go onto the street
> ready to fight with the others who have not had their hair cut.

No, once again it is possible to escape the unsparing honesty. Self-satisfaction is restored, being in love with one's own appearance, self-confidence in the 'battle with the others'. The look in the mirror has strengthened the ego once again, strengthened it for the battle of life. But all at once everything changes:

> But all at once
> the smooth certainty of your ironed shirt has gone;
> fear is there.

Fear sits in the dark depths of your nose,
with which you breathe in the air;
the brass by the chimney quivers slightly,
you hear it with your ears.

Say something!
Speak!
Prophesy how it will go on!
Will I die in bed, cared for, surrounded by an earnest professor, a white
nurse and sweet-smelling bottles;
or will I die a wretched death on a cold high road, all alone -
to the other vagrants I have sometimes spoken French,
because after all I was a bit better:
will I cough myself to death or sink back gently into my chair . . .
Red is slowly rising in the white of the eye
what compassion you have for yourself.
You worship yourself in a hating way

Speak!
Prophesy:
Success – respect – forgetfulness – lack of money – humiliation; they
glide by your well-fed comrades and clap you on the shoulder in an
encouraging way, with a touch of *Schadenfreude*.

Fluff. Kissed mouth. Animated ball of the head.
With mobilized muscles you both look at each other.
There's nothing to see yet. You're still both beautiful.
The anxiety nests deep down.

All at once everything is dominated by anxiety. What previously showed
itself as self-confidence and love of self is in reality a repression of anxiety
about life. And this anxiety is bound up with the question of death, or
more precisely with the manner of dying. Where will I end? I who am a
'all present and correct', content with myself, in the feeling of the 'healthy
marrow' of my life? What will the end be – tender care or a wretched
death? A wheezing cough or with gentle sleep? Granted, everything is still
in order. But self-hatred is mixed up with self-esteem, and love of self can
no longer suppress anxiety.

'Look,' says the Mirror Man to the other man,
'you have a hair on your jacket collar.

Can you see? It's gleaming in the light of the evening lamp – strange,
That's not allowed; please remove it –!'
I carefully remove the hair.

I go from the mirror.
So does the other –
There has been no conversation.
The eyes look into the void
with the mirror image
– without the other in the mirror.
Alone.

'Alone'. The narcissistic posing has led to nothing but knowledge of one's ultimate loneliness.

Against self-satisfaction

It is because of this quality that I cannot brush this text aside: the reflection of the self does not banish fears but rather arouses them: fear of time, which is a fear of the transitoriness, frailness and fragility of one's own body. Those who, like Tucholsky's man, look in the mirror, come away with a bit of self-knowledge, have got wise to themselves. This author's apparently effortless verses, easy to speak and enjoyable to listen to, are in reality a lure, a fragrance, comparable to a plant with a scent that invites insect to rest on it, and then proves to be a flesh-eater. So too with Tucholsky. Lyric parlando is a trap for the reader in search of satisfaction; humorous verses are a lure for those in search of superficial enjoyment. They notice too late that they have been drawn into the catch-question of the meaning of their life hitherto and the viability of a sense of self-worth which has been acquired laboriously. The riddle of human nature.

However, the Tucholsky text only sums up in a very pointed way what biblical texts already express when they speak of human beings. Even during my theological studies I was impressed by the realism with which the Bible speaks of human beings. It makes the most exalted statements possible about them: 'And God created the human being in his own image, in the image of God he created him' (Gen. 1.27). And at the same time it points out to human beings that they are not like God, that they are mortal, transitory, fleeting. Who are they in comparison with God?

What is man that you regard him,
or the son of man that you think of him?
Man is like a breath,
his days are like a passing shadow (Ps. 144.3f.).[2]

There is the same notion in another psalm:

As a father pities his children,
so the Lord pities those who fear him.
For he knows our frame;
he remembers that we are dust.
As for man, his days are like grass;
he flourishes like a flower of the field;
for the wind passes over it, and it is gone,
and its place knows it no more (Ps. 103.13–16).

These and other texts made it clear to me that the Bible does not present an illusory anthropology, but a sober anthropology of the right measure. And what could be more disillusioning than the story of the fall and the curse right at the beginning of creation? Adam and Eve, Cain and Abel – such figures do not derive from a naïve picture of human beings; they derive from an anthropology which knows how weak human beings are and how they can be led astray. On the very first pages of the Bible, human beings have been driven out of paradise: human existence on earth is an existence in exile! Human life? Hardly has it been created than it already stands under the creator's curse. For hardly has the creator's self-praise fallen silent ('Behold, it was all very good'), than the same God threatens human beings with pain, tribulation and mortality:

To the woman God said:
'I will greatly multiply
your pain in childbearing.
In pain you shall bring forth children.
Yet your desire shall be for your husband,
and he shall rule over you.'
And to Adam he said,
'Because you have listened to the voice of your wife,
and have eaten of the tree
of which I commanded you,
"You shall not eat of it."

Cursed is the ground because of you;
in toil you shall eat of it
all the days of your life;
thorns and thistles it shall bring forth to you,
and you shall eat of the plants of the field.
In the sweat of your face
you shall eat bread
till you return to the ground,
for out of it you were taken;
You are dust, and to dust you shall return' (Gen. 3.16–17).

I discovered that the description of this primeval fall and primeval curse has been a particular challenge to writers in our century, perhaps because often enough they themselves have had to live their lives in conditions of uncertainty, of exile, of catastrophe. Human existence as fallen, exiled, marked existence – this basic biblical notion recurs strikingly often in literary texts of the twentieth century. What happened then is repeated particularly in the catastrophic twentieth century. A fusing of horizons between the primal time of the Bible and present time – that is possible in this particular anthropological archetype.

2. What is the fall? Günter Kunert

One of the most acute analysts and most uncompromising diagnosticians of the riddle of human nature in contemporary literature is Günter Kunert. I got to know him in May 1986 when I was able to have a long conversation in Kaisborstel near Itzehoe, north of Hamburg, as a guest in his house, which used to be the village school.[3] By then it was ten years since Kunert, whose writing career was first promoted in East Germany, had signed the petition against the expulsion of Wolf Biermann, the writer and singer, and the best-known East German dissident. (This was an action which sparked off a wave of protest against the government and became the first unexpected signal of protest.) And he had paid for this deviation from the party line by being himself expelled from East Germany.

Abandoned without grace

I knew that Kunert – the son of a Jewish mother and an originally Catholic father – sharply rejected religion. And he confirmed this in our conversation: 'I grew up in a sphere which was completely void of religion and faith. Neither Christianity not Judaism have ever been significant to me.'[4] Indeed, in an autobiographical text from 1989, three years after our conversation, Kunert was even more specific. That year, on the invitation of a Protestant pastor, he had agreed to organize and take part in a series of lectures in St Peter's Church, Lübeck, under the title 'Writers Preach'. In the introduction Kunert describes his own situation:

What have I, an unbaptized person with a secular upbringing, to do with this church? My answer, which I intend to give myself, is that my prejudices are significantly less than those who in other respects are like-minded. That is probably because people have never pestered me with questions of faith. That pitiful state school which I was compelled to attend excused me religious education: I, the pagan of an origin declassified by the state because of my Jewish mother, was allowed to go home before the last lesson, while the other children were told something about which I was not curious. And the reports of my schoolfellows on the aforesaid instruction, about which they laughed, did not suggest anything worth further investigation. In my (extremely bad) reports, in the space indicating religion there was a strange word, which much much later took on an unexpected meaning, 'dissident'.[5]

I was particularly impressed by Kunert's major volumes of poetry from the 1980s, above all *Abtötungsverfahren* ('Extermination Process') (1980), *Stillleben* ('Still Life') (1983) and later *Fremd daheim* ('Strange at Home'). In *Stillleben,* one poem struck me. It is entitled 'Without Pathos' and this poem seemed to me to represent the whole basic attitude in which Günter Kunert writes. Here he achieves a unique mixture of a precise analysis without any intellectualism, an unsolemn language without any stiffness, and a disillusioned statement which does not lose its poetic elegance:

Too subjective – do not write it
Down: this painful lament
yet it is nevertheless the basic tone
of all
Constantly other faces
constantly the same longings:
One day to be as it ought to be

Honest for example and
at least not keep changing
the small coins of love
into ever smaller coins

But to give oneself

From oneself
from this made-to-measure dried-out
lump of clay
who gives a courteous greeting before
in God's name or his own
he decomposes into a few prescribed
last words.[6]

With such texts was Kunert once for all denying metaphysics, a disillusioned sceptic, who considered the question of meaning and hope closed? The question of religion – settled? But in the volume *Stillleben* in particular I found poems which did not just seem to be finally closed over the basic questions. For example the poem 'Götterdämmerung':

Not to be held fast: this day. Life.
Fabric dissolving, disappearing.
Whatever happens, you seek the meaning.
For that at least you will strive.

You cannot bear the intuition
from filth and fire a crazy birth
which tours incessantly all over earth
constantly fleeing such interrogation.

Recognize this: ourselves we cannot face,
no one we find like us, so godlike made
And no one who can give us aid,
abandoned to ourselves without grace.[7]

I found that there are unmistakable tensions in this poem. It is conceded that human beings seek meaning and always will strive to find such a meaning. The quest for meaning is to some degree essentially rooted in human beings. The reason is also given: the intolerable insight that we are nothing but a 'crazy birth' from 'filth and fire', which goes 'incessantly' over the earth. Thus there is a recognition that human beings cannot 'face themselves'; in plain language this means that human beings are an *abiding* riddle, an *open* question. But at the same time it is asserted in this poem that there is no 'aid' (the reference is probably to a transcendent origin) and that human beings are thus finally left 'without grace'. But how could the two insights be logically compatible? Human beings are an abiding question to themselves, so their ultimate detstiny is open; and at the same time human beings are to be completely without 'aid' and 'grace'. So how do abiding uncertainty and the resolution of uncertainty into a definitive assertion fit together? It has become clear to me that Kunert manifestly did not want to resolve this 'contradiction'. Moreover the aesthetic gain in this poem is its tangible state of suspension.

How does an 'unbeliever' read the Bible?

Moreover Günter Kunert's reception of biblical material has also been marked by unresolved tensions. I was struck that the Kunert who says of himself that he grew up 'in a sphere completely void of religion and faith', that for years he regarded any form of believing as 'opium for the people', and that the Bible had been no more than 'a fairy-tale saga' – can say of himself (again I am quoting from his preface to 'Writers Preach'):

> So 'at some time' some of the traditional and incredible facts (of the Bible) seemed to me quite parabolic, allegorical, and quite usable by the kind of writer whom I had become in the meantime; and also by someone who in any case thought with a secret terror that he could recognize in his surroundings, in his environment, in the world, the 'eternal return' of a basic psychological and sociological pattern.
>
> So I have made use of this foundation, drawn on this source, but at the same time I have also secularized and politicized the traditional material, used it in my own way, though without blasphemous intent, since as I have said, I did not suffer from any atheistic fury which I had to work off in this way. Possibly it was precisely my inner detachment, a certain degree of neutrality, which led me to open my door when the pastor . . . from Lübeck rang the bell.[8]

To discover that a writer reads the Bible means first of all understanding that here the Bible is no longer the 'word of God', but material to be used. For the biblical stories no longer have religious authority but existential authority. Without this they would not yield anything for an author. Kunert is an example of this. For him the 'traditional and incredible facts' can be used because they are 'parables' of the human situation. They have an abiding interpretative power which makes people clear-sighted. They manifestly contain primal truths about human beings and humankind which can even be discovered in a post-metaphysical age.

In other words, in the case of Kunert (and that of countless other authors of our century) the simple alternative – either believing, and then also using the Bible, or unbelieving, and then having nothing to do with the it – proves inaccurate. For Kunert 'the unbeliever', the biblical stories illuminate, rather, the 'it's always been like this' of human behaviour, what the author – in the face of the optimism over progress which he knew well enough from state socialism – calls 'the eternal return of a basic psychological and sociological pattern'. And because this is the case, the unbeliever can also 'make use of' the book of faith, draw on this 'source' and pursue his own interests with this material.

Adam, Eve and original sin

I can still remember very well how surprised I was when in our 1986 conversation Günter Kunert suddenly mentioned the biblical story of Adam and Eve. Previously, here too he had resolutely rejected any assumption of an 'overall meaning' of reality. The meaning could only be found subjectively. The individual could find what is so nebulously called 'meaning' 'only in himself and in his action'. For Kunert, the meaning of his existence was identical with his writing. There was no longer an overarching meaning, nor had there ever been. But now at least we knew this. I asked, 'Is this curse of existence what in theological terms could be called original sin?' And Kunert replied:

> Yes, you could describe our emergence from nature in that way. For the legend of Adam and Eve describes eating of the tree of knowledge and also knowing what is dead as original sin. As long as one was still part of nature, one did not know what is dead nor could one have other insights, because one is only part of nature. The biblical parable tells of original sin, but it is really no sin. For it is not our fault. Religion has a fixed notion of how the beginning was: there we are led astray into original sin, but in fact the emergence from nature took place quite by chance.[9]

At that time I could not work out what this statement meant, i.e. how fundamental this conviction was for Kunert. It only became clear to me later, when I studied other writings of his. The basic statement proved to be that for Kunert the story of Adam and Eve has preserved in legendary garb what still stamps the human condition. Adam and Eve's 'knowledge' is a primary recollection, fixed in literature, of a momentous event for human history: the detachment of human beings from their connection with nature. Of course for Kunert this cannot be imagined as an individual sin and therefore as individual guilt; for him, such talk of sin is part of the legendary garb. What is meant, rather, is that in the course of their evolution human beings detached themselves from nature as a whole, awoke to themselves, and thus began to objectivize nature as material. Now this event had far-reaching consequences.

Kunert reflects on these consequences for the first time in a text which appeared in his book 'The Last Indians of Europe'. It bears the title 'First Book of Moses. The Serpent and the Expulsion'. The very first sentences of this piece are a significant indication of how a contemporary writer perceives the Bible: 'The real riddle of the Bible, especially the Old Testament, consists in the fact that it is a collection of irresolvable contradictions.'[10] However, for Kunert these contradictions cannot simply be resolved by commonplace atheism: they have to be worked on. For example, one has to defend oneself against these texts and seek to break out of the value scheme which are hidden in them. Thus in his text Kunert not only works on a rehabilitation of the serpent but also forthrightly explains the sexual interpretation of the fall as a 'misunderstanding'. Instead, for him, the 'fall' means:

On the other hand, I regard the 'fall' . . . as an obscure reminiscence of the most important event in human history, the emergence from nature. Were this relationship only to be interpreted in sexual terms, it could hardly be said in the same text and before the expulsion, 'Be fruitful and multiply.' It seems to me that the recognition of one's own nakedness marks that moment when the human being leaves the security of nature and becomes aware of his or her defencelessness and helplessness. This is the moment of utmost dismay. For it is the moment of the recognition of one's own mortality – of what in principle separates us from the animal which does not know about its death. There is something touching about this terror and hiding away of the two innocent primal human beings. Compared with this, the punitive God, who at any rate with a twinkle in his eye gives them garments of skin so that they again become like animals, seems more like a disappointed and anxious superior evicting subordinates who are becoming a threat to him.

God too senses fear, the fear of the dictator when confronted by a possible pretender who could challenge his rule. And he recognizably expresses this fear: 'Look, Adam has become like us and knows what is good and evil.' Yes, yes – now Adam knows, and so he must go into exile.

The detachment from nature, even from our own, was a long and painful process: the fall, the insecurity which we brought on ourselves through an urge to know and a gain in knowledge. However, the loss of the unconscious, unperceived unity of all living beings is not to be expunged without anything to replace it; it is to be compensated for. The Old Testament already has the equivalents for this: domination of the woman who has brought about the forced exodus; domination of the earth which is to make itself subject; of the enemies of the chosen people.[11]

So for Künert the 'fall' of Adam and Eve as the emergence of human beings from nature has three consequences:

1. Recognition of one's own *mortality*. In this way the human being differs from the animal, which knows nothing of its death.

2. The *situation of rivalry* with God: now the human being too knows about good and evil.

3. The *urge for knowledge* and the *gain in knowledge*: there is a loss of the unity of all that is and a development of a knowledge and practice of rule: over the woman, the earth, the 'stranger'. The author once again spells this out in a letter to the Australian Germanist Kerry Dunne, to whom we are indebted for an illuminating study of the 'fall' as a parabolic key to the work of Günter Kunert:

Thus the biblical parables or images or stories, whatever one wants to call them, have really been very important material for me and still are. However, I have never used them or exploited them in a Christian sense. Basically I have always gone against the grain, i.e. used them in a literary sense which is appropriate for me. Sometimes I've stood them on their heads, inverted them. Thus I've used them in a very individual way. That is one thing. And the fall is really already a more historicizing approach. Thus for me the fall is the emergence of human beings from nature. But this fall was a very involuntary, a very unconscious one. And I believe that the whole of our present-day suffering and all the problems in industrial civilization stem from the fact that in a very distant, dark time we settled on the instrumental. In other words, the fall began the moment when human beings used the first flint as a tool.

A few days ago I read that the oldest flint knife has now been found in Europe, seven hundred thousand years old. So we can say that the fall took place seven hundred thousand years ago, with the use of the first tool . . . That means that our brain, our way of thinking, our logic, our reason became what is called instrumental . . . that's where the fall is. That was the sin, our emergence from being animals.[12]

So the 'fall' unavoidably, inescapably, shapes the human situation. The riddle of human nature is posed here, in so far as after the loss of the unity of all living things, human beings through their newly-gained instrumental practice of domination produced victims, losers, the oppressed, including themselves, their unconscious, their feelings, their drives.

Tired of one's own enigma

So I read Günter Kunert's poetry as a unique balancing act between relentless disillusionment and the longing to be able to decipher human existence; between an experience of the fall and the abiding quest for the meaning and significance of the human condition. In one of his last volumes of poetry, the poet has once again described this delicate situation of the human being, always fragile and endangered, in the form of an 'apocryphal self-portrait':

I am an utter stranger
To bush and leaf and tree,
No feeling: that machine there
Has no effect on me.

The world: chaotic pictures
Of people out of mind.
The days go by mechanically
A mediocre kind.

I think and yet I am not,
Though here, don't live the least.
Know nothing through all knowledge,
Die, yet am not a beast.

Tired of my own enigma,
Threatened by all that's new,
Exposed to all around me,
In debt to none. Thank-you.[13]

Here more than in any other poem Kunert has attempted to catch the many layers of his image of the human being. There is – a first level – the basic notion, familiar to readers of Kunert, that human beings are completely alienated from nature; the heart is like an unfeeling little machine; the world is a chaos of images; the days produce a mechanical rhythm, banal and mediocre. But there is no complaint about this. Rather – a second level – there follows a fundamental reflection on the structural ambivalence of the human condition. Although a thinking being, one is never identical with oneself; although one exists, one never really lives; although one attains a great deal of knowledge, the decisive questions remain obscure; although one dies like an animal, one is not an animal.

Weariness sets in during a process of ongoing reflection on oneself; in particular the future, with the 'threats' it contains, makes us sick. Moreover defencelessness seems to be the only adequate reaction. Nevertheless – a third level – here too a thanksgiving comes into play. The notion is surprising; there is nothing to prepare for it in the text. It is introduced by the last laconic line; and there are many unexpressed connotations. For one is indeed 'in debt' to no one, yet gratitude is manifestly appropriate. Thus the indication is probably that even the weariest and the most defenceless do not live only for themselves and from themselves. As a rule they are given even the little by which human beings live. So the poem ends in a surprising way with a pointer beyond itself: thanksgiving is expressed, with no indebtedness to another human being. In that case, thanksgiving to whom?

3. The beginning of all riddles: Wolfgang Hildesheimer

Just as important for me as my meeting with Günter Kunert was my meeting with Wolfgang Hildesheimer. Here too I want to begin with a personal recollection. In January 1989 I made the long journey to the little Swiss town of Poschiavo on the Italian frontier, where Hildesheimer has lived for many years.[14] This visit is unforgettable for me not just because our conversation was to be one of the last major interviews that Hildesheimer was able to give: he died on 21 August 1991 at the age of seventy-four. It is also important for me because right at the beginning of our meeting this author very directly said that the fundamental religious questions were the 'real' questions which now interested him. Too often, he said, he had investigated 'only' aesthetic, political and social problems; it was an explicit need now, at this point in his life, to adopt a standpoint on the basic religious questions.[15] This was all the more surprising when one considers the career and thought of this great writer.

Born in Hamburg in 1916, Hildesheimer comes from a Jewish family, and this fact initially determined his career.[16] After attending a boarding school (Odenwald school, 1929–1933), in 1933 he had to emigrate with his parents. First he went to England, and then to Palestine, where between 1934 and 1936 he was a carpenter's apprentice in Jerusalem. In addition he was trained in art and was given an education in furniture design and interior decoration. Later he worked in Tel Aviv as a teacher of English, and during the war as an information officer at the British government's Public Information Office in Jerusalem. Between 1946 and 1949 he took part in the Nuremberg War Crimes Trials as a simultaneous translator, and from 1948 he edited the whole record.

No meaning in creation

Someone who in his young years is, if not a victim, at any rate a product of the war and who minutes the official record of the cruelty of the concentration camps will be spiritually and intellectually wounded for ever. So it is no surprise that initially Wolfgang Hildesheimer identified intellectually with what also fascinated other intellectuals of the 1950s, the philosophy of the absurd. Moreover Hildesheimer first of all became *the* author of the 'theatre of the absurd' in Germany. In a brilliant address in 1960 he also proposed a theory about it. A key passage from this lecture runs:

> The absurd play confronts the audience with the impossibility of understanding life, its questionable nature. But the impossibility of understanding life cannot be depicted as an attempt at an answer, for that would mean that it could be interpreted, that life would be comprehensible. It can be depicted only by being disclosed in its whole magnitude and pitilessness and stand there almost as a rhetorical question: those who wait for an interpretation will wait in vain. They will not receive one until they have the meaning of creation explained to them by someone who is competent to do so, and that means never.[17]

The impossibility of understanding life; the inexplicable 'meaning' of creation; the impossibility of a binding 'answer': these words also characterize the atmosphere of Hildesheimer's first great novel, which was to be one of my most important reading experiences. *Tynset* appeared in 1965. As with the plays and radio scripts, the basic structure of this great prose work followed the lines of the 'theatre of the absurd'; life is understood as a collage of fragments and dissonances.

Moreover the novel is simply an epic montage of splinters of thought, pieces of narrative, and scraps of reflection, i.e. it is made up of last, ultimately interrupted attempts by the first-person narrator to make meaningful communication with the outside world. I am still electrified by the basic idea of the novel. It depicts the experiences of someone who during a single night, mostly lying in bed, goes through every possible space and time and yet keeps meeting only himself. He takes on the characteristics of what Walter Jens has called a 'meditating secular monk',[18] whose flights of thought are prompted above all by the strange-sounding name 'Tynset'. And 'Tynset' is simply a railway station in northern Norway which the hero of a night comes across by chance because he begins to thumb through the timetable of Norwegian Railways.

The sound of this word has always cast a spell on me. For the narrator of the book, as for me as reader, it conjures up fantasies of setting out, longings for something completely new, desires to flee into the 'wholly other'. What kind of a place must it be to sound so seductive? What kind of happiness must it hold to fulfil promises?

In the novel, 'Tynset' is only the seductive-sounding cipher for the impossibility of ultimately seeing through the world and its enigmatic nature. But how Hildesheimer describes this enigmatic nature is for me one of the most seductive pieces of prose in modern German literature, the magic of which can be addictive:

Part of the great riddle that is called Tynset. Now I'm getting very tired. Yes, Tynset is a good name for the riddle. Giving the unknown a name doesn't make it more known; the riddle doesn't disclose itself with the name, but it has been named, it has taken on a significance, which harbours, sums up, enciphers, the enigmatic element that hides in it, the sum of all riddles and at the same time their root. The word TYNSET will to some degree do justice to the sum and the root; at any rate I know of none better.

But what is it that I imagine by Tynset? What? – Nothing, be still, nothing. A mystery lies behind it. To investigate it, perhaps a journey wouldn't even be the right way. At any rate not yet. Later, yes, later, when everything else fails, later perhaps, when my fingers grow cold and stiff, when I get tired and the light goes out in the corridors, later, when the words seep through, even if I no longer find the pearls in the books, or the nothingness behind the Milky Way, if I no longer detect wind, get no more air, then perhaps nothing else will be left for me, and I will go there, perhaps with my last strength.[19]

It is easy to see from this text that the problems in *Tynset* represent an epic development of the philosophy of the absurd. And yet this short passage also betrays something of the contrary tendencies which similarly run right through the book. As in Kunert, there is on the one hand the experience of the meaningless and enigmatic nature of the world; on the other – presented with a strange urgency, a remarkable pathos ('I will go there, perhaps with my last strength') – the awareness of an abiding mystery in reality. Thus the conviction of an ultimate meaninglessness of the world does not simply still the urge to decipher the mystery, does not kill the need in the narrator perhaps to be able to decipher the 'cipher'. And one of the most stimulating passages for this unwearying questioning has to do with the biblical figures of Cain and Abel.

Why the riddle grins

In his nocturnal meditations the first-person narrator also recalls the biblical story of Cain, rejected by God. But in doing so, he raises critical questions, questions to human beings and questions about the order of the creator God, an order which has hitherto been accepted so unquestioningly:

> No. Not that, not Cain's prayer. Cain's prayer didn't smoke and didn't smoulder. Because it didn't ask for anything, it was a good, respectable prayer, perhaps one of the last good prayers – here I may be deluding myself – but definitely the first. Now it was meaningless, for the God to whom it was addressed was occupied elsewhere. It pleased him not to hear the prayer; that doesn't cast a bad light on Cain, but rather on his God. Why didn't God hear it? For a long time this riddle wouldn't let me rest. I've never heard or read any good explanation of it. And unexpectedly, even today it still shines red between the lines of some book or newspaper. It was the first riddle I encountered, and it made me stumble and fall. I got up wearily, hurt and astonished. I hadn't expected a riddle, at least not here, so near to the beginning and so early. I went on, a little more slowly than before, limping a bit, but hiding my slight limp as far as possible, since I was ashamed of myself. I looked back on the riddle, as I saw how it grinned at me. Evidently it had already tripped some others up and each time enjoyed the fall. It still grins today beneath all the grinning riddles, but it was the first, the beginning of all riddles. And it is also the beginning of all injustice, the beginning of the guilt of God, who for no reason did not look

graciously on Cain and scorned his offering of fruits of the field, let it smoulder on the ground in black smoking swathes, so that it made the person offering the sacrifice cough, almost choked him. But he allowed Abel's sacrifice, steaming flesh and blood of animals which he himself had slaughtered to the praise of God, bowels and entrails, to rise up to him, enjoying it and looking benignly on the one offering the sacrifice, who had recognized his God and read off his face the wish that God wanted meat. That's how it was, not otherwise. Cain felt that he could not bear this arbitrariness, God's hurtful joke. He had taken his creator seriously, had loved him, divinized him, and in fearful disappointment he smote God's favourite, his own brother. That's how it was, and he was damned for ever and ever by him.

It is written there that Cain had a violent, envious temperament and Abel was gentle and pious. But who wrote that? The jealous farmer and the pious hunter and killer: Cain evil and grudging, Abel good and righteous – no, that's not good enough, I don't accept this order from the creator of the two, far less from his chronicler. Nor do I know who would accept it except for the purchasing organizations, which are hostile to questions – I ask, and my question rings through the house, through the night, and even Celestina should sense it. I ask: what objects of mistrust, of envy, of wickedness, of vileness, of evil desires, of impure thoughts were there in the time of Cain? The earth just created, populated by no more than four human beings, two of them already unjustly punished, their lives squandered, what things and thoughts were there on which evil could have formed? What stood on earth around which it would have twined, and in what hole could it have nested? Where was the approach by which it could have devoured its way in, spread, and gone on devouring? Nowhere, nothing there but a deceptive paradise and wilderness and the blatant injustice of God, who was pleased to destroy Cain. A heavy burden, a stain, a sign on the forehead – that is attached, not to Cain but to his creator. Away with it![20]

It becomes clear that this author engages in biblical exegesis in the mode of the penetrating, doubting question – directed against the 'purchasing organizations which are hostile to questions'. This obviously refers to the traditional churches, which with the help of a trivializing exegesis tend to interpret away the contradictions from the Bible and the world. With a strategic aim the text chooses a painful point: for centuries this story of Cain and Abel has never been felt to be a problem by theologians, never at any rate a stumbling block to doing further theology. But with Hildesheimer's night figure a Bible reader emerges who no longer passes over this story but is irritated, affected by the manifest injustice done to a figure like Cain. He is a Bible reader who is no longer content with the justifications for the damnation of Cain and the fact that Abel is well pleasing to God: 'The Lord looked upon Abel and his sacrifice, but upon Cain and his sacrifice he did not look'? This biblical statement (Gen.4.4), which is thought to be so questionable, rather becomes the starting point for a question about the righteousness of God himself – in favour of the human being who is condemned. The history between God on the one side and Cain and Abel on the other, which was previously accepted without question, all at once becomes a riddle.

God in a bad light

Moreover the word 'riddle' occurs six times in the text, one after the other in close succession. This only reinforces the strategic purpose of the narrator: his text is meant to undermine the apparently assured world order with disturbing questions – with the slogan: I no longer accept the creator's order from him. Indeed this questioning culminates in an unprecedented reversal of the problem of theodicy. If the classical philosophical and theological theodicy from Augustine to Leibniz had been concerned in each case to demonstrate God's innocence and justice at the cost of sinful and guilty human beings, in other words, in the face of the existence of evil it had been concerned to relieve God of any responsibility and thus burden human beings, the first-person narrator undermines such an argument, indeed resolutely turns it round. Cain's repudiation by God is not justified by his guilt (where could it come from so shortly after the creation – with no more than four human beings on earth?) but is blamed on God. The 'blatant injustice' has been committed by God. God 'was clearly 'pleased' to destroy Cain. All the worse for God.

What we have here in literary form is a biblical exegesis in the tradition of the Jewish midrash. And Hildesheimer writes his midrash from the perspective of the damned. From this perspective God appears as a capricious arbitrary God who through his preference for Abel first gave Cain a reason for killing his own brother. Indeed in addition this God condemns a perpetrator who is basically his victim. Doesn't this God suddenly appear in a 'bad light'? That the world can go on like this – mustn't this rebound on its creator? It is precisely here that the narrator sees the grinning riddle which still has not disappeared. Of all the grinning riddles it is the most lasting, the most stubborn, and because of it, at an early stage all the harmlessness in the relationship between God and human beings disappeared. It is God who bears the mark of Cain 'on his forehead' . This should suggest by analogy that people should be careful about having dealings with such a God.

Diabolical grins flash out in the face of the manifestly unavoidable fact that from the beginning the creation has been anything but successful. Therefore we can explain 'the beginning of all unrighteousness' from the figure of Cain. All this came about too early in creation for one still confidently to be able to assent to the statement, 'Behold, it was all very good.' Guilt and fallenness come too soon after the optimism about creation; original sin, the fall, the curse come too soon after the harmony of creation. This has two consequences. First, from the beginning human beings discover in themselves the capacity to pervert the order of creation which was originally good; indeed they discover the monstrous potential of making this earth into a scene of fratricide. And secondly, from the beginning God is not part of the solution but part of the problem. That the world is as it is remains God's responsibility. indeed God is to blame. 'Away with it'?

Do not give them eternal rest

Hildesheimer's companion of the night could not say 'away with it'. For him this biblical story is in any case only the endorsement of an *a priori* conviction that history generally is full of such 'grinning riddles' and that no God will solve these riddles, because he is part of the problem. Therefore the midrash is not directed against God, but turns away from God. Here too, as with Kunert, biblical exegesis adapts to the post-metaphysical age. Yet it is exciting to see that the motive of a critical grappling with God in the author's work by no means disappears, but once again comes out strongly in the late works. Around twenty years after *Tynset* the author once again presents a new, unprecedented provocation of God; now he himself comes into play as the one asking the questions. In 1986 Hildesheimer was asked to enrich a public performance of Mozart's *Requiem* with texts, i.e. add his own commentary to the existing liturgical pieces. This task once again challenged Hildesheimer, the biographer of Mozart. Here he evidently saw himself having been given a unique chance to thematize basic questions which still concerned him in his old age.

What Hildesheimer sets down on paper are neither harmless and edifying meditations on the *Requiem* nor subtle reflections on musicology and the history of culture. His text on the *Requiem* becomes a passionate Anti-Requiem, which moreover bears the provocative title, 'Lord, do not give them eternal rest'.[21] Indeed the gripping weight of these texts – thus Walter Jens recently, and rightly, in a major essay – 'belongs among the great curses and lamentations of literature'.[22] It rests, among other things, on the insight that here the 'unbeliever' Hildesheimer deliberately puts himself in the role of the 'believer' and now begins to carry on a stirring dialogue with God – as if God existed. Cain and Abel suddenly appear again, but in contrast to *Tynset* their fall is now directly agreed with God – it should be noted, with the adoption of a role which has been carefully chosen:

> Why did you do this, Lord? Could you answer this question for me? Why did you hear Abel's sacrifice, but not that of Cain? But you do not answer any questions, certainly not those of an unbeliever. I can't say that I don't understand you here.[23]

I will never forget the evening of 7 January 1989 which I spent in the house of Wolfgang Hildesheimer in Poschiavo. For after conversation and supper Hildesheimer suggested that we should watch the video of his *Requiem* together. I knew the text and had already talked with Hildesheimer about it during our conversation. But I hadn't yet seen this performance. I shall never forget how Hildesheimer himself watched this performance once again, involved and spellbound. I felt that there he had made his most profound and important statement of these years. At any rate I had never heard an 'unbeliever' speak like this of God and to God. Later Hildesheimer was to say in a personal commentary:

> I am performing an act of fundamental self-alienation, i.e. I am acting as if I *believed*. Today that is no longer imaginable. Earlier I very much wanted to believe, but this was not granted to me. Today I no longer want to – but I make common cause with *genuine* Christians.[24]

However, for this author genuine Christians are no longer those who would damage the creation. And so his whole Anti-Requiem is one long invitation to God himself not to grant eternal rest to those who destroy nature and damage creation. God the judge is invited to meet those who 'unwaveringly intervene in creation' and withhold his grace from them. Again there is this strange mixture of unbelief and belief.

Were I a believer, I would want to cry out to the Lord, 'Do not let them share in your grace! Punish them before the end of humankind that they have prepared comes on the earth. For on this day the righteous will perish with them, the innocent. Give a sign, Lord' – that's what I would say if I were a believer – 'that you will really bring this *dies irae* upon them! We want to witness' – that's what I would say -'how you distinguish between good and evil'.[25]

What language for an 'unbeliever'! (Oh, if only God had such powerful believers.) As Walter Jens has again pointed out, Hildesheimer did not personally 'believe in such a turning point' brought about by God. 'Nevertheless, inventing new and ever more perfect interplays of word and image, quotation and variation on the quotation, sign and counter-sign, he never gave up the hope that now rests on the apparently para-doxical reversal of the dictum *spero ergo sum*. The quintessence of his forming and writing is that not hope – the finding always first, the inven-tion afterwards – but the capacity to be able to go on existing proves in the last decade that: I live, and that is a sign that I do not yet despair. 'Perhaps something hopes in me, and it is that which keeps me alive?'[26]

I got the impression that the Jewish heritage in Wolfgang Hildes-heimer, which is so often present in his work only in a broken, indirect and transformed form, had once again broken through powerfully in this Anti-Requiem. In the face of the ecological catastrophe which made this writer despair of writing (he had publicly announced that he would give up writing and concentrate on painting, and kept his word), he seized on what for him was an extreme possibility: the prophetic protest, complaint and accusation. The 'role' of the prophet was to give the message new weight, the concern great earnestness, the cause universal significance. It was Hildesheimer's experience that the planet earth is in the hands of exploiters and plunderers; that the creation is being most shamefully misused by 'unscrupulous vandals, despoilers of plains, levellers of hills, polluters of water, pestilences of the spheres'. He was utterly contemptuous of those who did this kind of damage to creation, indeed he commended them to God's judgment:

Not for those who manipulate and rob us eternal losers, not for these cynics, who exploit and rationalize, who under the cover of developing our world destroy it circumspectly and systematically. Lord, no requiem for them. And also no eternal life. For that is what they expect. They regard the earth as their property and live as if they are going to live for ever. They perpetuate themselves; they leave behind their offensive monuments as testimonies to their pernicious activity. The earth is subject to them. By the time that they finally disappear, we, their victims, will long since have disappeared. They will have the last word and the last action, and the last things. Are they really to have a share in eternal rest? If I were a believer I would say that they should not. They should be made to realize. Eternal light should not shine on them.[27]

The earth in the claws of vandals, polluters, planners, despoilers, pestilences; the creation in the hands of cynical profiteers; here the writer raises in particular the problem of human guilt and responsibility. And anyone who reflects on the human riddle will be able to do so only by including the question: Why must human beings incur guilt? And conversely, why do people so often fail to recognize their guilt, suppress it, not want to perceive it? I want to illuminate this problem of guilt in two dimensions, the dimension of creation and the dimension of the individual. We have to reflect – in the language of the poets – upon the question of human responsibility for our environment and the world in which we live and human responsibility for ourselves and for the life of others.

II. The exhaustion of creation

It is striking that in no period of German literature has the topic of the threat to creation and the annihilation of creation been so virulent as in the literature of the twentieth century, especially in the literature of our time.[28]

1. First visions of the end: Expressionists

This should not be surprising if we keep in mind a remark by Wolfgang Hildesheimer:

> It is the nature of the artist that he detects seismographically the currents and phenomena which affect his existence. He grasps their presence and recognizes their significance earlier than others. He therefore also recognizes the threatening element in the changes of nature, indeed experiences it physically, and, consciously or unconsciously, assimilates this with all his senses. An artist is not only someone who communicates himself but also someone who communicates with himself.

Hildesheimer concluded from this that the artist is particularly sensitive to the 'symptoms of the "end time"':

> It cannot escape the artist . . . that nature has begun to fail. The heavy human incursions are increasingly making it our enemy. 'The death of the forests' is not just talk . . . as everyone who has seen a dead or dying wood will confirm, it is also a sign the interpretation of which forces itself home on everyone. And it must force itself home on the artist like a nightmare, in so far as he is capable of exposing himself to this testimony. For to the artist in particular, any intimation communicates itself as an event the expression of which leaves its stamp on him and becomes the measure of his quality. Yet he is hardly the only one who goes through a wood that is still alive without asking, 'How long?' In

fact anyone who sees the blight in the pine forests, this growth as a sign of death, is shown an unsuspected variant of poetry made matter.[29]

The primal apocalyptic cry

'How long?' Those who ask this question are taking up the primal apocalyptic cry which resounds through the apocalypses of the Old Testament, for example the book of Daniel: 'How long will the abomination of desolation remain?' (8.13), a cry which can still be hear in the apocalypses of the New Testament: 'How long before you will judge and avenge our blood on those who dwell upon the earth?' – thus the slain martyrs of the 'fifth seal' from the Apocalypse of John (6.10).[30] So those who speak like that today betray some apocalyptic sensitivity. What is its specific character? Not just some sensitivity towards threat and unrest, but a sensitivity to the threat to the world as a whole, to the breaking off of all previous history. No less than the end of the present world-age is expected. From time immemorial apocalyptic texts have been disturbing texts with a global dimension, threatening texts of a cosmic scope – often suppressed by those who have got used to the *status quo* and seem to dominate the world order.

No wonder that the most sensitive of writers have been the ones who have used apocalyptic imagery to express their own perceptions. Poets often use apocalyptic language with deep feeling. For because of its existence on the periphery of, or below the surface of, the church and society, the language of such texts is the least worn-out in the biblical writings. Thus it is no coincidence that the first apocalyptically fruitful period of twentieth-century German literature was the period between 1910 and 1920, the time shortly before and after the First World War.

'End of the world' – with black humour

It was the generation of the early Expressionists, born at the end of the 1880s, who used the apocalyptic motifs in their poetry to hammer a bourgeois-everyday ritualized innocence. Georg Trakl, Jakob van Hoddis and Georg Heym were all born in the same year, 1887, and even before the First World War they all began to write a poetry of destruction – whether sarcastically with black humour or solemnly with the gestures of great visions. Jakob van Hoddis with his 'End of the World' poem stands for the first variant, and Georg Heym with his ballad 'People stand forward in the streets' for the other.

Let's look first at Jakob van Hoddis, whose poem, composed in 1910, would later open the most significant collection of Expressionist poetry 'The Twilight of Mankind', by Kurt Pinthus:

End of the World

From the citizen's head, wind blows the hood,
A kind of cry resounds through the air.
Roofs collapse – and form a pair.
And on the coasts – we read – a rising flood.

The storm blows, and the wild seas hop
On land to destroy thick dams.
It makes most people's ears go pop.
And from the bridges fall the trams.[31]

This text by Hans Davidson, the son of a Berlin doctor who wrote under the pseudonym Jakob von Hoddis, has been called apocalyptic in a nutshell. Hoddis was the founding member of the Berlin Expressionist group 'The New Club' and had made a name for himself in Berlin artistic circles through sketches in the 'Neopathetic Cabaret'. The effect of his poem about the end of the world on his contemporaries was unique – probably because of its threefold effect.

– It unmasked the *false security* of middle-class society. Here trivialities of everyday life seem to have been playfully mounted to form a harmless collage. But the apparent harmlessness is merely meant to reflect how the middle-class society has repressed so much that it has not yet noted its own proneness to death: 'People's ears go pop./ From the bridges fall the trams . . .'
– It displays *sarcastic humour*. This is produced by comic word-associations: 'The wild seas hop on land to destroy thick dams.' The comic effect that this produces is further intensified by the gesture of playful childlike naivety with which the scenes of terror are presented: 'Roofs collapse – and form a pair' . . .
– Comic word-plays and sarcasms produce a sense of *superiority and freedom*. It is meant to stop in their tracks those who in the recitation of these verses at the same time see through and enjoy the readiness of middle-class society for decline.

Those who investigate the history of the time will discover that when these 'playfully destructive catastrophe strophes'[32] were being written by

Jakob van Hoddis, the painter Max Beckmann was painting his picture 'The Destruction of Messina' – depicting in spellbinding colour a natural catastrophe in which in 1908 more than half of the 150,000 inhabitants of the Italian city of Messina perished. Hoddis too had seen the grisly photographs of mass death and misery in the *Berliner Illustrierte Zeitung*. Moreover Halley's comet had flashed past the earth in May 1910. It had disturbed the masses and caused fears of spring floods, inundations, polluted air and the threat of suffocation . . .

Ruin as a cosmic fall

All this may also be the background to the poem by Georg Heym (1887–1912), one of the most brilliant early Expressionists, whose death at the age of twenty-five in a ski-ing accident at the Havel shook the Expressionist community. With great solemnity and visionary gestures this poem describes ruin as a cosmic event, and with it Heym establishes himself as one of the greatest apocalyptists in German literature.

> People stand forward in the streets
> And look up at the heavenly powers,
> See the comets, trailing fiery sheets,
> Slip threatening round the jagged towers.
>
> Astrologers stand on every tile,
> Sticking their great tubes into the sky,
> And magicians, weird, from burrows in file
> Emerge to conjure up a galaxy.
>
> Through doors disease and illness creep
> In dark shrouds. And the beds bear
> With cries and moans the sick who cannot sleep,
> While those by the coffins rend their hair.
>
> Mass suicides by night go forth
> In search of their lost being in the gloom,
> Bent towards south and west and east and north,
> Sweeping the dust, each with their shabby broom.
>
> They are like dust, around a while,
> The hairs now falling on their way.
> They jump to die, and, over the stile,
> Are laid, with dead heads, in the hay.

Wriggling once again. And beasts of the field
Stand blind around and with their horns
Gore bellies. Corpses unannealed
Lie buried under the sage and the thorns.

The year is dead and, emptied of its gales,
Hangs like a sodden cloak where water seeps;
Eternal storms utter their mournful wails,
In cloud from deeps back to more echoing deeps.

The seas are still and in the waves
The ships hang rotting and morose,
Scattered, their hulls no current laves,
The doors are barred to the heavenly close.

The seasons do not change the trees,
Which remain, forever dead, in their end
And over the desolate ways one sees
How many long-fingered branches bend.

The dying man stands up with sweating brow,
And barely has a word been spoken,
when all at once he's gone. Where is he now?
And his eyes like glass are broken.

Shadows are many. Sad and hidden away
and dreams which creep by silent doors,
And whoever awakes, oppressed by another day
Must yawn heavy sleep from greying jaws.[33]

Under the cosmic threat of death the world is beginning to turn into its opposite. That is the theme of Heym's poem. When the great signs appear in heaven, sicknesses and monstrosities grow, suicides appear, the seas cease to dance and the trees refuse to follow the natural rhythm. Unmistakable motifs from the Revelation of John have crept into this text, above all from the scenes with the seven trumpet-calls by the seven angels in chapters 8 and 9: the dead sea (third trumpet), the falling stars (fourth trumpet), tormented people (fifth trumpet), and the plague scene from chapter 15, which speaks of the seven bowls of the wrath of God.

2. Apocalypses today and yesterday

It has become clear to me that the poets of this generation manifestly drew on a reservoir of imagery in the enigmatic and disturbing book of the 'secret revelation', which corresponded to their own experiences of unrest and which described in great style the threat that they sub-consciously registered. In a way unprecedented since the baroque period, once again they made the fate of the world the basic theme of literature.

The hour of wrath returns

And today? It is remarkable how quickly references to the texts of van Hoddis and Heym are appearing, and how quickly one can jump over the centuries:

And I saw
when the lamb broke the seventh seal,
the earth quaked with mighty thrusts,
the sun lost its light
and became as dark as a black sack,
and the moon began to bleed all around,
and the stars fell down from heaven to earth
like figs when the autumn storm comes
and sweeps through the branches.
The heaven rolled up
as if it were a book
and became tiny
and the hills and islands disappeared.
Nothing was any longer where it belonged.
And the lords of the world,
the kings, the great men,
the marshals and dignitaries,
the rich and strong,
all, the free and the slaves,
sought refuge in caves
and hid under the rocks of the mountains
and said to the stone and the mountain
Protect us! Cover us!
Hide us from the face of the one
Who sits on the throne,
the ONE

the UNNAMEABLE,
Protect us from the wrath of the Lamb.
For the day, the day of curse is here
the hour of great wrath.
Who, alas, could stand?

This text sounds like a poem from the 'Twilight of Humankind' which sketches the scenario of a destruction of the world in rhythmic prose. In fact it is part of the Revelation of John (6.6–17), which was published – not by chance – a few years ago in a new translation by Walter Jens.[34]

However, if we compare the original with its numerous variations in modern literature, we will note that the metaphysical horizon – which the Bible still takes for granted – is now darkened, indeed has often sunk. In the twentieth century apocalyptic language has detached itself from the horizon of the Bible and taken on a function of its own in the poetic secular sphere. What function? It serves:

– in a diagnosis of the time to detect social symptoms of crisis of global dimensions;
– to promote the self-enlightenment of the literary subject;
– to make the literary public aware of the disastrous interplay of human action.

Nothing is impossible for us

An essay by Günter Kunert entitled 'On the Apocalypse: A Reprimand', is characteristic of this:

I do not want to lose myself in philosophical considerations. I want to refrain from doing a solo dance on the end of a needle, something of which in any case only the angels are capable. Instead of this I want to keep to the original meaning of the word apocalypse. What it means is 'revelation'. The word only later changed its meaning to catastrophe, to the end of the world. However, I cannot speak of divine revelation like John, to whom God himself dictated the text of his vision. As we know, God has fallen silent and turned away from us, since we have undertaken to replace him. And we have managed this. The miracles we have produced are more astonishing than those once performed by him. Indeed they are really no longer miracles, but only successful solutions to problems in the sphere of the natural sciences. The revival of the dead has long been taking place in the intensive care units of our clinics. And surgery allied with medical techniques is succeeding in making the blind see and the lame walk on the conveyor belt. We are raising ourselves into a heaven that is increasingly becoming empty. We give psychiatric treatment to those possessed by demons. We produce purgatory and inferno by means of nuclear power. And if we wanted to, by pressing a button we could make the whole of creation disappear, in less than seven days or seven hours. Nothing, or almost nothing, is impossible for us. Should we not be thought to be like gods?[35]

This text is already a reflection of the changed situation of the 1980s and 1990s. And there are many reasons for a heightened perception of apocalypse at this time. The explosion of the atomic bombs over Hiroshima and Nagasaki had been all too quickly suppressed in the 1950s. Already in 1956 the philosopher Günter Anders was calling this 'apocalypse blindness'.[36] To the nuclear threat to the world there had to be added the ecological, chemical and biological threats for the collective consciousness of guilt to awaken. Carl Avery, with his book *The End of Providence* (1973), in which he took up and popularized the results of the study of the Club of Rome on the limits of growth and natural resources, was one of the first writers to understand the new situation.[37] Titles of films from the 1970s and 1980s like *Apocalypse Now*, *Atomic Café* or *The Day After* also signalled a new public awareness on a broad and already commercialized basis. Significant literature reacted in its own way. I shall attempt to illuminate the basic pattern by means of key publications.

3. Nothing will be as before: Christa Wolf

In 1983, with great journalistic success, Christa Wolf brought to life for our time an archetypal figure from antiquity: Cassandra, the prophetess of doom and disaster from Greek mythology.

From Cassandra to Accident

The rediscovery of Cassandra is also the rediscovery of a collective blindness which shapes the time in two respects. First there is the blindness to a millennia-old history of patriarchal domination over women: 'In Cassandra, we have one of the first female figures whose fate shapes in advance what is to happen to women for three thousand years: they will be made objects.'[38] Secondly, there is the blindness to an excess of nuclear weapons which can only be described with one word 'madness'. And for Christa Wolf there is a connection between the domination of women by the patriarchate and the domination of the world by weapons, between sexism and a mania for security. Therefore she revives Cassandra, the woman who as daughter of the Trojan king Priam once predicted the downfall of the city of Troy and found no one to believe her.

This is also an indirect depiction of the relationship between literature and the political public. But as in the case of the mythical Cassandra, in the case of the author too the intensity of the warning is inversely proportionate to its effect on the public. So Christa Wolf does not use *Cassandra* to work out a centuries-old history of sexist and political fear and domination. The book also restores to literature a symbolic figure with whom to identify, without this figure being allowed to become an excuse. For Christa Wolf wanted to show that today one need 'no longer be Cassandra':

Most people are beginning to detect what is to come by themselves. A discontent which many register as a void, as a loss of meaning, makes them fearful. We cannot hope that the worn-out institutions can provide new meaning. There is a zigzag course. But no escape is in sight. People feel left to their own devices. Australia is no way out.[39]

So literature is a refusal of escapism, of the flight mentality; it points beyond itself to the sphere of praxis in solidarity. In the face of the threat to the world, the unexpressed slogan of the book is 'Stand firm, do not flee!'

Three years after *Cassandra* the vision had become partial reality. For in April 1986, the Chernobyl catastrophe suddenly changed everything. Christa Wolf called her report on this one day *Accident. A Day's News*, tersely understating what could no longer be described in its terrible reality, with unforeseeable consequences. The core of a nuclear power station had melted down in the Ukrainian city of Chernobyl and had released a considerable mass of radioactivity into the air which then spread all over Europe. People were contaminated, crops destroyed.

The book takes the form of a diary made up of letters. The narrator is writing to her brother, who at the same time is having to undergo an operation for a brain tumour. And what she writes indicates a terrible awareness of a turning point: no familiar look at the green meadows, at the trees, the fields, the clouds, the milk, which does give her a strange feeling, a sense of anxiety and threat: the talk of the 'radiant heaven'. What sudden ambiguity! A whole tradition of poetry of nature, cut off, become waste paper. How could that happen?

Technology and anxiety

Moreover at the centre of the book stands the basic question 'where evolution, the humanization of human beings went wrong, so that pleasure and destruction were associated, so that development, technology, the domination of nature was inextricably bound up with a delight in killing'.[40] Thus in its association of individual history and the history of humankind, *Accident* is a contribution to the theme of technology and anxiety. If since the nineteenth century technology had emerged to free humankind from disturbing natural forces which for a long time it had not understood, seeking to control and dominate them in order to minimize anxiety, at the latest in the second half of the twentieth century a crisis of confidence in technology and science has spread to an unprecedented degree. Literature gives a poetic account of this crisis of confidence by reinforcing the widespread feeling that science and technology produce more problems than they can solve. The apparent rulers of the world are no longer its masters. And this inability to master it prompts new anxiety, now from science and technology themselves. What once promised a defence against anxiety is now encouraging the heightening of anxiety. We may follow the diagnosis of our time made by the sociologist Wolf Lepenies:

Science and technology entered on their triumphant course when they established themselves in the face of magic and religion as more effective and finally unrivalled mechanisms for coping with anxiety. In so doing they fostered the illusion that anxiety could be neutralized in science . . . This self-deception remained unproblematical as long as science and technology continued to make their spectacular progress in the knowledge of external nature and in the demolition of external fears. But this progress has now come to a standstill: gene technology and the splitting of the atom have produced consequences which no longer remove anxieties but cause them, the fear of the irreparable poisoning of our environment and the destruction of the world in which we live... If the achievements of the process of civilization are even to be preserved, technology and science will have to begin very rapidly indeed to learn to fear again.[41]

Literature can make its own contribution to this. Books like *Cassandra* and *Accident* have the character of an interruption. They seek to disturb in order to accelerate public disquiet over the fact that human beings can already 'produce' technologically more than they can imagine (G. Anders). That means that through technological inventions people have released forces the effects of which they cannot even suspect, far less control. In an extreme case the human race can already do away with itself with the means at its disposal. A post-human time has become imaginable. We learn what that might look like from a 1986 novel.

4. The nightmare of the end of humanity: Günter Grass

If the theme of Christa Wolf's works was the attempt to present cata-strophic disruptions as public disturbances and collective transgressions as acts of a new self-assertion of humankind over the origin and goal of its history, in his end-time 1986 novel *The Rat*, Günter Grass radicalizes the theme of the threat to creation once more in an unprecedented way. I confess that no novel of the 1980s so taught me fear and at the same time made me so impotent. It is here – with the problem of living on in an exhausted creation and the motivation needed to do this – that theo-logians must begin to grapple with Grass. And this question has lost none of its urgency, even if three years after *The Rat* there was a historical shift in Germany which first of all made it necessary to grapple with other questions. For German reunification has by no means exhausted the theme of living on against the horizon of a possible end to the world. It has now been further accentuated – against the background of the one nation.

The Enlightenment – a failure?

I feel *The Rat* as a burning wound in the German literary consciousness. For in a dream of the narrator, the reader is shown the possibility that the self-destruction of humankind has already taken place and that, after this end of the human period, only rats have survived. Grass once again presents world theatre – though with the difference that the curtain already seems already to have fallen on the last act of the drama of humankind. For the narrator, circling the earth in a space capsule, surveys the total devastation of the earth and what life is still left on an earth devoid of human beings. I do not want to go into the details of the

humanly possible and to be modest towards the remains of a destroyed nature? And a last question. Do we want to do what we could do: feed one another until hunger is only a legend, a bad story of 'once upon a time'?

The answers to these questions are overdue. And I cannot give them. But in my perplexity I nevertheless know that the future will be possible again only if we find an answer and do what we ought to do as guests on this globe of nature, by no longer making one another anxious, by relieving one another of anxiety, by disarming to the point of nakedness.[48]

The author's 'perplexity' intensified further during the 1980s, and *The Rat* is an expression of it. Above all in the face of the failure of the disarmament negotiations between the great powers in the 1980s, Grass gave up hope that human beings could really be ready to say no to their inventions in an act of renunciation, organize society globally in such a way that hunger disappeared, and shape their relationship to nature in such a way that they understood themselves anew as 'guests on this globe of nature'.

Struggling with the possibility of hope

Thus the end of *The Rat* is one long struggle with the possibility of hope. On the last three pages there is a gripping song of hope which could be the counterpart to the song of farewell with which the novel opens. Moreover the first lines of both songs are diametrically opposed: the first poem began 'I dreamed I had to take leave', and now the poem begins with the line 'I dreamed that I could take hope'. This hope is spelt out strophe by strophe. It would almost be infectious, were it not for the laughter of the She-rat, which shows up such hope as self-deception:

> I dreamed that I could take hope,
> barely a crumb or whatever is left
> on plates eaten clean, and hope that something,
> not an idea, more like an accident,
> supposedly friendly, was on its way,
> unobstructed by frontiers,
> that it was spreading, contagious,
> a salutary plague.

I dreamed that I could hope again
for winter apples, Martinmas goose,
strawberries year after year,
for my sons' incipient baldness,
my daughters' green, my grandchildren's postcard greetings,
for advances and compound interest, as though mankind
had unlimited credit again.

I dreamed that hope was permissible
and looked for words to justify it,
dreaming to justify my hope.
So I tried, I said good,
new, small hope. First cautious,
then sudden, I thought. I called it
treacherous, begged it to have mercy on us.
The last hope I dreamed
was consumptive.

I dreamed: A last hope is permissible;
there's sympathy and understanding.
People leave their ignition keys lying around,
they trust one another and leave their doors unlocked.
My hope did not deceive me;
no one ate his bread unshared; except that the merriment
I had hoped for, though all-embracing, was not
our kind of merriment: rats were laughing at us
when the very last hope was forfeit.[49]

But the narrator has not yet confessed defeat; he still contends with the She-rat over this, his 'last hope'. For despite all the rattish laughter, the narrator wants to maintain a perspective. And so the book ends at least with a hypothesis:

Only assuming that we humans are still . . .
All right. Let's assume
... but this time let us live for one another and peacefully, do you hear,
gently and lovingly, as nature made us.
A beautiful dream, said the She-rat, before dissolving.[50]

So what is the ultimate aim of this book? Historical fatalism and a radical renunciation of the Enlightenment? Is the destruction of humankind to some degree unstoppable? Is it coming like an apocalyptic horror which human beings can no longer influence? In his 'personal interpretations' of the novel Grass is as divided as in the overall conception of it.[51] On the one hand he depicts human beings in his book as defeated. For him as a narrator 'the arguments for the human position' to be advanced against the She-rat are 'bankrupt'. Unfortunately the She-rat is 'more convincing'. So his book is a 'catastrophic book at a catastrophic time'; it corresponds to 'our time, our situation', but he, Grass, is attempting to present the whole 'not in a melancholy way' but with his own means, including all the 'comedy' that there is in such a desperate situation. His book is not meant to be 'a book to fake hope, but to communicate insight, to convey terror'. For if people again want to have reason to hope, insight into and fear about the situation into which 'we' have got ourselves are indispensable presuppositions.

Such remarks already show that the last point of refuge of the argument in this book is the prevention of catastrophe. On the other hand, Grass thinks it very important to note that his novel is not an apocalyptic book in the classical sense. An 'apocalypse in the sense of that of John on Patmos' would mean the acceptance of a 'dark fate' imposed on us, which human beings cannot change. So his novel is 'not a book with seven seals'. The threat that is there is all 'human work'; including the 'self-destruction of the human race'. So it could also be 'only human work' if we wanted to avert it. As Grass points out: 'There is no excuse. We cannot say that the fate is imposed from above so that we cannot escape it. We could escape it if we acted against it.'

Thus acting against it might have been the author's ultimate motivation in writing this novel. There is an insistence on political action, though this now no longer stems from a political vision but from a desperate comedy. Grass's book still works by a poetics of catharsis – to some degree in a last act of trust in the Enlightenment: the possible reality of human self-destruction is meant to terrify and thus produce the opposite effect. At any rate readers are not to see their political fatalism confirmed by this novel and react to the apocalyptic maxim with the attitude that destruction can come – and the sooner, the better. So Grass is writing from a basic attitude of doubt which is not greater, simply because not to write would only accelerate the process of destruction and further the forces which are indifferent as to whether the world goes to the devil. The author himself points in this direction when, alluding to his poem, 'I dreamed I had to take leave', he remarks:

This poem, in a love for life, lists everything that gives joy, from the small things to the ideas which human beings have. That shows that I am very attached to life and do not know anything better than living.

And I also attempt to make something of this possibility of living consciously – with the means at my disposal. In writing *The Rat* it was not my concern to write a sinister book about destruction. There are very comic passages in this book, and I think that that is also conveyed to the reader. Because comedy, desperate comedy, is often also the most precise expression of despair. It goes with the book.[52]

5. Laughter as a prophylactic for cynicism: Kurt Marti

'Rats were laughing at us/ when the very last hope was forfeit.' It seems that the hope for a new 'being for one another' and a new 'peacefulness in love' can only be asserted to the sounds of sceptical and cynical laughter. And what is only hinted at by Grass is taken up, reinforced and heightened into new dimensions by the Swiss poet Kurt Marti. He too sees himself confronted with the basic question: how do we live on in an exhausted creation without allowing the 'beautiful dream' of human beings automatically to turn to cynical farewell laughter? Here I found important a volume of poetry, *Mein barfüssig Lob* ('My Barefoot Praise'), published a year after *The Rat* (in 1987).[53] When I read it, I felt that this poet had put my confusion, my impotence, my linguistic perplexity, indeed the whole split situation in which I find myself as a contemporary and a Christian, into verses which are personally closer to me than Günter Grass's 'world theatre'.

Chernobyl and after

Kurt Marti's slim volume of poetry, like the books of Christa Wolf and Günter Grass, taught me first of all to see. It compelled me to concede that in terms of time and creation we are undeniably at a great turning point, an epoch-making break of unprecedented dimensions. His very first poem in this book 'after the visit of the radioactive cloud' speaks of the experiences of a turning point which concerned both Christa Wolf and Günter Grass: the experience of a turning point which is associated with the name Chernobyl:

our garden
– defenceless the grass the bushes –
has lost its innocence
and will never be
as it was

our garden
defenceless the plants the weeds –
now stores up deaths in the life
of the roots: caesium strontium
crypton plutonium

our garden
– defenceless the trees the flowers –
will keep blossoming again
for us who in perplexity ask
what still blossoms for us.

Three simple strophes which not only show that a nature poem would be
groundless enthusiasm today without the technical jargon of chemistry,
but rather indicate (as Christa Wolf does) that despite all the life that
continues on the surface ('our garden will keep blossoming again') –
nothing will be as it used to be. The phrase the 'radiant heaven' – an age-
old cliché of German nature poetry: what ambiguity all at once of life
and death, of beauty and terror! There is also ambiguity where the poet
begins to play with words, and as a reader one does not know whether
one may laugh or whether laughter should die on one's lips:

A wastrel is
the modern man

waste is rising
up to our necks

sea earth air
so much waste

nuclear waste
will kill our grandchildren

waste age
waste age
so we waste
one another.

Two-line verses, the playfulness of which merely conceals the extent of the destruction which is their cause. It is this merciless confrontation with the catastrophes inflicted by human beings on creation which leads to the 'learning to see' in this book.

Understandable feelings of self-abdication

It is good not to get an over-hasty answer in these texts. It is good that the perplexity is conceded, that the author openly expresses his melancholy, that he does not spare his doubt and despair:

the finger still types
the olivetti
rebellious texts
into the blue

but the eyes
already no longer believe

lips
once stubbornly pouted
go thin

is there
still something
to say?

my delight
changes
to be no one

the captains
remain unswerving
on a course for destruction

the world
a tear – in whose
blinded eye?

Remarkably laconic lines, slowing down, fragmenting into short lines and nuclear words and provoking all the more intense reflection. I too know the mood of these verses: the seeming rebellion, seeing through delusion, bringing something about by language; this wordlessness used in words, this impotence of language put into language. I know the feeling of self-abnegation, of longing gently to take leave of everything, the desire to be no one and no longer having to be anyone. Yes, I too know this mood:

> have gone to the dogs
> everything for the cat
> my hurrah flew away
>
> from undepths
> i call
> god
> to me

With nonsense against madness

I live in an overdriven world which has gone quite mad. I cannot really see through its powers and structures, and its real rulers remain anonymous. Indeed my own life is somewhat overdriven, when I make it clear to myself that my good conscience is bought above all by overlooking the fact that I live beyond my spiritual means, because the repression mechanisms are still functioning well in me. It is truly laughable, so grotesque do I often feel the discrepancy between reality and possibility. The poet in particular must also cope with this situation. I understand that his situation as a writer is at least as split as mine is as an academic theologian. He writes verse – but what are poetic words in the face of the true spokesmen of the world? He is there on the literature market – and by his presence confirms those power mechanisms which he tries to unmask by writing. He lives not only in catastrophe but also by it. In short, he reproduces the reality that he seeks to escape by writing.

But in reading his texts I detect that he is aware how two-faced his role is, this one who treads the boundary between pastoralia and poetry. He writes from a nevertheless. And I note that this author attempts to protect himself from his consumers by striking up an almost crazy tune, the song of the hurdy-gurdy man ('O my dear Augustine, everything's gone'). He takes this to excess and drives it to the limits of madness. In other words, the madness of the misuse of creation is reflected in Marti in nonsense verses like these:

sad am i
go and lie
cover me
with your body

naked and helpless
lip to lip –
go outside
field and wood a tip.

Indeed, as in the naïve nihilistic hurdy-gurdy song, here too the normality of simple verse and rhyme and the shrill anomaly of reality coincide. As a poet Marti defends himself against the ecological madness with nonsense poetry:

Go close
go
Lyhyric
adieu
your head
drives in the sea
a food
wings blue
o sole
miaow

In other words, given the apocalyptic madness he has brought on himself, the poet evidently can speak of it adequately only if he puts his verses on the borders between sense and nonsense. Anyone who wants to speak about cruelty must not seek to flog it to death through verses. Anyone who wants to be heard must refuse consuming smoothness. Those whose theme is madness must not encourage this trivialization through 'beautiful literature'. They must write as if there were no more writing. They must speak as if words had come to an end. In short, they must force their speech to be silent, in order still to be audible, because silence could be misinterpreted as an agreement with the status quo.

Praising and laughing as brothers and sisters

Thus Kurt Marti shares the fate of modern poetry generally, the best representatives of which (from Gottfried Benn and Günter Eich to Paul Celan and Nelly Sachs) knew that the monstrosity of reality can no longer be put into words, but that one must speak if one is not to be guilty of the complicity of silence. So Marti too must put his verse on the borderline between sense and nonsense, of speaking and silence. What is left are lyric fragments, extremely terse, verses reduced to splinters of words and syllables; what is left is an author who under the fool's cap allows himself a ghostly delight in word-plays and twists of language so as to be able to hold up a mirror to the twisted world. Trust in time, praise of the present? In an age of apocalyptic madness this seems possible only in an awareness of folly. Praise and laughter have become sisters:

> who did not laugh
> when don quixote the fool
> nevertheless hurls himself blindly
> into the adventure of praise
>
> who did not laugh?
> who did not laugh –
> If a laugh
> is still there

This laughter has nothing to do with cheap optimism, with the suppression of problems or with covering over the conflicts of the world. In their laughter Christians do not live against the conflicts but in them, do not turn their backs on the problems but resist them. But laughter also expresses the capacity of Christians to live in a world without being oppressed by its contradictions and swallowed up by its abysses. So laughter is the expression of a co-existence in the world with all its contradictions, without abandoning oneself completely to the structure of this world or being insensitive to the contradictions. Laughter is a prophylactic against cynicism. Laughter means finding a form of reconciled coexistence with the contradictions and abysses of the world, without suppressing these or allowing oneself to be fatalistically oppressed by them.[54]

That is what I learn in this lyric school of seeing. Today declarations of trust in the world take the form of fool's talk; praise of creation seems possible only in awareness of one's own craziness. But in a poet like Marti this awareness of one's own craziness is no excuse for dropping out and turning one's back on the conflicts. The evocation of folly does not stem from a cynicism which thinks that it has seen through everything, in order to pretend that one may legitimately leave the world to itself and ultimately to the devil. No, in Marti the talk of craziness is neither pathology nor pose. Rather, it stems from a hope which has no rational foundation and which cannot have a foundation, but which is there indestructibly and undimmed – as a tradition of a crazy hope:

> it may be
> that I do not rightly understand
> what being born means
>
> it may be
> that I am waiting at a lost post
>
> it may be
> that it is crazy
> who still counts on miracles
> crazy like the women
> who in tomb of a dead man
> discovered the new birth

Thus just as much as Christa Wolf's accident report or Günther Grass's world theatre, Kurt Marti's nonsense poetry is borne up by a gulf stream of anti-fatalism – in keeping with the insight formulated by Grass: 'There is no way of talking oneself out of it. One cannot say that this sort of thing is imposed from above as a fate that we cannot escape. We can escape it if we act against it.'

III. The Unavoidability of Guilt

But how can one become active if people do not recognize their responsibility at all? What if they repress their share of guilt and constantly deny their guilty entanglement in an event? We must single out once again and at length what Grass, in search of the riddle of human nature, already indicated as a problem. What if people do not recognize at all that they fail? What if they constantly believe themselves to be in the right, aware of no guilt?

1. Vain quest for guilt: Max Frisch

Hardly any author of distinction in German-speaking literature after 1945 has posed and developed the question of guilt so constantly and in such a penetrating way as Max Frisch. Hardly a prose work (above all the two diaries), hardly a play (from *Now They Are Singing Again* to *Andorra*), hardly a novel or a story (from *Homo Faber* to *Bluebeard*) does not contain reflections on this problem.[55] So we should seek a dialogue with this author in order to become aware of the problems of diagnosing guilt and dealing with it.

Encounters with post-war Germany

Born in 1911, even as a Swiss citizen Max Frisch could not avoid being aware of the Second World War. From 1939 he had to do military service in the artillery, which consisted above all in protecting the Swiss frontiers against possible Nazi attacks. The question why a people like the Germans with their cultural tradition could resort to such barbarities occupied Frisch at a very early stage. Moreover, after the war he expected that those Germans who had survived intellectually in the struggle against National Socialism, for example the Christian poets Ernst Wiechert and Werner Bergengruen, would reflect critically on their entanglement in guilt. Would they embody 'another Germany'?

But when, at the age of thirty-five, in 1946 Frisch studied Wiechert's autobiographical account *Ein Totenwald* ('A Forest of the Dead') or Bergengruen's collection of poems, *Dies Irae*, he was disappointed. Certainly Wiechert had been concerned about the annihilation of the Jews, but his report did not 'anywhere contain a clear and sober question'. Unchanged as he was (as already emerged from the melody and the metaphor of his language), this author contented himself with 'laments of a dangerously bombastic kind'. And Bergengruen? He too certainly talked of guilt. However, his poem 'To the Nations', which was programmatically put at the end of the volume of poems I have mentioned, dissolved 'the German guilt in a religious way into general religious guilt'. The conclusion must be that Max Frisch failed to find prominent German intellectuals making specific political guilt a critical theme after the cruel war:

> We outsiders in particular, who remain aware that we have not suffered the distress directly, but only from the intimations of those who have been years in danger, would really have expected to encounter a completely different tone, a tone of deep sobriety, without hymns, without the insidious reverence for all that is unclear, which wherever one can name things by name contents itself with vagueness and become intoxicated with it: a tone without incense, a tone without the soothing sadness which is not just sadness but the enjoyment of sadness; a tone which does not resort to haziness, and escape into feelings.[56]

Frisch then presents his own political and moral struggle with the problem of guilt in one of his earliest plays, *Now They Are Singing Again*, from 1945. Here the author sees the moral question of guilt and responsibility closely bound up with the political and social question of the causes of guilt. In this play the young soldier Karl, a representative of the newest generation, has incurred guilt and is aware of his guilt. He has recognized that he cannot free himself from guilt over this war with the 'excuse of obedience'. Without any ifs and buts, Karl concedes:

> Obedience is no excuse. Even if one makes obedience one's last virtue, it does not free us from responsibility. That's how it is. Nothing frees us from responsibility, nothing. It is given to us, each of us, to each his own. One cannot give one's responsibility to another to control. One cannot shed the burden of personal freedom – that is what we have tried to do, and that is our guilt.[57]

The counterpart to this young soldier is his father, the teacher. He is portrayed as the representative of that unpolitical philistinism which played so pernicious a role in the Third Reich. So it is hardly surprising that Frisch was publicly attacked, indeed in a leading article in the *Neue Zürche Zeitung,* particularly over this figure. Challenged to defend himself, Frisch depicted the background to his personal choice:

> In recent weeks, when we were soldiers on the frontier and were talking with many Germans, with terrifying frequency I often met a third figure from the German camp, the teacher: the German feeling of innocence, the German hybris which presents itself as innocent astonishment as to why the world will not heal in the German way, the flight into the voluntary and temperamental, all these are things which, if we talk long enough, must often also be noticed by those Germans who regard themselves as respectable and innocent. The teacher's complicity consists in the lack of a bond between inner life and public reality. Too frequently there has been a lack of civil courage, and it is this which has made possible the last twelve years in Germany.[58]

However, the teacher does not get off unscathed. When his own wife dies in a raid and his son Karl commits suicide in despair, he too recognizes his blindness and accuses the rulers in Germany of their crime. Arrested, he is shot as a traitor . . .

Guilt distinguishes human beings from animals

Thus the motive for this drama is political and didactic: suppressed guilt should be recognized self-critically and this recognition should help towards the political analysis of the causes of guilt. The aim is not a cheap assignation of guilt or the perpetuation of guilt-feelings: the aim of the play is to arouse 'civic courage', the civic courage which, the author believes, would have made resistance against the demon of National Socialism possible had it been there earlier. Here Max Frisch is reflecting quite self-critically on his role as a Swiss observer of the political scene. But that does not prevent him from unequivocally taking up a position on German guilt:

> The suspicion that in the same circumstances we (as Swiss) could not have been equally guilty is not yet a reason for us to overlook or even forgive that guilt. Forgiveness, too, is arrogance. As Swiss citizens we

must realize that the German does not need us to become aware of his guilt; indeed, it could even happen that the righteous are taught by the guilty, in particular the self-righteous, and I have seen quite a few of these in Swiss uniform over the past week, when we have been guarding refugees and those who have come over. We do not have enough paper anywhere to tell of that. But if we are concerned with the tragedy of the German people, we are probably in agreement that they can investigate themselves only to a modest degree; on the best show-ing, our journalism, and even the play which has been attacked, can be no more than attempts to work on the clarity that we need and to guard ourselves against premature simplification.[59]

It is important here that Frisch does not see the concession of guilt as inhuman and thus as something that humiliates people, but as specifically human. The capacity for guilt distinguishes human beings from animals. Precisely because human beings acknowledge their guilt, they reflect on the spirit that distinguishes them from animals, a spirit which can ulti-mately also prevent them from sinking below the level of humanity:

> If guilt were not attributed to brutal inhumanity but to a failure of the spirit in the face of violence, we would be confronting an unconscious current which again turns truth into falsehood. What does that mean? We are probably agreed that an animal can never be guilty as such, no matter how bestially it acts. Why not? It is not endowed with spirit, which could and should have guided it otherwise. So only the spirit, the very thing that distinguishes us from animals, could and should have preserved us from our inhumanity.[60]

Thus in Frisch guilt become a theme at a very early stage, in the interest of political enlightenment, and to encourage civil courage, new reflection on 'spirit' and 'humanity'. This interest also underlies the writing of his novel *Homo Faber*, in which Frisch now radicalizes the problems of political guilt so that they pose a fundamental question about a particu-lar type of time. This time the focus is not the present but the past. And I have to confess that no literary text has been more important to me for the question of guilt than this novel, because here the author himself is already writing against a figure which is so typical of a particular spirit of the time, the bane of the time, that of 'not having been', i.e. of not feeling to blame or responsible for anything – according to the slogan: the others are always to blame.

2. Homo Faber – enlightened but blinded

For a better understanding, it is necessary to reconstruct briefly the complex narrative framework of the novel, especially as the narrative is itself the reconstruction of a failed life.[61] The Swiss citizen Walter Faber is waiting in an Athens hospital for an operation which will be a matter of life and death. And while he waits, he gives an account of the last three and a half months of his life. They were chaotic, beyond comparison with anything that he had experienced previously. It had all begun when as an engineer travelling the world on behalf of UNESCO he had had an emergency landing with a plane in the Mexican desert on the way to an exhibition in Caracas. Granted, he had emerged unscathed and after three days all the passengers were rescued, but Faber had made the acquaintance of a fellow-traveller who proved to be the brother of a former Zurich student friend of his. This former student friend, Joachim Henke from Düsseldorf, had evidently disappeared in the jungle of Guatemala, and the brother was on the way to try to find him.

Without really knowing why he is doing it, after being rescued from the desert Faber decides not to continue his journey to Caracas, but to join in the search for his friend. They set out on an endless and laborious journey through the jungle, and two weeks later find Joachim – who has hanged himself in a hut on his plantation in the middle of the primal forest. That is the starting point for the novel *Homo Faber,* which is set in 1957 and appeared the same year. It's a book which begins like an adventure story and continues like an adventure story, but towers above all its predecessors in that the question of guilt breaks into this commonplace stuff like a meteorite and in this way gives the novel anthropological depth.

An experiment in matters of guilt

With Walter Faber, Max Frisch wanted to depict not so much a complex individual figure as a type of the spirit of the age. And after the Second World War, the dominant spirit of the age is the spirit of the natural sciences and technology. The author makes his hero candidly confess what he makes no sense of: novels and dreams, landscapes and emotional experiences, folklore and flowers, religions and myths. Faber is depicted as a person who does not believe in 'providence' and 'fate' and regards life as a matter of probability. Even the improbable is still regarded as a limit case of the possible. Mathematics and cybernetics are enough for someone who as a technician is used to seeing things 'as they are' and as a rule trusts machines more than human beings. In short, in this novel Frisch has in view a person who can cope and for whom things are possible, who is a detached sceptic about everything: 'It's the same with the whole of man – the construction is possible but the material is no good: flesh isn't a material but a curse.'[62]

Walter Faber, unmarried and fulfilled by his work, could have gone on living as he did had not his history taken a surprising turn after the events in the primeval forest of Guatemala. For after finally carrying out his task in Caracas – contrary to his usual habits – he decides to return to Europe not by plane but by ship, from New York to Le Havre. On this journey he becomes infatuated with a girl twenty-years younger than he is; he makes her an offer of marriage, leaves her after their arrival, seeks her out again in Paris, and starts on a journey with her through Italy and Greece. Gradually Faber finds that the one whom he met so much 'by chance' on the ship is again someone who builds a bridge to his past, which had apparently been so well-contained.

The young girl, Sabeth, is in fact the daughter of a former friend of his, a German half-Jew, Hanna Landsberg, who similarly studied with him in Zurich and who had later married his friend Joachim Henke. And at that time Faber had even offered to marry her to prevent her being expelled from Switzerland. She had refused, although she was pregnant by him. Hanna had separated from him, and Faber had assumed that she would have the child aborted. Since then he had not seen her again. When Faber now hears from Sabeth who her mother is, he takes it for granted that she must be the daughter of the man whom Hanna married later, the child of Joachim Henke, who had just committed suicide in the primal forest of Guatemala.

But there are yet more 'coincidences'. When they arrive in Greece, on a walk by the sea Sabeth, who in the meantime has become Faber's lover, is been bitten by a snake and falls. In panic Faber takes her to an Athens hospital, which involves a wearisome car journey. The mother has to be informed, and suddenly – after twenty years – Hanna and Faber come face to face. She has meanwhile become an established, though embittered, art historian, who 'sticks the past together'[63] – as she says sarcastically – in an archaeological institute in Athens, with the help of fragments. The end of the shared history comes quickly: Sabeth dies, not from the snake-bite but from her fall, the severity of which the doctors underestimated. Furthermore, Faber learns from Hanna that he has had his own daughter as a lover, for Hanna had not terminated her pregnancy at that time. Faber, who once again sets off on an exhibition tour through South America, is suddenly smitten by a stomach illness, leaves his job, and returns to Athens, where he is preparing for his stomach operation in hospital and composing his 'report'.

Why Homo Faber is guilty and doesn't notice it

Make what we will of the plausibility of this story, there is no mistaking the fact that here the author himself is going to the limits of the probable. For him the improbable is clearly the limit case of the possible. I think it important to recognize that as in a laboratory experiment the author wants to show us how a hero of this kind behaves in crisis situations. Thus here we have a kind of experiment in matters of guilt, carefully devised, subtly and cunningly, by an author who uses his figure so to speak as a lure, as a trap for his invented character. And the degree to which this figure is caught in the trap becomes clear from the fact that to the end he cannot recognize that there is such a trap, i.e. that his life has opened up an abyss of guilt.

So that is one dimension of the novel, the subjective dimension of innocence. Frisch presents us with a man who subjectively deludes himself that he is innocent and to the end of his life is unaware of any guilty mistake. His 'report' is meant to show that he is innocent of the death of his daughter. Moreover Faber has some important arguments to support him: first, he had no idea that he had a daughter at all. Secondly, it is not forbidden to fall in love with a girl and make her his lover. Thirdly, the girl caused her own accident and the doctors who did not recognize that a fractured skull was the real cause of her death share in the blame. All rationally clear, plausible, reasonable grounds. What could he do about the death of this girl? 'What did I do wrong?'[64] This assertion of innocence is the outspoken-unspoken ground bass on every page of the book.

And yet there is a second dimension in this book, an 'objective dimension': that of guilt. And this can already be detected in the subjective dimension. The irritated tone in which Faber composes his justification itself makes it clear that he is on the defensive. The mere fact that there is a report at all suggests that its author is under pressure to explain himself. In writing, Walter Faber is already in the guilt trap which he has subjectively always denied. That makes him two-faced: although he 'really' has nothing to blame himself for, he feels accused; although he 'really' cannot do anything, he feels forced to unburden himself;

although he is 'really' in the right, he has to justify himself. Justify himself for what? Why? Before whom?

Walter Faber has to justify himself because in a conscious-unconscious way he feels that all the reasonable, plausible, illuminating arguments in the world cannot disguise the fact that his own daughter is lying on her deathbed after her father has made her his lover. The death of an innocent young girl stands at the end of a story in which Walter Faber was involved. Indeed, Faber shares the responsibility for the existence of this girl in the first place. Whether he wants to perceive it or not, he is entangled in the story of this girl and, when it ends catastrophically, he shares the blame.

If we have understood these two levels, it becomes clear why Max Frisch might have been interested in giving literary form to the problems of guilt once again in 1957.The figure of Homo Faber is meant to show up the mechanisms of exoneration and excuse in his modern contemporaries, their delusion of innocence and their addiction to exoneration. Just as the play *Now They Are Singing Again* has the past in view, so the novel *Homo Faber* has the present in view. A case study shows that assumed ignorance is no excuse for guilt, and self-justification can be based on suppression of guilt. But what should Faber have done?

Human beings do not determine their own lives

What insight does the novel seek into its hero? If I see it rightly, the failure of Homo Faber lies in his inability to use the breaks caused by the unplanned, the fortuitous, the impenetrable in his life as the occasion for a change in life, a change which does not just arise from weariness or illness, as in the last part of the novel, when Faber drops out, but from a new basic attitude to reality generally and thus to himself. So this is meant to be a demonstration of how a man who can cope with things is incapable of recognizing a reality which is more than he can cope with. Therefore Faber falls short of himself and his history.[65] In any case he had 'taken leave of' stories, myths, dreams and so banished them from his life. But when confronted by history, myth and dreams people learn a specific characteristic of their humanity, namely that they are dependent on others, that they have no control over time; they learn the deep truth about themselves that lies under the surface of what is technically possible.

A remark by Max Frisch, passed on by the film director Volker

Schlöndorff, points in this direction. While Schlöndorff was filming the novel in 1991 Frisch is said to have commented:

> His (Walter Faber's) guilt is that he believes that he can be master of his own fate, can control his life. The gods punish him by striking him and destroying him to remind people that they do not control themselves.[66]

So the guilt of the 'innocent' Walter Faber may be his inability to give up the delusion that he can control his own life, despite experiences of breaks in it. According to this novel, the humanity of human beings also includes the abandonment of a faith in technological control of one's own fate and sensitivity to the fact that we do not ourselves determine and guide our own lives. Therefore the 'coincidences' in this novel have an important anthropological function, as does the dimension of time, especially the dimension of the past. For they are realities which evade the capacity of human beings to plan and direct. It is also no coincidence that Greece is the setting for this tragi-comic crisis of Homo Faber. On the contrary, with a great sense of irony Frisch makes his hero travel through that very land which has an incomparable knowledge of guilty-innocent people. In the land of Sophocles and Aeschylus, Frisch presents us with a hero who does not believe in fate and yet experiences more 'destiny' than anyone else; who does not believe in 'coincidences' and yet is forced to stumble from one coincidence to another; who makes nothing of myths and yet more than anyone else before him falls victim to the fate of mythical heroes.

Therein lies the whole irony of this novel: for a man who believed that he could live 'timelessly', all at once the past which he had thought to be so past becomes a noose round his own neck. The twentieth-century technician, apparently without a destiny, becomes a tragic figure who – like mythical archetypes before him – experiences the truth about himself not as a liberation but as an abyss. For him, the disclosure of the truth becomes a process of fettering himself; deception is transcended and done away with in actual self-destruction. In short, the post-metaphysical man repeats the myths which he had long thought he had demythologized. Thus in Frisch the resumption of the theme of guilt is at the service of criticism of a spirit of the time which has prescribed that reality can be calculated and manipulated, and confuses the world with what is the case. To quote Volker Schlöndorff once again:

> Frisch once said to me: 'It is really good that the film is only being made now, now that the ideologies have been so thoroughly shaken and we

really are thrown back again on the existentialist attitude of the 1950s. Is there such a thing as guilt, or are we guilty simply by virtue of being born? We no longer have a positive utopia, we really have no more hope; but we do not want to be content with that, with life as it is.[67]

Here one insight is important in a theological discussion of Frisch: in this novel, too, guilt is not a religious, even a Christian, problem. For this author the theme of guilt has migrated from the sphere of religion and expanded into human life generally. It now has the function of being the problem which post-Christian individuals make of themselves – remarkably, resorting to the pre-Christian myths of classical antiquity.

3. The primal guilt of the sexes

'Is there guilt, then, or are we guilty simply by virtue of being born?' That this basic question concerned Frisch right down to his late work is clear from the story *Bluebeard*, which was published in 1982. For this story once again radicalizes the theme of guilt in a way which goes beyond *Now They Are Singing Again* and *Homo Faber*, though here we do not have an individual problem of guilt but the primal guilt of human existence generally.

Acquitted yet guilty

The starting point of the narrative is the murder of a prostitute which is being tried before a court. The accused is the fifty-four-year-old doctor Felix Schaad, the victim's former husband. He has no alibi and the evidence against him is strong, but he is finally acquitted for lack of proof. But it is when he has been acquitted that the discussion of his case really starts. The public 'acquittal' all at once becomes the occasion for him to make a quite personal search for the truth about his own life, to understand what his life been hitherto. Schaad already has six marriages behind him, all of which failed, and the seventh too was in trouble. 'Acquitted for lack of proof – how does one live with that? I am fifty-four years old?'[68] – that is the starting-point of this narrative.

What follows is the hero's vain attempt to find out 'the truth and nothing but the truth'[69] about himself. The narrative minutes the dialogue in 'a trial within'.[70] Sixty-one witnesses appear before the tribunal of conscience; dreams are alluded to, childhood memories conjured up, dialogues carried on with spirits. But the more that Schaad tries to penetrate into himself, the more he loses himself and his identity (there is no 'shared memory'). He does not achieve clarity; on the contrary, the more he confronts the shadows of his past, the more hopeless the situation he gets himself into; he sees himself entangled in an inextricable web of guilt. At the end, like Walter Faber, he lies in hospital, helpless and dumb after crashing his car into a tree. Granted, unlike Faber, Schaad had acknowledged his guilt (he had even attempted to confess the 'murder'), but this, too, was in vain, since the real perpetrator (a Greek!) had been discovered in the meantime. Here, too, the acceptance of guilt will not succeed because it lies deeper than any confessions can reveal. So in Frisch at the end of his life as a writer, guilt is radicalized in an unprecedented way as existential primal guilt, to be compared only with the situation of Kafka's heroes.[71]

Thus *Bluebeard* is a new variation on a primal theme of Max Frisch's: the identity crisis, the inability to accept oneself, the restrictive power of images, unavoidable guilt. As in *Homo Faber*, so too in *Bluebeard*, the quest for truth finally leads to an relentless unmasking of the self and an inescapable denunciation of the self: 'Ever since I was fourteen I have never had the feeling of being innocent,' the hero concedes.[72] And he has to be told by a judge: 'I should like to ask the accused whether he feels he has ever understood a woman. For this doesn't seem to me to be the case, Herr Doktor: you are always puzzling about women, and if a woman doesn't conform to your male interpretation, what then?'[73] So *Bluebeard* ends as an unsuccessful attempt of a possible perpetrator helplessly entangled in guilt to find himself. The book is about the question of 'guilt and innocence in a case where guilt cannot be demonstrated from actions'.[74] Thus the literary critic Joachim Kaiser may be right in his assessment:

What is oppressive about the book, if not compelling, is that here someone blames his hero, his *alter ego*. At the centre of this circumstantial process of clarifying whether the accused has a tendency to behave violently towards the other sex, there is unavoidably the accused's character in relation to partnership and society, i.e. his relationship to women. Here Frisch firmly takes sides – against his hero. At the end this hero even accuses himself (by no means just symbolically) of a murder committed by someone else. From this – and one has never read it as clearly, bitterly and Calvinistically in Frisch – there follows a comprehensive sense of guilt, a sense of guilt which extends far beyond the understanding (as opposed to senseless) and uncomprehending (as opposed to enlightening) behaviour of women to the depths of the gender. It is a guilt-feeling about the sex itself. That has little to do with 'misunderstandings', e.g., that there is 'no shared memory' – former partners remember things very differently. Rather, it springs from the awareness and concession of primal sexual guilt . . . In other words, in this man, from the beginning of sexual maturity, of desire, of so-called masculinity – there has been a sense of guilt.[75]

Guilt without expiation

Bluebeard, too, ends without a way out, aporetically like *Homo Faber*. At the end of *Bluebeard*, too, Frisch leaves his readers uncertain whether or not his hero dies; his doctor, like his technician twenty-five years previously, ends as a failure. But this is the purpose of the conception. Making his figures illustrations of aporia is part of Frisch's literary strategy. Here he differs fundamentally, for example, from the Christian and novelist Dostoievsky. Certainly, like the great Russian, this Swiss author shows in his novels that there is no human life without a shadow of guilt; certainly both show that human beings are interwoven in complex histories of life which make it impossible in the end to draw a clear distinction between guilty and innocent; certainly both show that human guilt reaches far deeper than anything that can be discovered and judged under the law. But in contrast to Dostoievsky, for Frisch there is no way of atoning for guilt. Neither of Frisch's heroes is capable, like the figures in *Crime and Punishment* or *The Brothers Karamazov*, of voluntarily taking guilt upon themselves in order to atone for it. As a twentieth-century author, Frisch has lost the confidence that guilt can be shown to be forgivable and capable of atonement at the level of literature. For him, the time of Christian literature is past, and the task of literature is simply truthful depiction, not the provision of moral solutions or messages.

But by deliberately not providing any moral messages, Frisch's novels and narratives point beyond themselves. Where? Above all to the authority of the reader. Readers are presented with the cases of the teacher, Homo Faber and Bluebeard. For them the Requiem is performed, the report written, the inner record of the 'trial within' composed. And as the readers are the authority before whom the attempts at justification are spread, they are called on to adopt a standpoint, to reflect on themselves and their own history, to test themselves in the mirror of the experiment that they have been shown. Readers are obviously to arrive at insights through the questionable character of the heroes themselves, to get rid of certain images and find themselves. The way in which Frisch distances himself from his heroes – often expressed even in decisions on form – is in fact meant to lead to an attitude on the part of the reader. And negatively, Frisch's failed heroes are meant to show the 'real' issue: the abandonment of projected images of oneself. But this 'really' is dealt with sparingly by Frisch in his writings, and so is left to the readers.

Human guilt towards humankind

Two insights from Frisch are important for a theological discussion. First, for this great contemporary author, too, there is no human life without the shadow of guilt. Guilt seems to be unavoidable, seems to be inscribed on the structure of the human condition. This also corresponds to the experience of Christians. According to the message of the New Testament, human beings are not automatically justified before God. Before the most high creator and judge human beings experience themselves as weak, inadequate, insufficient, in short as sinful. Therefore human life itself needs justification, purification, restoration through God's gracious concern.

The second insight is just as important: those who suppress their shadow side, who do not want to perceive their share of guilt, become questionable. Frisch shows that people who deny their guilt lose something of their humanity. They run after a false picture of themselves – like Homo Faber, enlightened and blinded at the same time. To confess guilt serves to humanize people, because those who know of their guilt at the same time know of their fallibility, their dependence on others. Such people, who have taken leave of the delusion of innocence and the craving for omnipotence, and have understood that one cannot be master of one's own fate, and cannot rationally control and direct one's own life, become more humble, more generous and more modest – to themselves and others. Indeed, in the experience and confession of guilt people truly become human. According to Frisch only the 'spirit' can incur guilt, and so only human beings can become guilty. Being guilty distinguishes human beings from animals.

These insights also have an analogous structure to basic human experiences from the perspective of Christian faith. For according to the message of the New Testament, there is nothing humiliating, desperate or worthless about human beings who confess guilt before God and their fellows. Confessing guilt leads neither to fettering oneself nor to destroying oneself. Confessing guilt takes place, rather, in the interest of a positive change in a person, which is classically called 'repentance'. It is God himself who does not want human beings to be imprisoned in their guilt but wants to free them from their guilt, a process classically called 'forgiveness'. And human beings are always offered the chance by God to make good their guilt, a process classically called 'atonement'. It is precisely this triad in the Christian understanding of guilt (repentance – forgiveness – atonement) that is focussed on a deepening of the humanity of human beings.

And yet despite all the positive functions for coping with guilt, we should not deceive ourselves about the depth of the vanishing point. Human beings have to incur guilt, they fail and become weak, because of the fragility of their existence. Human beings have detached themselves from the original harmony with God and opened themselves to the powers of evil. So in the question of guilt the vanishing point is in fact an abyss: it is the question of evil as the reality of that which opposes the good. And anyone who wants to reflect on the riddle of human nature has to confront the reality of evil. Horror about the 'riddle' of human nature finds its nadir in our dismay at what human beings can do to one another and to creation. And just as poets have coped with the question of living on in an exhausted creation and with the problem of the repression of guilt, so too they have faced experiences of evil. This too must be included in our discussion of human beings as reflected by literature.

IV. Experiences with evil

Anyone born, as I was, in 1948, born in Germany, has a personal memory of two genocidal wars, reflected in stories above all from my parents' generation. In the First World War my grandfather on my father's side, from Silesia, fell in France, more than six hundred miles west of his homeland. His grave is unknown; it will be one of the many mass graves on the Somme in Western France. At any rate, my father looked for this grave in vain when the longing came over him to find a last trace of his father. Also a Silesian, he had to endure the Second World War for six years, to the bitter end. He barely escaped death and years of imprisonment in a prisoner-of-war camp. War was never heroized at home. On the contrary, the shameful insight was communicated that wars swallow people up and that the catastrophe of the last war had been a punishment for the 'hybris of us Germans'. The history teaching at my school reinforced this attitude, and since then I have never lost my shame at what Germans have done to other peoples out of an arrogant nationalistic or even racial mania.

1. The veneer of civilization is thin

I recall particularly clearly how ashamed I felt when in 1978 I paid my first visit to the Holocaust Memorial in Jerusalem. At that moment it was physically almost intolerable to see all at once, among the numerous documents displayed there, some in German. In particular one saw displayed in great cases the so-called Wannsee Protocol, the decisions taken in 1942 at a conference at Wannsee in Berlin, at which the Nazis had resolved on the 'final solution' of the Jewish question. All at once, as a German one could understand everything directly. One's mother tongue – degenerated into cruel bureaucratic German, the jargon of death. Death – here was the 'Master from Germany' conjured up by Paul Celan.

Buchenwald next to Weimar

How was that possible in the land of poets and thinkers? German classics *and* German concentration camps, Weimar *and* Buchenwald, Goethe *and* Goebbels in one and the same people, who had been 'Christianized' for almost fifteen hundred years? Max Frisch made this the theme of his plays and essays at an early stage: none of the Christian and humanistic culture over two millennia was able to prevent Auschwitz. I have found this taken up and radicalized in a particularly impressive way by George Steiner. Of Jewish descent, Steiner added a special Preface 'To German Readers' to the German edition of his book *Language and Silence*:

> My whole work turns on the urgent question: are the roots of in-
> humanity interwoven with those of high civilization? Auschwitz did
> not come from the jungle or from the steppes. Barbarity overcame
> modern men and women in the centre of culture, the arts, universal
> education and the scientific miracle. Only a few miles from some of the
> finest museums, libraries and concert halls, Dachau polluted the air.
> People who tortured and hanged children by day read Rilke in the
> evening and listened to Schubert. That is an ontological riddle, the
> mystery of civilized ennui or evil, and for me it puts the whole future of
> humankind in question. If the humanistic sciences contribute nothing
> to humanization, if the same person can play Bach and set the Vilna
> ghetto on fire, what is left of civilization? Why educate, why read? Is it
> possible that there is a radical failure in classical humanism itself, in its
> tendency to abstraction and aesthetic value judgment? Can it be that
> mass murder and that indifference to atrocities which encouraged
> Nazism are not enemies or negations of civilization but its cruellest but
> most natural accomplices?[76]

These questions are fed by the shocking suspicion that – contrary to many assertions – the Holocaust was not a derailing of civilization but its consequence, and that therefore the hope of human beings for humanity needs to be examined. Indeed, this event stands for others (the Gulag Archipelago, Bosnia, Rwanda, Kosovo) in showing how thin the veneer of civilization evidently is and how ineffective the traditional moral notions are in situations of extreme lawlessness and political disorienta-tion. Thus the experience of the Holocaust is the experience of a breakdown in civilization which rids the more sensitive among our con-temporaries of the illusion that ethics is one of the assured ingredients of civil culture. In reality ethics is a thin veneer of civilization on an abysmal potential of bestiality which evidently can be 'aroused' in people time and again.

An oratorio against forgetting: Peter Weiss

I lost my innocence over this question at a very early stage. While still at school I had taken part in the college of my home town in a reading of Peter Weiss's oratorio *The Investigation*, a tableau of the Frankfurt Auschwitz trial which had come to an end in 1964. I remember how deeply ashamed this evening made me. I shall never forget the conclusion of the piece – the dialogue between the prosecutor and one of the witnesses:

> Of the 9 million 600 thousand persecuted
> who lived in the areas
> which their persecutors controlled
> 6 million have disappeared
> and it is to be assumed
> that most of them
> were deliberately exterminated.
> Those who were not shot beaten
> tortured to death
> and gassed
> perished of overwork
> hunger pestilence and misery
> In this camp alone
> more than 3 million people
> were murdered
> But to assess the total number
> of unarmed victims in this war of extermination
> we must add the 6 million
> killed on racial grounds
> 3 million Soviet prisoners of war
> shot and starved
> and 10 million civilians
> who perished in the occupied countries.[77]

The very last sentences of the 'oratorio' have also stuck in my memory. For here Weiss deliberately puts at the end the figure of one of the accused who 'representatively' indicates a 'mood' which was widespread in Germany then as it is now:

We all
I want to stress this again
did nothing but our duty
even if it was often difficult for us
and when we wanted to despair over it
Today
when our nation
has risen again
we should occupy ourselves with other things
than with charges
which must be seen as
long out of date
Loud applause from the accused

By making his series of scenes end like this, Weiss restores the problem to political and social discussion in post-war Germany. How is it possible that there are people in a land who even twenty-years after the Holocaust think that this crime against humanity can be dealt with by references to 'our duty' or 'the passage of time', and that there is a 'leading place' for the German nation in the world with its back to the closed documentation of the Holocaust? By deliberately concluding his work with a little triumph for the accused, Weiss makes the discussion of the Holocaust a politically and morally unresolved problem of the present. His work will not provide an aesthetic excuse for those for whom the problem of the Holocaust is 'settled' by the Auschwitz trial or this drama.

The church with its back to Auschwitz

Today more clearly than before we recognize that representatives of the Christian churches in Germany also encouraged this business of excuse and repression. In particular the official Catholic Church was able to reinterpret its policy, which so often tolerated or even supported Fascism, as a role of resistance. Or at least it was able to act as if the churches had escaped the dark anti-Christian powers with their moral fibre unbroken and could now again give moral guidance. As a church too, people largely lived with their 'backs to Auschwitz', as J. B. Metz put it. People did not realize that the 'ontological riddle', the mystery of a 'civilized ennui or evil', could also put in question the church's preaching, indeed the Christian picture of God and humankind. In the church, too, things went on as if theologically nothing had happened . . .

In this situation, Rolf Hochhuth's play *The Representative* (first performance 1962) came as a shock. Having grown up a loyal Catholic, to begin with I, too, was indignant about the author's apparently shameless and excessive polemic against 'our pope', Pius XII. The pope had been dead only three years and we still regarded him as a morally perfect, almost superhuman figure. And were we suddenly to imagine him in the twilight of the Holocaust? As a failure? As an accomplice? I remember seeing a performance of *The Representative* in the theatre of my home town when I was still at school, and how this play provoked almost instinctive defensive reactions among 'us Catholics'. What might not be could not be . . .

2. Evil has fun: Rolf Hochhuth's devil

Later I grappled with this play time and again.[78] It had become clear to me that not only I as an individual but the whole of cultural Catholicism had reacted to it in an almost exclusively apologetic, counter-polemical way. People could see it as anything but slander of the pope, a tirade against the Catholic Church, indeed even an incitement of the public against clericalism and Catholicism.

Auschwitz or the question of God

However, a careful interpretation – which I made in my book 'Representative of Christ? The Pope in Contemporary Literature' (1980) showed me that there could be no question of this being an anti-Catholic or even an anti-Christian play. On the contrary, here the criticism was not simply of 'the pope' or 'the papacy', but specifically of *this* pope, of a papacy exercised like *this*. There can be no question of this being an anti-papal play, simply because its whole effect depends on the pope being the only one of the great figures in the drama of the world at that time who had been entrusted with a decisive task: the prevention or at least the diminution of the annihilation of European Judaism.

The same is true of the charge that the play is anti-Catholic, indeed anti-Christian. That is beside the point, because for Hochhuth – here as in the next work – the church always has two sides. Over against the church of the pope and the officials stands the 'martyr church'; over against the *ecclesia triumphans,* which acts diplomatically, stands the *ecclesia sub cruce,* which goes to Auschwitz. So for Hochhuth this pope becomes questionable not because he acts in a Christian way but because the way in which he acts is not radically Christian enough. The point of his play is that the pope, confronted with Christ's demand for unlimited love of neighbour, does not becomes a 'representative' of Christ but a governor for Pilate. Like Pilate at that time, here and now this pope sacrifices an innocent man out of political calculations. Paradoxically enough, in the people of the Jews silently handed over to extermination, the representative has betrayed his primal image: what should have been discipleship of Christ becomes political governance. I thought that I had understood that the play essentially revolves around the question of how radical discipleship of Christ should have been in the age of the Holocaust.

In 1991 I had to grapple with Rolf Hochhuth again. I had accepted the invitation to give the Laudatio on the award of the Elisabeth Langgässer Prize to Hochhuth in the town of Alzey. As I occupied myself with this play once more, it dawned on me that talk of 'radical discipleship of Christ', too, did not go far enough. For the real theological challenge of the play is not merely the question 'Who is the true representative of Christ under the conditions of the Holocaust?' The real challenge stems from the question how this excess of evil can be reconciled with the righteousness of God.[79] So *The Representative* is ultimately focussed on the questions of anthropodicy and theodicy: how was it possible for such evil as we encounter in the Holocaust to be unleashed among human beings? And what does this mean for faith in God? This desperate, perplexed question is explicitly raised in the fifth act of the drama, 'Auschwitz or the Question of God'. It could equally well have been entitled 'Auschwitz and the Question of Human Beings'. For here Hochhuth risks the highly explosive aesthetic experiment of staging the reality of a concentration camp and depicting dramatically what in the play itself is called the 'Hellish cynicism' of Auschwitz.

The situation at the start of the fifth act is as follows. After Pope Pius XII – although fully informed – cannot bring himself to make a public protest against the 'Final Solution' of the Jewish question; after the representative of Christ has been unwilling to expose the world criminal Hitler to the world public for reasons of church and state politics, a Jesuit father (invented by Hochhuth) named Riccardo Fontana takes on the cause of representing Christ. After a passionate but fruitless dialogue with the pope, to whom he had managed to make his way because his father and the pope were close friends, this Jesuit father himself stitches the Jewish star on his soutane and in Rome climbs aboard a train deporting Jews, which brings him directly to the platform in Auschwitz. His arrival there at first causes confusion among SS officers. A Catholic priest was not planned for by the Nazis in the programme of annihilating Jews. But then the 'doctor' (an only slightly stylized imitation of the butcher Dr Mengele) seizes him, to make him an example in Auschwitz on matters of belief in God.

Evil is willed

Here the stereotyped designation 'the handsome devil' would not have been needed to disclose the devil, i.e. God's adversary, in this 'doctor'. For here the diabolical element manifestly lies in the cold self-control with which the man abuses men and women for his own intellectual and sexual purposes and enjoys this abuse. He is not following his bestial instincts; he has mastered them. He shows that there is a deliberate evil, indeed that evil can be an end in itself: he sleeps with beautiful Jewish women before he sends them to the gas chamber; with cold laughter he carries out experiments to gain knowledge about the birth of twins, which can then be applied to increase the 'German-Aryan race'.

Here in literature we have, concentrated in one figure, what the American historian Daniel Goldberg brought out as a basic feature of 'Hitler's willing executioners'. The methodology and historiography of this book are disputed, but in my mind the main thesis cannot be refuted. It can be summed up like this: the perpetrators wanted this, and they enjoyed it. As Goldhagen comments:

> The Germans' voluntaristic cruelty, the Germans' beatings that were the 'invariable daily fare' for the Jews living in camps, the Germans' 'sport' practised upon the Jews, the Germans' symbolic cruelty perpetrated upon the Jews, were an integral and typical feature of the Germans' actions. The Germans often used Jews as playthings, compelling them, like circus animals, to perform antics – antics that debased the Jews and amused their tormentors. Of their treatment at the hands of the Germans, the Jews could say, paraphrasing King Lear, 'As flies to wanton boys are we to the Germans, they kill us for their sport.'[80]

In Hochhuth's Auschwitz act 'the doctor' argues sharply and rationally above all in matters of theology. Over against the Jesuit father his role is to provoke God. His mass executions ultimately followed only the one goal, of compelling God to reveal himself:

Since July '42, some fifteen months ago,
weekdays and Sundays, I have been sending men to God.
Has he shown any sign of recognition?
He hasn't even aimed a thunderbolt at me.
Can you understand that? Of course you *must* know . . .
Nine thousand in *one* day not long ago . . .
A martyr would always rather die than think.
Valéry was right. He said, The angel –
maybe you are an angel –
(*laughing.*)
differs from me, differs from the Devil,
purely through the act of thought
which lies ahead of him.
I shall expose you to this act of thought,
as a swimmer to the ocean.
    . . . History! A vindication of divine providence,
the final theodicy – really?
(*He laughs like a torturer.*)
History: dust, altars, suffering, rape,
where every reputation mocks its victims.
Creator, creation, creature, all these three
Auschwitz negates.[81]

Why the devil laughs

Already in this brief extract it is striking how often the doctor talks of
laughter. And if there is a devil, then he may indeed have his hallmark
in the laughter of this torturer. It is a quite special kind of laughter, a
mixture of coldness and pleasure; of cynical thoughtlessness and delight;
of terror at the victim and at the same time enjoyment of this terror. We
can hear the proverbial laughter of hell in the laugh of this devil. For as
we know, hell laughs at all human attempts to establish the good – laughs
at the futility and self-deception. Hell laughs because human beings are
deluded fools who do not yet know that in the end everything is destined
to collapse, literally to go to the devil. Hell laughs because – as Goethe's
Mephistopheles already put it in his inimitable way:

> All that gains existence
> is only fit to be destroyed: that is why
> it would be best if nothing ever were created (*Faust*, lines 1339–41).

So this 'devil' pours all his scorn on a pope who in all seriousness thinks that he can get by with political calculations in the style of the classical diplomacy of the greatest monstrosity of hell, Hitler's Fascism which destroys Jews. Moreover at no point does the doctor's laughter ring out more crazily than when he wonders why the representative of Christ is silent, instead of giving a sign of protest or devotion, a sign which would have made him a representative in the discipleship of the cross:

> Yes . . . but the Representative of Christ
> must *speak*. Why is he silent?
> (*eagerly.*)
> Something you can't yet have heard:
> last week two, three bombs
> which killed no one, fell in the Vatican gardens:
> for days the great sensation of the world.
> The Americans, the British and the Germans
> are all falling over themselves to prove
> they could not possibly have dropped them.
> You see again: the Pope's a holy man
> even to heretics. Exploit the fact –
> challenge him – what is the matter?
> Sit down.
> (*He takes Riccardo by the shoulder, Riccardo has sunk on to the bench.*)
> You're whiter than the walls of a gas chamber.
> (pause.)
> Riccardo (*On the bench, with difficulty.*).
> I have already asked the Pope to protest,
> But he is playing at politics.
> My father stood by me . . . my father,
> Doctor (*with the laughter of Hell*)
> Politics – yes, that is his level, -
> politics, with the gift of tongues.[82]

The provocative point of this scene is thus that the pope is involuntarily doing the work of the devil by not protesting with full moral authority against the war being waged by Fascism and the annihilation of the Jews. He is not throwing his own destiny in the scales in a literal discipleship of the cross, in support of hundreds of thousands of people who are being gassed on a production line. A pope who engages in politics instead of giving a political sign is worth only the scornful laughter of hell.

Indeed the scornful laughter of this devil can ring out all the more shrilly when he has seen that is the church itself which has prepared for experiences of hell in this world with its pictures of hell in the next. At any rate, the 'doctor' can cynically and cheerfully point out to his Jesuit conversation-partner that in the end it was representatives of the church who prepared all this satanic and hellish stuff:

> It was your church first showed
> that one could burn a man like coke.
> In Spain, alone, and without crematoria,
> you incinerated three hundred and fifty thousand,
> and nearly all alive: for *that* one needs –
> the support of Christ.[83]

And as one of the pieces of evidence of diabolical cruelty in the church the doctor takes pleasure in quoting from the *Spiritual Exercises* of the founder of the Jesuit order, Ignatius Loyola, which the Jesuit Riccardo carries around with him. In the fifth of his exercises Ignatius has recommended 'Reflection on Hell', the 'inner sense of punishment' which the damned suffer – with the aim that the 'fear of punishment' may not lead those who contemplate it to fall into sin if they forget the love of God. Ignatius Loyola's fantasy of hell is:

> *First point*: To see in imagination the great fires, and the souls enveloped, as it were, in bodies of fire.
> *Second point*: To hear the wailing, the screaming, cries and blaspheming against Christ our Lord and all the saints.
> *Third point*: To smell the smoke, the brimstone, the corruption and rottenness.
> *Fourth point*: To taste bitter things as tears, sadness, and remorse of conscience.
> *Fifth point*: With the sense of touch to feel how the flames surround and burn souls.[84]

Moreover the doctor can triumphantly hold up these statements to his priestly conversation-partner:

> Oho, Ignatius Loyola,
> the *Exercises* – *fire*side reading.
> Much read at the stake
>
> . . .
>
> 'The devil on the throne of smoke and fire attracts

like a seducer' – I know, aha, here: 'I see with
the eye of imagination the powerful glow of
the flames, and the souls, imprisoned in burning
bodies. I smell with the smell of imagination
smoke, sulphur, excrement and
rotting things.'[85]

What remains after so much infernal cruelty cherished with such pleasure? All that is left for Riccardo, at any rate, is self-sacrifice as a representative of Christ. This takes place when he is shot by the SS guards as he is attempting to shoot the doctor. Previously he had cried out against the doctor in an act of ultimate revolt – and here the theological problem is focussed with ultimate density:

Your grimaces of lust, and filth and idiocy
sweep every doubt aside . . . every one.
If there is a devil then there is a God:
Or *you* would long ago have won.[86]

Appeal to compassion

This is a classical quotation from Thomas Aquinas's *Summa contra gentiles*, *Si malum est, deus est*: if there is evil, there is God. Perhaps this is in fact the last possibility of theological withdrawal in the face of the hellish and diabolical in this world: the belief that the devil can only exist if and as long as he consumes God's substance. Perhaps this is the *ultima ratio* of all theology which seeks to oppose the devil and his power in the name of God. Hochhuth's personal interpretation – given many years later – goes in the same direction. In 1991 I was able to have a lengthy conversation with him in Tübingen and ask him directly about *The Representative*. I asked him not only what the 'religious message' of this play was (his answer was along the lines of Schopenhauer's 'appeal to compassion'!) but also what he personally would do in the face of the triumphant statement by the 'Doctor' ('Creator, creation and creature are refuted by Auschwitz'). Hochhuth's answer was clear:

I have attempted to depict the doctor, who was in fact a Mengele type, in the way that Schopenhauer requires of a dramatist. Schopenhauer has written in his *Aesthetics* that only the bad playwrights portrayed the devil and then put themselves alongside him and pointed their fingers at him. In truth one must give every figure on the stage its due as long as that figure is speaking. It must be totally convincing and attempt to convince from its own standpoint, which can be quite false. Unfortunately I had more compelling arguments in depicting the doctor than in depicting Riccardo. It is no coincidence that you have remembered the statement you quoted: precisely because it is striking. But that is no reason for it to be right. Riccardo then replies, 'If there is a devil then there is a God: or you would long ago have won.' We must maintain this hope, and perhaps it is not a hope; perhaps it is simply an observation that even the worst evil conjures up the boldest as its counterpart.[87]

However, on closer inspection I found that Hochhuth's Auschwitz act is aesthetically too garish and does not avoid crude dramatic effects. The aesthetics of horror and the diabolical is remarkably conventional in this play in particular. This is indicated by the stereotyped designation 'the handsome devil' for the doctor or the designation throughout of Auschwitz as 'underworld' with the 'reflection of a great fire'. Hell-fire shines constantly in this act, and the victims moan, cry, rant and roar. Moreover by such clear, tabloid personalization of evil Hochhuth suggests that evil is to some degree 'visible', 'tangible' and thus comprehensible. One need only attempt to put a stop to this devil and already the problem of evil is removed. And that is the remarkable paradox in Hochhuth's depiction of the devil: by direct personalization of evil he unintentionally contributes towards a trivialization of evil.

Thus Hochhuth's drama raises the basic question how a writer today can depict 'evil', 'the Evil One', without at the same time trivializing it aesthetically. And in my experience there are only two great works of literature in which this seems to have been done successfully, precisely because they also contain reflection on the failure of literature in the face of this incomparable reality. One is Alexander Solzhenitsyn's *The First Circle* and the other is Thomas Mann's novel *Doctor Faustus*. Both novels show simultaneously both the greatness of literature and also its poverty in the face of a reality which even it cannot 'manipulate'.

3. Hell – the first circle: Alexander Solzhenitsyn

Alexander Solzhenitsyn's novel *The First Circle* appeared in 1968 and immediately was a talking point for all those interested in literature. I had already read *One Day in the Life of Ivan Denisovich* with great excitement: it is a first literary treatment of Stalinism and its concentration-camp system (which Solzhenitsyn later called the 'Gulag Archipelago'). I sat down to read this new novel immediately. Its theme did not fit into the climate of the student movement of the time, which had inscribed on its banner political and sexual liberation, dreams of a better society, dreams in the spirit of neo-Marxist utopianism. It ran counter to this because it did not fit into the picture of human beings which 'we' tacitly presupposed at that time, namely that people can be educated and improved if only the social structures are changed. Solzhenitsyn showed precisely the opposite: people are capable of making hell for others on earth and misuse socialism in particular to do so.

Human beings in hell – unsuspecting

Only later did I understand what was unique about this book as literature. It is its unpretentious form, which refuses any connection with a traditional aesthetic of horror. Here the infernal is not portrayed with garish effects, as it is with Hochhuth, but consists in its uncanny invisible presence. What is the book about? It tells the story of prisoners in the camp of Mavrino near Moscow. Here a technological and intellectual elite is forced together and kept occupied with nothing more than refining surveillance methods. On the one hand scrambling apparatus is to be constructed which allows telephone conversations with the Kremlin that cannot be bugged, and one the other deciphering apparatus that makes it possible for the secret service to identify telephone conversations which they hear. That leads literally to a 'hell', an enclosed vicious circle: prisoners are directed to construct apparatus which will produce new prisoners. Moreover the external action of the novel is governed by precisely the same circular movement. A promising young career diplomat by the name of Volodin had made the mistake of warning an acquaintance by telephone about prohibited contacts with people abroad. This telephone conversation had been overheard, and from it the secret service discovered who the speaker was. Volodin, unmasked by products of Mavrino, becomes a new prisoner in Mavrino. Thus the first circle of hell is closed.

However, the uncanny thing is that the transitions from the outer world into the first circle, and also the transitions into the various other circles of hell, are fluid. It is no longer possible to make out where this hell begins or where it ends. Even the outside world becomes a pre-hell. This is the difference from Dante – whom Solzhenitsyn both takes up and contradicts – , to whose *Divine Comedy* (composed around 1307–1321)

Solzhenitsyn alludes in his title. For Dante had claimed that he could visualize hell precisely in nine circles. For him these are graded by the degree of guilt of the delinquents. The first circle of hell contains the righteous pagans and unbaptized children: here for example one meets Homer, Plato and Cicero. The last, ninth circle, the centre of hell, is formed by the three-headed Lucifer as the devouring counterpart to the Trinity, in his jaws the three arch-traitors of world history, Judas, Brutus and Cassius.

There is nothing of this in Alexander Solzhenitsyn. In his work hell is only hinted at, and only its first circle can be seen. But here already its infernal quality consists in the subtle interchangeability of perpetrators and victims. All are prisoners of this world, the prisoners and the warders alike, the minions of the secret service and those whom they interrogate and beat. They all belong among those who are blinded and blinkered. The effectiveness of hell consists in their repression of it: no one speaks about it and no one understands it. Here is an underworld *in* the world above, a beyond *in* this world, an invisible world *in* the visible world.

An expression of this blinding is the fact that many of the prisoners fall victim to self-deception. They have already got used to life in the 'first circle', and as technical specialists they enjoy high privileges. They have already repressed the fact that this is 'hell'. 'Perhaps it's all a dream? I believe – I am in paradise', says one of the prisoners. Another replies:

> No, my dear sir, you are in hell, but you have graduated to its best and highest circle – the first circle. You asked me what kind of a place this is. Remember how Dante racked his brains to know where to put the sages of antiquity? As a Christian he was in duty bound to consign them to hell. But as a man of the Renaissance he was troubled in his conscience at the thought of throwing them in with all sorts of ordinary sinners and condemning them to the torments of the flesh. So he designated a special place for them.[88]

Other victims of self-deception are all those who cannot or do not want to see the totalitarian dictatorship that there really is in this system. The end of the novel is a satirical jab at the Western press. Prisoners are transported from the first circle of hell into further circles: 'only the very worst awaits them'. They are transported in a van which has the words 'Mjasso – Viande – Fleisch – Meat ' written on it. On the way the van passes a Western correspondent:

The correspondent read on the delivery van: 'Fleisch – Meat.' He remembered having seen several trucks like this today in Moscow. Taking out his notebook he wrote with his dark-red fountain pen: 'Now and again on the streets of Moscow you meet food delivery vans, clean, well designed, hygienic. One must admit that the city's food supplies are remarkably well organized.'[89]

The disconcerting banality of evil

A comparison of motifs[90] has shown me that none of the great authors has made hell seem so uncanny, precisely because this novel renounces all the effects of the uncanny. No previous literary text about hell has to my knowledge so lucidly described the infernal nature of human conduct, precisely because Solzhenitsyn does not depict the devil in human figures but the banality of evil in all the guards, administrators, collectors and perpetrators, whose level of spiteful banality can hardly be surpassed. No great author has so relentlessly presented hell an artificial reality of gracefully ordered lies, totalitarian spying, organized falsehood and collective blinding so unsparingly as Alexander Solzhenitsyn, experienced in the way of the prison camp, without ever resorting to the requisites of the horror genre. In fact – as the literary critic Karl Korn once pointed out – 'he does not use any artificial literary means, because the most trivial reality has its own demonic nature or because Solzhenitsyn knows how to release it from the real or translate it into the dimensions of the macabre philosophical.'[91] Mavrino is the allegory of hell under the sign of Stalinism.

Solzhenitsyn's novel made it clear to me that if hell exists, it is a state of totalitarian oppression, which human beings must affirm as a state of happiness. In that case it is the reduction of the human being to a piece of meat, which those concerned have to claim to be the wisdom of their statesmen. It is that form of terrorist dehumanization which one has to praise officially as state socialism. It is then madness turned into bureaucratic administration, totalitarian rationality gone crazy; it is anarchy planned and legally safeguarded to the last . . .

Resisting evil

But Solzhenitsyn's giant novel in particular raises even more acutely the question: Can evil be understood? What is its nature? Why does it exist? To describe the effects of evil and its uncanny nature is one thing; to understand it is another. Granted, Solzhenitsyn wrote his novel with an

ethic of resistance. The hells of Stalinism are recalled in order to make it
possible to oppose evil – at least after the event. Precisely in Solzeh-
nitsyn's case it is true that literature also has its rights in restoring dignity
to the victims of evil and snatching the butchers of hell from anonymity.
Literature prescribes for itself the work of recollection, so that justice
does not perish in the cynicism of the perpetrators. This is the decisive
reason why this author has built gigantic cathedrals of remembrance in
the literary landscape of the twentieth century: the torturers must not
escape; the victims of these hells must not remain unatoned for; truth
must be given its due in the face of the satanic state.

That is why Solzhenitsyn was and is no seeker of faith (in the Western
intellectual sense), nor does he despair of faith; rather (more in the
tradition of Russian Orthodoxy), he is a witness to faith, a preserver of
the faith. Therefore the Russian literary critic Igor Winogradow is right
in describing the quintessence of 'moralism' in Solzhenitsyn as follows:

> The central spiritual situation in Solzhenitzyn's work is not the quest
> for faith, the struggle for faith, but life in faith. Solzhenitsyn, too, as we
> know, underwent a 'change of convictions', and in the camp and
> in exile was transformed from an atheist and Marxist into a deeply
> religious Christian. However, in his books we find at least a faint echo
> of this process: there he shows us a world in which revelation has
> already happened, the choice has been made and faith has been
> achieved. There it is rather a matter of persevering in this faith.
> Persevering, because it has been fought for on the periphery of human
> existence. However, to remain true to faith one must be in a state of
> absolute all-permeating evil, where life in faith irresistibly calls for
> action, namely the life-and-death struggle with this evil . . . Therefore
> it is also the lie which is Solzhenitsyn's main enemy, against which he
> has to summon up all his human and artistic courage; for the lie as a
> poisonous sting, as the evil mask of evil, is also the most effective
> weapon of that 'Satanic state' in which Solzhenitsyn sees the 'earthly
> representative of the father of evil'.[92]

So it is not the delight in cruelty, the enjoyment of terror, which moti-
vates the visions of hell in great literature. That devils live among us, that
hell is human work – this is what shapes serious literature, not in the style
of nerve-tingling horror poetry or sensationalist horror stories, but as the
basic moral question about the state of our world, indeed about the
meaning of God's order of creation generally. Great literature is already
an aesthetic critique of that cheap aestheticizing of horror which only

makes the nerves tingle, satisfies the desire for sensations and exploits anxieties commercially. But great literature is a judgment on the mass products of the repulsive commercialization of horror. Evil cannot be enjoyed aesthetically, but has to be banished and overcome in the act of showing it up relentlessly.

But once again: how are we to understand evil? Even a reference to the fact that a man like Solzhenitsyn is utterly steeped in a Christian ethic does not do away the problem why there has to be evil. It raises this question, even for a 'deeply religious Christian' like Solzhenitsyn. For does not the very existence of evil altogether put in question that 'life in faith'? Can the 'quest of faith', the 'struggle over faith' ever come to an end here? Isn't the very existence of evil the most abysmal attack on faith? Wasn't Theodor W. Adorno right when in one of the key philosophical works of this century, with the programmatic title *Negative Dialectics* (1966), he said with specific reference to Auschwitz:

> The earthquake of Lisbon sufficed to cure Voltaire of the theodicy of Leibniz, and the visible disaster of the first nature was insignificant in comparison with the second, social, one which defies human imagination as it distils a real hell from human evil. Our metaphysical faculty is paralysed because actual events have shattered the basis on which speculative metaphysical thought could be reconciled with experience.[93]

Real hell from human evil – isn't this in fact unimaginable, incomprehensible? And doesn't it shatter all talk of faith, hope, grace?

4. Speaking of grace nevertheless? Thomas Mann

One of the greatest authors of twentieth-century German literature, Thomas Mann, asked himself these questions. We are indebted to him for what is so far the deepest and most comprehensive grappling with the problem of evil in literature, above all in his novel *Doctor Faustus*. And we shall understand this novel only if we first attempt to understand Thomas Mann's grappling with Fascism. Fascism is the background to this writer's reflections on the essence and effect of evil. Let's look at them more closely.

Against the diabolical par excellence

November 1938. Thomas Mann is already in exile in America and from Princeton is involved in a plan for an anti-Fascist political manifesto to which contributions are to be made by prominent representatives of the 'whole moral and spiritual world'. A draft has already been composed, but as a result of difficulties both in the United States and later also in France, the planned publication fails. The text is later used by Thomas Mann for his own purposes and today bears the title 'To the Civilized World'.

It is worth noting because here – not for the first time, but in a uniquely programmatic way – Thomas Mann gives a particular interpretation of Fascism. Words are used like 'diabolical lie', the 'diabolical', 'enemy of humanity', 'adversary'. With all the rhetorical passion of which he is capable, Thomas Mann uses the language of exorcism:

> Do not be afraid! Do not allow yourselves to be intimidated and confused by the programme of lies which has so far helped him to play his game and which, thanks to the folly of many powerful people, will go on helping him for a while. He also speaks of 'Bolshevism'. You have to choose, he claims, between him and 'Bolshevism'; he is the only bulwark against it, so all must hide behind him. The world must fall to him so as not to be swallowed up by the red spectre. – Now we know very well that you too, those whom we are addressing, the waverers, the shaken, those impressed by the success of evil, at least half-heartedly believe in these lies, the most effective lies of the enemy of mankind. Will you listen to the truth?[94]

What Thomas Mann is aiming at with the use of religious language becomes clear: to make the seriousness of the situation clear to a mass public and to emphasize the universality of the concern which involves all nations. Hence the seemingly naïve recourse to the apocalyptic dualism of good and evil; hence the deliberately simplifying dualism of truth and lies, God and Satan. Hence the rhetoric which seeks to unmask Fascism as 'spiritual excrement', as a 'grimace', as 'the diabolical', the 'primal crime' and the 'rejected'.

Moreover this interpretation of Fascism with 'metaphysical' categories is constantly maintained throughout Thomas Mann's numerous political statements. He often speaks of 'diabolical lies',[95] of 'ludicrous infernal twisting of the truth',[96] and of resistance to 'Satan'.[97] Indeed, with the beginning and end of the Second World War one can note an intensification of the dualistic and demonological rhetoric in Thomas Mann. Especially in the year 1942, when the German wave of expansion reached its climax (after the subjection of Poland, Denmark, Norway, Holland, Belgium and France and the attack on the Soviet Union), the author's statements become more radical. What would it mean for mankind – he asks, for example, his audience at the University of Berkeley in California at that time – if Fascism were to win? His answer is:

> You have no idea of the moral destruction it would bring if the world were compelled to accept the final triumph of evil in the world, the triumph of lies and force. Recall the impact that a mere natural event, the great Lisbon earthquake, had on people in the eighteenth century. This natural catastrophe cost the Lord God many thousands of believers, for people understandably said that it was impossible that an all-good and all-wise God could rule over a world in which something so terrible could happen. I venture to state that this anti-religious effect of the Lisbon earthquake would be child's play compared with the morally destructive effect of Hitler's final victory.[98]

Therefore Thomas Mann was firmly convinced that one must not allow the 'definitive triumph of absolute evil'.[99] There was 'good and evil' in this war – and he said this 'without fear of being accused of painting in black and white and of moral simplification'.[100] Indeed, when in 1942 Thomas Mann gave an address to Americans of German origin, it burst out from him once more:

> It will mean something, dear friends, that I have left Germany, that I could no longer live there. Basically nothing, no change of government, no political change, no revolution, should have been able to drive someone like me, a basically unpolitical person, out of Germany – nothing in the world would have been capable of it but this one thing, only that which calls itself National Socialism, only Hitler and his bands. For that is no politics and no state and no form of society; that is the evil of hell, and war against this is the sacred self-defence of mankind against the absolutely diabolical.[101]

Diabolical lies, an infernal twisting of the truth, the triumph of evil, the wickedness of hell, the diabolical *par excellence*, the devilry of evil: the texts impressively indicate how much Thomas Mann, the man of the

Enlightenment and modern critic of religion, suddenly sees himself confronted with a reality the existence of which tends to be domesticated by theology or explained away by a critique of religion: the reality of evil. Talk of the hellish and the diabolical is no longer the reserve of backwoodsmen who resist the Enlightenment, but a challenge which is historically unavoidable even for critical intellectuals.

So a writer of the stature of Thomas Mann had to deal with two questions. First, why did the German people in particular fall under the spell of evil? Are there points of contact in the German tradition for this proneness, reasons of cultural and intellectual history? And secondly, what is the 'essence', the 'nature' of evil? How can it be grasped, indeed understood, in literature? He now attempts to answer both questions in a great new novel. And these two questions now make the novel *Doctor Faustus* an unavoidable theological challenge. It bears the sub-title 'The Life of the German Composer Adrian Leverkühn, Told by a Friend' and was written between May 1943 and January 1947. The text reports on the time between the end of the nineteenth century and the beginning of the 1940s, in other words the periods in which German history in this century were shaped.

Germanhood, demonism and music

To understand the specifically German problems in the novel it is enough to point out here that Thomas Mann believed that there is a secret bond between the German disposition and the demonic. This is already striking with Luther, but no less so in that material which becomes the most German of all historical material: the story of a doctor by the name of Faust which already became popular in the late Middle Ages. At its centre stands a man who out of an excessive urge for knowledge sold himself to magic and the devil. In an essay which he wrote in the middle of working on the novel, entitled 'Germany and the Germans', Thomas Mann described it like this:

> Where the arrogance of the intellect espouses itself to spiritual anti-
> quarianism and a bond, there is the devil. And the devil, Luther's devil,
> Faust's devil, seem to me to be a very German figure; the bond with
> him, signing oneself away to the devil, in order for a while to gain
> all the treasures and power of the world in return for surrendering
> the salvation of one's soul, seems to me something quite peculiar to the
> German spirit. A solitary thinker and scholar, a closet theologian and

philosopher, who out of a longing to enjoy and rule the world signs away his soul to the devil – is it not the right moment to see Germany in this image, today when Germany is literally going to the devil?[102]

So it is no coincidence that at this moment Thomas Mann took up once again material which is more Ur-German than anything else: the story of a man who from the abysses of his inwardness conspires against the world and takes the devil as his ally.

There was only one dimension which Thomas Mann did not find in the Faust material, which he similarly regarded as quite decisive for understanding the German demonism: the dimension of music. In the same essay, 'Germany and the Germans', Thomas Mann reverts to this allegedly 'great mistake' of the original Faust saga: that Faust is not brought into contact with music. Really this Faust must have been musical, must have been a musician. Why?

Music is a demonic sphere – Søren Kierkegaard, a great Christian, showed that most convincingly in his painfully enthusiastic article about Mozart's *Don Giovanni*. It is Christian art in a negative key. It is at the same time the most calculated order and the most chaotic opposition to reason, rich in invocative, incantatory gestures; number magic, the art which is remotest from reality and at the same time the most passionate of arts, abstract and mystical. If Faust is to be the representative of the German soul he would have to be musical, for the relationship of the German to the world is abstract and mystical, i.e. musical – the relationship of a professor with demonic tendencies, unskilful and in this way governed by the arrogant consciousness of being in the 'depths' superior to the world.[103]

Music was also a happy choice as a paradigm of German existence because at the beginning of the twentieth century it was stylistically in a creative crisis of epoch-making dimensions. From Johann Sebastian Bach to Anton Bruckner every style seemed to have been tried, every possibility of composition used up, all forms composed to the end. A great crisis of productivity had erupted, which none of the great musicians at the end of the nineteenth century experienced more existentially than Gustav Mahler.[104] Thus a composer who did not want to understand himself as merely reproducing elements of tradition was close to despair. His creativity threatened to become sterile. Moreover Thomas Mann describes precisely this as the basic condition for the inner drama of his novel: the experience 'of sterility', the innate despair of the artist, which predisposes him to a pact with the devil.[105] For only this despair explains the urge to regain new productivity with the help of the devil, the resolve to make a special pact with the devil.

But who or what is 'the devil'? Strangely, the devil appears as the most understood and at the same time the most incomprehensible figure in the whole novel. Thomas Mann does not make the mistake of clumsy personalization. His devil is present from the beginning, but without taking form. Moreover the author regards it as his task 'to allow what is intimated from the beginning slowly to take shape, to assume more and more form and presence' – from the 'experiments' in alchemy which Leverkühn's father already made, through Leverkühn's theological studies in Halle, to the real appearance of the devil to Leverkühn in the Italian town of Palestrina.[106] I cannot reconstruct all these individual phases here, but must limit myself to the decisive scene which so far is unique in the German literature of the twentieth century.

Pact with the devil: death of love, a cutting cold

This is Chapter 25 of *Doctor Faustus*, which later became famous. The basis of the narrative by the biographer, Serenus Zeitblom, are Leverkühn's notes on a real conversation with the devil in bodily form. A conversation with the devil? Even Zeitblom hesitates to accept the reality of this conversation, because he knows what that would mean: 'I would have to be crazy to believe it.' The mere idea that the devil could appear to anyone upsets him, so that he is willing to concede its reality 'only conditionally and as a possibility'. But the other possibility is also 'gruesome' for Zeitblom to think about, namely that the conversation with the devil came from 'the soul of the one who had been visited'. So whether objective reality or subjective projection, metaphysics or psychology – the devil is a terrifying reality.

We learn that while Leverkühn is reading Kierkegaard's work about Mozart's *Don Giovanni* in his room in Palestrina, a figure suddenly sits opposite him. The room has grown cold. Hardly has this guest been perceived when he begins a witty game on the question of reality or imagination with clever cultural historical reflections on his origin from old German: Imperial Saxony, Wittenberg, Wartburg, Leipzig. But then the point is quickly reached, the question of art and its future. The topic of the exhaustion of music is debated, and that produces the decisive point of contact for the pact of the devil. For Leverkühn makes a pact with the devil in return for the promise that over the next years the devil will help him to compose brilliant works of art. He accepts the condition:

> My condition was clear and direct, determined by the legitimate jealousy of hell. Love is forbidden you, in so far as it warms. Thy life shall be cold, therefore thou shalt love no human being.[107]

This draws the analogy between musicians and German fate in the twentieth century. The price of gaining new brilliance is the loss of love, unthinking loneliness and utter coldness in relationships. Thus Leverkühn has finally become the symbolic figure of German fate under the sign of Fascism: the one who is greedy for the supreme achievement is at the same time the one with the cold soul. Only someone whose soul is cold is capable of turning the world into a hell.

What is this hell? According to Thomas Mann's devil it is the reality for which no language is any longer sufficient, which can be indicated only in symbols: 'cellar', 'thick walls', 'soundproof', 'forgetfulness', 'no escape'. All 'mercy, all grace, all sparing, every last trade of concern' has disappeared:

> True it is that inside these echo-less walls it gets right loud, measureless loud, and by much over-filling the ear with screeching and beseeching, gurgling and groaning, with yauling and bauling and caterwauling, with horrid winding and grinding and racking ecstasies of anguish no man can hear his own tune, for that it smothers in the general, in the thick-clotted diapason of trills and chirps lured from this everlasting dispensation of the unbelievable combined with the irresponsible.
>
> Nothing forgetting the dismal groans of lust mixted therewith; since endless torment, with no possible collapse, no swoon to put a period thereto, degenerates into shameful pleasure, wherefore such as have some intuitive knowledge speak indeed of the 'lusts of hell'.
>
> And therewith mockage and the extreme of ignominy such as belongs with martyrdom; for this bliss of hell is like a deep-voiced pitifull jeering and scorne of all the immeasureable anguish; it is accompanied by whinnying laughter and the pointing finger; whence the doctrine that the damned have not only torment but also mockery and shame to bear; yea, that hell is to be defined as a monstrous combination of suffering and derision, un-endurable yet to be endured world without end.
>
> There will they devour their proper tongues for greatness of the

agony, yet make no common cause on that account, for rather they are full of hatred and scorn against each other, and in the midst of their trills and quavers hurl at one another the foulest oaths. Yea, the finest and proudest, who never let a lewd word pass their lips, are forced to use the filthiest of all. A part of their torment and lust of same standeth therein that they must cogitate the extremity of filthiness.[108]

All this recalls the world of Fascist and Stalinist terror; indeed the cellars describe the torture chambers in which Himmler and Beria, those sons of hell, practised.

Away from society, over the next few years in fact Leverkühn composes great musical works, which find their climax in the symphonic cantata *Doctor Faustus' Lament*. Now this piece is already the work of someone who is completely desperate, who seems to be on the way to helpless damnation. It is a 'monster work of lament', the composition of which is stamped by the painful death of Leverkühn's beloved five-year-old nephew Nepomuk. Then comes the end. At this end, like Doctor Faustus before him, Leverkühn gathers his few acquaintances around him to give an account of his life and play from his last work. As he does, he collapses:

> We saw tears run down his cheeks and fall on the keyboard, wetting it, as he attacked the keys in a strongly dissonant chord . . . He spread out his arms, bending over the instrument and seeming about to embrace it, when suddenly, as though smitten by a blow, he fell sideways from his seat and to the floor.[109]

Adrian Leverkühn suffers a paralytic shock, his time is up. After years of suffering he dies in 1940, like Nietzsche, in spiritual darkness and the syphilitic ravaging of his body.

We need to have become clear about this story of the pact with the devil and its contemporary background in order to see the basic statement of the novel. For after all this the question now arises with almost logical compulsion: where is everything in this novel heading? Towards a surrender to evil? And thus to hopelessness, madness, decay? Did Thomas Mann write this novel about the downfall of his hero because he was convinced of the all-pervading and all compelling power of evil? Does the hero of the novel fail finally because human beings fall victim to evil – unstoppably, irrefutably, and because one can only fail before evil?

The speculator as his own executioner

One might arrive at this idea if one kept strictly to Leverkühn's perspective in this novel. For his last composition, conceived – as we heard – as 'a monster work of lament', as a 'giant lament', is meant to be none other than a summary of all the accusation and lament of which human beings are capable. Moreover, literally up to its last notes this composition is to offer 'no other consolation than what lies in voicing it, in simply giving sorrow words; in the fact, that is, that a voice is given the creature for his woe'. So no consolation, no reconciliation and no explanation. Adrian Leverkühn's symphony – it is conceived from the composer's perspective as a counterpart to, indeed as the reverse of Beethoven's Ninth Symphony, which could still end with a 'Hymn to Joy'.[110] That is now past: in view of the personal and political situation, the end of the good, the noble and the humane in art can now be shown. And this end of an era is at the same time also the end of the artist, who in a self-sacrifice takes the guilt of the time on himself – and, like Nietzsche, goes into the night of madness. What then?

Strangely enough, at the end of his own history Leverkühn commends himself to the grace of God. Certainly, copying his late-mediaeval hero even down to the language (which is already itself an impressive signal of the beginning of his downfall), Adrian reveals to his assembled friends first of all that he has made a pact with the devil and that therefore all the compositions that he has produced are to be seen as the work of the devil. But at the same time Leverkühn asks for an understanding of his situation: that art has become too hard and therefore 'God's poor man no longer knows where to turn in his sore plight'. But that is the 'fault in the times', and if one invites the devil as a guest to get beyond it and make a breakthrough, one is taking the fault in the times on oneself, so that one is damned.[111] Perhaps for that reason the possibility cannot be excluded that he is spared damnation? This is literally what Leverkühn says, in a caricature of Old German:

> So the Evil One has strengthened his words in good faith through four-and-twenty years and all is finished up til the last, with murther and lechery have I brouhgt it to fullness and perhaps throuh Grace good can come of what was create in evil, I know not. Mayhap to God it seemeth I sought the hard and laboured might and main, perhaps, perhaps it will be to my credit that I applied myself and obstinately finished all – but I cannot say and have not courage to hope for it.[112]

So Adrian Leverkühn's relationship to God stands under the sign of the 'Perhaps', 'Don't know', 'Not the courage to hope'. Why does Leverkuhn not have this courage? Because – we learn – his sin goes even beyond the pact with the devil. Reflective man that he is, Leverkühn had already speculated with God's grace. As an ex-theologian he knows the key statements of the doctrine of grace: where sin is greatest, grace is strongest. Seeing through this relationship between sin and grace, in his rejection Leverkühn had already calculated with God. He had become intoxicated with the idea that his greatest sin must also draw down the greatest grace, and that the more rejected one is, the more one must provoke God to an activity of grace. But at the same time Leverkühn is capable of despising this speculative and provocative intellectualism, which makes his consciousness of guilt and his self damnation all the deeper. The speculator becomes his own executioner:

> My sin is greater than that it can be forgiven me, and I have raised it to its height, for my head speculated that the contrite unbelief in the possibility of grace and pardon might be the most intriguing of all for the Everlasting Goodness, where yet I see that such impudent calculation makes compassion impossible. Yet basing upon that I went further in speculation and reckoned that this last depravity must be the uttermost spur for Goodness to display its everlastingness. And so then, that I carried on an atrocious competition with the goodness above, which were more inexhaustible, it or my speculation – so ye see that I am damned, and there is no pity for me that I destroy all and every beforehand by speculation.[113]

However, one must understand the subtle refractions in what Leverkühn says about himself in order not to seize on them wrongly as the basic statements of the novel. Here we do not have the well-known 'miserable sinner' speaking. We do not know whether the man to whom the author gives a voice here is still in control of his senses or has already fallen victim to madness. We are not sure whether the man is Faust or only playing Faust. Here a highly complex intellectual is speaking and we are not certain whether he is really conscious of a sin or whether he is just enjoying the pose of self-humiliation. No one, not even his biographer, can ultimately judge whether Leverkühn is thirsty for grace or merely playing with grace. And the second possibility cannot be excluded on the basis of the text itself. Evil seems finally to be triumphing.

However, the striking thing about this novel is that if one looks for clear answers as to how the 'essence', the 'nature' of evil is to be defined, the novel remains remarkably vague. Only one thing can be inferred from it with certainty: evil is a reality, but it cannot be grasped intellectually, nor can it be dealt with in literature. All that comes through is the cold-ness and sharply analytical intellect of the devil. They seem to be forms of expression of evil. But the 'essence' of evil is not grasped here, nor even its whole form. Indeed the paradox of Chapter 25 lies in the fact that evil can appear bodily, without becoming more tangible and more under-standable as a result.

Here we have a fact which is also theologically remarkable: the Faust novel is an artistic attempt to describe the different figures of evil, which in the end founders on its final explanation. Evil remains incomprehens-ible, and reflecting it in art, Thomas Mann shows that human beings are no longer capable of discovering ultimate structures of meaning in the face of this reality. Therefore already in its form the novel is written in gestures of self-withdrawal and self-relativization. We constantly hear complaints about the inadequacy of the project, about the inability to understand such an event in a narrative way. Only one conclusion can be drawn from this: there is a connection between the formal failure of the novel as a narrative work and the inability to comprehend or even under-stand evil in its reality.

In this way the greatness and the limits of the novel become visible. Its greatness lies in the way in which it treats the problem of evil in the sphere of art; but this theme at the same time shows the limits immanent in such a project. Even this novel cannot explain what the 'diabolical' and the 'hellish' really is. Even if one cheerfully fights against evil, one has not exposed its source; even if one explains evil as a necessary part of the order of creation, its nature remains enigmatic.[114] But because the novel fails with explanations, it has come to an end as an instrument for inter-preting the world. Here I follow the literary critic and Thomas Mann specialist Helmut Koopmann:

The validity of classic notions of art has come to an end, and Thomas Mann notes this end in the face of his own attempt to write the novel of his era in the person of Leverkühn. For him it is the bankruptcy of the novel hitherto, the failure of traditional narrative art, the epic work of art . . . The end of this narration, which is so demanding in its wealth of relationships, came when it proved inadequate in the face of the diabolical events of the time. The downfall of the traditional novel: that is also the theme of *Doctor Faustus* from Chapter XXV on . . . Here the novel no longer has what has made it so important in modernity: the capacity for exegesis. It lacks power of expression: German history could no longer be interpreted by it. And it is striking how from now on this insight also governs the composition of novels: one's own statements are now strikingly replaced by borrowings, and the novel becomes a large-scale parody. We know the suppliers: Schoenberg's and Adorno's theories had to pay for taking up the thread of thought again. But everything diabolical, with which the author had really been concerned in his history of German inwardness, remained largely unexplained and inexplicable. A theory of evil was replaced with something else: a theory of the musical work of art.[115]

This failure of the novel as exegesis of the world in the face of evil is theologically of the utmost importance. For if the explanations of the world communicated by art end in fragments, in the unfinished and the unfinishable, in its failure the work of art points beyond itself. If the interpretation of the world can no longer be given conclusively in the work of art, the work of art relativizes itself and becomes a penultimate authority on meaning. Then art hands on the interpretation of the world and coping with the world to other authorities. The question thus arises: are there in this novel traces of a self-transcendence in respect of the question of meaning? Does the novel itself contain references to a necessary transcending of the experience of evil? Here the talk of grace and hope, which in the novel are probed in a way that is exciting for the theological reader, come into play.

A miracle which transcends faith

Leverkühn – as we saw – had already spoken of the grace of God. Perhaps it can make 'good' what it has corrupted. This may be the reason why in retrospect even Leverkühn's biographer Zeitblom feels justified in similarly putting his friend's fate under the sign of grace, and at least hearing in the self-accusations and self-condemnations the longing for deliverance; even interpreting the last work of his friend, *Doctor Faustus's Lament*, in the direction of hope, grace and light.

How deliberately Thomas Mann wanted to bring this second perspective, which is expressly one of grace, into the novel, is shown by the struggle over this passage during the time of composition, specifically over the conclusion of the penultimate Chapter 46. This struggle over a credible expression of hope in an age of cynicism, goodness against the horizon of evil, grace in the context of gracelessness, is of the utmost significance for any theological talk of grace. Here we can literally go to the school of language if we want to learn to understand worn-down words like 'hope', 'miracle', 'faith', 'meaning', 'light' with existential weight. Thomas Mann's correspondence over this with the philosopher and musicologist Theodor W. Adorno (at that time Thomas Mann's neighbour in California) is an abiding model here. Right at the beginning of this chapter I mentioned Adorno's negative dialectic.

In his autobiographical background account 'The Origin of Doctor Faustus', Thomas Mann himself reported that initially he had wanted to give the interpretation of *Doctor Faustus' Lament* by Serenus Zeitblom an essentially more positive and hopeful form than actually came about and can now be read. But Adorno, whom the author in any case had used as an adviser on questions of musicology and the history of music while working on *Doctor Faustus*, thought that at this particular point in the manuscript he had to make a firm criticism:

> And yet I am tempted to say that his (Adorno's) main service over the chapter does not lie in the sphere of music but in that of language and its nuances, when right at the end in the end they court the moral, religious and theological. When I had finished the section after working for two weeks on it, or thought that I had finished the section, one evening I read it out to Adorno in my room. He found nothing memorable in the musical part, but was cross about the conclusion, the last forty lines, which after all the darkness were about hope, grace, and were not as they are now, but were simply misconceived. He said that I had been too optimistic, too generous and direct, had kindled too much light, had laid on the consolation too thickly. I had to recognize that the objections made to it by my critic were justified. The next morning I set about thoroughly revising the one and a half or two pages and gave them the cautious form that they now have now. Only now did I find the phrases about the 'transcendence of despair', the 'miracle that is about faith', and the much-quoted final cadence which occurs in almost every discussion of the book, with the change of meaning of what sounds like sorrow into 'light in the night'. Only weeks later, again with Adorno, did I read him the changes and ask him whether they were all right. Instead of replying, he called his wife to hear them too. So I read out the last two pages once again, looked up – and did not need to ask any more questions.[116]

In fact the interpretation of *Doctor Faustus's Lament* by his friend Serenus Zeitblom, which also satisfied the Adornos, now read like this:

But another and last, truly the last change of mind must be thought on, and that profoundly. At the end of this work of endless lamentation, softly, above the reason and with the speaking unspokenness given to music alone, it touches the feelings. I mean the closing movement of the piece, where the choir loses itself and which sounds like the lament of God over the lost state of His world, like the Creator's rueful 'I have not willed it.' Here, towards the end, I find that the uttermost accents of mourning are reached, the final despair achieves a voice, and – I will not say it – it would mean to disparage the uncompromising character of the work, its irremediable anguish to say that it affords, down to its very last note, any other consolation than what lies in voicing it, in simply giving sorrow words; in the fact, that is, that a voice is given the creature for its woe. No, this dark tone-poem permits up to the very end no consolation, appeasement, transfiguration. But take our artist paradox: grant that expressiveness – expression as lament – is the issue of the whole construction: then may we not parallel with it another, a religious one, and say too (though only in the lowest whisper) that out of the sheerly irremediable hope might germinate? It would be but a hope beyond hopelessness, the transcendence of despair – not betrayal to her, but the miracle that passes belief. For listen to the end, listen with me: one group of instruments after another retires, and what remains, as the work fades on the air, is the high G of a cello, the last word, the last fainting sound, slowly dying in a pianissimo fermata. Then nothing more: silence, and night. But that tone which vibrates in the silence, which is no longer there, to which only the spirit hearkens, and which was the voice of mourning, is so no more. It changes its meaning; it abides as a light in the night.[117]

In the darkness God is closest

How are we to understand the connection between artistic and religious paradox described here? Only in this way: just as it is true of a work of art, however radically negative its content may be, that through the expression itself, through the entrusting itself to the expression, a hope appears (the work of art in its existence at least as a triumph of being over non-being), so too it is true for the world of the religious that where the negativity is most radical, a sphere for faith can open up in a wonderful way, i.e. one which cannot be controlled by reason. Where the darkness is densest, hope can become virulent. Where the disaster is deepest, longing can germinate from this experience – if only as the 'gentlest question'.

In fact all this is only conceivable as 'paradox': as an experience for which there is no rational foundation. Rather, radical despair first makes room for the expectation, and radical darkness for an expectation of the light. A sentence by Thomas Mann from his account of the origin of *Doctor Faustus* helps us better to understand this: 'A serious work of art brings God nearest, like battle, distress at sea and danger to life, by producing the pious search for blessing, help, grace, a religious mood.'[118] And Zeitblom thinks that he can hear precisely this in his friend's last work of art, so that in his view Adrian Leverkühn does not in fact appear as someone who cynically plays with grace, but as a desperate man thirsty for grace.

And because this is the case, Zeitblom can feel justified in entrusting his friend to the grace of God. Moreover, knowing that the fate of his land is reflected in Leverkühn's fate, Zeitblom accomplishes what his friend did not have the courage to do in the face of radical self-condemnation: *in prayer to hope totally in God,* for himself, his friend and his fatherland. His report, and thus the novel as a whole, ends with sentences of self-transcendence, precisely because it is aware of failure. At the end stands the reference to an authority beyond the novel, precisely because in the face of evil, all explaining and enlightenment has come to an end. An age-old theological insight is artistically achieved: in the end evil cannot be understood and explained but it can be opposed – in trust in the grace of God:

> Germany, the hectic on her cheek, was reeling then at the height of her dissolute triumphs, about to gain the whole world by virtue of the one pact she was minded to keep, which she had signed with her blood. Today, clung round by demons, a hand over one eye, with the other staring into horrors, down she flings from despair to despair. When will she reach the bottom of the abyss? When, out of uttermost hopelessness – a miracle beyond the power of belief – will the light of hope dawn? A lonely man folds his hands and speaks: 'God be merciful to thy poor soul, my friend, my Fatherland!'[119]

Thus Thomas Mann, slowly, carefully groping, constantly including the negative as an opposite pole, had consciously ventured to talk of grace. Adorno's criticism in particular (which is still valid for any theological discourse today) had once again made it clear to him how much talk of transcendence, light, consolation, is in danger of being artificially exposed, of having a flat effect which is alien to life. Here in fact in a naïve way one can be 'too optimistic', 'too generous', 'too direct'. One can kindle 'too much light' and lay on consolation 'too thickly'. In that case one has squandered the great words, has made them cheap toys, has reduced them to propaganda slogans. Thomas Mann's revision of the conclusion to his *Doctor Faustus* is an example of the theological critique of language and religious sensitivity to language. It shows that the great words preserve their existential seriousness, gain their depth and allow their power to be felt only when they are opposed by counter-experiences, when they are wrested from the negative, when they are indebted to their opposite. Words like 'grace' once again begin to be illuminating when one has sensed what the chill of the absence of grace means. A word like 'goodness' comes alive once again if previously one has portrayed a world to which this word has become as strange as a piece of moonstone.

Therefore the novel *Doctor Faustus* can only be understood adequately as a radical critique of the illusions of modern civilization. Only a few texts in twentieth-century literature expose so relentlessly how thin in fact the veneer of Western culture is, the patina of civilization over human bestiality. No one shows so relentlessly the fragility and corruptibility of moral existence. Thomas Mann is no less in pursuit of the 'ontological riddle', 'the mystery of civilized ennui or evil', than George Steiner. He too could not give answers which made the questions disappear.

V. Sketches of a human poetics

We have come a long way, and now it is time for an interim survey.

1. The facets of human nature

We have made the acquaintance of many aspects of human nature. We might recall:

- Kurt Tucholsky's Glass Man, who in his reflection of himself does not get rid of the anxiety about the fragility and finitude of his body which lives in his soul;
- Günter Kunert's quest for the primal human sin, which took place in the 'moment' when the human being detaches himself from the context of nature and objectifies, controls and violates the world as a reified world;
- Wolfgang Hildesheimer's meditating secular monk, who cannot get over the way in which so early in human history human beings became fratricidal and how this puts the creator God in a bad light. At the same time we might think of the rebellious meditations in which the author slips into the role of a believer in order to be able to commend the polluters of creation to the mercilessness of God and to invite God not to grant the wicked in his creation eternal rest;
- Human beings as the potential destroyers of their creation, as Christa Wolf, Günter Grass and Kurt Marti describe them, all three struggling over the possibility how, in the face of the threat of destruction which they have brought down on themselves, they can still engage in politics, still have hope.
- The unavoidability of guilt, which is there even when it is denied or suppressed, and in the light of which Max Frisch paints a critical portrait of the Homo Faber who in his delusion over power believes that he can be lord of his own 'fate'.
- The terrifying knowledge of how thin the veneer of modern civiliza-

tion is, and how the terrible, murderous and destructive can keep
breaking through, to change the world into a hell, described in a
unique way by Rolf Hochhuth and Alexander Solzhenitsyn;

- The proneness of human beings to their drive to power and their desire
for success, the prize of which is the cold soul and which ends in self-
destruction. Thomas Mann has described this and at the same time
struggled with the problem how the human being who delivers himself
to self-destruction can still hope for the grace of God.

2. My God, human beings . . .

Writers confront human beings with themselves, their contradictions,
their abysses, but also their hopes and expectations. The poetics of the
human in twentieth-century literature is a poetics of conflict, of fragility,
of self-doubt, of the fear of destruction, of the penetrating quest for
meaning. When human beings are described in twentieth-century literature, they are described as human beings in all their depths and their
uncertainty. Literature reflects the whole palette of the risks of human
existence, all that undermines self-confidence (the man in the mirror) and
trust in the world (experiences of the apocalypse and of evil). In contrast
to a bourgeois culture of experience and any mentality which seeks
security with no risks, it shows human beings as those who take risks,
who cannot be explained, who are an abiding riddle to themselves and
others. Uncertainties, latent or open, are the material of literature, under-
currents of anxiety, the fragilities of human projects and sketches of
history, threats in which Genesis can turn into apocalypses; inabilities to
control life and acknowledge guilt.

The riddle of human nature – as early as the texts of Thomas Mann
this found its adequate expression of disillusionment with civilization. In
a 1938 speech – the author's despair over the break-through of Fascism
can be detected even in the language – we can hear Thomas Mann
exclaim:

We are so familiar with human nature, or better, with human beings,
and far from having illusions about them. That is established in the
sacral saying, 'The desire of the human heart is evil from youth up.' It
is expressed with philosophical cynicism in the saying of Frederick II
about the 'accursed race' – '*de cette race maduite*'. My God, human
beings... Their injustice, wickedness, cruelty, their average stupidity
and blindness have been sufficiently shown; their egoism is crass, their

lies, cowardice, unsociability are our everyday experience: iron discipline is needed merely to keep them in order. Who would not attribute all blasphemies to this lost race, who would not often think quite hopelessly about its future and would understand that from the day of creation the angels in heaven have turned up their noses over the incomprehensible part that God the Lord plays in this questionable creature?[120]

None of these are 'yesterday's' insights. Today in particular the experiences of evil are again part of a social, indeed a philosophical, discussion. I would refer to the work of Rüdiger Safranski, who has made a name for himself as a biographer of Schopenhauer and Heidegger.[121] He has written a philosophical study on 'evil', [122] and what this philosopher said in a 1994 article about 'the return of evil' was an anticipation of this. Safranski's criticism is of the 'whole world of the welfare state', a 'postmodern contentment', an 'experience society' in which aesthetics has replaced ethics. His criticism here is of the assurance mentality which is being expressed, a mentality which asks to be effectively insured against all possible risks in life.

Here this philosopher sees a mixture of triviality and infantile narrow-mindedness, indeed a threatening infantalization and inability to achieve maturity. For maturity includes acquaintance with the evil in and around us, and the courage to resist it. The well-cushioned experience society and the dominant logic of the satisfaction of needs are bad presuppositions for this. People believed that they had discovered the power of civil society when in the midst of this same society there opened up an abyss of hatred, neglect, xenophobia and a lust for killing, which are lamented by a 'helpless political pedagogy'. But it is 'political Biedermeier' to resolve the problems by more information and the provision of meaning, presupposing the 'good' in human beings.[123] Safranski retorts:

Probably we shall have to learn again what earlier centuries took for granted: that civilizations are no more than the civilizing of a latent readiness for violence. Violence is not a substitute for something else; precisely the opposite: civilization, if it succeeds, may 'replace' the violence which always lurks underground in the soul and society. Civilizations are attempts to domesticate evil, and Freud has kept warning against overestimating the reliability of safeguards. He wrote of the orgy and killing and destruction in the First World War: 'In reality they (human beings) have not sunk as deep as we fear, because they had not risen as high as we believed.' We must reckon with the return of evil, with the de-sublimization of the potential of violence which is bound by civilizations – all the more so because the imaginary world of the media already transports us every day to a universe where anything goes. If a society opens up opportunities for setting free 'evil desires', we will experience, Freud says, that human beings commit acts of 'cruelty, malice, treachery and roughness the possibility of which people reckon to be incompatible with their cultural level'.[124]

3. We all live and die in the riddle

Nevertheless, literature does not begin from a tenacious, dark stream of pessimistic contempt for human beings. The world is not described as hell and history as disaster and catastrophe in order to kill off any will to change through the forces immanent in history. The negativity has heuristic value and may not be misunderstood as an ontology of nega-tivity. In the end the negativity may put us on the track of the 'wholly other'. And precisely because the negative is fathomed in all its depth, a return to future and hope is all the more credible. Thomas Mann said that we are closest to God in the dark. And we should also not forget that even the most sceptical text remains text, i.e. derives from a confidence in language. Even the most abysmal experience is literature, comes from trust in writing. The hope which literature has to give is identical with the fact that it still exists. The poem is a message in a bottle, the novel a Noah's ark in the flood.

But the basic question remains: if evil is still the human in its worst excesses, if the radical freedom of human beings tends towards radical perversion, if the free men and women of creation time and again become those who hurt and torture it, must not then the 'notion of creation' come into play?[125] Must not the experience of evil penetrate to the question of the creator, who evidently put both in human beings? This basic question seems to me unavoidable. Thomas Mann, Wolfgang Hildesheimer and Rolf Hochhuth already got to it. In once of his last letters, written in March 1955, Thomas Mann maintained his lifelong restraint over the word 'God' and preferred to speak of 'nature'. What, he asked, could be made of a God whose actions were absolutely incomprehensible and unfathomable'? But at the same time he adds that he is by no means a 'believing atheist'. That too is 'ridiculous'. Why? Finally, after all, there is the question 'of the ultimate origin of nature and life, the whole tremendous cosmic affair'. And no human being will 'ever answer' the question. Thomas Mann evocatively adds:

We all live and die in the riddle, and if one likes, we can call this feeling religious. It is a somewhat demanding word, but the consciousness of hopeless uncertainty amounts to a kind of piety.[126]

We shall be sharpening up these questions about the 'origin of nature and life' connected with the 'riddle of human nature' in the next part: the abyss of the mystery of God.

B. God the Abyss

Never let go of God! Love him!
If you cannot, then argue with him,
accuse him and dispute with him like Job,
indeed, if you can, blaspheme him,
but – never let him go!

Theodore Haecker

The state of creation poses a question not only to human beings but also to God, the creator. Only late in my theological career did it dawn on me that this critical discussion was necessary even with God himself, indeed that there are theological traditions which explicitly encourage this. Such questions were never put at any time in my religious education. I was not encouraged to ask these questions by the church. I had to be taught them, too, by literature. They led me to thoughts of a relentless argument with God, a critique of God – in the interest of God. That is what I shall be relating in this section – in the awareness that there are quite other ways of approaching the experience of the character of God as abyss (like mysticism). However, this character will not be put in the foreground here, but – by deliberate choice – the dimension of complaints and accusations against God. This will hold the very different texts in this part together.

I. Criticism of God becomes taboo

Time and again I have looked in the officially approved church prayer books and hymn books for texts in which questions were put to God. I have searched the Catholic prayer book and hymn book used in all German-language dioceses since 1975, entitled *Gotteslob* (= GL: 'Praise of God') and the new completely revised Protestant hymn book (*Evangelisches Gesangbuch* = EGB), approved for the whole of the Protestant Church in Germany. Hymns like 'I stand before you, Lord, with empty hands/ strange are your ways to me and strange your name' (GL 621/EGB 382), are the exception which proves the rule. Verses like 'Rouse dead Christianity from the sleep of certainty' (GL 644/EGB 262) have to be sought like needles in a haystack. In particular the dimension of human lament is almost completely absent, let alone that of accusation of God, both from the prayers and from the hymns.

1. The assuaging of doubt: prayer books

My investigation of the prayer sections produced the following results. Among the thirty-five numbers under which 'personal prayers' are to be found in *Gotteslob*, there are just two which at least address a possible situation of existential conflict: 'In need and darkness' (no.9), and 'In sickness' (no.10). But even here, figures of speech like surrender to God, humble petition for support and readiness 'to bear whatever comes' (No. 10/1) dominate. Granted, the texts of some prayers mention perplexity, doubt and desperation, but in the end there is always a shift towards trust in God.

Do with me what pleases you?

The following text is characteristic; it is a collection of little quotations from the work of the Protestant theologian Dietrich Bonhoeffer:

> Lord God, great distress has come upon me. My cares are about to
> choke me. I do not know where to turn. God, be gracious to me and
> help. Give me power to bear what you send me. Do not let fear rule
> over me; look after my loved ones with fatherly care.
>
> Merciful God, forgive me all the sins I have committed against you
> and others. I trust in your grace and give my life wholly into your
> hands. Do with me what pleases you and what is good for me (GL 9/2).

The findings in the *Evangelisches Gesangbuch* are similar. Among the
forty-four numbers in the prayer section, just one is devoted to 'distress
and sickness' (EGB); here too the motif of practising confidence in God
and trust in God's grace stands in the foreground. The prayer with which
it is suggested that a Protestant Christian should cope with the death of a
child is particularly striking:

> Incomprehensible God! We bring to you our despair. You have taken
> our child from us. It is difficult for us to comply with your will. Help
> us, we are at the end of our strength. Strengthen us to trust in you even
> when we do not understand you. Now let our child be with you. God,
> do not forsake us (EGB 831).

In this critical analysis my concern is not to dispute the possible
significance of such texts in pastoral emergencies or even make mock of
people who live with such prayers and cope with their crises in a religious
way. Those who believe that they are stronger than others in such situations should take heed less they fall! It is not the texts in themselves which
are the problem, but the fact that in an official church book they are the
only ones with which Christians may come before God. Other dimensions of the relationship with God are not present, evidently because the
church does not want them. For in none of our texts is the person who
prays offered the possibility of complaining to God in situations of existential crisis, far less of accusing God directly, which would be quite
understandable in the face of the death of a child.

But all these texts act as though the crises were a human problem and
as though God can be made exclusively the one who copes with crises; as
though talk of God could emerge unscathed from these existential
conflicts in his creation. As if one could not sort out this suffering with
God oneself. As if there were not a form of innocent suffering which one
simply cannot accept in humility any longer, and where one would show
contempt for oneself, if one allowed oneself to be consoled with the

statement which *Gotteslob* commends to Catholics 'in distress and darkness': 'Do with me as it pleases you.'

Suppression of complaints – exclusion of accusations

The findings in the two hymn sections are similar. Among the hundreds of hymns in the two church books there are very few which can explicitly be understood as a complaint to God. For example this one:

> My God, my God, why do you give no answer?
> So King David once sang and that is my complaint.
> A shadow and no longer human; you are far,
> my God, my God, why do you give no answer? (GL 308/EGB 381).

But in the face of the mass of other hymns, such a text and thus its content is completely marginalized. The situation is even worse with the element of accusation of God. One has to search for a very long time to find it at all. The *Evangelisches Gesangbuch* finally offers this text based on Psalm 13:

> How long will you forget me,
> where is your help and grace?
> How long will ills beset me
> so cut off from your face?
>
> How long must I bear sorrow
> and torment, day by day?
> When comes the bright tomorrow,
> that joy for which I pray? (EGB 598).

Certainly, in individual hymns suffering, despair and human need are addressed; indeed, in the index of key words the *Evangelisches Gesangbuch* has explicitly included 'primal words' like 'anxiety' and 'despair'. But if one looks more closely, in all these texts, usually the saving, gracious, merciful God is immediately conjured up, as if people feared fear or as if one might not confront God with this truth. Certainly, human crises and darkness are addressed in some hymns, but nowhere do they become a problem of talk about God. Answers, soothing words, consolations occur all over these texts and hymns, but nowhere is doubt radically sustained; nowhere are the aporias of human beings before God endured, the questions left open. A theology of answers which rests upon itself is the dominant feature.

My concern – and the point to which the conversations with the writers in this section will lead us – is expressed by a text from the Christian philosopher and journalist Theodor Haecker, which is interspersed (unfortunately without reference) as an interim text in the *Evangelisches Gesangbuch*. Suddenly one is confronted with these sentences, the theology of which is completely different from that of its surroundings, and which in this way seems like an alien body:

> Never let go of God! Love him! If you cannot, then argue with him, accuse him and dispute with him like Job, indeed, if you can, blaspheme him, but – never let him go![1]

This evidence, which I have produced on the basis of church prayer books and hymnbooks, is not random. It reflects the history of a systematic exclusion of the dimension of protest, of complaint and accusation in reflecting on the problem of theodicy: from the theology of the patristic period to that of the present day.

2. Why God has been spared

The more I investigated the problem historically,[2] the more I recognized that one of the most effective reasons why the creator God is spared questions about the history of suffering in the world may have had to do with the battle against dualism in the early church. For from the second century on, the theologians of the early church were confronted with rival philosophies and religions which propagated a dualistic picture of the world: Gnosis, Manicheism and Priscillianism. Above all the religion stemming from the Persian Mani (216–276/7), a world religion of that time with influences from Spain to China, had become a challenge of epoch-making dimensions for Christian theology. Manicheism had put forward a doctrine of the origin of evil that convinced many people. The world is dominated by the unbridgeable opposition of two eternal primal principles: light and darkness, good and evil, spirit and matter, God and Satan. Evil could be explained rationally as a reality split off from God which owes its existence to an independent cause through a second metaphysical principle, Satan. In this way God is kept free of all evil. He belongs to the world of light, diametrically opposed to the kingdom of darkness, where all that is bodily, material and worldly belongs.

Warding off dualism

The reaction of church orthodoxy certainly averted dualism, but at the price of a loss in the human sphere. To be specific, on the one hand the first great ecumenical assembly of the church, the Council of Nicaea in 325, could resolutely reject dualism – 'We believe in one God, the Father almighty, creator of *all* that is visible and invisible' – thus ruling out a dualistic division of the world into a good kingdom of the invisible and an evil kingdom of the visible was ruled out. All that exists, owes itself exclusively to the creative power of the almighty and good God and not to any other evil powers or principles which rival God. Moreover, around eighty years after Nicaea, in 400, the Synod of Toledo quite clearly asserted:

> Whoever says and believes that this world and all its institutions have not been created by the almighty God, let him be anathema . . . Whoever says or believes that the world has been made by another God than the one of whom it is written 'In the beginning God created heaven and earth' (cf. Gen. 1.10), let him be anathema (DH 191, 199).

And this view was once again explicitly endorsed by Pope Leo I in a letter of 447 (to bishop Turribius of Astorga in Spain): 'True faith' is 'that the substance of all spiritual and bodily creatures is good and that there is no nature of evil; for God, the creator of all, has not made anything that is not good' (DH 286).

On the other hand, this anti-dualistic development of doctrine completely repressed questions to the creator God. Anyone who had doubts about God's good order came to be suspected of dualism and enmity with God. Especially under the epoch-making influence of the theology of Augustine, at the latest after the fifth century the unshakeable conviction became established in the formation of church doctrine that:

1. All that exists owes itself to the creative will of the good God.
2. All that exists is fundamentally good.
3. The evil that exists has no substance of its own; it is simply a 'lack of good' *(privatio boni)*.
4. Evil does not come from God but through the free will of human beings.

However, in the course of the history of theological reflection the fundamental questions could not be suppressed: if evil has no author of its own and no substance, if like all that is created it comes from the creative hand of God, has not God then willed evil as much as good? Is not God then contradictory in himself or even responsible for the existence of evil? Questions about the relationship between divine foreknowledge, divine predestination and human freedom arise, and thus above all the question of moral evil.

Foreknowledge, yes; predestination, no

As early as the ninth century, at the synod of Valence in 855, the church made clear statements about the problem of predestination and freedom:

> Furthermore the foreknowledge of God has not imposed necessity on any evil (*nulli malo*), so that he (the human being) could not be otherwise but would know like God, who knows all that that (person) will become of his own will before it happens, on the basis of his almighty and unchangeable majesty. 'Nor do we believe that a man will be condemned on the basis of his (= God's) prior judgment, but on the basis of his own unrighteousness.' 'Moreover these evil men do not perish because they could not have done good, but because they did not want to be good, and through their vices remain in the mass of corruption either through original or through actual sin' (DH 627).

Again there was a decisive shift in the church's teaching on the relationship between divine predestination and human freedom: God is not burdened with the actual existence of moral evil; only human beings are. And God's foreknowledge does not change anything, since evil is not forced on men and women by God. God does not condemn people definitively to evil from eternity. God gives scope to human freedom, allowing men and women to refuse evil or to be open to it and thus to oppose God's original will for good. Certainly God knows the human will in advance, including the will to evil, but he respects the freedom of the human will.

So what is decisive for church teaching is the difference between foreknowledge of evil and predestination to evil. This too was already stated quite clearly by the Synod of Valence:

> But in the condemnation of all those who will perish, guilt precedes God's just judgment. 'But God has established by predestination only what he himself wanted to do either through his gracious mercy or through his just judgment', in accordance with scripture, which says,

'He has done what will be' (Isa. 45.11): but in the case of the wicked he has foreknown their wickedness, because it comes from them themselves, but not predestined, because it does not come from him (DH 628).

Thus it is clear at a very early stage that in the church's view human beings alone are the source and cause of moral evil and therefore bear all the blame for the existence of this evil. But God's foreknowledge of evil is not a determination of God to evil. The actual existence of evil is connected with the actual existence of human freedom.

Evil is only allowed by God

But how do the two sets of statements go together logically and theologically? On the one hand, all that is, is good, because it owes itself to the creative will of the good God. On the other hand, evil has its cause in the human will. Must not the existence of evil also rebound on God, the creator of *all* things? Indeed, must not God ultimately be blamed for the failure to achieve salvation, since while he gives all human beings sufficient grace, he manifestly does not give them all effective grace? Can God really be acquitted of all responsibility if he created a human being who was capable of evil and could constantly fall into the trap of his freedom?

To resolve this dilemma, under the influence of the theology of Thomas Aquinas recourse was had to a distinction between God really doing evil and merely allowing it. This distinction found its way into church teaching for the first time at the Council of Trent. In the famous 'Decree on Justification' (1557), there is a formulation which is unmistakably directed against Calvin's strict doctrine of predestination.

Whoever says that it is not in man's power to make his works evil, but that God brings about the evil works as well as the good, not only by allowing them (*permissive*), but also in the real sense and through himself, so that the treachery of Judas is no less God's work than the calling of Paul, let him be anathema (DH 1556).

This doctrine that God allows evil persists constantly in the doctrinal tradition of the church. The existence of moral evil, the source of which is the perversion of human free will, is theologically justified as a means allowed by God to a higher end: in particular to maintain the moral order (e.g. for the punishment, testing or education of human beings). A particular figure of theological argumentation becomes characteristic: on the basis of his love and righteousness God cannot really want evil; he can only allow it because he takes account of human freedom and has the wisdom also to make good come out of evil. The fact of evil is therefore not a charge against God, because it serves a just purpose and aim of God (which is often hidden from human beings). The sting is drawn from any doubt in God's righteousness by a reference to the limited capacities of human knowledge. Thus even the question of theodicy *de facto* becomes heresy.

It has become clear to me that for centuries, millions of Christian men and women have lived with these theological answers. They have internalized them, spiritually and psychologically. They seem content to deal with evil by a spirituality of the cross, a theology of recompense, or a moralizing and pedagogical approach. Certainly this has proved successful in warding off a dualism which is pessimistic about the world, the notion that evil stems from an evil principle contrary to God, or can and may be put ontologically on the same level as the good. But the consequence of this theology was always an unburdening of God and a burdening of human beings. Evil really never became a theological problem but only an anthropological one. On these presuppositions a protest against God as the cause of evil could not arise. And this theological theory was reinforced not only by the Reformation but also by the early Enlightenment, the most brilliant representative of which was Gottfried Wilhelm Leibniz. In his *Theodicy*, which appeared in 1710, Leibniz now revived the classical theological arguments about a harmony and order in the world, in which evil has its function and significance (as a lack of the good), and rationally supported them in great style. Leibniz was the first and last great philosopher of any status to justify God.

But in the middle of the eighteenth century, such an optimism over theodicy began to collapse for many people in Europe, especially intellectuals. The Lisbon earthquake on 1 November 1755 which killed 30,000 people set off a shock wave which shattered such optimism. Here was an experience of unjust, boundless suffering, which showed up any talk of evil as a function of the good to be hollow phraseology. As if one can go on understanding such boundless suffering of innocent victims as a necessary evil, imposed on people to test or to punish them! That would have been cynical, at least as far as the victims were concerned. And after such catastrophes God's order of creation, too, could no longer be described with Leibniz's term 'the best possible of all worlds'. On the contrary, the mass of unmerited suffering breaking through here for the first time became the occasion for many people in Europe to doubt not only the meaning of suffering, but the meaning of creation generally.

3. The protest against God as atheism

In short, questions about the creator God became unavoidable. Given all the share of human responsibility for the establishment of evil and hells on earth (we recall the laughing devil in Hochhuth and the terrifying banality of evil in the punishment camp described by Solzhenitsyn), can the one who willed this creation to be thus and not otherwise be relieved of all responsibility? The theological debate is over the fact not that God created human beings, but that God has created his creation (including human beings) in this way and not otherwise: with all its capacities for perversions, cruelties and anti-godliness. Despite a fundamental affirmation of creation and the freedom of human beings as 'actors' on the stage of the world, can God any longer be kept out of a play of which he is author and director?

Necessary questions to God

Furthermore, the need for such questions also arises from the mere fact that by the misuse of their freedom human beings not only trample on God's commandment but also often enough misuse their freedom in the name of God. How much unbridled inhumanity has been practised in the name of God, from the persecutions of heretics, through Jewish pogroms, the burning of witches, the Inquisition, to wars of faith and religious fanaticism of every kind! To serve God, human beings have hurt, tormented, tortured other human beings and robbed them of their happiness and life. In the name of God (already in the Bible!), wars have been waged, mass murders committed, those of other faiths put to death, dishonoured and discriminated against. And is the creator God himself to be acquitted, exonerated, excused responsibility for all this, justified?

The modern consequence of these experiences is a criticism of religion and atheism. In the literary works of Georg Büchner (1813–1837) this is concentrated in a way which is hitherto unprecedented in German literature.[3] And it is significantly in a play about the French Revolution, i.e. about a period of crisis, chaos, blood and murder, that Büchner formulates his radical counter-thesis to all optimistic theodicy in the style of Leibniz. As early as 1833, at the age of twenty, under the impact of his study of this part of French history, Büchner had written:

I find in human nature a terrible equality, in human relationships an inescapable violence bestowed on one and all. The individual only spume on the wave, greatness mere chance, the rule of the genius a puppet show, a ridiculous struggle against an iron law, to recognize it the highest thing, to control it impossible.

Two years later, in his play on the French revolutionary Danton (*Danton's Death*) Büchner put his own personal view into the mouth of his hero: 'What is it in us that whores, lies, steals and murders? We are puppets of unknown forces. We ourselves are nothing . . . The world is chaos. Nothingness is the world God who is to give birth.' And it is no coincidence that it is in a prison scene, while prisoners are waiting for their execution, that Büchner makes one of the figures formulate a renunciation of God and his creation:

You can only prove the existence of God if you deny the world is imperfect. Do away with the imperfect, only then can you demonstrate God. Spinoza tried it. You can deny the existence of evil but not pain. Only false reason can prove God. All true feelings rebel against it. Anaxagoras, why do I suffer? That is the rock of atheism. The slightest twinge of pain, even if only in a single, and creation is smashed, from top to bottom.

Farewell to Leibniz

'One can deny evil but not pain; only the mind can prove God, feelings rage against it': these two statements formulate a farewell to any rational demonstration of theodicy. Leibniz's metaphysics are seen through as mental gymnastics which in no way correspond any longer to human feelings: the feeling of living in a world in which the experience of evil cannot in any way be integrated into the world order as a harmony of contrast. On the contrary: evil has a power and vigour which – despite all intellectualizing explanations – ruptures the harmony of the cosmos. The experience of pain and suffering is so strong that any theory of privation amounts to scorn of suffering men and women.

Indeed, it is similarly no coincidence that in Büchner's play the classical tradition of theodicy from Augustine to Leibniz is shattered by that experience which people had dealt with previously either through a harmony of contrast or in a moralizing pedagogical way: the experience of unjust, boundless suffering. This suffering can no longer be understood as a merely necessary evil, imposed on people to test them or to punish them. Now this suffering becomes the 'rock of atheism', in other words, an occasion that can no longer be discussed away to doubt whether not only suffering but the creation generally has any meaning. In the creation things ultimately do not hold together: a rift runs through creation, the rift of suffering, the rift of pain, the rift of evil. This rift can no longer be explained rationally or used pedagogically, but becomes a point of accusation against the omnipotent creator himself.

4. But God also suffers

However, prominent representatives of contemporary theology begin at precisely this point and dispute the need to accuse God by referring to God's suffering over his creation. Basically, the argument goes like this: classical theology (from Augustine and Thomas Aquinas to Luther and Calvin) acquitted God of all responsibly for evil, including innocent suffering, so that his superiority over the world and his omnipotence could be preserved. The divinity of God himself was to be respected. But the price for that was to make God unmoved, uninvolved and unaffected in the face of the suffering in his creation. Thus all those who wanted to justify God in this way had, contrary to their interests, exposed God even more to the protest which is critical of religion – the protest against the majestic lack of involvement of a God who turns his back to the cries of his children. Granted, there was an intrinsic legitimacy and plausibility to the traditionally 'theistic' understanding of God. But atheism followed this theism like a shadow and was relatively justified here, in that it was rebelling against God's lack of involvement in the name of the suffering of the innocent and in the end denying the existence of such a God.

However, if one could prove that a genuinely Christian understanding made it possible to speak of a God who in no way is enthroned high above all suffering but is involved in the suffering of creation, indeed can himself suffer, could one then protest against such a God in the name of suffering? On the contrary, could it not then be possible to think of God and suffering together without contradiction, so that the foundations were so to speak removed from protest atheism? But how?

Suffering – the price of love

The foundation of all this is a theology of love, now in fashion, which thinks that it may dare also to speak of God's capacity to suffer. This theology of love is developed from the suffering and dying of Jesus Christ the Son of God. It is thought legitimate to draw the conclusion that what happened on Golgotha is an expression of God's capacity to suffer and an impotence made possible through love. Has not God precisely in the cross of his Son shown himself to be a weak, impotent God who can suffer and die for love? And does not such a theology of suffering for love in fact remove the basis from modern protest atheism?

Moreover in present-day theological schemes we can find the conviction expressed that one can no longer protest against a crucified God in the name of the crosses of world history: one can no longer sue a weak God for one's own weakness; one can no longer play off one's own suffering against a God who suffers with us out of love; one can no longer rebel against a dying God in the name of all unjust deaths. This seems to be an answer to the theodicy question. Thus in a 1982 book of Catholic dogmatics one reads this sentence:

> The 'sympathetic' God who is revealed in Jesus Christ is the final answer to the question of theodicy on which both theism and atheism come to grief. If God himself suffers, then suffering is no longer an objection against God.[4]

And here 'final answer' can only mean that with the theology of the cross, an answer can be given to the question of theodicy, an answer which solves the question that has been posed. Thus the Christian theology of the cross makes the question of theodicy disappear.

Indeed, present-day Christian theologians are not afraid of taking Augustine's line and explaining human suffering not only as the price of freedom but even as the price of love. They say: in creating human beings, God also creates the possibility for evil to happen, although as the holy One, God absolutely does not want evil. But God's love of men and women stems from this will for freedom. We read in a contemporary Catholic theologian:

> If God therefore wants human freedom as a condition for the possibility of love between him and the creature, and the human being is essentially bound up in a world which corresponds to him, there is a negative background to this freedom; in that case there is necessarily structural suffering. And for our question about the compatibility of suffering with the Christian image of God, that means that the fact of suffering does not tell against the good creator God and against the

goodness of creation. Rather – from the perspective of our reflections – suffering is the price of freedom, the price of love. A God who prevented suffering by his omnipotence and goodness would make love (which presupposes freedom) impossible.[5]

The main arguments of such a position are therefore:

1. God's omnipotence is the power of his love. In his love God gives human beings a sphere of freedom which they can use for good or ill. In the light of this understanding of omnipotence it is senseless to appeal to God to prevent suffering through 'intervention' or to shorten the process of suffering by his almighty word. For in accordance with this understanding, God has voluntarily renounced his omnipotence out of love of human beings.
2. Suffering is therefore not a contradiction of the good creator God or the goodness of creation, because it is simply the price that human beings pay for the freedom that has been given them by God in love.
3. The notion that human beings can suffer by exploiting their freedom is therefore no objection to God, and is tolerable, because God, too, suffers in any suffering in order to transform it from within.

The stilling of protest

Here I have been concerned to set out the concepts objectively in an argument, although emotionally the question of theodicy affects me deeply. And I want to credit all these theological efforts with being concerned with the connection between belief in God and the experience of suffering, which has become extremely difficult in the face of the modern critique of religion. It has to be noted that they do not want to make the experience of evil the 'rock of atheism' again, but want it to lead to tested, mature talk of God.

Here in particular the notion of the 'inner transformation' of suffering through faith in God's nearness, indeed compassion, seems to me indispensable. People affected by suffering can hear from the New Testament that their suffering is not an expression of God's curse, rejection, coldness or punishment, but can be an expression of God's nearness. Suffering men or women are at least left with the comforting thought that the God of Jesus Christ is near to them even in their suffering; that their suffering does not take them away from God but leads them to God. From that they may gain the strength to accept their suffering creatively, to endure it boldly, or even to overcome it.

However, we are to make a completely different assessment of the claim that a theology of love and suffering gives 'the final answer to the theodicy question' in which suffering is said to be 'no longer an objection to God'. That is a false conclusion. For such a theology of love and suffering does not solve the theodicy problem, but sharpens it. If God indeed knows compassion and love and has also constantly 'proved' this down history, the question of the sufferer becomes more intense: Why me? Why like this? Why now? Where are the love and compassion of God in my particular situation, whether in the case of a pernicious illness, a disastrous accident or a natural catastrophe? So any theology which seriously thinks that suffering and the Christian image of God are 'compatible', in the sense that the fact of suffering does not tell against the good creator God and the goodness of creation, is deluding itself.

For precisely the opposite is true: those who maintain the possibility of God's love and compassion (which for me is an indispensable notion) do not solve the theodicy problem but raise it. The more there is talk of God's love, the more 'conditions' put this love in question. The higher the moralizing of God, the deeper the fall of the person concerned when the crises come. Nothing is gained by explaining suffering as the price of freedom, the price of love. That must sound cynical to any innocent sufferer. Is it in all seriousness possible to put up with a God who out of love could literally look upon all that suffering without preventing it? Even a dialectical manipulation of the concept of omnipotence does not do away with the question: can we believe in a God who would look on Auschwitz 'in love', simply because he respects human 'freedom'? Auschwitz – a 'price of love'? Such a God would fall below the ethical level of any father, any mother, who respect the freedom of their child, but do everything their power if a child gets into situations of horrible misfortune or itself produces such situations.

But what is the alternative to dealing with the theodicy question credibly – beyond the crazy alternative: denial of God or love of God? Is there a third way which does not fall victim to the false conclusions of either atheism or the love-suffering theology? I have sketched one out with my Tübingen colleague, the Old Testament scholar Walter Gross, in a book entitled 'I Create Darkness and Doom!' Is God Responsible for Evil? (1992). It is based on the theological legitimacy of lamenting to God and accusing God in the face of the bottomless mystery of the question of theodicy. Here – in conversation with the poets and writers – I want to endorse and develop this outline. And here the conversation with these writers is particularly important because the theological tradition has largely made this dimension taboo. What the analysis of the official Catholic and Protestant prayer books and hymn books produced, endorsed by information from the history of theology, is also confirmed by an investigation by the great Protestant Old Testament scholar Claus Westermann. On the basis of an analysis of Christian commentaries on the Old Testament book of Lamentations, he comes to the conclusion that 'in almost all commentaries and investigations' the lamentation is either 'devalued' or is spoken of 'only in a derogatory way'. This devaluation in no way stems from the 'interpretation of these texts', but is rather grounded 'in a pre-understanding'. 'To lament before God is inappropriate; it is not the right attitude to God. Lamentation disturbs or diminishes the pious attitude to God.'[6]

II. How do we speak of the incomprehensible?

So it should not be a surprise that resistance to talk of God which waters things down or harmonizes them, or direct protest against God, has been discovered outside theology. The writers have made themselves advocates of such an experience, which has been domesticated and blunted within the church. Great literature articulates the resistance in the light of basic experiences: the collapse of religious security in people's view of the world (F.Dürrenmatt and M.L.Kaschnitz); the blatant innocent suffering of the individual (H.Heine); and finally the experience of the mass extermination of the people of God (E.Wiesel, Z.Kolitz). In all these cases the 'old conversation' has been broken off; its place has been taken not by atheism but by a new experience of God as abyss. At the end of the section the significance of this experience of the writers for present-day theological talk of God will be evaluated.

1. An author deletes the word God: Friedrich Dürrenmatt

Here I have to tell a story and the story of this story. None illustrates more clearly for me what it means to break off the 'old conversation' about God. The piece in question is Dürrenmatt's story 'The Tunnel' . When it appeared for the first time in 1952 in the prose volume *Die Stadt*, it had the following conclusion:

> 'And you?' asked the twenty-four-year-old. I am the senior conductor, answered the other, and I have always lived without hope. Without hope, repeated the young man, who now lay comfortably on the windscreen of the driver's cab, his face pressed over the abyss. We were still sitting there in our compartments and did not know that already everything was lost, he thought. It seemed to us that nothing had changed,

yet already the shaft had taken us into its depths and so we were rushing like Korah's gang into our abyss . . .

What are we to do? Nothing, replied the other mercilessly, without turning his face from the deadly scene, but not without a ghostly cheerfulness, showered with splinters of glass which came from the broken control panel, while two lumps of cotton-wool, caught in a current of air which now suddenly forced itself in (a first split appeared in the windscreen), swept like an arrow into the shaft above them. Nothing. God made us fall. And we are falling to him.[7]

Twenty-six years later, in a new edition of his text, Dürrenmatt deleted the following phrases:

> . . . and so we were rushing like Korah's gang into our abyss . . .
> . . . from the deadly scene . . .
> . . . but not without a ghostly cheerfulness . . .

And above all Dürrenmatt deleted the last sentences of all:

> God made us fall. And we are falling to him.

What is this narrative about? And what has happened for Dürrenmatt to want to drop the word 'God' above all from his literary text?

A train rushes into the abyss

The story is about a twenty-four-year-old student who – as had been his custom for a year – gets into a train for the two-hour journey between his home and his university city. In the packed train he fights his way to the last coach, finds a seat there and shares the compartment with a red-haired girl reading a novel and a fat man playing chess. After a while the train goes into a tunnel, and this too is so usual that the passengers do not even notice it. Only when the journey through the tunnel and thus the darkness in the compartment last longer than usual does the young man become 'confused'. But the lights are on, so his two fellow-passengers peacefully go about their business again.

However, the young man has become restless and goes out of his compartment into the corridor, only to note that the other passengers evidently have not noticed anything unusual. They go on reading newspapers and chatting as before. Is he perhaps in the wrong train? But the

ticket collector, who soon afterwards checks the tickets, assures him that
all is well. However, the student wants the conductor of the train. When
the student finds him, the senior conductor asks the young man to go
with him to the front of the train. The senior conductor seems to be
the only person who has noticed a deviation from normality. For this
senior conductor not only notes that the tunnel 'is unending'; he has
also registered that the train – though only apparently – is going 'downwards'. In any case there is no question of stopping.

Both go to the driving cab of the locomotive, which means clambering
laboriously and dangerously over the locomotive, close to the rock walls.
For in the meantime the train is still going forward, and the journey into
the abyss is accelerating. When they reach the driver's cab it is empty;
the engine driver had long since jumped off, along with the staff in the
luggage van. The speed increases now, to become a headlong rush, and
all the attempts of the senior conductor to do his 'duty' and warn the
people comes to grief on the fact that the train is now pointing downwards and travelling at headlong speed into the heart of the earth. What
can one do? The senior conductor and the young man are agreed: one can
do 'nothing'.

Erroneous interpretations

That – in a few lines – is the action of this short story. How has it been
interpreted? An *autobiographical-existential interpretation* is popular:
here Dürrenmatt, it is claimed, has above all wanted to draw a self-
portrait of himself as a student (corpulent, spectacles, much travelled,
the journey from his home city of Bern to the university city of Zurich)
and reflects an attitude of 'cheerfulness' which at an early stage made it
possible for him to cope with perceptions of catastrophe. This cheerfulness is his saving virtue, as it is the 'breath of boldness', for the twenty-
four-year-old is the 'only bold, clear-sighted person' on this train. Thus
in this narrative, too, that 'basic question' is raised which 'the existence
of a Dürrenmatt puts to us: how does a person who is naturally cheerful,
and endowed with clear sight, endure our world?'[8]

The interpretation of the story as a *critique of society* represents an
extension of this autobiographical-existential interpretation. If for the
first interpretation the sentence 'but not without a ghostly cheerfulness'
is a key to understanding, now the key lies in all the sentences which
describe the lack of suspicion among the passengers. Above all:

At the other end of the carriage the doors opened. In the garish light of the dining car one saw people drinking to one another, and then the doors closed again.

These sentences are supposed to make the text 'a parable which is a critique of society'. In the narrative Dürrenmatt is said to have wanted to depict the 'worst possible turn' in an everyday event in the contemporary context of Switzerland. The focus of this shake-up is a 'society saturated and enjoying itself in the process of the economic miracle, and apolitically trusting in the regularity of the official running of everyday life', embodied by the passengers in the train. The 'brilliantly written' text could therefore be interpreted as a 'parable which is a critique of society'.[9]

Alongside the autobiographical-existential interpretation and the social critique stands the *religious and theological interpretation*. Its key text is the last sentence: 'God made us fall. And we are falling to him.' Theological interpreters have seen here a Christian confession of the merciful God on whom human beings set their hope and with whose help they can also endure the absurd world. Dürrenmatt has depicted a person successfully accepting a God who has put off the traits of the Old Testament avenger and shows himself to be a helping God.[10] Other interpreters of this ilk speak of the 'clear confession of a Christian God or a Christian world order' or want to deal with the faith of the twenty-four-year-old by means of the category of the 'omnipresence of God'.[11] God is said to work unceasingly through all creatures, to be omnipresent and all-active in nature and history, as the dark, hidden God for whom no human accusation and no theodicy is appropriate. And indeed, does not the allusion to 'Korah's gang' above all speak for a religious interpretation of this story? Here Dürrenmatt is clearly and deliberately taking up a scene from the book of Numbers, where a group of people is described who fall under judgment because of their rebellion against Moses, God's lawgiver. According to Numbers 16.31 God opened up the earth before them and in this way made them and their families hurtle to their death . . . So is Dürrenmatt's 'The Tunnel' similarly a threat, with destruction as God's penal judgment on a sinful humankind?

None of these interpretations does justice to the story. And because they had become established, Dürrenmatt evidently felt it necessary to intervene himself by making corrections. Certainly the narrative displays traces of autobiography: the parallels between the twenty-four-year-old and his author can be substantiated autobiographically (the regular train journey between Bern and Zurich in the winter and summer of

1942/43), and in addition Dürrenmatt frequently refers to reading Jules Verne's *Journey to the Centre of the Earth* in his early youth.[12] But Dürrenmatt himself evidently did not want to give his story an exclusively existential point. Therefore he deletes the key sentence for this group of interpreters: 'not without a ghostly cheerfulness'. The same goes for the religious interpretations. Dürrenmatt deliberately deletes all biblical and theological phrases in his text. But the social-critical interpretation also falls short. For a critique of society is always at the service of another, better, 'more progressive' society. And for Dürrenmatt this is not in prospect, either in this text or elsewhere. The point of the narrative is different, and only in the light of this point do the interpretations in terms of existence, social criticism and religion take on a new function – above all for the reader, the recipient.

The terrible as a possibility

The point of this narrative appears at the moment when it is about the experience of 'terror', the 'monstrous' and the abysmal, and people at the same time can no longer explain this phenomenon or prevent it through actions. This discrepancy between the incursion of the terrible and the collapse of all plausible explanations of it, or necessary modes of action, might be the decisive feature of this text. Therefore not only is society shaken here (in favour of a new and better one), but the world generally. Here the fact of the 'world' is being debated, and the fact that human beings fail in the attempt to keep a grip on their 'world' when 'terror' comes.

For at first an attempt is made to grapple with the incursion of terror in a quite conventional way: through rational explanation and a rescue attempt. Indeed, to begin with the twenty-four-year-old himself seeks rational explanations. Perhaps he is on the wrong train? Perhaps previously he had not noticed how long the tunnel was? And rational explanations are provided above all by those around him: the fat chess player, for whom Switzerland statistically has more tunnels than any other country! So why get excited? Or an Englishman, who here (he is caricatured as Simpel) thinks that this is the 'Simplon' tunnel, in fact the longest tunnel in Switzerland. Or the ticket-collector, who explains the darkness outside as bad weather or a gathering storm. And as a rescue attempt there is the attempt of the twenty-four-year-old to use the emergency brake, or the suggestion of the senior conductor that he should do his 'duty' and prevent a panic among the passengers, or the way the two officials jump out of the luggage van and off the locomotive. But all this is vain. The fall cannot be stopped. The traditional pattern of explanation and action fails in this case, is meant to fail. The prevailing plausibility of the order or practice of the world is meant to be shaken here, is meant to be brought toppling down – played out in a fictitious story which is written on the basis of the motto, 'What if . . .'

Only a few people perceive the terror at all: the senior conductor and the twenty-four-year-old. We learn from the senior conductor only that he has 'always lived without hope'. We are to believe that he belongs to the group of those who have never had illusions about the possible state of the world – unlike others. We learn more about the twenty-four-year-old. In the very first lines of the text it is reported that perhaps his only gift was 'to perceive the terror behind the scenes'. His bulky body is ironically explained by the comment that it prevents the terror 'from coming too close to him'; indeed he is fond of stopping up the 'holes in his flesh', since the terror could stream in through them in particular. So the twenty-four-year-old usually carries a cigar in his mouth (Ormond Brasil 10) and has cotton wool in his ears. With these he arms himself against 'the terror behind the scenes', because as one of the few he must guard against the terror getting too close to him.

So from the beginning we learn that the terror exists 'behind the scenes' of the normal world and can break into this world at any time. It is a *possibility* – at any time and in any place. At any time, for example, the world can open its maw and let a train rush into the abyss. And if this happens, if the world really displays itself in its fragility and abysmal nature, there is literally 'nothing' to be done. In that case the world is out of joint. The world is an abyss. And to play through this possibility in fiction as a worst case may have been a challenge to Dürrenmatt as an author.

So only if we have in view the possibility that the world is an abyss is the dimension of the text which is a social critique given its right status. For beyond question this narrative *also* describes the discrepancy between the perception of the terror, which is given only to a few, and the normal business of the world, of handing oneself over to people in naïve trust. The picture sketched by Dürrenmatt is a fascinating and uncanny one. While their train is rushing into the abyss, people are going on as if nothing had happened: 'Wienerschnitzel' and rice continue to be served in the dining car and people toast one another in cheerful mood. Without question such a scene also has a dimension which is critical of society, because it opens up the extent of the repression of terror as a possibility:

We were still sitting there in our compartments and did not know that already everything was lost, he thought. It seemed to us that nothing had changed, yet already the shaft had taken us into its depths.

If one has perceived the possibility that the world is an abyss, one can also rightly assess the existential dimension of the narrative. For without question it is *also* about the basic attitude of people in a world invaded by the terrible and the uncanny. But in the text there is no mention of boldness or relaxation in face of the absurd. Dürrenmatt was right to delete that reference to 'cheerfulness'. It is not a matter of coping with anxieties about catastrophe in an educated and psychologizing way. On the contrary – the twenty-four-year-old in this narrative feels strangely attracted by the abyss, is remarkably fascinated by it. Not once does he become anxious; not once does panic break out. Indeed still at the height of the tension, when he and the senior conductor have already reached the locomotive, the young man thinks of his Ormond Brasil cigar. Anyway, there is a lot of smoking in this text: we know why. And the student also finds clambering on the locomotive an adventure; his enquiries about the speed show an interest in technology. When the twenty-four-year-old is pressed against the windscreen of the driver's cab by the speed, we are specifically told that he 'saw the abyss below him with eyes which were now wide open for the first time'. So the young man is more electrified than scandalized by the abyss, more fascinated than fearful. Moreover he had expected such a moment – as we learn. He had lived 'for this moment, which had now been reached, this moment of invasion, this sudden leaving of the earth's surface, the adventurous fall into the interior of the earth'. All at once the terror which exists 'behind the scenes' was there. The possibility had become reality. So the cotton wool could disappear from his ears.

And finally: only when it has been accepted that the world can be an abyss can the religious challenge of this narrative be seen. Originally it was still directly on the surface of the text. Originally Dürrenmatt may have meant to be provocative about religion with the sentence 'God made us fall. And we are falling to him' – opposing the world order as understood by traditional Christianity. An autobiographical reminiscence clarifies one of the backgrounds against which this text must be written. Dürrenmatt describes his parents' 'world' which may still have been very much in his mind at the time when the text was written:

I grew up in a Christian world which later did not let me go: my son has become a pastor. The people with whom my parents had to do were God-fearing; everywhere I came up against Christianity like a wall of faith, whether I was staying in the Christian seminary in Bern during the holidays, or looking after the cattle and helping with the haymaking for a farmer with whom my parents were friendly.

The adults who surrounded me and practised a bourgeois-country Christianity, were not mendacious, as people today so easily believe. In the eyes of these people the order in which they lived and in which they believed was right, and where it was no longer right, the fault lay with unbelief. It was an order willed by God, which also embraced the state: patriotism and Christianity did not stand in contradiction to one another. But the different classes among men and women were also divinely willed: just as there were different races, so too God had created the citizen, the farmer and the worker, the rich and the poor, and given each his dignity, burdens and obligations.[13]

Why 'God' had to be deleted

The young Dürrenmatt is evidently directing his text against this 'wall of faith', against this 'divinely-willed order' of the bourgeoisie and Christianity. It is meant to prod a milieu which tends to console itself with harmonizing confessions of faith over the fact that the world is an abyss. The provocation is manifestly meant to lie here: God does not guarantee order, but can be like an abyss which swallows one up. God himself is the *possibility* of the terrible and the uncanny. The talk of 'God' at the end of the first version may thus originally have meant that the invasion of the terror was being described as an act of God. It is not human work and so cannot be remedied by human work either. Something is not right with the world as a whole because that is how God wills it. He made us all and so are we falling to him.

Dürrenmatt, who in his student days planned a dissertation on 'Kierkegaard and the Tragic' (and instead composed his first play, 'It is Written') is aware here of his indebtedness to reflections by Søren Kierkegaard on the absolute intervention of God in human existence: the re-establishment of paradox and scandal.[14] The same is true of Karl Barth's 'theology of crisis'; Barth's *Commentary on Romans* had a considerable influence on Dürrenmatt's early prose style.[15] So originally Dürrenmatt wanted talk of God which shook the traditional certainty of faith, shattered the traditional plausibilities, and revived the dimension of the terrible, the uncanny and the abyss for talk of God. God is not a 'standpoint' which human beings can adopt in order to be able to be

assured in the world; the reality of God is not civic security to which one
can devote oneself in superficial enjoyment. The reality of God is not the
ordered world which functions by laws that can be examined by reason.

Dürrenmatt, who as a student used to add 'nihilist poet' to the name-
plate on the door of his room, once described the original theological aim
of this story in his reminiscences of that time:

> They (the linguistic means) were not to be learned from the classics.
> I could not cope with Thomas Mann; his middle-class world repelled
> me. It was the same with Herman Hesse – he seemed to me petty-
> bourgeois in the face of the general collapse beyond the frontiers. His
> rebellion against the bourgeois world was too harmless for me. The
> important thing was to protest against the world in itself, to attack
> God in himself.[16]

However, Dürrenmatt evidently thought that the theological reception
corrupted this theological point of his text. It robbed the narrative of its
religious sting and trivialized its provocativeness. Theological interpreters seized on the word 'God' and saw their own religious certainties
confirmed 'by the poet'. Instead of being disturbed by this God-talk, they
put Dürrenmatt's text on the asset side of their faith. As early as 1972
Dürrenmatt was therefore resolved to delete the last sentence from his
story. In an interview he answered a question about this as follows:

> Today I would delete it. I do not believe that one needs to attach a
> moralistic sentence to a narrative – that weakens the content.[17]

Here we find the remarkable fact of an author banishing the word God
from his text in order to give new point to the 'content'. And we understand why this author *had to* delete the world 'God' – to some degree
for the sake of God, i.e. to make it possible for God to remain the
uncontrollable, the incalculable. And if we want a biblical parallel to
this, it does not lie in talk of being safe in the 'hands' of the merciful God,
but in an experience expressed in the letter to the Hebrews: 'It is terrible
to fall into the hands of the living God' (10.30; cf. 12.21, 29).

So if one has prevented any commandeering of Dürrenmatt's text for a
traditional certainty of faith, one can emphasize all the more clearly,
without misunderstandings, its theological relevance for the reader who
is interested in religions. For with the deletion of the word 'God' this text
loses none of its theological explosiveness. It need not be imputed directly

to the author, but is a matter for the recipient, if he or she is open to religion. And in fact the deletion of the word 'God' does not 'water down' the narrative, but gives it more point, precisely because what is now the last word of the narrative, 'nothing', leaves the conclusion open. Question upon question is opened up. Why is the world so out of joint that human beings can make literally 'nothing' of it? And where do human beings fall if the earth really opens up its jaws? Into infinity? Into chaos? Into catastrophe? Into destruction? Into God? Which God? So the openness of the conclusion makes a bunch of questions possible which similarly may originally have been aimed at, but which were resolved too simply by the conclusion, which could be misunderstood in 'moral' terms.

However, in defending himself against a 'watering down' of his text, Dürrenmatt was at the same time arguing for the content to be sharpened. And this content is that human beings are always confronted with the possibility of the invasion of terror. What lurks behind the scenes can come on the scene at any time. People live in a world in which abysses can open up, in which the uncanny can constantly break through an order which superficially seems secure. And this possibility of invasion cannot be changed by politics, by morality, or by religious convictions. It is connected with the fact of the 'world' generally. The world *is* the sphere of the unsafe, the chaotic, the abyss. The world provides no answers, but is an unresolved question, a question which points to a last primal ground which proves to be an abyss.

The old conversation has been broken off. But in that case how are we still to talk of God and to God? Change of scene.

2. Neither believing nor without faith: Marie Luise Kaschnitz

In September 1951, six years after the war, writers gathered in the Evangelical Academy in Tutzing near Munich to discuss the theme 'Whither poetry?'. Representatives of traditional Christian literature in Germany like Rudolf Alexander Schröder and Manfred Hausmann met representatives of another generation of writers, including Marie Luise Kaschnitz, who was then fifty years old. She had drawn attention to herself in the literary world before 1945 with love stories which were relatively conventional in form, like *Liebe beginnt* ('Love Begins', 1933) and *Elissa* (1937); however, it was now impossible to ignore her as a writer after three volumes of her poetry published after 1945 (*Gedichte* ['Poems'], 1947; *Totentanz und Gedichte zur Zeit* ['Dance of Death and

Poems on the Time'], 1948; *Zukunftsmusik* ['Music of the Future'],
1950) and regular contributions in the journal *Die Wandlung,* edited by
Dolf Sternberger and Karl Jaspers. When on 9 September 1951 she began
to read as yet unpublished poems, it must have become clear to the audience that now at the latest a break between the generations had come
about. The guests of the Evangelical Academy heard texts which 'cause
disturbance, perplexity and alienation' and which brought the charge
of 'blasphemy' down on the poet.[18] Published separately for the first
time in 1953, in 1957 they formed a separate section in the volume
Neue Gedichte ('New Poems') under the title 'Tutzinger Gedichtskreis'
('Tutzing Poetry Cycle').[19]

New experiences of God

One could already have guessed about the world from which this woman
came from reading 'Poems on the Time' (1948). In 1946 she had passed
through Frankfurt am Main, terribly destroyed by bombs, and none of
the German lyric poets was as capable as she was of capturing in verse the
human misery and the extent of the destruction in a great city. One has
only to read poems like 'Great Migration', which speaks of packed
trains, of the homeless, of refugees, of the injured, the blind, those
believed dead. Once can read the cycle 'Return to Frankfurt', in which
Kaschnitz depicts the city, once so familiar, as a ruined landscape,
without falling into depression and despair. What is typical of the author
is rather that in all the misery and all the destruction she also perceives
another side of life: the strength, the courage, the will. She sets something
undestroyed and indestructible over against the destruction. For her the
world – images from nature often dominate her poetry – consists of the
great contrast between light and darkness, beauty and terror, death and
life. Life is terrible, but also 'glorious'. Nowhere does that become as
clear as in one of her poems from the cycle 'Conjuration':

> I lay in the bunker with many,
> None got any rest,
> And one hand robbed me
> And the other covered me.
> And I went on the street with many,
> Because we were told to walk,
> And one hand pushed my cart
> While the other prodded me.

And I did not know what to say,
what kind my neighbour was,
Nothing could be calculated any more
In the old terms
And there was no more talk
Of pleasure
Only the wretched glorious life
was in us all.[20]

God is rarely mentioned in all these texts. If God is mentioned, it is in a peculiar, alienating sense. In the same cycle 'Conjuration' there are the remarkable lines (referring to those who are hurled into 'wretched glorious life'):

Burnt up in the world
And desert-wide
Was only the body
Which still bore itself
and stood upright,
was only the heart,
which beat and beat,
abandonment.

And God was there,
so they said,
Not as at home
In the spring wind,
In the noise of the herd,
In the word of love.

He was as once
He divided sunlight
From blackness
And sea from land.
A beginning.
They went
And gave themselves
Into his hand.[21]

'Nothing could be calculated any more In the old terms' – that is evidently also true of talk of God. Now God can no longer be experienced 'as at home', but is manifested in a different way under new conditions. God is 'a beginning' which can probably only be understood in this way. So this time of great upheaval is at the same time a time for experiencing God in a new and different way, in the midst of this 'wretched glorious life', indeed as an expression of this 'wretched glorious life'.

We can become clearer about this understanding of God by means of a text which appeared in a 1945 collection of Kaschnitz's essays entitled 'People and Things', entitled 'On the Experience of God'.[22] This is a quite basic text, since nowhere before or afterwards has the poet reflected so systematically on her understanding of God. It is striking here how much the author attempts to maintain equidistance: from 'believers' on the one hand and 'unbelievers' on the other. The certainty and arrogance of 'believers' repels Marie Luise Kaschnitz, and also a lack of cheerfulness (among the religious people who are still struggling). Those who live by the laws of religion have had their originality 'throttled' by the 'heavy tablets of the law', have had the life in them destroyed. However, for the author 'the God of the dark days' is not one of those who wrote on tablets or whose commands one can have read in books. Nor is this God a strict tutor, for whom one can never do anything well enough. This God is not bothered about what one does and does not do.

And the godless? They repel the author because they enjoy the 'grandiose loneliness' with which they confront their fate. They regard themselves as a 'speck of dust' in the infinitely circling global mist, and it is precisely from this smallness and unimportance, this 'complete lack of responsibility', that they gain their confidence and their courage. Others elevate themselves to the stars and attach to human beings what formerly was the property of the gods. Over against these 'faithless' ones Marie Luise Kaschitz brings her 'certainty about a life after death' into play, and she guards this certainty like the possession of a 'precious treasure'. In the 'happy capacity to surrender to a power transcending the earth' she feels 'filled with a tremendous mercy, like the one who sees in the midst of blind people'. And on the last two pages of her essay the author defines this 'surrender to a power transcending the earth' with great clarity.

For her, another term for 'power transcending the earth' is 'the power of love'. And this word should not be trivialized. For Kaschnitz concedes that there were times when she could not clearly distinguish and separate this power of love from the forces of decay and annihilation. She could not separate it from the forces of nature whose 'blind activity' one constantly senses. To surrender to this power of love, to be fused with it, seems to her to be the 'origin and end, the significance of death, a nameless, unspeakable happiness'. Then follow the decisive sentences:

In our own breast we fight the fight that God endures with himself. In the wonderful moments of harmony we have an inkling of the perfection of our origin and our end, between which the chaotic centuries of the earth lie like a single stormy day.

But there is no escape from the immediate experience of God which strikes the heart like a bright thunderbolt and which all at once reveals all that is terrible and beautiful about creation. Certainly we sense in them the fulfilment which awaits us in being no more. We sense in them the moments in which the world with all its beauty touches our senses, and no less so where the divine creative drive of the human being has shaped human tones, words and material and elevated them to a higher reality. But we have no notion that can reach God, no law which can express him. And for me, to share in his nature means that we partake in the incomprehensible oppositions of his nature.

Convinced of this, I feel myself removed from the pride of the faithless and the certainty of believers. For my present affirmation of life and death is a fearfully personal relationship, a terrifyingly indirect surrender to the compulsion to change, to which we are subject in God and which we must endure with him. Sometimes I see the hecatombs of the battlefields as a sea of flames, a mighty fire which burns for our expiation, and it seems to me as if the divine in our imagination were emerging, wonderfully purged, from the terrible wars. I see his light on every human birth as on every seed that breaks out of the earth. But human death seems to me to be greater and more holy than the falling of the leaves in autumn and the dying of creation. For the human share in God's work is greater. And his way to the Western garden of paradise, which will one day blossom and smell again in a miraculous way before it sinks back into God, is longer and more difficult.[23]

It is easy from this essay on the 'experience of God' to build a bridge to the 'Tutzing Poetry Cycle'. It was striking that in Kaschnitz's earlier poetry the word 'God' appeared very rarely. But the essay showed that for her, talk of God had a specific sense. Now the conviction of participating in the 'incomprehensible opposites' of the nature of God and the concern for poetic expression fuse into something unique in German literature. And even from a present-day perspective we can trace how the verses which were now written must have shaken a traditionally

Christian public. For the 'Tutzing Poems' are a hitherto unprecedented
argument with God, born of a radically changed experience of the world:

> I began to speak with the Invisible.
> My tongue uttered the tremendous Thou,
> Reflecting old familiarity.
> But whom was I addressing? Whose ear
> Was I attempting to reach? Whose breast
> to touch – that of a father?
> Father, you dying giant,
> Perishing beyond the Milky Way,
> Father, you shimmer of air,
> Twinkling of the fleeing star.

Those who allow these opening verses to work on them can already
recognize an inner rhythm which will remain in the following strophes:
movement and counter-movement; negation and affirmation; on the one
hand, on the other. On the one hand the 'old familiarity' of talk of God
is 'gone'. God is no longer the loving 'father' whose 'ear' one could reach,
whose 'breast' one could touch. This 'father' is manifestly in the process
of perishing in cosmic space. The religious term 'father' has now been
replaced by scientific and cosmological terminology: 'shimmer of air',
'twinkling of the fleeing star'. And if words like the familiar second
person, and 'Father', are still used, the old familiarity is no longer there.

On the other hand the familiar second-person form of address, the
metaphor of father, remain and at least seem indispensable as a quotation. In this way the talk of God in this text becomes strangely paradoxical: the religious metaphor seems to have died out when confronted
with cosmic space, but God is once again alive in language as the 'tremendous Thou'. What we have here is quite unusual: a prayer as anti-
prayer, a conjuration of God which comes from the consciousness of the
death of God, a trust in the invisible which at the same time is an act of
mistrust, indeed a desire to understand which stems from complete
incomprehension:

> I began to speak with the Invisible
> And said: I understand nothing,
> I am like a stone lying there, a goggle-eyed obstacle.
> I cannot even get over the street.
> Your voice pierces my ears, tears at my entrails.

You fearful accelerato makes me shudder.
You have made me from your old earth,
Which is no longer to count. In my breast
You have aroused the old feelings
Which no longer have any importance in time.

This sketches out the new scenery from which the author speaks. Her experience is the contemporaneity of voices of God which are no longer compatible, and this leads to incomprehension and paralysis. On the one hand there is the 'fearful accelerato', a reference to the technological acceleration of tempo and the economic upheaval at the beginning of the 1950s. And this acceleration in the course of technology and urbanization is regarded as an expression of God's 'voice'. But on the other hand there are still the old experiences of God, described with the metaphors 'old earth', 'old feelings'. However, these have no value, have no importance in a new time. The relationship between God and human beings has radically changed because the world has been subject to radical changes. This contemporaneity of old familiar and confusingly new experiences of God which overlap is a peculiarity of all the Tutzing texts. And the following strophes, 3 to 14, describe this contemporaneity in ever new cascades of verse.

God in the upheaval and in the destruction

The texts are too rich merely to paraphrase them. In any case, how could one want to 'dissolve' poetry into prose? Already in the 1950s an equally famous poet, Erich Fried, spoke of the 'great open form' of the Tutzing poems. 'Derived from psalm and elegy, but never simply imitating', this form could take in a great deal: 'Montage, here perhaps influenced more by Eliot than by Benn, conjuration, a vision of anxiety, preaching, poetic image and contemplation.'[24] However, a few lines should be described to help us to understand. The dominant motif in the first great section (strophes 3–14) is described with the sentence: 'All that means a new beginning is right by you'. The phrase 'a new beginning' specifically relates to the industrial and technological changes which the author sees in her Frankfurt surroundings and which are of an unprecedented extent. After the destruction that she had experienced, now came the headlong rebuilding: moreover the text also speaks of the 'grab arm' of the crane, the 'wandering flame writings' of the advertisements, of pipes in the street, of wires, of elevators, of 'stamping pistons', of incessant conveyor belts, of rattling wheels and thundering aeroplanes. The new time is marked by tempo, noise, demolition and reconstruction. And it all seems to be an expression of the will of God: 'You have pleasure in the work of wheels which do not stand still.' The tempo seems God's tempo; the noise God's sound; demolition and reconstruction God's enjoyment. 'All that means a new being is right by you.' Indeed, in these circumstances God becomes a kind of monster who manifestly has his intoxicating pleasure in the 'refugees' bundles' and the 'steps of the exiled'.

> When the young men on their clattering wheels
> roar through the streets at midnight, you smile.
> You love the thundering aeroplanes more than swarms of white doves.
> All that means a new beginning is right by you.
> The refugees' bundles are your sacrificial gifts,
> You count the steps of the exiles by your heartbeat,
> You drink your fill of the deadly farewells (strophe 5).

But since this 'fearful accelerato' is manifestly an expression of God himself, in the religious sphere this leads to a break. Moreover the notion of incomprehensibility in strophe 2 recurs in strophe 6, but now God is made directly responsible for it:

> The one who goes out to be judged no longer finds a judge.
> The one who goes out to enquire of the old gets no answer.
> You have broken off the old conversation.
> When we ask to what end,
> You are silent.
> When we ask, why so fast?
> You are silent.

But one may not conclude from the silence that God no longer exists. Those who prematurely think this are punished by God, who manifests himself to them in destruction:

> When we go and act as if you were not there,
> You let us build the tower to the top storey,
> Knock it down by barely breathing on it (strophe 6).

This responsibility of God for all the new beginnings which swallow up so much, this presence of God even in destruction leads to a feeling of homelessness. It is as if God himself had moved the house which previously promised certainty and security.

> You are like a householder who is clearing out – yesterday the old
>   proverbs,
> Today the pictures, tomorrow the safe bed.
> What are we to sleep on? You no longer sleep.
> What are we to eat from? You no longer eat.
> Whither are we to travel? You set out long ago,
> No footprint in the sand, no branch bent (strophe 8).

What is the consequence? The first consequence is a de-ethicizing of God. The 1945 essay already said that Kaschnitz's God did not write on stone tablets or know moral 'tasks', and was not bothered about what people did or did not do. Now the 'Tutzing Poems' say that the one who goes out to be judged no longer finds a judge. And where there is no judge there is no guilt. God is also made responsible for that.

> You have taken away your guilt from us,
> To which we could hold fast, the lead weight,
> And quenched the dark counter image
> From which we could escape into your bosom (strophe 10).

The second consequence is that the old religion has decayed into a reserve: the familiar religious objects have become museum pieces. And because this is the case, the traditional language of praise of God is to some degree throttled:

> The language which once rang out to praise you
> draws itself together, no longer sings
> In our vinegar mouth. It is already a great deal
> When we take things into protection,
> Shut them up in glass cases like peacock butterflies
> And look at them on holidays.
> Somewhere else behind seven seals
> Your psalms stand recently written,
> A landscape of logarithms, forests full of the unknown.
> Roots of creation. Equation of the Last Day (strophe 12).

What is decisive here is that it is evidently God himself who does not want, or prevents, the traditional praise of God and makes it so impossible for people to honour him the familiar religious way ('before your altars', 'in your fair valleys'):

> With those who want to acknowledge you
> In the old way you do not deal gently.
> Before your altars you make their hearts desolate,
> In your fair valleys you strike them
> With blindness. At the feet of those who try to praise you
> You wash up a bloated corpse.
> The words of those who begin to speak of your love,
> You twist in their mouths, make them howl
> Like dogs in the night (strophe 14).

Let's stop here and attempt to make out what is unique about these poems. From countless Christian texts, particularly in the 1950s, we know two reactions to the secular, industrial-urban world: Christian rejection and secular praise. The creator God is still praised by Christians – despite all upheavals and experiences to the contrary. And Christian poets like Rudolf Alexander Schröder and Werner Bergengruen have written an abundance of such texts. At the same time technological progress in the course of headlong urbanization is usually criticized for being godless; the secular world is accused of apostasy from God; technology and industry are branded by the criticism of the time only as forces destructive of faith. By contrast, secularists are fond of pointing to technology as progress and in the course of their domination of the world regard a critique of religion and a denial of God as the pinnacle of human progress. With her 'Tutzing Poems', Marie Luise Kaschnitz goes an independent third way between these two options, a way which is already indicated in her essay 'On the Experience of God': a way beyond Christian traditionalism and atheistic secularism. These texts, too, maintain equidistance from 'believers' and 'unbelievers'. For they neither offer the expected praise of God (combined, for example, with a culturally conservative critique of secularism), nor do they take the side of those who traditionally deny God – in the face of the breakthrough of technological civilization.

Hers is a different way: from the experiences of breaking points the author begins a critical discussion with God, presents questions, complaints and accusations. Certainly God has broken off the 'old' conversation, but that is manifestly no reason for the poet to stop the conversation from her side and to stop looking for possibilities of carrying on quite new conversations, unprecedented conversations, with God. These verses seem to me to focus on this exploration of unprecedented other presences of God in a new time, which call for new conversations about and with God. They are not about the 'experience of the *deus absconditus* which oppresses us on all sides', nor about suffering over 'the presence of the absence of God', as a theological interpreter thought,[25] but about investigating and discussing hitherto unheard-of presences of God. For in this text God is in no way *absconditus,* unknowable, hidden; God is in no way absent; God is constantly manifest, but in a way which is familiar and at the same time radically strange, alienating. That has earned the author criticism, accusations and questions. Making God a riddle turns into accusing God.

God's coldness and God's confusion

For in the following strophes Marie Luise Kaschnitz once again intensifies this accusation of God. In strophe 2 her formulation was still completely subjective: 'I understand nothing'. By strophe 6 the perspective had already shifted: now it is God himself who has broken off the 'old conversation' and withdrawn into silence or destruction. In strophes 15 and 16 this is accentuated once again: perhaps God does not want any talk of him? Certainly, once upon a time in history God fed on the 'flesh and blood' of the victims, 'on the praise' of the priests. But now? Evidently God feeds on silence! Perhaps God prefers 'our paralysed tongues' to 'the dancing flames' of the miracle of Pentecost? Is God's silence and our dumbness then a deliberate withdrawal of God, another form of his presence which we no longer understand? Or does everything rest on a deliberate 'confusion' by God? The remarkable thing is that the place where people earlier recognized God, the mountains, the valleys, the waves of the sea, are still there. The beauty of nature (the rose, the wind ruffling the sand dunes, the lily and the larkspur) – has not been exterminated, even from human hearts (strophe 17). But how does all this fit with the perceived other experience of God? In the face of the headlong technological seizure of power over the world, God manifestly 'has quite other concerns': 'the flowers which no longer smell, the fruit without taste, the icy play of the northern lights over the slope' (strophe 17).

The basic experience is therefore being left alone by God:

Sometimes it seems as if we had to
Call on you, say what has become of us
Suddenly left alone . . .

It has pleased to dry us out
Like yellow cod. Without tears (strophes 18 and 21).

The basic experience is the coldness of God:

And sometimes it seems to us as if we had
To bring before your face all that you have made,
Raise it up against your coldness.
I want to cry out to you as at the fair.
The poplar leaf which stands silver in the breeze,
The scaly shine of the fish, the curious eye of the kid
The beautiful maple leaf spotted with mould.
As the Aeolian harp sang in the trees,
Like the shepherds' flutes in Argos,
I want to cry out all this and last of all
The joy of my love,
I, your memory (strophe 19).

The basic experience is the deliberate incomprehensibility of God:

You will no longer make yourself understandable to us
Nor resolve your perplexity,
Repeat the days when silently
We hid our heads in your gardens (strophe 25).

But even this is not the last word. The last three strophes (26–29) once again concentrate the argument so far in a way which is paradoxical and unprecedented. For the author makes a last effort to interweave the old and new experiences of God dialectically. She thinks through the bold notion that possibly God wants to be praised precisely in our brokenness – precisely by those who are called 'unbelievers'. These are quite manifestly the new conversations which God expects of us.

And nevertheless you will require us
To show incessantly as we are
In these poor garments, with these dull eyes,
With these hands which no longer know how to shape,

With this heart without comfort or dream.
You will call up legions of unbelievers
With your soundless voice day by day,
Their members will hear,
Their bosom will hear,
They will eat and drink you,
Their lungs breathe you in and out (Strophe 26).

Indeed, the thought is taken seriously that it is in his opposite that God longs to recognize himself:

You will long for us, the loveless of this earth,
To be your love.
The ugly your beauty,
The restless your rest,
The wordless your speech,
The heavy your flight (strophe 27).

And perhaps that is God's 'last mystery':

Your distance your nearness,
Your ending your beginning,
Your coldness your fire,
Your indifference your wrath (strophe 28).

But who is to understand all these bold dialectical interlockings? It is striking that if the poems began with a confession of complete incomprehension ('I understand nothing, I am like a stone'), they end with a forward-looking perspective. They hold out the prospect that in the future there will be at least some who will make God 'sometimes moveable, quicker than your machines and artificial lightning'. There is a prospect that there will be at least some people who neither cling to the old and familiar nor allow themselves to be oppressed by the technological domination of the world, but rather manage to understand change as the context of the experience of God and to recognize in the leavetaking an expression of love:

And some will sometimes make you move
More quickly than your machines and artificial lightning,
They will outstrip their anxiety.

They will become travellers. Joyful.
Rich and full of sweetness will be
The encounter, the passing greeting.
They will nest in their homelessness
And love themselves in valleys of farewell.
Comfort your dying.

Conflict in Tutzing

From the beginning, this conversation with the Tremendous caused
conflict. And now we can understand better why. Already in Tutzing
Kaschnitz noted in her diary: 'Conversation about my poem (Tutzing
Poems). How did Rilke address God by comparison? Sometimes very
compassionately . . . conversation in Tutzing about the negativity in
present-day poetry (Curtius calls it "from the whining corner"). The
longing for salvation, raising up . . .'[26] The author had evidently come
upon a Christian milieu which wanted nothing from poetry but 'salvation' and 'raising up' . Doubt in God, even accusation of God, seemed
immoral – almost blasphemous to it. The phrase 'whining corner' is
meant to express contempt. Evidently no objective content of truth is
allowed to the complaint about God; it is reduced to a failure on the part
of the individual writer. This failure is like a dog whose whining one
cannot bear. This confirms what Claus Westermann said about the
milieu of Christian theology: 'To complain before God is inappropriate;
it is not the right attitude before God. Complaint destroys or diminishes
the pious attitude to God'.

As early as 1949, in an article for *Die Wandlung* entitled 'The
Vocabulary of Poetry', Marie Luise Kaschnitz had already reflected
on the dialectic between terror and beauty, chaos and order, truth and
truthfulness. Alluding to Rainer Maria Rilke, for whom 'praise' was the
real task of the poet, here she is already criticizing readers who in 'raw
anxiety' clung to the last poets who still knew how 'to praise'. She
objects:

The honour of the eternal is not attacked, and a spot of oil on the
asphalt reveals all the beauty of the world with its iridescent gleam.
Where people become small, the size of the universe grows, and those
who think they are describing meaninglessness perhaps discover again
a secret meaning precisely there. Those who attempt to give form with
the seriousness of truthfulness already create order, even if chaos is its

subject. What is to be conjured up must be mentioned; what makes us anxious must put in an appearance.

For each individual the poet engages in a search for truth which today is different from yesterday and tomorrow will be different from today. For each individual he discovers the changes in the relationship between human beings and God, their fellow human beings, nature. Whoever spoke yesterday of love as a possession must today unveil the hatred, the coldness and the loneliness; whoever yesterday still thought themselves bound to nature will today achieve only the cry of the lost for home and the great lament.

That the poet nevertheless sits in the hand of God is the mystery which shines though all his taunts and keeps getting hold of us . . . The poet merely attempts to rid them (the readers) of their nightmare. For him dust and refuse, the noise of motors and the rifle-fire of machines are faces and voices of God, who is accomplishing his work of transformation.[27]

Dust and refuse, the noise of motors and the rifle-fire of machines – faces and voices of God? Here in 1949 there is an indication of what developed into great poetry in the poems of 1951: God accomplishes his 'work of transformation' with all parts of his creation. His presence is not bound to our aesthetic canon of taste, nor can it be domesticated ethically. Moreover the ethical dimension is completely bracketted out in this talk of God – in favour of a radicalized aesthetic dimension. That means that for this author God's presence is everywhere – even in the dust and the refuse; God's voice can be heard everywhere – even in the noise of motors and the rifle-fire of machines. That is the aesthetic experience of God (not to be confused with a cheap aestheticism), directed against any ethical reining-in of God. And precisely this may have caused offence in Tutzing. God in the rifle-fire of machines? And the cries of the victims? Are these also cries of God? Does God also drink his fill of their blood? Here theo-poesy stands over against theology.

Religious life as quarrelling with God

The author clearly did not get away from the controversy which broke out here. And two years later, in her book *Engelsbrücke. Römische Betrachtungen* ('Bridge of Angels. Roman Reflections', 1955), there is a remarkable chapter which can only be interpreted as a reaction to this and similar criticism. It is entitled 'Justification of a Lachrymist'.

Lachrymist? The word (from the Latin *lacrima* = tear) is evidently meant to take up the charge made in the expression 'whining corner', for here the author tells of an 'old friend' who ridiculed a young Austrian poet with this very label:

> In C's eyes, to bewail the world was a painfully unworthy attitude, unworthy of the one so confronted with the beauty of the outside world, the possibilities of love and the strivings of the human spirit. C's repudiation of doubt and lamentation was characteristic of Goethe, not in deliberate imitation but out of a similar kind of gratitude, and out of the conviction that it was the expression of the negative that first really helped evil to exist. So for him 'lachrymist' was more than a personal attitude of lamentation; it produced evil and was intrinsically evil. Though he might despise the dumbness and indifference, he feared despair in all its manifestations as only one who is deeply threatened can fear.[28]

After this psychological analysis (those who condemn doubt and lamentation are usually themselves 'deeply threatened' and therefore do this out of anxiety), Marie Luise Kaschnitz self-consciously opposes it, and spells out the function which the negative statements in the poems have for her:

> That the negative statement brings about a faith, albeit a painful one, and a love, albeit one which is eternally defective, will not dawn on the idealist longing for comfort, far less that one can be a lachrymist and yet on a sunny day by the sea can have one's really bright joy. Say it anyway, they chide, and taunt the poet with his malicious silence. But *it* speaks from the poet and *it* feels the discrepancy between the perfect and the hopeless; a personally rich life cannot change that, nor can a personal sense of humour . . . The epidemic must be expressed, the dreaming stopped, especially by those who love life most passionately.[29]

So Marie Luise Kaschnitz herself sees no contradiction between doubt, complaint and despair, and faith and love. Indeed very much along the lines of the 'Tutzing Poems', in later works like *Wohin denn ich?* ('Where am I going?', 1963), she has called the dispute with God and the rebellion against the creator expressions of a living relationship with God. The opposite to strife and rejection would be indifference.

I have often put to myself the key question, what do you think of religion? How could I be indifferent to the Last Things, since I have already half fallen for them, with my better, nobler self? Now I had with them, or they had with me, what some people may declare disputation, rebellion and raw trust. Someone who is indifferent does not taunt, does not quarrel, does not doubt, though that would make up my religious life, were I not in grace, that means in a state which I would not want to call by that name, but cannot call by any other.[30]

When these lines were published, Marie Luise Kaschner already had the greatest catastrophe in her private life behind her. And it is stimulating to note how the texts from the 'Tutzing Poetry Cycle' then also 'catch up' with her privately. For in 1951 she could as yet have had no inkling of what would lie before her personally, how in 1956 her beloved husband, Guido von Kaschnitz-Weinberg, professor of archaeology, would be torn away from his successful work as Director of the German Archaeological Institute in Rome. An inoperable brain tumour was diagnosed. The illness lasted two years and Guido von Kaschnitz-Weinberg died in Frankfurt on 1 September 1958.

This experience of a malicious illness and a wretched death, which hit the author in a quite unexpected way and condemned her to complete helplessness, was one of the most shattering experiences of her life, which hitherto had been unusually happy in the private sphere. When two years later her young sister-in-law was similarly snatched away after long and painful suffering, and the same year her elder sister died of cancer, Marie Luise Kaschnitz also had personal reactions which refer back to the Tutzing Poetry Cycle. After these experiences she could exclaim: 'All honour to the good God, but must he always strike where everything is beautifully in order and full of joy and love?'[31] This was an experience which she was later once again to describe with the term quarrelling. In her notes *Tage, Tage, Jahren* ('Days, Days, Years', 1968), there is the sentence: 'What God does is far from being done well, and those who quarrel with other people and themselves also quarrel with him. I do that constantly, but it would never occur to me to deny his existence.'[32] Put in concrete terms at a later point where she reflects whether she should not entitle her notes the title 'God and the World':

I then thought 'God and the World' a quite appropriate title. It did not offend me in the least that there is virtually nothing about God on these pages which have now already grown into two bundles. I am not an atheist. Where the world is, there too is God; not a particularly dear God, but a God who constantly manifests himself, in every destruction, in every reconciliation, who is always more than we ourselves are and can be, so that whoever depicts the phenomena of each day also paints him on the wall and his beautiful fallen angels with him.[33]

So perhaps we should follow the interpreters who see the 'Tutzing Poetry Cycle' as the most important religious poetry of Marie Luise Kaschnitz, a cycle which in fact 'half a century after Rilke's diary has stated modern men and women's relationship to God with relentless radicalism'.[34] Indeed these texts must be counted not only Kaschnitz's most important religious poems, but the most important in twentieth-century German literature generally. For here a unique attempt has been made for which there are virtually no parallels in German literature: 'an accusation against God is formulated in the form of a hymn, almost blasphemously' but it is 'still credible in rejection'; an 'invocation of God, Promethean in resistance, but – the paradox may be maintained – without a Promethean sense of self'.[35]

III. Does God himself produce the farce?

Still believing though rebellious? I personally encountered this unique mixture for the first time in the poetry of Heinrich Heine. Already during my studies I came to know him as the great poet who made a witty critique of religion. That was a stroke of luck for me, and I love him more than almost any other poet. I simply had to learn many of his verses by heart, because they freed me from a musty way of thinking, a narrow-minded indolence. And above all, they made me familiar with wit and laughter in religion, too.[36]

1. Protesting return to God: Heinrich Heine

Who could ever forget the opening verses of 'Deutschland. A Winter Tale'? When Heine wrote it in exile in Paris in 1844, he appeared as the 'apostle of a new religion'. It was the time of his friendship with Marx and Engels and his belief that societies really can be changed by political revolutions, that a 'new race' could arise – 'with free ideas, with free pleasure' – which would understand Heine's concern: a synthesis of sensuality and politics, of beauty and social justice. None of the great poets had celebrated so compellingly, in the face of all Christian pessimism about sin, the rehabilitation of the flesh, the divine rights of human beings, the abolition of sin, redemption from the moral law, the dethronement of an other-worldly lawgiver and the foundation of pure autonomous human blessedness:

> A different song, a better song
> will get the subject straighter.
> Let's make a heaven on earth, my friends,
> instead of waiting till later.[37]

But in 1849 a great turning point came in Heine's life, when the onset of a paralysing illness confined the fifty-two-year-old poet to his Parisian 'mattress tomb'. He had to vegetate there for seven long years. In this time Heine speaks of 'transformation', of return to God, of 'revival' of religious feeling. This did not mean a pious folding of his hands, but a desperate assault on God. Indeed we can say that now Heine needs God; in his illness he needs to speak of God; he uses God as the one to whom he addresses his complaints, his cries, his biting questions. It is the 'desperation of the body', as he writes in a letter, which makes him say: 'Thank God that I now again have a God, since I can allow myself some curses and blasphemies when the pain is too much; the atheist is not granted such refreshment.'[38]

The sick man: Lazarus and Job together

Some remarkable texts were written in these seven years before his death in 1856. Of all these, those collected under the title 'Lazarus' are the most impressive for us. The very first volume of poems which appeared after the onset of the illness, *Romanzero* (1851), contains in its second book, which Heine programmatically calls 'Lamentations', taking up the Old Testament tradition of lamentations, twenty Lazarus poems. Certainly we must guard against reading the problems related to dying in Heine's late work in terms of a purely individual psychology, indeed an individual pathology. Even in this very last phase of his life Heine remains a political poet who never separates private experiences from political experiences. Heine's despair is always more than a purely private matter: it also extends over the course of the worlds, the development of humankind and the fate of the revolution. The literary critic Georg Lukács has rightly described the basic motif of almost all the texts of *Romanzero* as the sorrow 'that in this reality the bad triumphs over the good, always and everywhere', and sees this thrust in Heine: 'it is the desperate quest for a hope, for a bright perspective, the desperate clinging to any illusion, and finally the bold, reasonable and ironic destruction of this illusion which he himself creates and never completely believes'.[39]

But at the same time a political reading of the text may not suppress the fact that now Heine also carries on a very personal argument with God. In his postscript to *Romanzero*, dated 1851, the author himself makes it clear how much his picture of God has changed in the meantime. For the first time he now openly concedes that he has returned 'to God like the prodigal son'. Attacked by 'all the high clergy of atheism' and already commandeered by church believers, Heine wants to protect his quite individual step from misunderstanding. He now unambiguously confesses:

If one is lying on one's death bed, one becomes very sensitive and maudlin, and wants to make peace with God and the world ... Yes, I have returned to God, like the prodigal son, having tended the swine for a long time with the Hegelians. Was it misery that drove me back? Perhaps a less miserable reason. A homesickness for heaven came over me and drove me through woods and gorges, over the most vertiginous mountain paths of dialectic. On my way I found the God of the pantheists, but I could make no use of him. This poor dreamy being is interwoven and overgrown with the world, as it were imprisoned in it. It gapes at me, without a will and impotent. To have a will one must be a person, and to manifest it one must have one's elbows free. If one desires a God who can help – and after all, that is the main thing – one must also accept his personality, his other-worldliness and his holy attributes – all-good, all-wise, all-righteous, etc.[40]

Furthermore, earlier Heine had reflected and pleased himself in role figures like the martyr of love ('Book of Songs') or the martyr of the political idea ('Travel Pictures'). Now it is 'roles' like those of Lazarus and Job by which Heine will explain to himself how he is experiencing a special fate. Now he belongs to those who are specially smitten and visited, and thus belongs negatively among God's chosen creatures. Lazarus is an example. Heine's identity and the way in which he differs from the biblical-Christian world can be clarified through this figure in particular. For Heine takes from the New Testament Lazarus story (Luke 16.19–31 and John 11.1–44) only the lowliness of this figure. Like the Lukan Lazarus, as a sick man Heine, too, is more than ever dependent on the 'crumbs' of the rich man; like the Johannine Lazarus he too is in fact already in the tomb, to some degree a dead man, one who is dead to the world. Indeed Heine's life is now marked by a paradox: as a 'leper' – the 'Lazarus clapper' in his hand, so that people can get out of the way in time – one is an outcast, one of the living dead; but at the same time all Germany cheerfully sings and pipes its own songs:

> Sometimes in my troubled dreams I believe that I can see the poor cleric of the Limburg chronicle, my brother in Apollo, and his suffering eyes stare strikingly from his hood; but at the same moment he scurries from there, and, like the echo of a dream, I hear the jarring tones of the Lazarus clapper.[41]

By contrast, the dimension of hope in the Lazarus story is not taken over: the exaltation of Lazarus to Abraham's bosom after his death (whereas the rich man vainly pleads for relief in the torment of hell), or the resurrection from the tomb with the restoration of life in this world. Instead, there follows in Heine a critical controversy with God which nowhere is carried on more sharply than in the collection 'Poems 1853 and 1854'. It is no coincidence that here once again the author includes eleven poems under the title 'On Lazarus' to emphasize continuity with his own tradition of lament in the *Romanzero*. But now the figure with whom he identifies is not so much Lazarus as Job, and thus the tradition of rebellion against God. Certainly in the initial phase of Heine's illness there were indications of patience and acceptance which we *also* find in the book of Job. Thus in his Draft Testament of 13 November 1851 he had written:

> O God, you wanted me to perish and I perished. Praised be the Lord! He has cast me down from the pedestal of my pride, and I who in my dialectical darkness had thought myself a god and cherished feelings and practised virtues which only befitted a god – now I lie on the floor, poor and wretched, and curl up like a worm. Praised be the Lord! I patiently bear my torments and I learn to drink the cup of humiliation to the last drop without pursing my lips. But I know that I shall rise from this humiliation justified, hallowed and celebrated.[42]

Yet in the course of the years primal questions to God broke through with Goethe, just as the Job tradition was now introduced critically in quite a different way. In March 1854 Heine can write:

> But why must the righteous suffer so much on earth? Why must talent and honour perish, while the braggart buffoon lounges on the cushions of happiness and almost stinks of contentment? The book of Job does not solve this wicked question. On the contrary, this book is the Song of Songs of scepticism, and in it the most terrible snakes hiss and pipe their eternal Why?[43]

Rebellious prayers from the mattress tomb

We can now understand better why Heine introduced his new collection 'Poems 1853 and 1854' with a poem which is written in this rebellious spirit of Job and the psalms of lamentation:

> Scrap the holy parables,
> Ditch the pious hypotheses –
> And try solving these damned questions
> Point-blank, no digressions, please.

Why do good men drag round bleeding,
Wretched with some heavy cross,
When, like happy conquering heroes,
Villains trot on their high horse?

What's to blame? Perhaps our Lord's
Not almighty all this while?
Or does he produce this farce?
Christ, that would be really vile.

So we put our endless questions
Till some unknown with a handful
Of earth stops our craws at last.
That's supposed to be an answer?[44]

One can hardly put the famous question more tersely and pertinently, or theologically more boldly. In twelve lines the whole problem of theodicy in modern times is sketched out in such a way to put an end to all optimism about theodicy in the style of Leibniz. Indeed, as we heard, for Leibniz theodicy meant that God's righteousness can be described rationally by human beings: human beings can justify God in the face of the evil of the world with the aid of their own reason.

Heine 'screams' from the mattress tomb – as no other German poet before him – his experience to the contrary. The 'damned questions' are unsolved for those concerned, indeed they cannot be revoked either by pious parables or by philosophical speculations. The questions persist until death, which does not silence the questioning but makes it more acute. Heine thus wrote one of the first anti-theodicy poems in German literature. Job prevails over Leibniz: God cannot be justified by human beings, if at all, God justifies himself, God has to justify himself. Therefore – on the model of the Old Testament lamentation texts (as we shall see) – God is challenged, indeed provoked, to hasten this process of justification. Thus God can be attacked, assailed, by human beings – either in his omnipotence (perhaps after all he is 'not completely almighty') or in his goodness (perhaps after all he is 'base').

What Heine here 'stages' so lyrically in the role play is certainly the return of a prodigal son; not, however, of a son who kneels before his father conscious of his guilt, but of a son who calls his father to account on his return. The return to God has not broken the rebellious goad, but forced it in again. The creator himself is now the one to whom the objection is made. Indeed, the *Posthumous Poems*, which were similarly composed in these last years, including thirty-four poems which once again reinforce the theme of 'Lamentations', show just how boldly at this time Heine could carry on a direct conversation with God. Perhaps the most gripping of them was later published under the title 'Miserere':

I do not envy the sons of bliss
For living in such state
I envy them alone their deaths
A painless speedy fate.

With splendid garb, garlanded brow
And laughter all around,
While sitting at the feast of life –
Death fells them to the ground.

In party clothes, with roses decked,
A glow that never fades
The favourites of Lady Luck
Enter the realm of shades.

Sickness has never marred their miens,
They are the handsome dead
Welcomed by Lady Proserpine,
Into her palace led.

Their fate to me is envious,
For seven long years now I
Have writhed up here in agony
And yet I cannot die.

O bring my torment to an end,
That they may bury me,
Dear God, you know I don't intend
A martyr brave to be.

On your inconsistency, O Lord,
I cannot fail to brood.
You make the happiest poet, and now
Rob him of his good mood.

The pain so dulls my sense of cheer
And makes me melancholic
That if the painful fun won't end
I'll just end up catholic.

Like other Christians good I'll rant
And rave, and clench my fists,
O miserere, you have lost
The best of humorists.[45]

I learned from the late Heine that there is a way of being religious which has nothing to do with 'medicine' and 'hidden poison' in Goethe's sense. I learned that there is a controversy with God in which even the terminally ill person, worthy of compassion in his creatureliness, must lose nothing of his wit and worth. Heine was probably the first poet who succeed in rhyming 'Catholic' and 'melancholic' . . . I understood that Heine's enforced 'return to God' under the painful posterior sclerosis was not the cheap 'creeping to the cross' of a former mocker of religion which is known well. Rather, it was a return to God in the act of protest; faith in the creator in the form of resistance; a revival of the religious in the garb of rebellion, a prayer to God which summons up a great deal of irony. God, it can't be your policy to let me suffer here so much. Am I to go on lying here with my noise in your ears? After all, the 'good Christians' already do that enough. Why so 'inconsistent', Lord? Originally you created me as the 'happiest poet' – and now my whining? You too should be more interested in a cheerful poet than a depressive one . . .

I learned a second thing from the late Heine. Just as death is not an answer to anything, but simply remains a question-mark, so too 'God' is never simply 'the answer' to all the crises in our lives and the questions about our existence, not even the basic question of the meaning of the suffering of the innocent. For it is precisely the person who believes in God who experiences the contradictions, the rifts, breaks and abysses in God's creation all the more painfully; experiences above all the often intolerable degree of innocent suffering as disturbing and outrageous in a special way. Those who believe in God must perceive the contradictions in the world even more strongly because their faith in the creator presupposes that this world originally rests on a good and just order. God himself does not put on the 'farce' – as a kind of cynical player in heaven who takes his delight in seeing us human beings in misery, and who clutches his belly laughing at all the cries and prayers.

Subjecting God's fun to respectful criticism

From Heine I learned to reckon with this uncanny possibility; possibly God is in no way the 'dear Father' concerned for his creation, but a 'being' who out of impotence or sarcastic fun does not care a jot for the world. It is strange how early Heine toyed with such a possibility, how early his trust in creation encountered the abyss. At the age of twenty-seven, in a poem entitled 'Götterdämmerung', he describes the fundamental changes provoked by technology and industrialization. Heine depicts the consequences in the form of a vision of terror:

> I see your defiant giants' sons,
> Primeval brood, mounting from dark clefts
> And swinging red torches in their hands; -
> They set up their iron ladders
> And wildly storm the fortress of heaven;
> And black dwarves clamber after them; – and noisily
> Scatter all the golden stars up there.
> With impudent hands they rend the golden curtain
> From God's tabernacle, howling cast down
> The pious hosts of angels on their faces.
> On his throne sits the pale God,
> Tears the crown from his head, ruffles his hair – .[46]

So perhaps in the face of a creation which has developed against him, God has really gone pale with terror, incapable of opposing this development? Or perhaps God is as Heine described him in his book 'Ideas. The Book Le Grand' (1826):

> Life is indeed so pleasantly sweet, and the world is so attractively confused: it is the dream of an intoxicated God who has slipped away from the carousals of the gods *à la française*, and lain down to sleep on a solitary star, and does not know that he has also created all that he is dreaming of – and the dreams are often amazingly mad, and also harmoniously rational – the *Iliad*, Plato, the battle of Marathon, Moses, Venus de Medici, Strasbourg Cathedral, the French Revolution, Hegel, the steamships and so on are individual good ideas in this creative divine dream – but it will not be long before God wakes up and rubs his sleepy eyes – and our world is shattered – indeed it has never existed.[47]

Uncanny possibilities, which explain why to the end of his life Heine kept reflecting on the meaning of creation, used to speak of the 'great irony of God', of the 'great irony of the poets on the world stage', and reflected on the possibility that, faced with a sheerly irredeemable creation, God might perhaps one day grasp 'the madness of despair'. In Heine's late 'Notes' we find the comment:

> How much has God already done to heal the evil of the world! In Moses' time he did miracle upon miracle; later, in the figure of Christ, he even allowed himself to be scourged and crucified; and finally, in the figure of Enfantin he did the most tremendous thing to save the world: he made it ridiculous – but in vain. In the end perhaps he is seized with the madness of despair and smashes his head on the world, and he and the world fall to pieces.[48]

And it is no chance that in Heine's 'Confessions', which take stock of his situation in the winter of 1854, two years before his death, the motif which already governed the 'Lazarus' poem returns: the possibility that God himself is 'producing the farce' with us. Couldn't that be it?

> Ah, God's mockery is a heavy burden on me. The great author of the universe, the Aristophanes of heaven, wanted to show up the little earthly, so-called German Aristophanes, whose wittiest sarcasms were only poor mockery by comparison with his own, and demonstrate how lamentably I must fall short of him in humour, in colossal joking.
> Indeed, the sarcastic scorn which the master pours over me is terrible, and his pleasure is horribly cruel. I humbly confess his superiority, and I bow before him in the dust. But if I lack such supreme creative power, the eternal reason shines out in my spirit and I may even bring God's fun before its forum and subject it to respectful criticism.[49]

I understood that belief in God is not a matter of standing still but of sharpening up the questions. Why is the world as it is, since God has created it 'good'? So 'God' cannot simply be an answer to the question of the meaning and meaningless of creation which would silence the question. And this is the case, not because the madness in creation remains even with and before God. 'God' must be understood as being too much for human beings to take, as one who puts the basic questions of their life in a forthright way: before God – against God. Why, God, are there so many cruel places of terror in your creation? Why so many mattress tombs in which people vegetate in such an undignified way? Why so many massacres and catastrophes? Basic questions which can be taken so far as to put our own existence is question, as the biblical Job did. Why must we be put in this world at all, if this fate awaits us?

> Why did I not die at birth,
> come forth from the womb and expire?
> Why did the knees receive me,
> why the breasts that I should suck?
> For then I should have lain down and been quiet;
> I should have slept; then I should have been at rest (Job 3.11–13).

Feelings which the terminally ill Heine also knows, in one of his texts now longing for the grave as the place of happiness:

> O grave, you are paradise
> for fastidious, tender ear.
> Death is good, but better it would be
> for mother never to have borne us.[50]

Thus in Heine we have a remarkable simultaneity of scepticism and trust, blasphemy and submission, blasphemy and humility. So we can we echo the literary critic Wolgang Preisendanz, to whom we are indebted for important contributions to the interpretation of Heine's late work: 'His poems remain decisive, and they quickly make clear what this personal God meant for him: someone to whom to address not a single prayer, but lamentation, accusation and blasphemy, someone to address of whom Heine says that it is a relief to know someone in heaven to whom he can direct his sighs and lamentations in the long night after his wife has settled him down. Once again there is no Christian surrender to the unfathomable counsel nor a Promethean rebellion; Heine persists in the honest irony of a failure to understand which in pain, misery, disgust and despair still quarrels like Job and seeks justification with the wicked question 'Why?'[51]

2. God facing judgment: Elie Wiesel

A century later the question of the suffering of the innocent had become even more radical for Jewish writers, when their people had almost completely fallen victim to the anti-Jewish anti-semitic destructive mania of the Nazis. And of the writers of our century, no one has put these questions to God so stubbornly and so deeply as the Jew Elie Wiesel, who himself barely escaped the Holocaust. His literary and theological work for which he won the Nobel Peace Prize in 1986 is one long cry to God.[52] In his autobiography, *All Rivers Run into the Sea*, first published in 1995, Wiesel summed up his lifelong concern:

> I will never cease to rebel against those who committed or permitted Auschwitz, including God. The questions I once asked myself about God's silence remain open. If they have an answer, I do not know it. But I maintain that the death of six million human beings poses a question to which no answer will ever be forthcoming.[53]

Of all his numerous texts, Elie Wiesel's play 'The Trial of Schamgorod', published in 1979, has moved me most.[54] For more than in any other text before and after, here Elie Wiesel as expressed his indignation against 'Him' in a unique way, Moreover those who see this play witness a striking event: in the face of a quite intolerable history of violence, people set about putting God on trial, arraigning the creator of heaven and earth before the bar of human judgment.

A tribunal against God

The original idea – like almost everything in Wiesel's work – came from his personal experience in the concentration camps of Auschwitz and Buchenwald to which he had been deported in 1944, at the age of sixteen, from his home town of Sighet in Hungary. In the camp Wiesel had once worked with a man who before the war had been head of a Talmudic school somewhere in Galicia. While they were dragging stones, one day he turned to the young man and asked why they shouldn't study. And in fact they began to go through the Talmud and Midrash during work, from memory. One evening the man said to Wiesel:

> Come close to my bed tonight. I went. Now I know why he did it: because I was the youngest and he must have thought that because I

was younger I had a greater chance of surviving and telling the story. And what he then did was to convene a rabbinic tribunal and accuse God. He had added two other learned rabbis, and they resolved to accuse God, in appropriate, correct form, as a proper rabbinic tribunal would, with witnesses, arguments, etc. . . . The proceedings of the tribunal went on for a long time. And finally my teacher, who was president of the tribunal, pronounced the verdict: 'Guilty.' Then silence reigned – a silence which reminded me of the silence of Sinai: an endless, eternal silence.

But finally my teacher, the rabbi, said: 'And now, my friends, let us go and pray.' And we prayed to God, who a few minutes beforehand had been pronounced guilty by his children.[55]

Later we shall have to speak at length about this apparently contradictory connection between the pronunciation of guilt and the act of prayer. Here the biographical context is of prime importance for me. On his release from the camp, Elie Wiesel began to describe the experience of the Holocaust in literature. And he could not get the story of the tribunal against God out of his head. But what literary form was he to give this story? That of a novel? He wrote one, but threw it away. That of a play? About Auschwitz? He also rejected this idea. That of a cantata? That too did not satisfy him. Later Wiesel realized why: because as aesthetic forms, neither theatre nor novel nor cantata could do justice to the monstrous event of Auschwitz. So Wiesel, while keeping the form of a play, transferred the story from the twentieth century to the middle of the seventeenth century, to the time of the Chmielniecki pogroms in Russia, in which the whole Jewish population of Eastern Europe had been decimated in a terrible way.

Moreover the scene of the play, *The Trial of Schamgorod*, is a Russian village in 1648, near to the river Dnieper. Only a few Jews live in this area, since Ukrainians, Tartars and Cossacks have just carried out a pogrom on the Jewish inhabitants. Among the survivors is the farm-hand Berisch, who is eking out a wretched existence with his daughter Hanna and his servant Maria. Hanna has gone mad, since the pogrom raged on her wedding day. Her bridegroom had been murdered in a bestial way, and she herself had been raped. And the 'Christian' pogrom mob had raged on, as there were still a few Jews alive in the place. There is still unrest and anxiety: waiting for an event which seems to be very near.

The play is set on the eve of Purim, that Jewish festival which is meant to recall the miracle of the deliverance of the Jews from annihilation by the Persian minister Haman as reported in the book of Esther. According to Jewish custom, on this festival people changed clothes, put on costumes, donned masks, had games and processions: there was drinking, celebration and feasting. So Purim is the Jewish Feast of Fools, of children and beggars, the feast on which circumstances can change once gain in play, in which once again 'anything goes'.

On this evening of the year 1649, three members of a small troop of players enter the shabby house of Verish the herdsman, and want to perform a cheerful Purim play. The herdsman agrees, but because of his traumatic experiences he makes one condition:

> You want to play a Purim game? Very well. I'll define the content: a Din-Toive, this evening we'll hold a religious trial . . . of the Most High King, the Supreme Judge, the Lord of the Universe! That's the play you're to perform this evening. That or nothing. Choose![56]

The players are shocked. A trial of God? But Berisch can win them over by referring to the tradition of the Purim game. For in the Purim game one can say things under the fool's hat that no one has said before, ask questions which no one has so far dared to raise.

Thus dramatically a 'play within a play' is possible, and this raises the tension tremendously. The farmhouse turns into a hall of judgment, the comedians become judges, the shepherd the prosecutor. And once again unexpected difficulties arise: no one is prepared to take on the role of defending God. The game would almost not have come off, had not suddenly a man called Sam entered the room and offered: he is a cold but courteous intellectual. He is accepted as defender without any questions asked: people are glad finally to be able to begin the trial. Berisch now presents the charge once again:

> I, Berisch, Jewish innkeeper from Schamgorod, accuse the Lord of the Universe of hostility, cruelty and indifference . . . I am saying what I think and I say it because I think; either he does not love his chosen people, or he is mocking them. This much seems certain: our fate leaves him cold. Why has he chosen us? Why us in particular and no other people for a change? In short, either he knows what awaits us or he does not. Either way, he is guilty.[57]

The devil defends God

From this point on a brilliant rhetorical duel develops between the defender and the prosecutor of God. Point by point Sam attempts to drive Berisch on the defensive: certainly crimes were committed in Schamgorod, but aren't things fine with Berisch personally? Can't he go on serving his customers, doesn't he still have a roof over his head? Certainly blood flowed in Schamgorod, but is that to be blamed on God? Haven't human beings been massacring other human beings? Certainly murders were committed in Schamgorod, but isn't God to be sought among the victims rather than among the murderers? Certainly there have been dead in Schamgorod, but can the prosecutor really speak in the name of all the dead? Are the dead all witnesses to the charge? Can we exclude the possibility that the victims were fortunate to leave the ugly and blood-soaked earth in order to enter the world of truth and eternal life? Indeed, mustn't the dead be grateful that God spared them supreme suffering or shame or remorse? And anyway, God is God, and his will does not depend on human wills.

And what is the human cause? Is it to submit to God, at all events to accept God's will? Is God guilty? What do human beings know, that they can judge God with such certainty, indeed arrogance? Haven't former generations experienced precisely such catastrophes and yet not ceased to praise the righteousness of God? Is the present generation wiser than they were? Every time the catastrophe was a punishment for human transgressions. And are things to be any different today? Triumphantly the defender adds: 'Who are you, then, to accuse the Creator of the Universe or to put him on trial? Nothing but dust. You're just a speck of dust.'[58]

Such counter-arguments are not without their effect on the judge. And Berisch too is clearly forced on the defensive. Moreover, by his dialectical skill in argument, by his acute mind and his brilliant rhetoric, Sam is able to make a brilliant defence of God's cause. However, the external threat to the small community of Jews increases hour by hour. Again an attack by the 'Christian' mob is imminent, and the Jews barricade doors and windows, put out their candles. General hysteria develops. And suddenly those present beg Sam, who is such an eloquent 'man of God', to save them from danger:

> You're a righteous man, use your influence on our behalf . . . You've the power, use it . . . You're close to heaven, pray for us. Your faith can do much. Call on him, and ask him to rescind the order.[59]

In the end turned into a wonder rabbi by projections of anxiety, someone to whom magical powers are attributed, all at once Sam reveals his true self. When all – for Purim – put on their masks, Sam also takes a mask from his bag. Then all utter a cry of dismay: it is the mask of the devil. Sam breaks out into terrible laughter and bids them farewell with the words:

> You took me for a saint? A righteous man? A wise man, made to be venerated? A herald of faith? Poor fools! How blind you are? If only you knew, if only you knew . . .[60]

And with these words he raises his arm as if to give a sign, whereupon the Christian mob now finally storms into the room. The play ends.

The end of classical theodicy

Elie Wiesel has succeeded not only in making this trial of God a gripping play but also once again in taking up the classical elements of theodicy and at the same time developing them *ad absurdum*. For if we analyse Sam's speech in God's defence, five classical arguments in defence of God can be reconstructed.

1. The history of the suffering of the many must be relativized by the history of personal happiness. As long as one is spared oneself, one has no right to accuse God.
2. The history of suffering is not God's fault but only the fault of human beings who have caused other human beings suffering.
3. Through the history of suffering God himself becomes a victim of creation which has rebelled against his original will.
4. The victims may not be made witnesses to the charge against God since none of the survivors can really adopt their perspective.
5. God's will cannot be judged by human categories. The anthropocentric perspective must be given up in favour of the theocentric perspective. In any case obedience must be shown to God's will, and guilt must be sought in human transgressions.

Against these classical arguments, Elie Wiesel ventures to think through radically an idea which previously had been taboo even in Jewish circles: the notion that God is guilty of the unjust mass suffering of his 'children'. Here the classical theodicy argument is not just countered rationally. The surprise effect of the play, which is also staged skilfully, lies in the insight that the arguments for theodicy presented here in the end prove to be the devil's arguments, i.e. their sole purpose is to deceive men and women about God's real being. Only in this way can the 'devil's ' laughter or his cryptic remark 'If only you knew' be understood. So with this play Elie Wiesel leads classical theodicy into a crisis of unparalleled radicalism: those who in the face of boundless suffering of the innocent justify God with such arguments are doing the work of the devil, God's adversary. Indeed, the conclusion is suggested that a God justified in this way would look very much like the devil.

But in Wiesel's work the crisis of classical theodicy never leads to a shift towards godlessness. The talk of 'God's guilt' is not a metaphor for the intrinsically enigmatic character of the world in a post-metaphysical age, as it is for Wolfgang Hildesheimer, but the expression of an ultimate trust in God. The specific theological point of the play is that theodicy is rejected with a reference to the guilt of God. God can no longer be justified in the face of the mass suffering of the innocent. From a human perspective, theodicy can be refused only because God's righteousness simply cannot be reconciled with such pogroms. But this refusal takes place before God, and by his accusation the hero of this play holds fast to the existence of God. The accusation is not that God is dead, but that God is silent.

Above all from Elie Wiesel's theology I have learned that there can be a legitimate protest against God – before God. Marie Luise Kaschnitz and Heinrich Heine realized this in their own ways. Here all have made it clear that this protest is an expression not of indifference or arrogance but of a last respect to God. Elie Wiesel in particular has always thought it of the utmost importance that his theology of accusation is backed by religious traditions of his people. Hence the recourse to the Purim game, which allowed him to play out the protest against God in role play without having to fear the charge of hybris or blasphemy. The Purim game gave him the necessary legitimation to rebel against the tradition within the tradition. Therefore Wiesel saw even a tribunal against God as being 'completely in accord with the Jewish law and with Jewish tradition'. It may be difficult for Christians to understand this, Wiesel once remarked, and even more difficult to accept it. But Jews could, and Jews had:

Abraham did it, and Moses did it, and the Talmud is full of rabbis who protested against God. In the Hasidic literature Rabbi Levi-Yitzhak of

Berdichev constantly accused God. We may say no to God. Provided that it is for other people, for the sake of humankind. We may say no to God. For me that is a great innovation, bold, revolutionary, in the Jewish tradition.[61]

IV. Waiting for God's justification

Elie Wiesel may have been right in saying that it is difficult for Christians to accept a protest, let alone a tribunal against God. To show why this is the case would need a separate major study which would certainly bring together many lines of argument.[62] However, one thing now seems to me to be certain: the difficulties of Christians are also caused by the fact that they have largely cut themselves off from the biblical-Jewish tradition. It is time to examine this situation and revise it self-critically in Christian theology. It is time to remember again that for Christians the 'Old' ('First') Testament is not only a historical document of the 'prehistory' of Christianity but the living word of God.[63] Certainly Christians will ultimately seek to understand God's history of revelation granted to the people of Israel in the light of the Christ-event and to deepen it. But that does not dispense them from taking Israel's experiences of God seriously. They are and remain authentic experiences of God, which are not made obsolete, irrelevant or out-of-date by the testimony to Christ. For Christians they are certainly as authentic as the experiences of God communicated through Jesus Christ. They have their own justification and their own worth. They have their own riches which are supplemented and deepened, not done away with, by the New Testament 'christo-logical' experiences of God.

1. Rebellious texts in the Bible

If we look closely, the texts of the Hebrew Bible indicate an uncommonly varied relationship between human beings and God, and one of the possibilities in that relationship is complaint and accusation. Israel did not feel this to be blasphemy or hybris; it was a legitimate possibility for believers to tell God to his face, completely freely, what made them indignant and sad – in their situation, as individuals and a people. Otherwise these texts would never have been handed down. I want to demonstrate this by three key texts. Above all I just want to document them, and in this way to let them speak for themselves, not interpreting them with any great exegetical effort. They may be around two thousand five hundred years old, but in my experience they have lost none of their spiritual power. These texts in particular make it possible to fuse the horizons of then and now. They illustrate how in Heinrich Heine, Marie Luise Kaschnitz and Elie Wiesel, talk of God – for all the modern difference – has deep roots in the biblical tradition.

My trust has gone: Lamentations

I have chosen a text from the tradition of Lamentations. In it someone speaks who has experienced suffering and can only understand his suffering as an expression of the wrath of God:

> I am the man who has seen affliction
> under the rod of his wrath.
> He has driven me and brought me
> into darkness without any light.
>
> Surely against me he turns his hand
> again and again the whole day long.
> He has made my flesh and my skin waste away,
> and broken my bones;
> He has besieged and enveloped me
> with bitterness and tribulation (3.1–5).

But since the man does not accept his situation, he accuses God. And the surprising thing is that nowhere does he indicate that he feels that he is to blame and thus accept his situation of suffering as just punishment. This traditional pattern of explanation, which we frequently encounter elsewhere in the Hebrew Bible, is quite alien to this text. On the contrary: the sufferer does not make himself responsible for his situation, but God. God seems to him to be like a lurking beast, who robs him not only of all joy in life but also all unfolding of life. God has so to speak immured this man in suffering, condemned him to fetters.

> He has made me dwell in darkness
> like the dead of long ago.
> He has walled me about so that I cannot escape;

he has put heavy chains on me;
though I call and cry for help, he shuts out my prayer;
he has blocked my ways with hewn stones,
he has made my paths crooked.
He is to me like a bear lying in wait,
like a lion in hiding (3.6–10).

Furthermore, God's silence – despite all the crying and prayers – is evidently part of God's purpose to torment people and destroy their happiness. And this torment includes the experience that the sufferer is also isolated socially, that he stands in his situation as one who is mocked.

I have become the laughing-stock of all peoples,
the burden of their songs all day long.
He has filled me with bitterness,
he has sated me with wormwood.
He has made my teeth grind on gravel
and made me cower in ashes.

My soul is bereft of peace,
I have forgotten what happiness is;
so I say, 'Gone is my glory,
And my expectation from the Lord' (3.14–18).

So this lamentation culminates in the experience that it is God himself who has robbed the person of peace and destroyed his happiness. Indeed we can say that it is God himself who has destroyed all trust in God in this person.

Yet one unshakeable fact remains: even the bitterest accusation against God takes the form of a prayer, i.e. a discourse to God and with God. Even the bitterest of charges ('My soul is bereft of peace') is made against God. Thus this lamentation is a text against God – but before God and for God.

Why did I have to be born? Job

Job above all, the man from Uz, has lost his 'trust in the Lord'. He is not the most patient man in the Bible, as he as often been portrayed in the past, but above all the greatest rebel against God.[64] His speeches are disputations: the submission speech is a fragment of them – towards the end. The basis of Job's dispute with the Most High is that God has become completely incomprehensible to him. God can torment a man without having any obvious occasion; he can heap suffering on a man, although hitherto – like Job – this man has lived a 'blameless and righteous' life before God. So what kind of a God is it who thus robs the innocent of their happiness? Who does not stand on the side of right and whom does even the righteous not escape? 'Without reason' this God feeds on his 'wounds', does not let him 'draw breath', sates him with bitterness (9.17f.). Certainly Job feels himself utterly 'guiltless' (9.21), but what use is this innocence to him before such a God who evidently persecutes the guilty and the innocent in the same way?

And then, in chapter 10 of the book of Job, there follows one of the boldest passages in Old Testament discourse about God. In the figure of Job a human being hurls against God all the indignation he has in him, culminating in the bitterest accusation that human beings could make against the creator God: Why did you ever draw me from my mother's womb? It would be better if I had not been born!

> I loathe my life;
> I will give free utterance to my complaint;
> I will speak in the bitterness of my soul.
>
> I will say to God, do not condemn me;
> let me know why you contend against me.
>
> Does it seem good to you to oppress,
> to despise the work of your hands
> and favour the designs of the wicked?
>
> Although you know that I am not guilty,
> and there is none to deliver out of your hand?
>
> Your hands fashioned and made me;
> and now you turn about and destroy me.
>
> And if I lift myself up, you hunt me like a lion,
> and again work wonders against me.
>
> You renew your witnesses against me,
> and increase your vexation towards me;

you bring fresh hosts against me.
Why did you bring me forth from the womb?
Would that I had died before any eye had seen me,
and were as though I had not been,
carried from the womb to the grave (10.1–3, 7f., 16–19).

In this text, too, the basic experience is like that in Lamentations: Job is at his wits' end, not knowing why he has God as his enemy. He asks what use it is for God to favour the sinner and scorn those who are not sinners. Indeed the logic of the creator God becomes a completely riddle to him. After all, God has created him, the human being, and now God evidently wants to annihilate his own creature. And this too is inconsistent: as soon as human beings arise against God, God directs all his miraculous power against them and constantly reactivates his wrathful energy. But where are the miraculous power and energy of God when Job is sitting in misery? Why now no 'fresh troops' who can rush to the aid of God's righteous? Why only God's troops to annihilate human beings, and not to rescue them? So it is only consistent for Job after all this to raise the basic question: why in the face of such a life must one be born at all? Is such a life still worth living?

Here it becomes clear that Heine's rebellious prayers (thus the ironical question about God's self-interest) are not his personal invention, but have been formulated in prayer texts of the Hebrew Bible, Job's words:

Does it seem good to you to oppress,
to despise the work of your hands
and favour the designs of the wicked.
Although you know that I am not guilty,
and there is none to deliver out of your hand?
Your hands fashioned and made me;
and now you turn about and destroy me

match those of Heinrich Heine:

On your inconsistency, O Lord,
I cannot fail to brood.
You make the happiest poet, and now
Rob him of his good mood.

I cry to you: the protest of a sick man

Psalm 88 is the most important of the psalms for our question. A man sick from childhood does not suppress his questions to God, but addresses God:

Lord, why do you cast me off?
Why do you hide your face from me?

Afflicted and close to death from my youth up,
I suffer your terrors; I am helpless.

Your wrath has swept over me,
your dread assaults destroy me.

They surround me like a flood all day long,
they close in upon me together.

You have caused lover and friend to shun me,
my companions are in darkness (88.15–19).

This text could even more have been the original form of Heine's 'Miserere'. The speaker in this prayer does not think of attributing his sickness to a sin and accepting it as a punishment for sin, after the model of other texts about sickness in the Bible (cf. Psalm 41). How could he, since he has been lying there sick 'from early youth'. On the contrary, in the face of his hopeless situation, his incessant crying into the apparently deaf ears of God, this speaker dares to attack God directly as the cause of his state:

You have put me in the depths of the tomb,
in the regions dark and deep.

Your wrath lies heavy upon me,
and you overwhelm me with all your waves.

You have caused my companions to shun me;
you have made me a thing of horror to them;
I am shut in so that I cannot escape.

My eye grows dim through sorrow.
Every day I call upon you, O Lord,
I spread out my hands to you (88.7–10).

After this clear description of his own situation, and after the naming of God as the cause of the sick man's state, a third motif is emphasized in this text: the appeal to God's self-interest. The tone becomes somewhat sarcastic, because God is to be provoked finally to change his attitude. God is to be stirred up to shorten this suffering, for it should be in God's interest to deal with a man who praises him with a happy heart and does not moan from the depths of depression:

> Do you work wonders for the dead?
> Do the shades rise up to praise you?
>
> Is your steadfast love declared in the grace,
> or your faithfulness in Abaddon?
>
> Are your wonders known in the darkness,
> or your saving help in the land of forgetfulness?
>
> But I, Lord, cry to you,
> in the morning my prayer comes before you (88.11–14).

And a fourth motif is important: despite all his previous experience, this suppliant presupposes that God wills people's salvation and not their annihilation. Thus despite all the misery and all the vain crying, this text lives by the 'God of my salvation'. Moreover this appeal stands right at the beginning of the text like a positive key signature:

> Lord, my God, I call for help by day;
> I cry out in the night before you.
>
> Let my prayer come before you,
> incline your ear to my cry (88.2f.).

We can follow the Tübingen Old Testament scholar Walter Gross, who describes the unique feature of this text like this: 'The peculiarity of this psalm is that without any final note of reconciliation it ends in terror before this God, in accusation of him. Certainly the suppliant has prayed and continues to pray; however, the psalm does not indicate any certainty of being heard, but ends in remoteness from God and desperation. Nevertheless, near to death, the suppliant calls this Yahweh 'God of my salvation'! . . . Perhaps even more astonishing than this text is the fact that it has been included among the 150 prayers of the Psalter, Israel's book of prayer and meditation, a decision which the church too has endorsed by using this Psalter in the liturgical and the private sphere down to the present day. By accepting this text into its collection of prayers, post-exilic Judaism indicated that this psalm is an acceptable, indeed, commendable prayer. A person facing a misfortune equal to death can and in some circumstances must speak to God like this.'[65]

2. Waiting for theodicy

It has become clear that the common element in these texts from the Hebrew Bible is that the situation of human suffering leads neither to a denial of the existence of God (along the lines of the modern critique of religion) nor to pious submission and unquestioning acceptance. Instead, radical criticism of God, indeed provocation of God, are legitimate forms for expressing faith. For the world of the Hebrew Bible, lamentation to God, indeed direct accusation of God, are accepted forms of the human relationship to God, and have also left their traces on the New Testament (Mark 15.33–39; Heb.5.7–10; Rev.6.9–11). Such texts were evidently not excluded as being offensive, but were given their due place as one way of dealing with God in the cosmos of the Bible.

Why complaint and accusation are legitimate

Moreover the theological legitimacy of complaint and accusation in the Old Testament is conditioned by the following factors:

– their specific *existential context*. Complaint and accusation to God are not legitimate in every situation. In the Old Testament it is the situation of the boundless (and therefore incomprehensible) suffering of innocent men and women: collectively (as a people) or individually;
– belief that *God is responsible for ev*erything that goes on in the world. It is God himself by whose activity everything is determined and who thus bears responsibility for everything. So this responsibility can be called to account;
– *existential urgency*. The Old Testament suppliant does not have hope in a resurrection at his disposal. 'Comfort in a beyond' therefore cannot bring any solace in situations of suffering; a turning point in intolerable circumstances is therefore called for here and now;
– *previous experiences of trust in God*. Thus we can recognize a threefold

temporal structure in the Old Testament texts of complaint and accusation which looks like this:

In all texts a past is presupposed in which there was an unbroken trust in God. Someone who – like the suppliant in Lamentations – feels that 'My soul is bereft of peace', who has 'forgotten' what 'happiness' is, and sees his 'trust in the Lord' shattered, must once have experienced peace, happiness and trust in God. Someone who – like Job – rebels, does so because he has a history of happiness with God behind him. And even someone who has been sick from childhood explicitly appeals to the God of his 'salvation'. All that allows the conclusion that none of these texts suggests that God has always had deaf ears, has always pursued people with his wrath. Rather, all start from the assumption that God in principle wants human 'salvation', and that there have been signs of God's happiness and 'trust in the Lord'.

Only on the basis of this history of trust and happiness can the rebellious protest be made, here and now, in the present; only on the basis of a former 'comprehensibility' is God's incomprehensibility now called to task. The basic presupposition in all these texts is that on countless occasions (in the past) God has cared for men and women, that he has spared them much and has earned their trust through righteousness. But now God seems to be blind to human fate, insensitive to human suffering, deaf to human lament and arbitrary in exercising his righteousness. God has become a monster who threatens life, destroys happiness and disrupts security.

Hope that God will establish himself

The complaint is made to God in order to change this; God is accused in a challenge to him to be positive. Here trust from the past is projected on to the future. As a rule the texts expect God to have the power to change destiny once again. They are an expression, not of a passive fatalism or a paralysing cynicism, but of an inalienable hope that God himself will do justice to the innocent sufferer, i.e. restore happiness in life. Complaints to God and accusations against God are thus ultimately an expression of confidence in a new, happy self-assertion by God in the face of the evil of the world – in favour of human beings.

This self-assertion by God corresponds to a self-justification by God. I deliberately choose this theological category in order to distinguish it from the modern understanding of theodicy. As a rule the word theodicy is understood as an objective genitive, *anthropocentrically*: God is justified by *human beings* in his righteousness in the face of the evil in the world. In the perspective of the Bible the word theodicy must be understood *theocentrically* as a subjective genitive: *God* himself justifies himself in the face of the evil in creation. This is a statement of radical hope: God hears the accusations of human beings and will enlighten them over the incomprehensible riddle of his 'good creation'.

3. Loving God – despite God

We also meet this line of human lament and accusation of God in the Jewish tradition, the tradition of the rabbis as we find it in the Talmud and the Midrashim, and in the tradition of the wise, as we find it in Hassidism. Here again I shall follow Elie Wiesel, who in his numerous biblical-Talmudic-Hassidic writings has specifically brought to light this rebellious tradition among the pious scholars of Israel. Here are a few examples.

The stories of rebellious rabbis

In his 'Talmudic Celebration' (1991), Wiesel presents to his readers the case of Rabbi Elisha ben Abuja, a fascinating and complex Talmudic scholar from the second century. The rabbinic tradition condemned this man, and excluded him from the Jewish community as 'other', since to the dismay of those around him, Rabbi Elisha, the son of a well-to-do father and a brilliant pupil of eminent scholars, had apostasized from the Jewish faith during the time of the Roman occupation of Palestine at the beginning of the second century. Traditional explanations put the blame on his mother and father. Elie Wiesel is not content with this and seeks to understand Elisha's step in an impressive portrait. This rabbi had started from the following conviction:

> After all, God should have protected the people that the Torah was meant to protect. Men and women are sacrificing themselves at that time in order to seal this covenant with their life and blood. But God, the God of Israel, does not seem to respect it. His children allow themselves to be killed, his elect are put to death, and He does not intervene.
>
> Nevertheless, many Jews do not give up hope and cling with all their might to God, who seems to have forsaken them.

Elisha ben Abuja rebels, not against the executioner but against the one who through his silence, perhaps even through his assent, is in league with the executioner.[66]

Granted, no personal testing can be demonstrated in the case of Rabbi Elisha; he personally did not experience any persecution; he personally did not suffer any injustice. Yet the problem of theodicy is the key to Rabbi Elisha's radical change. Tormented by this problem, he does not rebel against the creation but against the creator. The story of individuals, but also the history of his own people under the Roman occupation, is the occasion for this. Thus it is reported of Elisha that he had once witnessed something monstrous: a man had climbed a date palm and, although it was the sabbath, had robbed a bird's nest. He had taken the mother bird, but left the young. That was a flagrant transgression against one of the central commandments of the Torah – and nothing happened to the wicked man. He was able to return home safe and sound. That same evening, when the sabbath was already over, Elisha had watched a second man climbing another date palm. Here he had also found a bird's nest, and – in accordance with the Torah – had taken the young but let the mother go free. However, when he reached the ground again a snake bit him and he died on the spot. This is one example of many in God's creation: one who offends flagrantly against a divine commandment gets off unscathed, while another who acts in conformity with the Torah is suddenly snatched away. This is Elie Wiesel's conclusion about Rabbi Elisha:

> Elisha felt repelled, despaired in the divine righteousness and ceased to believe in it. Since the righteous suffer in the kingdom of God while the godless happily enjoy life, Elisha resolves to turn his back on God and join the hosts of the godless. He does not claim that God is not a judge but that God is a bad judge. He does not proclaim that the law is unjust but that God hardly obeys it, which means, in other words, that God does not keep his promises.[67]

It is the same with the persecutions of his own people. Here too Elisha rages against his God, who through his silence seems to indicate his assent to the executioners, indeed to be in league with them. What remains of God's covenant with his people in the face of these persecutions? Men and women sacrificed themselves to authenticate this covenant with their blood and life. But God seems to have forgotten his own covenant. His children are killed, his elect slaughtered. He does nothing and lets it all happen. For Elie Wiesel it is understandable that Rabbi Elisha already asks himself:

But who is to blame? God? Yes, says Elisha in keeping with another Talmudic school of thought. Tormented by the problem of theodicy, Elisha rebels, not against the creation but against the Creator himself.[68]

We need not pursue the case of Rabbi Elisha further here. In the course of his portrait Elie Wiesel engages in a quite critical discussion with him. However, this is not because Elisha rebelled against God; it is because in his indignation against God he also treated his fellow human beings (his Jewish brothers) scandalously. He became an informer for the Romans, and got entangled in tales of murder. So Elie Wiesel finds the moral condemnation in the Talmud understandable:

Against God? Had it only been that, we would have understood him. But he sinned against his own brothers, and I rebel against that. If you dispute with God, all right, that's your affair and his – but how far are your brothers to blame? If you rebel against God, well and good, but why do you show your indignation by turning against your own people? Why do you become an accomplice of the executioner? One has to be very harsh and inhuman to think and act like this. Our tradition justifies only a single cry, the cry that we utter for our fellow human beings, not against them. Only the indignation that helps the victim is allowed. That which encourages the executioners is vain, because it is inhuman. In other words, Elisha's injustice lies in the fact that he rebelled against human destiny and merely contributed towards devaluing it. [69]

One must not give in

Elie Wiesel sees an opposite case in the tradition of Hassidism, the case of Rabbi Moshe Loeb from Sassow. In contrast to Rabbi Elisha, not a negative word has been handed down about this Hassidic master. Rabbi Loeb is always depicted as a perfect human being, extraordinary in his readiness to help inside and outside the synagogue, unsurpassed in his zeal for study, unique in his love of human beings and God. For this rabbi, life meant clothing all speech and action in love. And this love was been all-embracing for him; it knew no preference for anyone.

Elie Wiesel already feels distant from this rabbi; he finds this allegedly all-embracing love which leaves out nothing and no one 'almost irritating'. All these reports that make this rabbi seem so perfect cause Wiesel to be mistrustful. Does this man never get angry? Can he never be enraptured? Is such a person still human? Instinctively Wiesel prefers 'the sorry and the dark' in the Jewish tradition, people who have 'dark secrets'. One day a brief text falls into his hands which suddenly casts another light on this rabbi:

> Rabbi Moshe Loeb had another reading for the psalm verse 'Happy the man whom God has chosen for chastizement', namely, 'Happy the man who dares to chastize God,' i.e. who has the courage to put hard questions to him and to remind him of his duty to his people.
>
> Did he too dispute with heaven, did he too argue with God, the God of mercy and love? If so, he will not have been as serene and cheerful as he seems to have been. If he put the God of mercy on trial, then he too felt himself to be at his wits' end. This again put in question everything I believed I knew about him.[70]

Elie Wiesel investigates further and comes upon other traditions. He discovers that inwardly this rabbi must have been a broken man; only a few suspected it. He had been so concerned to spread joy that no one had noticed any of his sorrow. The mask which he wore had been a good protection. It had hidden a secret: the grief of this man. This is attested by a story handed down by the son of Rabbi Loeb. At the age of five he had been taken by his father to a Rosh Hashanah celebration. He had hidden under his father's prayer shawl and heard him say in the middle of a solemn prayer:

> Lord of the Worlds, for years, for generations, for centuries we have been addressing our pleas to you, and you have still not sent us the Messiah. You know very well, you must know it: we cannot take any more, do you hear me, Lord of Heaven, we cannot take any more.[71]

Another story is similar. In one family several children died one after the other at an early age and the mother conveyed her grief to the wife of the wise man of the place: 'What sort of God is the God of Israel? He is cruel and not merciful. He takes what he has given.' But the woman had tried to calm her down: one must not talk like that; the ways of heaven are unfathomable; one must learn to accept one's fate. At this moment Rabbi Loeb had appeared on the doorstep and had said to the unhappy woman:

And I say to you, woman, one must not accept it! One must not submit to it! I advise you to call, to cry, to protest, to demand justice. Do you understand me, woman? One may not accept it.[72]

In all these texts the cry to God is uttered in confidence in God; the indignation against God in expectation of God; the rebellion before God out of love of God. According to a sentence which he often quoted, 'The opposite of love is not hatred but indifference; the opposite of life is not death but a lack of feeling,'[73] this Jewish author shows figures from his own tradition who in their pain over a deeply contradictory creation do not give way to indifference and insensitivity towards God. Rather, their rebellion is their form of prayer, their quarrelling their form of saying yes. Precisely by being incomprehensible, God remains God of the living, in whose power one trusts that there will be a turning point.

What do we get in return, God?

For Elie Wiesel, no other figure from the Hassidic tradition shows this tension more impressively then the figure of Rabbi Levi-Yitzhak of Berdichev, whose impressive portrait we find in Wiesel's book 'Hassidic Celebration' (1972). For there is also a remarkable second side to this rabbi, who was born in Galicia in 1740 and died in Berdichev in the Ukraine in 1809, and who was revered by all. First of all Wiesel makes it clear that the significance of this rabbi for the Jewish tradition is overwhelming. Sayings have been handed down like, 'God is a *Zaddik* up there and Levi-Yitzhak is one down here', or that the angels and seraphim are jealous of Levi-Yitzhaq's piety. For others he is the light of Israel; for yet others someone who opened the gates to the sanctuary of love which were closed again after his death. In short, Rabbi Levi-Yitzhak must be imagined as a friend of all rabbis and rabbi of all their pupils. He did not belong to a clan, but rather stood above the power struggles, and refused to get involved in disputes which split the Hassidic movement. So he was an authority standing over the parties, towering in his knowledge, exemplary in his way of life.

And yet there must also have been another dimension to this man: severe attacks of depression, of sorrow, of flight into loneliness, of madness. All this was made taboo in the tradition, and in this case the censorship was especially rigorous. For Hassidism had not wanted to show Rabbi Levi-Yitzhaq, of all people, as tormented, broken, defeated. Anyone else, but not him. It was not right for this great rabbi to suffer a

defeat, even a transitory one. All others could endure crises, but he had
to stand there as a model, full of faith, power and creative inspiration.

Here, too, Elie Wiesel establishes a counterpoint and brings other
traditions to light which report a collapse of Rabbi Levi-Yitzhaq, his
desperation, indeed his revolt against God. That is the moment when
God is blamed and it is indicated that the people of Israel does not just
need to receive forgiveness from God but also needs to forgive its God:

> Doubtless others before him had also had arguments with God. But
> none had been so bold as to set himself against God. No one had gone
> so far as to condemn him, to threaten him: 'Should Ivan blow the
> shofar!' cried Levi-Yitzhaq in the middle of the Rosh-ha-Shanah
> service. 'If you prefer the enemy who suffers less than we do, then he
> should sing your praises!' The rabbi had no scruples about reminding
> God that he too has to be forgiven by his people for the suffering that
> he has imposed on them. Hence the plural form Yom Kippurim: the
> prayer for forgiveness is based on mutuality.[74]

Indeed, it is reported of another rabbi: 'If we accept that the argument
of the rabbi from Berdichev is correct, then there is no Jew before whom
God has not incurred guilt.'[75]

And secondly there is the element of refusing to pray to God:

> Once he (Levi-Yitzhak) stood dumb before his desk from morning
> to evening, without moving his lips. Previously he had warned Him:
> 'If you refuse to hear our prayers, I shall stop saying them.'[76]

So Levi-Yitzhak had allowed himself to threaten God that he would
break off communication. Indeed this rabbi had loved to demonstrate
that one can be a Jew with God, in God and even against God; but not
without God. It was not enough for him to ask questions, as Abraham
and Job did. He wanted answers, and when he did not get them he drew
his own conclusions. He had – a third element – required something in
return from God:

> Levi-Yitzhak had important arguments: Since you concluded the
> covenant with your people, you have worked stubbornly to break it,
> by putting the people to the test. Why? Remember. On Mount Sinai
> you peddled your Torah like a tradesman who cannot get rid of his
> rotten apples. You offered your commandments to all people, but they
> turned away from them full of contempt. Only Israel declared itself
> ready to accept them. But what does it get in return?

Another time he made the horrifying remark: Be sure that if your kingdom does not bring grace and mercy, we shall know that your throne is founded on deceit!

And he said: If a Jew sees *tefillim* (prayer beads) lying on the floor, then he rushes to pick them up and kiss them; is it not written that we are *tefillim*? Are you never going to pick us up?[77]

Here too Elie Wiesel thinks it extremely important that this rabbi did not incur the charge of blasphemy for his revolt. For two reasons. First, he never persisted long in a state of rebellion. When he had poured out his heart, he returned to God. When the charges had been levelled, the threats uttered, he resumed the prescribed liturgical prayers a free and liberated man. His questions often remained open, but he could continue the relationship with God, begin again, and build on the ruins. Secondly, the Jewish tradition allows people to say anything to God that is good for them. The only question is the framework in which people quarrel with God. Within the community everything can be said. If one is detached from it one loses this right. For the revolts of the faithful are not the same as the revolts of the apostates, those of the unbelievers or the godless. So to legitimate a theology of revolt from the Jewish perspective, Wiesel uses two criteria:

- The revolt may not be absolutized: the relationship with God can be false if it is reduced to revolution, indignation and protest. Conversely, revolt, indignation and protest are not hybris or blasphemy, but for believers a legitimate form of the relationship with the living and incomprehensible God of the abyss.
- The rebellion against God does not take place as apostasy from God but in a last trust in God. It is protest against God – before God; haggling with God – before God's 'throne'; a cry to God – out of love of God.

What happens next? Zvi Kolitz

For me, no one in the twentieth century has expressed more grippingly this unique interweaving of rebellion and humility, faith and protest, acceptance and dedication, than the Jewish writer Zvi Kolitz with his 1946 text 'Jossel Rakover Turns to God'. Born in Lithuania in 1918, the son of a rabbi and Talmudic scholar, Kolitz came to Palestine in 1939 and fought as an underground agent, against the British occupation and

for the state of Israel. In 1946 he was in the Argentinian capital Buenos
Aires as a delegate of the Jewish World Congress. Unrest had broken out
among the Jews there, since more and more ex-Nazis had come to
Argentina. Later Kolitz was to settle in New York, where he led the life
of a journalist, film maker, producer, businessman and lecturer. His
greatest public success was the film *Hill 24 Does Not Reply*, the first film
of the young state of Israel, which won international prizes in Cannes
and Mexico.

Zvi Kolitz knew only from stories the terrible fate of the Warsaw
ghetto, which the SS razed to the ground in spring 1943. He himself had
never been in Warsaw. Now in Buenos Aires he wrote a story which
convinced countless shaken readers that it was an authentic document,
because it was so lifelike. It was the story of a Jew called Jossel Rakover,
who had to look on as the Warsaw ghetto perished and his own family
was also massacred. Zvi Kolitz's story, which appeared in 1946 in the
Jiddische Zeitung of the Jewish community of Buenos Aires, later became
detached from its author and as an authentic document led a stubborn
life of its own, which is a separate adventure story in itself . . .[78]

Jossel Rakover – we learn – is the descendant of a great Hassidic
rabbinic family and begins to write when the Warsaw ghetto is in flames
from the bombardment of the German troops. On his flight into the
ghetto he had already lost his wife and three of his children, including a
seven-month-old baby. With his three surviving children, he succeeded in
escaping into the ghetto, but here too murder soon caught him up. He
lost ten-year-old Rachel, thirteen-year-old Jacob and fifteen-year-old
Chave. Jossel expects that at any moment the last house which is not yet
on fire, and in which he is writing his notes, will be blown up. In this hour
before the destruction Jossel – who is forty-three and can look back on a
'splendid life' – turns to his God and tells him 'to his face' what he is
thinking at this time.

Here it is striking that Jossel Rakover's talk of God displays the same
basic structure as the Old Testament texts of lamentation and accusation: past – present – future. For Jossel Rakover's complaint against God,
too, presupposes a trust in God which is grounded in the past:

> I've served God devotedly and my only prayer to him was to let me
> serve him 'with all my heart, with all my soul and with all my strength'.
> Now I can tell him – after all that I have experienced and endured –
> that my attitude to God has not changed. With absolute certainty I can
> tell him that my faith in him has not changed at all.[79]

In fact, it is not the fact of faith in God which has changed, but the relationship of this believer to his God, as a result of the events of the present. Here Jossel Rakover wants nothing special of God, no preferential treatment. He does not want to be 'the exception which proves the rule' and does not expect God to reveal a 'special relationship' to him. This Jew, too, is by no means a broken coward. In long passages he fantasizes on the possibility that God will take vengeance on the enemies of Israel, that he will avenge himself because of the crimes committed against his people: 'I am convinced that you will repay them mercilessly, inexorably, without compassion,' he tells his God. Yes, Jossel does not leave the slightest doubt that he is proud of being a Jew, simply because he would be ashamed of being 'a member of the nations who had given birth to and brought up those criminals'. He knows that it is difficult, very difficult, to be a Jew, and yet for him it is 'an honour' to be a Jew:

> I believe that being a Jew means being a fighter, one who swims eternally against the seething, criminal human stream. The Jew is a sign, a witness, he is confiscated, God's prisoner: his property, holy . . . I am fortunate to belong to the most unfortunate of all the peoples of the world – whose Torah contains the supreme law and the finest morality. But now this Torah is more hallowed and perpetuated in its humiliation and violation by the enemies of God. One is born a Jew as one is born an artist. One can never free oneself from being a Jew. That is the divine brand on us, which marks us out as his chosen people.[80]

So in all this nothing has changed. But what has changed for Jossel Rakover? What has become different in the relationship to his God? What has changed is the conviction that now God owes this innocent sufferer something, indeed a great deal. Earlier this Jew had always had the feeling of owing God something. Now he feels that God is standing there guilty and that therefore he has the right to 'admonish' God. Furthermore, Jossel Rakover is no longer prepared to accept and approve the blows as an expression of the just will of God. For:

> To say that we deserved the blows that we get means scorning ourselves and desecrating God's name. Those who shame our name also shame the name of God. Those who curse us curse God. To despise ourselves means to despise God.[81]

Thus this Jew's protest against God arises from the rejection of any contempt of himself. He wants to 'have things out with' God one last time in his life, not because he has finished with God, but because he has maintained an unshakeable trust in God:

> I tell you this because I believe in you, because I believe in you more than ever before – because I now know that you are my God. For you cannot be the God of those whose terrible acts of violence are so full of godlessness. For if you are not my God, whose God are you? The God of the murderers? If those who hate me, who murder me, are so dark, so bad, who am I – if not someone who bears something of your light and your grace in him?[82]

On the basis of this literally unshakeable trust, this Jew pours out his desperate questions: 'Tell us, what has to happen before you show your face to us again?' On the basis of this unshakeable trust he asks God: 'Where are the limits of your patience?' On the basis of this unshakeable trust he warns God not to take things too far, since the rope that holds them together could one day break. Indeed, on the basis of this trust he ventures to invite God to 'forgive' those who have turned away from God in their unhappiness and anger. But all this still remains in the framework of those structures which are provided by the rebellious prayers of the Old Testament: human rebellion against the manifest incomprehensibility, the coldness, the silence, the indifference of God.

You have done everything to stop me believing

However, here Jossel Rakover goes one step further: he formulates the most monstrous of accusations that a human being may make against God. And the most monstrous thing is to accuse God of being himself responsible for human lack of faith; he himself has done everything to destroy faith in him. One has to be a Jew to be able to follow completely the paradox which comes next: God is played off against his Torah. All at once this Jew claims that he prefers his Torah to God:

> I believe in the God of Israel even if He has done everything possible to make me not believe in Him. I believe in His laws even if I cannot justify His action. Now my relationship to Him is no longer that of a servant to his master but that of a pupil to the teacher. I bow my head before His greatness, but will not kiss the rod with which He smites me. I love Him, but I love His Torah more. Even if He has made a fool of me and I have been deceived in Him, I will go on guarding his Torah.

His Torah means instruction in life. The more we die for this instruction, the more immortal we shall be.[83]

If one reflects on this text, the paradox possibly resolves itself. For it is precisely the Torah, in which God has bound himself irrevocably to the people of Israel, that provides the basis for quarrelling with God. Without the Torah as a criterion one could not talk with God like this at all. Only because God in his commandments has committed himself to righteousness can one call this righteousness to account. Only because God has decreed commandments can one require him, too, to accept these commandments. Therefore it is logical to say that 'God' means 'religion' generally and in the abstract, but the Torah means instruction. In other words, despite all appearances there is a basic moral order in the world.

Moreover in a short meditation the French scholar Emanuel Lévinas, who also comes from Lithuania, has interpreted this 'beautiful and true' text as an expression of a 'reliable Jewish science' and 'a deeply authentic experience of spiritual life'. Even if this interpretation might seem to one to be all too forced, it is worth recording. What is decisive for Lévinas is that the danger of God's concealment is not negative, but the experience of being adult before God. A God for adults manifests himself particularly through the emptiness of the childish heaven:

God who veils his face is in my view neither a theological abstraction nor a poetic image. It is the hour when the righteous individual finds no other refuge, when no institution gives protection, when even the comfort of God's presence in a childlike religious feeling fails, when the individual can conquer only in the consciousness, i.e. necessarily in suffering. There is a specifically Jewish sense of suffering which at no moment takes on the value of a mystical penance for the sins of the world. The situation of the victim in a world that is out of joint, i.e. a world in which the Good does not succeed in winning, is one of suffering. It reveals a God who, by renouncing any helpful manifestation, appeals to the maturity of fully responsible human beings.[84]

Moreover precisely at this point Lévinas thinks that he can recognize the 'special physiognomy of Judaism'. The relationship between God and human beings is no 'sentimental communion' in the love of an incarnate God, but a relationship between spirits by means of an 'instruction, the Torah'. It is a non-incarnate word of God that bears witness to a living

God among us. The trust in a God who makes himself known through no
earthly authority can rest only on the 'inner evidence and the value of an
instruction'. Therefore now Lévinas can also interpret the words of Jossel
Rakover ('I love him, but I love his Torah even more'), as trust, indeed
as 'inner evidence of the morality which the Torah brings'! Lévinas
concludes his meditation with these words:

> To veil his face in order to ask everything of human beings – in a super-
> human way – to have created a person who is capable of answering,
> capable of approaching his God as a creditor and not always as a
> debtor – what truly divine greatness! In the end the believer has trust
> *par excellence*, but he is also the one who is not content with the
> withdrawals of the debtor. Our monologue begins and ends with this
> repudiation of resignation. Capable of trust in an absent God, human
> beings are also adults who assess their own weaknesses: the heroic
> situations in which they find themselves validate the world, but also
> bring it into danger. Matured by a faith that has come out of the
> Torah, they accuse God of his monstrous greatness and his exaggerated
> demands. They will love him – despite all the attempts that God has
> made to discourage their love. 'But you must not stretch the rope too
> far', exclaims Jossel ben Jossel. The religious life cannot be perfected in
> this heroic situation. God must unveil his face; righteousness and
> power must come together: there is a need for just institutions on this
> earth. But only the one who has recognized the veiled God can call
> for this unveiling. How powerful is the dialectic in which equality is
> established between God and human beings precisely in their dis-
> proportion![85]

The story of Jossel Rakover ends with a final dramatic twist. When the
ghetto threatens finally to fall, all at once Jossel remembers a story which
a rabbi told him. The story is set in the fifteenth/sixteenth century and is
about a Jew who fled the Spanish Inquisition with his wife and child. On
the stormy sea, in his small boat he had landed on a stony island. When
safety seemed in sight, a bolt of lightning came and struck his wife; then
a storm, which threw his child into the sea. Only he was left, stark naked,
stricken by the storm, terrified by thunder and lightning. When he landed
on the desolate rocky island the Jew raised his hands to God and spoke:

> God of Israel, I have fled here to worship you undisturbed: to do your
> commandments and to hallow your name. And you are doing every-

thing possible to make me not believe in you. But if it should seem to you that you are succeeding in turning me from the right way with these tribulations, let me tell you, my God and God of my parents, that it will be of no use to you. You may hurt me, you may strike me, you may take away from me the dearest and the best that I have in the world, you may torment me to death – but I will always believe in you. I will always love you, always, you, you, alone, despite you!

And those are also my last words to you, my angry God. It will be of no use to you! You have done everything possible to make me go astray, to make me stop believing in you. But I die as I have lived, with rocklike faith in you.[86]

V. Sketches of a theopoetics

Here too it is time to engage in some interim stocktaking and look back on the way that we have covered. I chose the procedure of recontextualizing. I wanted to bring texts to life by connecting them with their contemporary background and sphere of personal experience. It proved possible to show that for all the authors invoked here, talk of God arose out of a reaction to historical and personal upheavals. No armour of indifference and unshakenness surrounds these authors, nor even the demon of a leaden fatalism. Their talk of God came from the thin-skinned perception of shattering experiences which led to the following consequences:

- in the case of Friedrich Dürrenmatt, who deletes the word God from his text in order to do justice to the subject-matter, the shaking of the 'fact of the world', it led to asceticism in language,
- in the case of Marie Luise Kaschnitz, who concludes from the conviction that God's presence is given in the light and darkness of creation, embraces all moods, tones and light, and thus explodes our canon of ethical and aesthetic values, it led to the exploration of unprecedented conversations with God;
- and it led to the sketches of ever newer theologies of rebellion by Heinrich Heine, Elie Wiesel and Zvi Kolitz, who are guided by the conviction that one can also respect God by quarrelling with him.

These theopoetic texts are markers of a theopoetics that needs to be developed, i.e. a theory of what style is appropriate in speaking of God and adequate to today's awareness of language and time. Poetics differs from poetry as theology differs from faith. Just as theology is a reckoning with faith which is systematic, subject to scientific control, and capable of being tested by argument, so poetics is an account of the conditions of successful, appropriate poetic discourse (forms, stylistic means, technique). And theopoetics is giving an account of an appropriate discourse about God which corresponds to the present-day consciousness of language and time. If we let the theopoetic texts that have been selected here as examples work on us, the question arises: can principles for a talk of God which is appropriate today be derived from them? At the end of this section I want to contribute some reflections on this.

1. Work on language – in awareness of failure

The linguistic level of literary texts requires a different linguistic level of theology. Anyone who has been to the language school of the poets, returns with a sensitivity to language. A sensitivity to language means an' awareness of how well-worn the images of the tradition are, how stereotyped the phrases, how threadbare the linguistic conventions. A theology that has gone to the language school of the poets will break out of its own language-pattern and move forward to another language. However, this other language is possible only if talk of God still gives some intimation of the endangering of the existence from which it comes and makes it possible to detect something of the doubts which accompany the use of the great words. That would be a language in which people indicate the way in which they feel threatened, their readiness for risk, their lack of possessions, the fact that they are on the way – a vibrant language.

Great theologians have similarly required this other sense of language. One of them was Karl Rahner. In a moving speech on his eightieth birthday in 1984 he attempted to sum up his 'experiences' as a Catholic theologian. He died soon afterwards, so this speech became a kind of testament. In it Rahner programmatically emphasizes something that is constantly forgotten in the practice of theology: theologians speak of God, of God's existence, of God's personality, of three persons in God, of God's freedom, God's will which puts human beings under obligation (and of course they must do this). However, they usually forget that such talk is to some degree legitimate talk of God only when at the same time we as it were keep retracting it, maintain the 'uncanny fluctuation between yes and no' as the true and fixed point of our knowledge, and thus keep letting our statements drop 'into the silent incomprehensibility of God himself'.[87] But what about what is said from the cathedras, pulpits and 'hallowed dicasteria of the church'? It is not very obvious that they are stirred by an ultimate creaturely modesty which knows the only way in which we can really speak of God, which knows that all talk of God can only be the last moment before that blessed silence. And Rahner added:

I do not want to talk here at more length about the incomprehensibility of God, which is the true subject-matter of theology, nor can I. I only

want to testify to the experience that the theologian is really a theologian where he does not calmly think of talking in a clear and trans-
parent way, but is afraid of the analogous suspension between yes and
no over the abyss of God's incomprehensibility, and at the same time
experiences it and testifies to it in a blessed way. And I only want to
confess that as one poor theologian, in all my theology I think too little
about this analogous quality of all that I say. We spend too much time
in *talking* and in all this talk basically forget what we are talking about.[88]

2. Wresting the unutterable out of the speechless

That the suspension between yes and no is 'uncanny' has in fact to do
with the 'silent incomprehensibility of God himself', with what Karl
Rahner calls the 'abyss of the incomprehensibility of God'. For a theologian to talk of the 'silent incomprehensibility of God' builds a bridge of
understanding to poetry and literature. For poetry, too, comes from
advances to the extreme limits of what can be expressed in language.
Great poetry and literature, in particular, knows that any talk can come
only from the primal ground of silence, and is responsible to this primal
ground. What is said must be wrested from the unsaid and the unsayable.
But it is a dialectic in favour of what can be said, in the interest of speech.
And so God's incomprehensibility too is certainly a silent one, i.e. a
reality in which no language is adequate that could be deciphered or
eliminated by human language. But at the same time language is needed
in order to understand talk of the 'silent incomprehensibility'. Language
is needed to make it possible to express the failure of language. Thus trust
in language is needed to articulate mistrust in any language.

The same is the true of Christian theo-logy. It too ultimately stems
from the awareness that God's reality escapes any linguistic interpretation, that God remains beyond our control, inexpressible, incomprehensible. But Christian theology is worthy of its name only if it gives talk of
God and to God priority over silence. The prologue to the Gospel of John
does not say 'In the beginning was silence' but 'In the beginning was the
word'. That is an extraordinary bold statement, but its boldness dawns
on us only when we have experienced the fascination of wordless, object-
less meditation and the meaning of a disgust with language and the
impotence of language in theology. Thus the evangelist John has
formulated the creed that what God is, takes the form of a word. So the
word is not an external, even inferior, dimension of God, but God's
being. Thus 'God' is not identical with a mysterious enigmatic silence.

God is manifest – in the word. That is at the same time a consolation and a burden. That constitutes the greatness and the misery of any human talk of God.

So a reference to God's silence must not become an excuse for disqualifying talk of God, although this continually disqualifies itself. Reflecting on an ultimate importance of language before God must to lead to contempt for language, to an over-hasty surrender of speech. Max Frisch once described this two-sidedness of the power and impotence of language in his first 'Diary' under the heading 'On Writing':

> What is important is what cannot be said, the white between the words, and time and again these words speak of incidentals that we really do not mean. Our concern, our real concern, can at best be paraphrased, and that means quite literally that we write round it. We transpose it. We make statements that never contain our real experience – that remains unspeakable. They can only frame it, as closely and as accurately as possible, and the real, the unspeakable, at best appears as a tension between these statements.
>
> Presumably we make an effort to express everything that can be said; language is like a chisel which cuts away everything that is not mystery, and all saying amounts to a removing. It should not terrify us that everything that becomes word falls victim to a certain emptiness. We say what life is not. We say it for the sake of life. Language works like the sculptor when he uses the chisel, by forcing the emptiness, what can be said, against the mystery, against the living. There is always the danger that one will shatter the mystery, or, alternatively, that one will stop too soon, will leave it a lump, that one will not grasp the mystery, free it from all that could still be said, in short, that one will not penetrate to its last surface.
>
> This last surface of all that can ultimately be said, which must be one with the surface of the mystery, this immaterial surface which is there only for the spirit and not in nature, where there is no line between mountain and heaven – is that perhaps what is called form?
> A kind of sounding frontier – .[89]

It follows from this that if talk of God were successful in having in view both the dangers of language (as flogging the mystery to death) and the dangers of the cowardice of language (as ignoring the mystery), then it would be completely minding its own business. If theology were done (in analogy to poetry) in the awareness that not knowing is the basis and result of all talk of God; if it took seriously the fact that it has no control over what it thinks; that it does not have as an object that to which it testifies; that it can only point away from itself to a mystery in which ultimately no speech suffices, then it would not need to worry whether it was relevant.

The Tübingen Old Testament scholar Fridolin Stier, of whom we heard in the Prologue to this book, once envisaged such a theology. In his notes he wrote on 28 November 1970:

> If theology were born à la Samuel Beckett,
> and if such a Samuel Beckett came to Jesus of Nazareth,
> and Jesus called him,
> and he went with him,
> went further and further with him
> to the limits of language,
> and beyond,
> where the unspeakable strikes speech,
> and –
> if then this Samuel *theologus,*
> from there, from over there
> returned to the limit, to where
> language is still silent
> and the silence already begins to speak –
> then! Then?
> If theology
> if that happened to theology,
> if, if, if . . .[90]

The presupposition would be that one had learned from the poets and writers. The armour of indifference and unassailability needs to be stripped off; theologians need to show their own vulnerability, not to suppress doubts, not to keep quiet about their tribulations. What would need to be overcome would be a full, self-confident theological language, a triumphant certainty of salvation and a self-certain confidence in the law. What would need to be overcome would be any theological and spiritual jargon, any verbosity and the morass of language which has accumulated over the centuries, all the tacky pathos and the empty formulae of a domestic theological language which is like a secret code for the initiated. What would be required in view of the riddle surrounding God would not be a triumphalistic theology but a negative theology; not a theology constructed in a doctrinaire way but a narrative theology related to existence; not a theology that was officially safeguarded, but a theology that had been endured existentially. This would be not so much a theology in the spirit of rationalistic scholasticism as one in the spirit of the uncertain existential school of life.

3. The abyss of the incomprehensibility of God

Our theopoetic texts are an expression of a third option. The 'old conversations' about God and with God have been broken off. Dürrenmatt's deletion of the word 'God' from his own text is a symbol of that. This deletion was an act of protest against commandeering and trivialization by theology. It had to be done because the word 'God' had been misused by Christian theologians simply to endorse their views. In the 'old conversations' God is always the rock-solid guarantor of meaning and order, of persistence and security. The poets and writers reject this expectation without expressing a leaden godlessness. They pursue a third option, the option of being shaken and made uncertain through God and before God. God is not a standpoint that human beings could adopt in order to go into the world securely; the living God is not identical with bourgeois security. The reality of God is not to be identified with an ordered world which functions according to rules that can be seen by reason; the reality of God the abyss has nothing to do with religious feelings of harmony, peace and relaxation that one enjoys on Sunday morning. We read something different in the texts of the poets and writers. And the metaphor of the 'abyss' denotes, say in Friedrich Dürrenmatt, the possibility of a terror that God himself wills, a questioning of the 'fact of the world'. The 'abyss' stands for the silent unfathomability of God.

Granted, the texts of Marie Luise Kaschnitz, Heinrich Heine, Elie Wiesel and Zvi Kolitz do not speak directly of God as the abyss, but in their own way they do express the incomprehensibility of God. Marie Luise Kaschnitz's 'Tutzing Poems' are the expression of a riddling over God and a complaint about God. But they are also the expression of a quest for unprecedented conversations with God, for a presence of God in all the dimensions of creation. For her, to participate in God's being means to have 'a share in the incomprehensible oppositions' of God's nature. This author sees the light of God 'over every human birth as over every shoot which breaks from the earth'. The monstrosity and incomprehensibility of God consists in the discovery that dust and refuse, the noise of motors and machines, are faces and voices of God. Kaschnitz's texts are the expression of a radical aestheticizing of God while at the same time withdrawing the ethicizing of God.

We find the opposite movement of thought in Heine, Wiesel and Kolitz – along the lines of Old Testament texts of lamentation. The incomprehensibility of God is an experience of the present. God seems to be blind to human destiny, insensitive to human suffering, deaf to human complaints and arbitrary in showing his righteousness. God has become a life-threatening monster who shatters happiness and destroys security. But this experience presupposes a criterion from the past. God was once a God on whom one could rely, whose righteousness was trustworthy, whose concern for human beings was touching. And this trust from the past is projected on to the future. For people rebel against God because they trust in God's obligation to himself. People quarrel with God because they are waiting for God's justification of himself. People seize hold of God because they do not let go of him. People attempt to stir God up because their feelings for him are not dead and their hopes have not been killed off. Despite God they love this God.

The challenge to theology posed by theopoetic talk of God can be taken up. And here talk of God as the abyss helps to clarify things. In normal terminology the word has purely negative connotations. It prompts dismay, terror, fear. And in fact the abyss can be understood in this way: as devouring vengeance, as a pitfall of chaos, as a shaft of destruction. So theologians prefer not to speak of God as an abyss but as a ground, as the ground of all grounds, in order to express that God is ultimately reliable, trustworthy and gives orientation.

But talk of God as ground can be misunderstood (the history of Dürrenmatt's story makes this abundantly clear): harmonizing, trivializing, soothing. As if God were always and in any case a reliable basis on which one could rely; as if God were the reliable partner with whom one could go untroubled through life; as if God were a kind of assurance against risks in life.

The phrase 'God the abyss' attempts an intellectual synthesis. On the one hand it seeks to maintain that God is not simply a crisis-free basis on which one can naively rely. God as abyss means that even as the power in which faith is grounded God remains free, incalculable, incomprehensible. The great Christian mystics have spoken of God as abyss in this sense.[91] According to Meister Eckhart:

If God sees that we are his beloved sons, then God comes so powerfully to us and he rushes so fast and acts as if his divine being would break and annihilate itself in itself, so that he reveals to us the whole abyss of his deity and the fullness of his being and his nature.[92]

According to Johannes Tauler, too, one must speak of a groundlessness of God which is inaccessible to reason. Indeed, Tauler speaks of the 'abyss of the groundlessness of God' and says that 'the created abyss flows into the uncreated and becomes one with this there: a nothing in the other nothing.'[93]

Talk of the abyss must be understood in this sense of an unreachable, unfathomable depth of God, an incomprehensibility and hiddenness of God. God is the ground of the world, but in a way which is appropriate for him. God is not a ground on which human beings can build or think. God grounds in a way that accords with him, in freedom, incomprehensibility and hiddenness. Talk of the abyss is meant to preserve this dimension of a last withdrawal of God. Karl Rahner once gave a fine description of this notion:

> The real God is the absolute, holy mystery to which one can really point only in prayer and silence – to himself as a ground which keeps silent, which is the abyss and thus grounds everything in the world and our knowledge of the world. God is the one beyond whom by definition one cannot go, because in any discovery of a 'formula for the world' (which would then no longer really be explicable) one would certainly not even get beyond oneself. The formula for the world itself, were it to be understood, would once again remain in suspension in the infinity of the mystery.[94]

4. The theological legitimacy of an accusation against God

Conversations need to be carried on between theologians and writers about these experiences of God as the abyss. Conversations need to be carried on about 'trembling' talk of God and vibrant talk of God, about the need to talk of God and at the same time constantly to withdraw this talk as inadequate; about the doubt and tribulation which first makes one's own history of faith a history of faith; about the monstrous suspension between yes and no; as the 'true and only fixed point in our knowledge' . . .

Critical discussion with the theopoesy of the poets and writers shows that talk of God cannot mislead people about the 'abyss of the incomprehensibility of God'. Theopoesy must be understood as 'mystagogy' in Rahner's sense: as an initiation or guide to the mystery of God the abyss. Here doubt is the brother of faith. For faith in God is not a silencing of the questions but an accentuation of them. If God's creation is indeed 'good', the perversities keep putting this in question, monstrosities which can simply drive people to despair about God's very incomprehensibility.

This produces situations of quarrelling with God. In many writers it gives rise to a basic attitude of simultaneity (already anticipated archetypally by Heinrich Heine). This is a simultaneity of trust and scepticism, surrender and blasphemy, humility and rebellion. It gives rise to situations in which the cry to God can be a last act of trust: indignation against God feeds on expectations and the quarrelling that comes from love – in keeping with the sentence by Elie Wiesel that I have quoted often: 'The opposite of love is not hatred but indifference; the opposite of life is not death but a lack of feeling.' In Jewish authors in particular we were able to see that the rebellion of human beings against God can be their form of prayer; quarrelling their form of saying yes; protest their declaration of love to God.

5. Against a 'lying optimism'

What follows from this for a contemporary theology, particularly for a Christian theology? On the occasion of Karl Rahner's eightieth birthday, mentioned above, the German Protestant theologian Eberhard Jüngel gave a lecture on 'The Revelation of the Hiddenness of God'. In it Jüngel first warned about a distinction which is important for the biblical and Christian understanding of God. The hiddenness and incomprehensibility of God as expressed in the gospel of Jesus Christ cannot be compared with the darkness of the abyss or a reserve to which there is no access. Rather, it is to be compared with an excess of light. According to I Timothy, God, 'whom no human being has seen and can see', dwells 'in light inaccessible' (6.16). This metaphor of light for God is inadequate in that it has a twofold content: light stands for life, power, knowledge; but at the same time – if light is too intense, as with the sun – it stands for terror, blinding, pain, annihilation. Even as 'light', God thus remains unfathomable, incomprehensible, indeed terrible. And precisely here Jüngel sees a possibility of complaint and accusation. Complaint and accusation can be a mode of glorifying God:

> The glorification of God is the basic determination of right human talk of God – including the dimension of complaint to God . . . God is not dishonoured, but glorified, when people talk with God in such a way as to address their complaints or even accusations to him. God would be not be honoured, but rather the reverse, and we would be refusing

him the glorification which is his due, if we did not also address our complaints and accusations to him if it were to come to that. Silence would be blasphemous, for we would then fail to offer him the truth. But one cannot dishonour God in a worse way than to fail to offer him the truth.[95]

Practical conclusions can be drawn from these fundamental reflections. Here too I shall keep to guidelines laid down by Karl Rahner. At an early stage he rightly required a theologian – say in preaching – to show 'in a relaxed and brotherly way that he too suffers tribulations in faith' and is someone who 'time and again must prove faith to himself'.[96] The preacher must know something of a 'mystical' distress in faith, which for Rahner means, existentially: 'Faith as enduring the silence of God, the "night" of faith; the apparent "shrinking" of faith as a concentration; faith (despite the material difference in its content) as silence about God; the recognition of the Lord only in the "breaking of the bread" for the "stranger" (Luke 24.31); the permanent resurrection of faith from the tomb of unbelief.'[97] So Rahner could require:

> The preacher must not speak as if his message could change the world and the existence of the individual into empty light and harmony, which can be accepted only in faith. Basically, the 'solution' given by Christianity to all questions of life is resolutely to hold them open without the short cut of radical pessimism and scepticism, and without a lying optimism which thinks that it now already 'has' the solution, is 'hope against all hope', salvaging all that is incomprehensible, not in a transparent solution but in the incomprehensible mystery of God and his freedom. That does not 'solve' anything, but is unconditional acceptance of the impossibility of solving the mystery that is called God. And that means believing and hoping and loving.[98]

So where faith forgets or denies that doubt is its brother, it is in danger of becoming an ideology which confuses God with idols. But since the incomprehensibility of God is the ground and abyss of all faith, true faith also includes a protest against all too easy reassurances. It consists in the courage to rely on the incomprehensibility of God, even if it has sides which are dark for human beings. Belief in God firmly resists all too easy certainties and all too self-certain unbelief. Along these lines, in his programmatic farewell lecture at the University of Münster in 1993, one of Karl Rahner's most influential pupils, Johann Baptist Metz, called for a 'disturbed' theology:

Talk of God always comes from talk to God, theology from the language of prayer . . . the language of prayer is not only universal but also tense and dramatic, much more rebellious and radical than the language of the discipline of theology. It is far more disturbing, far more uncomforted, far less harmonious. Have we ever perceived what has accumulated over millennia of the history of religion in the language of prayers . . . the crying and the jubilation, the lament and the song, the despair and the mourning and the final dumbness? Have we perhaps orientated ourselves too much on a language of prayer which has been tamed by the church and liturgy, by the one-sided images from the biblical tradition? What about Job's lament 'How long?' . . . The Son's cry of desolation, and Marantha, as the last word of the New Testament? This language is far more capable of resistance, far less malleable and ready for use, far less forgettable than the language of Platonism and idealism, in which theology is concerned about how compatible it is with modernity and with which it tests its perplexing firmness in the face of all catastrophes and all experiences of non-identity.[99]

And Jesus, the Christ? We shall have to go on a third journey and see how great authors have dealt with the figure of the man from Nazareth. We shall see that talk of God as abyss and reflection on the figure of Jesus Christ are not very far from each other. To point the way forward, I shall end this section with a remark by one of the greatest writers of this century, Franz Kafka. If we are to believe the conversations he had which have been recorded by Gustav Janosch, this is what Kafka said – and his remark allows us to think of the metaphors of abyss and light together in a congenial way:

'What is faith?' *And Kafka answered*:
'Whoever has faith cannot define it, and the shadow of un-grace burdens those who do not. Therefore the believer cannot speak and the unbeliever should not. The prophets really speak always only of the supports of faith and never of faith alone.'
'You are talking about the faith which is silent about itself.'
'Yes, that is so.'
'And Christ?'
Kafka bowed his head.
'That is an abyss full of light. One has to close one's eyes so as not to fall into it.'[100]

C. Faces of Jesus

And you, master, prepare for the cruellest
execution,
so that human beings may become open to goodness and compassion,
so that they may perceive the fundamental difference
between the rational and the irrational,
for laborious is the way of man on earth,
and evil is deeply rooted in him.

C. Ajmatov

I. The rebel spared

He was forty-six when homesickness drove him back to Germany. For twelve years now he had been living in Paris, and he had not seen his homeland in all that time. Years of success and conflict lay behind him: the battle against the powers of the Metternich restoration; above all the state religion, where potentates and clerics attempted arm in arm to exterminate the democratic-republican spirit; the exhausting battle against censorship and the prohibition of his own writings, especially in Prussia, against spies and informers, former friends and old enemies . . .

What he saw on his way through Germany in October 1843, whether in Aachen or Cologne, Paderborn or Minden, Hanover or Hamburg, led him to write a satirical poem made up of dreams: *Deutschland – A Winter's Tale*.

1. Dialogue with the 'poor cousin': Heinrich Heine

Suddenly – by no coincidence, near Catholic Paderborn – he encountered the man on the cross in the form of a wayside shrine. This gave rise to an *Ecce homo* poem in six strophes, which has archetypal significance in German literature and thus also anticipates in both style and content the German literature of the twentieth century:

> Poor cousin, it always makes me sad
> when I recall your behaviour;
> you wanted to redeem the world,
> you fool, to play the saviour!
>
> They played a nasty trick on you,
> those high Establishment Pharisees.
> Criticism of Church and State
> was the worst of all possible heresies.

If only you'd written a *book* to show
that religion needed renewing.
But printing wasn't invented then,
that was your undoing.

The censor would have cut what fell
in his worldly jurisdiction.
Censorship would have lovingly
preserved you from crucifixion.

If only your Sermon on the Mount
had shown no political bias –
you had talent and intellect enough
not to tread on the corns of the pious.

You even whipped from the temple courts
the bankers and money-changers –
hapless idealist, there you now hang
to warn us ideals have dangers.[1]

This is in fact a unique conversation between the baptized Jew Heinrich Heine and his poor Jewish 'cousin' from Nazareth, unique in style and pointed content, which in future would also stamp the 'modern' literary picture of Jesus: an interpretation by the artist in terms of self-identification; a political universalization of the 'cause'; the discrepancy between Jesus and the church.

The portrait of Jesus as a self-portrait

The note of irony in this text is unmistakeable, and for its author irony seems the only possible way of dealing with an event like the cross, which loaded the Christian tradition theologically and charged it sacrally. This theological load is what Heine wants to free the cross from. He points forward to modern literature particularly in the way in which he detaches talk of the crucified Jesus from any dogmatic and sacral context and earths it historically. *Ecce homo*: the man on the cross is not the redeemer of the world, but a fool who has got his quittance for something as foolish as the message of the kingdom of God. And he, Harry Heine, has seen through the structure of the thing: the innovators always become fools because they engage in actions instead of tactics, practise confrontation instead of compromise. One can only laugh at this kind of 'saviour of humankind'!

And yet very soon one notices that in this text the ironical superiority is only an apparent one, put on show and played out. In reality the baptized Jew from Düsseldorf who had himself baptized without ever being able to become a Christian, and who seems to have seen through the 'unfortunate enthusiast' on the cross (the adaptation was not sufficiently refined; in the end one is oneself to blame for such an end), is not 'outside' but in the middle of things. The split in the story of Jesus is his own. For what at first sight could be understood as a mocking trivialization of the event of the cross is in Heine basically an attempt at a self-portrait in which he sees himself, to use Ernst Bloch's phrase, 'distorted to the point of being recognizable'.

Thus in reality the Jesus irony in this text is the self-irony of a man who has got wise to himself. If we look at it closely, strophe by strophe connections can be recognized between then and now: hadn't he himself once set out to redeem the world? Hadn't the 'high lords' similarly played with him as he had similarly spoken so 'recklessly' of church and state? Doesn't he have dealings with bankers (Baron Rothschild) now, in Paris? Indeed, isn't his own survival an expression of refined adaptation to circumstances which he fought just like the 'poor cousin' of those days? How 'merciful' censorship is today by comparison with the crosses of former times! *Ecce homo*: the man on the cross is himself, though he cannot in his own person claim the consequences of passion and cross. For all the distance from the Good Friday man (such an end was not necessary), the irony is only the mask of someone who did not draw such consequences; the mockery disguises respect for a way which the Jew from Nazareth took consistently to the end. One feels related to Jesus as to a cousin, but does not want to be as 'poor' as he was . . .

Golgotha is everywhere

But this identification and self-interpretation of the artist is possible only on the basis of his insight into the laws of political balances of power. Heine is one of the first writers to read the Jesus story above all politically. For him, Jesus' basic conflict is a universal one, because it is then repeated structurally whenever the message of freedom, equality and brotherhood comes up against the forces of repression, thinking in terms of class, class-selfishness. There are crucifixions everywhere and at all times, as is said in Goethe's *Faust* about the great spirits of humankind:

'The foolish few who, with such knowledge, failed
to keep their wealth of intuitions in their hearts

revealed their feelings and their visions to the rabble,
have in all times been crucified and burned (lines 591–3).

Heine, who revered Goethe, was familiar with this passage, and it stands
behind his own political universalization of the Jesus story. Moreover for
Heine his Jewish fellow-sufferer Baruch de Spinoza, whose life was 'as
pure and spotless as the life of his divine cousin, Jesus Christ', stands in
the same line: 'Like him he suffered for his teaching, like him he wore the
crown of thorns. Wherever a great spirit expresses his thoughts, there is
Golgotha.'² *Ecce homo*. The man on the cross is Everyman.

Jesus, yes; Christ, no

And a third thing becomes clear: if anywhere in German literature, then
already with Heinrich Heine, the conviction has become established that
for writers it is not the Christ of churches and dogmas, not the Christ of
theologians and priests, Christ the Redeemer and miracle-worker, the
eternal Son of God, a second person of the Trinity, but the concrete Jesus
of history who is still of interest and importance – in that remarkable
mixture of identification and universalization. If anyone in German
literature has made the antithesis 'Jesus yes – Christ no' an independent
theme, then it is this man on the frontiers of Judaism and Christianity.
Jesus – yes: he belongs in the great human, democratic and republican
history of freedom, which is certainly always also the history of failure
and the cross, yet its failure does not contradict its truth. This Jesus is a
redeemer – certainly, but a rebellious, enlightened, provocative redeemer
who 'freed his brother from the ceremonial law and nationalistic religion
and founded cosmopolitanism'. But at the same time he becomes 'a
victim of his humanity' – 'and the city magistrate of Jerusalem had him
crucified and the mob mocked him'.³

And the Christ of dogma? How have things been in the history of
dogma? Nothing has emerged from this, Heine thinks, but 'dogmatic
pedantries' in which the sophistry of ancient Greece has announced itself
once again. Nothing but 'disputes over disciplinary and church interests',
in which the legal casuistry and ruling skills of ancient Rome have
established themselves with new forms and means of compulsion.⁴ No,
Heine cannot see anything exalted and edifying in the history of dogmas,
far less any trace of a struggle over depth and truth in understanding
Christ. . . For him, political intrigues, a perception of interests and
power-plays are at work everywhere in history, and particularly in the

origin of the dogmatic edifice of the church. For what really stands in the background of such questions as 'Was the Logos *homoousios* with God the Father? Was Mary to be called mother of God or mother of man? Did Christ hunger for want of food because he wanted to hunger?'[5] What really lies behind such questions? Heine replies:

> Behind all these questions lie sheer court intrigues, the solution of which depends on what is whispered and giggled in the chambers of the sacred palace, whether e.g. Eudoxia or Pulcheria is pleased – one lady hates Nestorius, who betrays her love affairs, and the other hates Cyril, whom Pulcheria protects. In the end everything relates to women's gossip and chatter, and in the dogma it is really the man, and in the man a party, which is being persecuted or promoted. It's the same in the West: Rome wanted to rule; 'when its legions fell it sent the dogmas into the provinces'.[6]

2. Jesus and writers today

In the adoption of an attitude to Jesus of Nazareth one does not need to look far in contemporary German literature to find Heine's influence directly or indirectly. In my conversations with writers I have encountered the following quite representative remarks. 'I have difficulties with Christ', says Wolfdietrich Snurre, and immediately adds: 'not with the historical Jesus, who was a terrorist, a revolutionary and an innovator. No, I have trouble with the Christ figure.'[7] 'For me Christ stands in the line of the rebels, heretics and outsiders,' remarks Karin Strick. She continues: 'What I cannot understand is the fact that the outsider in our culture has been made an insider. The outsider becomes so to speak the dutiful person.'[8] Ingeborg Drewitz's remarks are similar: 'Jesus too is bound up with a tradition in a society which had become almost chauvinistic. In this society he went against all the rules. He quite deliberately shattered the burdens which rested on people, whether by addressing the socially disadvantaged in precisely the same way as the rich, indeed treating them with greater involvement and tenderness than the Pharisees; or by breaking through barriers; or by approaching the main power, the Roman forces of occupation, in precisely the same way as he did the Samaritan who had been also cast out and was a stranger. Jesus put everything in question in the knowledge that every human being has the same right to exist; also that those who are privileged have a greater obligation not to keep themselves to themselves.'[9]

It is clear that it is the revolutionary element in Jesus, his role as a heretic and outsider, which links the writers of our time with Jesus of Nazareth: the amazing abolition of conventions and class barriers, the egalitarian and the democratic, the social and the philanthropic. Whether consciously or not, that is the spirit of Heine's spirit. 'For me,' remarks the Swiss writer Adolf Muschg, 'Christ is the anti-church, anti-institutional existence *par excellence,* and is also indispensable for artistic work and social contexts. And I would like, more than I can today, also to make that readiness for surprising behaviour which I read in the Gospels the maxim for my life.'[10]

Whatever may be theologically or historically accurate or inaccurate in these personal statements, whatever of them can be agreed with or must be disagreed with, they are to be taken seriously as testimonies to experience and life. They signal two things:

An unbridgeable gulf from dogma

The discrepancy between the Jesus of the literary figures and the Christ of the church and dogma is not only terrifying but also in principle seems unbridgeable. Is a wider gulf conceivable between what challenges writers (who here represent countless critical contemporaries) in Jesus and what theologians and church representatives say and preach about him dogmatically? Here the heretic and rebel, there the divine redeemer, God-man and Second Person of the Trinity; in short, here the social outsider and there the dutiful religious person? And indeed, where is there an author of our time for whom the Christ of the theologians, pastors and priests is still an issue, let alone an occasion for literary productivity? Where is the Christ poem in contemporary literature which shows Christ as prescribed by purely orthodox doctrine, a poem of the kind that representatives of traditional Christian literature like Reinhold Schneider, Rudolf Alexander Schröder and Getrud von Le Fort could still write? Where is the Christ epic of our time which, like Klopstock's *Messiah,* could still show Jesus as a divine mediator who has solitary conversations with God about his role as redeemer of the world? Where is there a writer of the present for whom words like 'catechism' and 'dogmatic' are not synonymous with hostility to the Enlightenment and a prohibition on thinking? That leads to a second point.

The man from Nazareth is spared criticism

For writers of contemporary literature, too, Jesus Christ, whether affirmed or disputed, remains an archetype of unadapted, rebellious, provocative humanity, an authority to refer to in whom the discrepancy between utopian ideal and wretched reality is unsparingly exposed, and in the light of whom the political and social realization of promises is found fault with. I have discovered that if there is one theme in the literary concern with Jesus among writers of our time, it is *the sparing of Jesus*. In other words, despite all the criticism of the church which is often so bitter, in most cases Jesus himself is spared criticism, treated gently, indeed often himself made the sharpest critic of a church and society which is all too confident of being legitimated by him. And more than anything else in Christian culture, the topic of Christmas is well suite to demonstrating this simultaneity of a radical criticism of society and the sparing of a utopian Jesus.

II. Christmas: the utopia and its betrayal

We can best see the profile of twentieth-century literature if we set it against backgrounds from the last two centuries.[11] Once upon a time there was a unity of literature and church belief, of poetry and theology. And once upon a time there was a unity of literature and religious feeling, literature and Christian morality. Let's examine this.

1. What was possible for former centuries

In the middle of the eighteenth century an author like Christian Fürchtgott Gellert (1715–1769) could still write a Christmas song which was programmatically composed as a church hymn. It appeared in Gellert's 'Spiritual Odes and Songs' in 1757 – Goethe was eight years old, Schiller was to be born two years later. This university teacher and poet who worked in Leipzig was extremely popular in his time; he used every literary possibility to influence the lives of his fellow citizens, educating them and moralizing with fables, games, poems, letters and a novel.

Gellert kneels before the miracle

Moreover many of his poems belong to the repertory of German middle-class Christianity far beyond Gellert's time, made popular not least by many settings, including Beethoven's 'The Heavens praise the Eternal Glory', and also our Christmas hymn:

> This is the day that God has made,
> to him be all due honour paid.
> Glory to him, through Jesus' birth,
> from all that is on heaven and earth.

Lord, praise for you will never cease,
Immanuel and Prince of Peace,
Christ, whom the fathers longed to see,
now born a man we worship thee.[12]

In seven strophes Christmas can still be illustrated along the lines of church dogma as a great act of salvation and grace, as a great miracle for mankind. Men of letters still make no claim to originality in matters of theology. In complete innocence they put themselves at the service of church faith, which they want to illustrate fully and beautifully with the help of their texts. There is not a trace of doubt in the content. Completely secure in the Christian certainty of salvation, the poet with his work understood himself to be the mouthpiece of the church; a a moral teacher of Christianity; a guide of the people; an educator of the masses . . .

Eichendorff's vision of a reconciled world

A good century later the content of dogma could no longer be described like this in literature. What challenged the new generation of poets was more to describe the emotional effect of Christmas. And the great unity of faith and feeling which was expressed in Romanticism with a religious bent could be put into verse in a unique way when it came to the topic of Christmas. In 1837, eighty years after Gellert, a poem entitled 'Christmas' was written by Joseph von Eichendorff, who at that time was an adviser to the Prussian government:

Streets and market stand forsaken,
Gently shines each home with light,
As I pass by church and steeple
On this solemn, holy night.

Garlands made by loving mothers
Hang by every window pane.
Quietly joyful, sisters, brothers
Greet the season come again.

From the walls, outside my roaming
Leads into the countryside.
Awe and wonder in the gloaming,
Silence reigning far and wide.

Clear on high the stars are swinging,
From the snow's bright, lonely face
Rise the sounds of wondrous singing.
O you time so full of grace![13]

This poem is no longer a prayer, composed of theological themes from
the incarnation to messialogy, which invites us to bend the knee piously
before the Christian wonder, but a view from outside. At the centre
stands a solitary traveller who is intoxicated by the effects of the Christmas
feast. This traveller is to embody not the intellectual harmony of faith
and reason but the feeling of harmony between the inner world and the
world outside. Eichendorff's figure observes Christmas from the streets,
alleyways and country, and at the same time an inner dramaturgy is
constructed. But it follows an expansion of space which is inconspicuously achieved in this poem.

Thus the gaze of the traveller (and with him the reader) goes from the
market place and the streets over the open country to heaven and the
stars. This external expansion of space is matched by an inner intensification of feeling: from the senses through awe to an almost ecstatic
exclamation, 'O you time so full of grace!' This dynamic of expansion of
the Christmas mood is repeated with the persons mentioned in the poem:
I – mothers – children; and it is repeated in the setting: 'every window
pane' – 'countryside' – 'snow's lonely face' – 'stars on high'; and it is
repeated in the lights and tones of the poem: the 'quiet joy' of the happy
children is taken up and intensified in the 'wondrous singing' which
now resounds throughout the world. In his own way Eichendorff
thus introduces a universal cosmic dimension which had always been
associated with Christmas in the Christian tradition: the birth of Christ
as a new time of grace which transforms this world inwardly. In the
silence, light and song at Christmas, the vision of a reconciled world is
developed, a world without economic conflicts, without social rejections,
without spiritual distortion and political disputes – in a poem of
enthralling simplicity, still tenderness and inconspicuous happiness.

Storm's Knecht Ruprecht takes stock

Indeed, in the first half of the nineteenth century the Romantic poets still
delivered what was expected of them: the great unity of faith and feeling
advanced in literature. And later also the great unity of faith and morality.
The shift from illustrating dogmatics through synthesizing the world of

feelings to the propagation of morality is also typical of the second half of the nineteenth century – in literature often stamped by middle-class Protestantism. We are indebted to Theodor Storm for such a text in connection with Christmas, which with good reason is one of the favourite texts of middle-class Germany. Here Storm stands in the tradition of giving an educational function to the feast of Christmas, a development which is evident above all in the figures of the 'Christ child' or 'Nicolas' and 'Knecht Ruprecht'.

From comprehensive research into folklore and custom we know today that:[14]

- since the Counter-Reformation the figure of Nicolas has been associated with visits to children's homes;
- since the second half of the seventeenth century in the German-speaking world the best-known companion of Nicolas is 'Knecht Ruprecht';
- 'Knecht Ruprecht' is a dark, shaggy, black figure of terror who points back to the devil and thus is a numinous negative figure from the 'realm of evil';
- the main purpose of such a companion is to discipline badly brought up children through terror, at a very early stage with three possible levels of punishment: pulling their hair or beating them with the rod; then the threat to carry them off to a distant place; and finally the announcement that disobedient children will be killed or even eaten.

Moves for educational reform in the Enlightenment, which opposed such excesses in this custom, did not bring about much fundamental change in this widespread practice: it persisted in middle-class circles even in the nineteenth and twentieth centuries. On the contrary, the educational means of pre-Christmas visits to children by figures of terror who instilled anxiety became increasingly important in the subsequent period. From around the middle of the nineteenth century onwards it was predominantly the middle-class educational system that unthinkingly used Nicolas and his companions as an instrument of discipline. Where parental admonitions over the year had not helped, and instruction at school had borne little fruit, Christmas Eve promised educationalists the necessary effect. Here was an opportunity, with the help of a mysterious visitor surrounded by an aura of omniscience, to engage in a moralizing stock-taking, to encourage or intimidate, indeed to reward or punish children's behaviour. Nicolas, Knecht Ruprecht and Father Christmas thus became fixed features in the repertory of family educational measures.

This has found literary expression in the Christmas story 'Under the Christmas Tree' which Theodore Storm, at that time a local magistrate in Heiligenstadt, wrote in 1862.[15] For this text, too, is governed by a moralizing dualism of good and evil. Here too 'Knecht Ruprecht' is the helper of the Christ Child, who is to divide the good children from the bad, and whose rod is an appropriate instrument:

'Is your sack all ready here?'
I said, 'Yes, it will bring good cheer,
For pious children love to eat,
Apples, nuts and chestnuts sweet.'
'Do you have the rod here too?'
I said, 'The rod is here in view
But only for bad girls and boys
Who spoil for others all their joys.'
The Christchild spoke: 'A start is made;
Then go with God, my faithful aide.'
From forest deep I shall appear,
I tell you, Christmastide is near.
Now say, who shall I meet with here,
Children bad or children dear?'[16]

Here the moralizing of the Christmas theme within middle-class Christianity comes to a literary climax. Through the language of lowliness adapted to the children's world ('Christchild') glimmers a punitive pedagogy. Alongside 'apples, nuts and chestnuts sweet' there flashes the bare bottom which the rod can strike. Like the motto which in the story is put in the mouth of Knecht Ruprecht, 'Do they not tell you in this town, bow the head and trousers down'?[17]

This unity of literature and church faith, literature and middle-class feelings, literature and middle-class morality has been shattered in twentieth-century literature. At the latest with the catastrophe of the First World War, authors begin to use the theme of Christmas in quite a different way. Literature now stems not from the unity of the worlds but from the split between them, from the conflicts, the contradictions, the abysses in society. Christmas is told of as non-Christmas. The holy time is related as an unholy time. The images are set against counter-images, the expectations countered by events, the utopia of Christmas is combined with a wretched or false reality.

2. Cracks in the scenery

The first breaks are recognizable in one of the greatest novels in German literature, which stands as a giant portal at the beginning of this century, Thomas Mann's *Buddenbrooks* (1901). Anyone who has read the Christmas scene in the house of the Senator's family in 4 Mengstrasse, Lübeck, will never forget this rift, indeed the indications of abysses in the middle-class world, which Thomas Mann demonstrates with narrative mastery in this particular Christmas scene.[18] All the trimmings of Christmas are still present in this middle-class world: the family party and the songs, the wealth of presents and the giant Christmas tree with the 'realistic crib at its feet'. All the familiar sounds ring out in this world: 'Rejoice, O Daughter of Zion'; 'Rejoice, Jerusalem'; 'Silent Night' – in three parts, 'O Christmas Tree'. And the Christmas chapter from the 'great Bible' is read out as it always has been: 'and to men goodwill'.

Not a whole world in Buddenbrooks: *Thomas Mann*

But all this is described in such uncanny and perceptive detail that the reader is meant to recognize the ambiguity of the scene. Everything is still there, but nothing is genuine any more; it's all a staged scene. Christmas is a world which once a year is put on to deceive oneself and others. Family harmony? That's imposed, artificially generated; in reality it has broken. Those taking part in the festival? They come together once again, but act like players on a stage.

– Frau Consul Buddenbrook, mother of the now 'ruling' Senator Thomas Buddenbrook, needs this Christmas festival every year to preserve the illusion of a whole family. The 'consecrated programme' which her dead husband 'had appointed for the ceremony' must be maintained.

– Tony Buddenbrook, the sister of the ruling Senator, has two failed marriages behind her, and the marriage of her daughter also threatens to end in a catastrophe, because her husband, Director Hugo Weinschenk, has been accused of fraudulent manipulation in a current trial. While the 'consecrated programme' runs its course, it leads the family to have 'un-Christmaslike thoughts'. And just think: a member of the family has been 'accused of a crime against the laws, civil order and social honesty, and perhaps will incur shame and prison'. It is really inconceivable, 'a Christmas Eve for the Buddenbrook family with an accused man in their midst'.

– Christian Buddenbrook, the brother of the ruling senator, is an unproductive, unreliable roué. Significantly, he had 'almost forgotten' the familiar Christmas festival. And hardly has he appeared than he feels the urge to mock the mood of Christmas Eve with frivolous profanities. He tells of a Christmas Eve which he spent 'in London in a fifth-rate variety hall' and caricatures the procession into the room in which the presents will be given out 'by lifting his legs' when marching 'like a jumping jack' and singing 'O Christmas Tree' in a stupid way; at dinner he then tells of the Christmas celebrations in his club, which were 'very jolly': 'Those fellows drank Swedish punch like water.'

– Hanno Buddenbrook, the only son of the ruling Senator, is put to bed at the end of the second Christmas evening and as he goes to sleep he sees – anticipating the fate of the family – 'the misfortune of the previous year'. While Sesemi Weichbrot, Tony's teacher and a friend of the family, was speaking at the Christmas celebrations, three times uttering emphatically the Pauline 'Rejoice', a transparency over the door garlanded with a branch of fir bearing the inscription 'Glory to God in the highest' had gone up in flames. Mademoiselle Weichbrot had stood there, a comic figure, 'who with a little shriek and a sidestep of unexpected picturesqueness and agility managed to avoid the rain of sparks which descended on her'. Moreover the author makes Hanno end this Christmas evening – recalling this grotesque scene – like this: 'For several minutes he was totally seized with laughter, irritated and nervously amused, gently sinking back on his cushion . . .'

Kurt Tucholsky's Christmas melancholy

Hanno Buddenbrook's chuckling over the Christmas catastrophe is like an anticipation of scornful laughter at the downfall of the whole family. And this 'downfall' anticipates the fall of the whole middle-class world which is to follow a few years later. The First World War is *the* break in this century. After that, nothing in Germany was the same again. This inevitably had consequences for the topic of Christmas in literature. Moreover the most significant Christmas poem in this period looks very different. It was published on 19 December 1918 in the *Weltbühne*, a few months after the end of the Great War. It was written by Kurt Tucholsky, who had taken part in the war, and is the mourning and lamentation of someone returning home to find himself in a 'Fatherland in ruins'.[19] 'Christmas' sets off in him childhood memories full of sorrow and melancholy:

> Back in this ruined German city
> I quietly sing my Christmas song.

No longer need I heed or pity
the distant world's great load of wrong.
That is for others. Ours the tears.
I gently hum, quite as can be,
a tune from childhood years:
O Christmas tree.

But then the poet abandons all resignation. 'Knecht Ruprecht' reappears, but now given a political function by Tucholsky, the political satirist. With the help of the popular Knecht Ruprecht myth, this 'popular educationalist' indicates that the Germans are obviously quite unteachable. For even an appearance by Knecht Ruprecht with his rod would be of no use to the Germans:

Were I Knecht Ruprecht now returning
back to this scene of grief and pain
– the Germans will accept no learning –
God knows I would turn round again.
No bread or flour left in the house.
Noise in the street, crude jollity.
I'd love to hang them on your boughs,
O Christmas tree!

The third and final strophe poses the political questions even more acutely. Now for Tucholsky the Christmas tree is no longer a symbol of bourgeois idylls but of political resistance. As one gazes at the candles, the question of guilt arises. Who is to blame for it all – the war, the misery, the sacrifices? This question is raised with great indignation. Anger rises up. And this anger born of unspeakable disappointment is directed against a people which is evidently bearing its fate passively with the patience of a lamb, and instead of bringing about better times is waiting for them. Against that background the 'old dream' is dreamed that with the help of the revolution one may finally be able to conquer the pitch darkness. The situation must change; trust in the ruling elites (the army, financiers, industry, church leaders) must finally be renounced. And only after the achievement of political freedom can one sing the Christmas songs freely. Then 'Christmas' can no longer be used as a narcotic, to lull the people into temporary bliss. Christmas feelings have a place when they are an expression of real freedom:

I stare at the twinkling candles:
Who is the cause of all our misery?

Who brought on us the blood and scandals?
Us lamblike Germans, patient as can be.
The candles do not suffer, do not strain.
A dream of old comes back to me.
O people, put an end to all this pain!
Never believe these men again!
Then joyfully you'll sing the glad refrain:
O Christmas tree, O Christmas tree!

Erich Kästner's satire

But circumstances did not change. Tucholsky, as we know, was in despair over them. The class conflicts became more bitter, harsher, more fanatical in the course of the 1920s. The pitch darkness did not end. Political extremists exploited the wretched social situation of the masses for their own ends. 'Christmas' remained a reserve of middle-class bliss and thus came to contrast in increasingly grotesqueness with the social reality of millions of people. Erich Kästner attacked this – even more bitterly and sarcastically than Tucholsky. In the first volume of his poems, published in 1928 under the title *Herz auf Taille* ('Heart to Measure'), there is a text titled 'Christmas song, chemically purified'.[20]

The Christmas song 'Children, what will come tomorrow' is part of the collective memory of the German middle class. It was probably composed at the end of the eighteenth century and expanded in the course of the nineteenth century. It gives children a vision of Christmas Day. It conjures up the memory of 'last year' and projects it on what is now very near: a time of rejoicing, a brilliant festive season, a time of gifts, a time of unalloyed enjoyment – and (here too nineteenth-century moralism left its traces) a time of moral armament. This Christmas song, too, is ultimately an educational song. Not so aggressively violent as Storm's song of Knecht Ruprecht, it still ends with the moralizing admonition:

What a happy day is dawning,
Full of bright new Christmas joys,
planned by parents on this morning
for their dearest girls and boys.
But such pleasures won't await
those who don't appreciate.

Erich Kästner, political satirist and parodist, felt called to write a counterpart to this. Strophe by strophe, against the image of middle-class security and responsibility is set the counter-image of the social reality in Germany. With Kästner, the 'tomorrow' of the traditional children's Christmas song which refers to the Christmas Day so longingly expected sarcastically becomes a day after tomorrow, a metaphor of the consolation for those who fall short in this life and must not expect a Christmas worthy of the name. In the style of a political agitation poem, excuses are picked up. How can one rationalize away the longing for a full Christmas: roast goose? But he makes objections. Dolls – anyway, they're no longer modern. Father Christmas? He only passes by:

> Children, just forget tomorrow,
> Only those who have get more.
> Life's enough for you, and sorrow,
> Whom your mother sadly bore.
> Soon enough will come your day.
> It will not be far away.

> Don't be sad. Beyond all question
> Wealthy folk love to be poor.
> Roast goose gives you indigestion,
> Dolls aren't modern any more.
> Santa's coming with his sleigh
> But only passing by your way.

> Go to town and watch the people,
> Lots of turkey and mince pies.
> Christian faith, rung from the steeple
> Makes the smallest children wise.
> Shake your head at all you see
> No need for a Christmas tree.

In this poem, all at once the attitude has changed, as with Kurt Tucholsky. The experience of a discrepancy between promise and reality is not to degenerate into a passive ritual of mourning but to lead to reflection on the political and social situation. Not sorrow, but rebellious laughter is announced. And rebellious laughter comes from clear sight and a readiness for enlightenment. One shouldn't complain about one's own situation but change it, actively remove the cause. The blockage which hinders perception of reality should be removed. 'God' as an excuse will not hold. On the contrary, God's goodness is quite compatible with rebellious resistance. The poem ends:

Christmas tree with lights in hordes,
Show your pride, hold your head higher.
From the stars tear down the boards,
We need wood to stoke the fire.
Silent night and holy night,
Stop your tears and laugh outright.

Children, just forget the morning
If you've nothing, all the same
Learn and heed the solemn warning:
God alone is not to blame.
God's great goodness is so wide.
O you blessed Christmastide.

3. The Christmas play as a drama of life

But the disaster continued. The Nazi megalomania in 1933 led not
only to the abolition of democracy in Germany but also to a terrible
machinery of discrimination and finally also killing, directed against
Jewish fellow-citizens. And perhaps the most gripping story which brings
together the topics of Christmas and the killing of Jews was written at
that time by Ilsa Aichinger, an Austrian professor of Jewish provenance.
This is a chapter from her novel 'The Greater Hope', which was
published in 1948.[21]

Jewish children seek lodging: Ilse Aichinger

The heroine of the book is the eleven-year-old half-Jewish girl Ellen, who
at the beginning of the novel is hiding in the American consulate of a
German city under the Third Reich, She wants a visa for America, where
her mother has already emigrated, while Ellen is staying behind with her
grandmother. For this child, America is the land of the 'great' hope, of
freedom. But the consul succeeds in convincing the girl that the visa
which he authorizes always ultimately disappoints people: they never
find the freedom that they hope it will bring. There is a 'greater' hope.

Later Ellen joins a group of Jewish children who are playing the
'reparation game': they want to save a drowning child from the river
so that the mayor will in recompense forget the guilt of their 'false
grandparents'. The symbolism of the novel becomes denser when the
Jewish children play hide and seek in a cemetery, the only place that the

Fascist society has still left them. Game and reality suddenly enter into an uncanny reciprocal relationship; the harmless children's game can turn into grim reality at any time. The children play in this cemetery between the tombstones and in role-play anticipate their fate.

However, this anticipation in role-play is demonstrated most impressively with the help of a nativity play. The scene could not be built up more dramatically. The Jewish children play on a roof the game of the world, of war and peace, of the search for lodgings, of the kings and the flight, while every moment they are aware that the secret police are waiting outside the door to deport them in trucks to the annihilation camps in Poland. Every sound at the door (effectively introduced three times in the play) can be the signal that decides death and life. Every stranger who appears can be the expected secret policeman.

But a remarkable thing happens. Instead of anxiously creeping away the children learn to understand something of 'a greater hope'. In the role play of the Christmas story they begin to improvise, and in the act of identification accept their imminent fate. They understand that the game being played with them is what they themselves are playing: just as Christ was already persecuted as a child and threatened with death, so too are they. And as already in the New Testament, so too in this story the theme of Christmas is interwoven with the theme of the cross:

> There was a sound.
> And in the half light, hands on their knees, cold and motionless, they had to go on enduring the old uncertainty whether we are nothing or kings. And they dared not take off their coats, because they were afraid, still afraid. The slightest movement could betray them. Their guilt was having been born. Their anxiety was being killed and their hope was being loved: the hope of being kings. One is perhaps persecuted for this hope.
> Joseph feared his own anxiety and looked away. Mary bent down and with a silent movement picked up the bundle again. Nothing should hinder a mother. She snuggled up to Joseph, who looked away, as the king in her arms would snuggle up to the cross, to which he had been nailed. While the children were afraid, they had an inkling of his teaching, to snuggle up to what one is nailed to, and they feared this inkling more than the shrill rapid sound at the door.[22]

In this chapter Ilse Aichinger achieves literary and theological depth by playing off the great promises of the Christmas story – peace, light, joy –

against the situation of these persecuted children threatened with annihilation. The nativity play becomes world theatre, the Christmas play a drama of life. This climax is reached when the children admit a stranger who reassures them with the news: 'It's all blown over. The deportations to Poland have been stopped.' The man urges them to go on playing and even allows himself to be drawn into the game. In the role of the vagrant looking for an inn, he is told: 'You poor man, I can still tell you how God's love glows.' And suddenly the children see how the man is shaken and weeping. They understand that this man is in reality an official of the secret police, who had been ordered to keep the children occupied until they could be deported. The man is so concerned that he wants to warn the children to run away: their meetings have been discovered. But the children remain. Where are they then 'to go to seek peace'? The chapter ends:

> The stranger felt the ground beginning to tremble under the fleeting steps of 'the world'. He heard the noise of the windows and only wanted to remain lying here. He saw in the glow of the lanterns how 'Mary' was handing over her child 'to the world'.
>
> He heard the warning of the angel, and when it sounded the third time, he was the last to jump up. As in a dream he brushed the dust off his coat and adjusted his tie. He had to play the role of the unholy king to the end. For there are only three holy kings. 'Take off your coat.'
>
> The silver threads shone happily. None of the children noticed him; they rushed to the door.
>
> Like a great dancing flame their game came together over them.[23]

Has Stalingrad refuted Bethlehem? Peter Huchel

As we know, the Nazi madness did not just rage in the mass destruction of European Jewry. The Nazis also sought to force the rest of the world under their rule. In 1943 they suffered their first heavy defeat before Stalingrad. After that, things went steadily downwards until Germany again lay in ruins. In his 1963 volume of poetry, *Chausseen, Chausseen* ('Highways, Highways'), the poet Peter Huchel connected the vision of Christmas with these experiences of the war in a unique poem. The utopia of Bethlehem is set alongside the counter-utopia of Stalingrad, two poles of German reality, which had never been connected with such powerful language. The poem is entitled 'December 1942':[24]

Like winter storms with a thunderous din
Shells blast the stable of Bethlehem's inn.

Mary with shattered flesh and bones
Lies, bloody hair frozen to the stones.

Three lancers, ears muffled tight, go by,
Hear not a sound of the infant's cry.

Their last sunflower seed will not go far
They seek the way and see no star.

Aurum, thus, myrrham offerunt..
Around the bare farm wander crow and hound.

quia natus est nobis dominus.
From the pale skeleton shine oil and rust.

To Stalingrad the high road does not go.
It leads to a death chamber of snow.

Everything is different, is the motto of this poem; everything is turned
into its opposite. Here in the first strophe the stable in Bethlehem, and
there in the last Stalingrad: it is hard to think of a more abrupt antithesis.
In fourteen lines an archetypal image, that of peace among the nations
under the sign of Bethlehem, is set against its grim caricature in the
counter-sign of Stalingrad. The stable is shelled; peace between the
nations has turned into war between the nations; where there was
worship there is killing; where there were life, warmth and friendliness,
now death reigns. Mary, the mother of life, is dead and lies on the stones
with bloody hair, no longer a life-giving woman but a frozen corpse.
There is no mention of Joseph; he seems to have disappeared. The three
kings have turned into lancers – soldiers who do not hear the cry of the
child, preoccupied as they are with creaturely wants, down to their last
sunflower seed.

'Quite different' – that is not only the case with human beings; things
are also 'quite different' among the animals and the other elements of the
Christmas story: instead of incense, gold and myrrh, the remains of iron
rations; instead of the friendly stable the bare barn; instead of ox, ass and
cow, crow and dog, lost animals wandering around. Indeed, as the poem

goes on, the contrasts become more blatant, the confrontation more direct. The quotation from the Vulgate stands out of the Christmas story like a fossil in a ghostly scene of oil and rust. Drips from tanks instead of the unguent; the rubbish of the war machine instead of the shining gold.

What is the point of these contrasts and negations? To put it bluntly, does the poem want to blot out Bethlehem with Stalingrad? Has the reality of Stalingrad finally refuted the vision of Bethlehem? Is the utopia of Bethlehem, 'Peace all over the world', finally suppressed by the counter-utopia of Stalingrad, 'annihilation of the whole world'? I think that the poem is meant to be read against the grain, in the manner of Brecht. The author, a pupil of Brecht's, does not want to confirm us in our political fatalism; rather, his poem encourages us readers to think the story through to the end. If we do so, the logic immanent in the poem becomes manifest: Bethlehem must be presupposed so that the grimness of Stalingrad can be understood rightly in all its horror. This utopia must shine out at least once more before it can be described as threatened, endangered. It is not Bethlehem that is betrayed; rather, Stalingrad is unmasked as a betrayal of Bethlehem. The utopia holds, but it can shine out only in the poem only as a dismembered utopia. Thus Huchel's text shows in a dialectically impressive way how fragile is the utopia of Bethlehem, and how in world history the grimness of genocide can apparently establish itself in the face of the vision of peace among the nations. The poem does not speculate on the readers' 'it is thus and not otherwise', but on their rebellious hope that the Stalingrads of world history may not finally triumph over 'Bethlehem'. Christmas as the inextinguishable hope of a pacified world; of a state of peace among the nations. Peter Huchel conjured up this vision in historical perspective; Heinrich Böll did so in the private sphere. For me there is no more impressive Christmas story which shines out in the inter-personal realm (without being unpolitical) than Heinrich Böll's story 'So there was Evening and Morning'. The Christmas message is here reflected in the microcosm of a marriage which has become a non-marriage, but in the sign of Christmas festivities it experiences a tiny revival of true human fellowship.

Incarnation through a word: Heinrich Böll

'So there was Evening and Morning', written in the 1950s,[25] is the story of a husband who does not dare to go home to his wife on Christmas Eve because for weeks she has refused to say a word to him. Anna, the wife, had suddenly turned to stone when her husband had once deceived her about his behaviour. It was an apparently small, stupid everyday lie which other women might perhaps have laughed about, passed over. But this woman had turned to stone, become lifeless, seemingly dead. The close relationship had been broken in a flash: his marriage – which he had previously so taken for granted – all at once became strange to the husband. The death of talk ensued; a leaden time dawned.

So on Christmas Eve the man is wandering round the railway station of his home town as though he were homeless. He has put the Christmas present for his wife in the left luggage office and is incapable of getting it out and deciding to go home. What will he do at home if a chilly welcome awaits him? Middle-class Christmases pass before his eyes, now sharply observed from the perspective of the outsider. A drunk staggering past sings, 'Every year the same'; in a shop window decorators begin to swap Father Christmases and angels for other models: women with plunging necklines, their bare shoulders sprinkled with confetti, their wrists fettered with paper streamers; the wings and hair are being taken off one model, and the husband is surprised how quickly an angel can be turned into a mixer. Christmas has ended here before it has begun. Memories well up in him, full of melancholy tenderness about his relationship with his wife.

Perhaps I was too young to marry, he thought, perhaps I should have waited until Anna had got less serious and I more so, but he already knew that he was serious enough and that Anna's seriousness was right. That was why he loved her. For the sake of the hour before going to sleep he had said no to the cinema, to dances; had not kept appointments. In the evening when he lay in bed, piety came over him, peace, and then he often repeated a sentence the precise wording of which he no longer knew: 'God created the earth and the moon, had them rule over day and night, divide between light and darkness, and God saw that it was good. So there was evening and morning.' He had planned to read the sentence through again in Anna's Bible, but he kept forgetting it. That God had created day and night seemed to him at least as generous as the creation of the flowers, the animals and human beings.

He loved this hour before going to sleep more than anything else. But since Anna had stopped talking to him, her dumbness lay like a weight on him.[26]

With this fragmentary recollection of the biblical creation story the husband decides finally to go home. However, it is now so late that the left luggage office is closed. He cannot get hold of the Christmas present and the last tram has gone. With the last money in his pocket he takes a taxi. He goes through a world which is celebrating its Christmases everywhere, but he no longer relates to it: 'In the houses behind the lightened windows he could see the candles on the Christmas tree: Christmases, what he understood by them as a child and what he had felt on this day, seemed to him far away: what was important and serious happened independently of the calendar.'

When he gets home and enters the house, his wife has, as always, done her duty. A Christmas tree stands on the table where it belongs; gifts are there for him as they should be, the meal has been prepared, as it should be . . . But his wife has already gone to bed. Then comes the end of the story:

But the bedroom door was open, and he called gently into the dark rectangle without much hope: 'Anna, are you asleep?' He waited for what seemed to him a long time and thought his question was falling infinitely deep and that the dark silence in the dark rectangle of the bedroom door contained everything that still awaited him in thirty, forty calendar years – and when Anna said 'no', he believed that he had misheard her. Perhaps he was deceived, and he spoke quickly and loudly: 'I've done something stupid. I left your present at the station for safe-keeping and when I wanted to get it it was closed and I didn't want to wait. Is that bad?'

This time he was certain that he had heard her 'No' rightly, but he also heard that this 'No' was not coming from the corner of the room where their beds had stood. Evidently Anna had moved her bed under the window . . . (He) listened for the answer, but nothing came from the dark rectangle. However, when he asked, 'Are you pleased?', the 'yes' came more quickly than the two previous 'noes'.

He put out the two kitchen lights, went into the dark and lay down on his bed: through the curtains he could see the Christmas trees in the house opposite, and down in the house they were singing, but he had his time again, two 'noes' and a 'yes', and when a car came down the street the headlights showed him Anna's profile from the darkness . . .[27]

Christmas appears in many facets in this story. The 'Every year the same' of the drunk on Christmas Eve points to the coldness of relationships in a society in which certain people can evidently bear holidays only by drowning their soul in alcohol. The changing of the Christmas decorations in a shop window points to a Christmas of empty ritual and ritualized emptiness, a substitute provided by a world of consumers and commerce, a commodity which is offered and exchanged.

However, what seems most terrifying is the Christmas room to which the husband returns when he gets home. His wife has done her 'duty' at Christmas and has constructed an apparently ghostly set: Christmas tree, gifts, food. Nowhere does it become clearer than it does here how much the dead lifeless Christmas objects reflect the lifelessness of human relationships. Nowhere is the difference between what Christmas really means and what it has become more detectable than here: duty instead of gift, emptiness instead of love, alienation instead of nearness.

But then comes the surprise: the one who without a gift and with empty hands stammeringly confronts his wife is all at once the one who receives a gift. Not, however, the traditional objects, but – strangely enough – a few basic words: two 'noes' and a 'yes'. The are little words, but they are enough in this case to break the ice of the soul. The Christmas which takes place here has nothing to do with 'The same every year' and does not manifest itself in the traditional festive objects. The exchange of Christmas presents which takes place here has nothing in common with the material world and does not exhaust itself in all the things we usually 'give' one another. Christmas takes place here as a resumption of a dead relationship between two people, exchanging presents in the form of a gift of words, unexpected, as a complete surprise. It is a word that creates life and allows people to become human again, a ray of warmth in a cold current.

Therefore the recollection of the creation story in this Christmas story is not random, but completely in place: and there was evening and morning. Every day of creation in the book of Genesis ends with this formula: the first, second . . . fifth, sixth day. Alluded to in quotations, in this everyday story a span is constructed from the creation of this world to Christmas here and now. The story thus recalls quite inconspicuously the great theological dimensions of the feast of creation: the creation of the world by the word of God and the incarnation of that same word of God belong together; the coming into being of the world and the incarnation, primal creation and new creation in Christ, form a unity.

In concrete terms that means that by becoming human the creator God gives the old worn-out creation new power, and in the spirit floods the exhausted creation with new life. That is why our Advent hymns, too, are full of images of new life, the new creation that we expect at Christmas: 'Drop down, dew, from heaven'; 'A rose has spring up from a tender root'; 'The thorns have born roses'; 'A flower blossoms in the depths of winter'. That means that with God what is frozen among us bursts out; the root that was believed dead begins to shoot again; the thorn bush which seems to have died unexpectedly produces new blossoms; the winter cold cannot prevent the surprising growth of small flowers. As the brave Friedrich von Spee, fighting against the witch craze of his time, wrote in 1622: 'O earth, bring forth, bring forth, O earth, that hill and valley may all become green. O earth, bring forth this flower, O Saviour, spring from the earth.'

And that is precisely what happens in Böll's marriage story: new creation through the word, the embodiment of the word and thus the incarnation of human beings. Through his wife's few words this confused man again becomes human, the dead comes to life, and what has died off begins to live again. The heart begins to thaw. That is the point of this story: where a cold fossilized relationship warms up again, again comes to life, there is creation, new creation, incarnation. There is Christmas – in this story paradoxically in Christmases despite Christmases.

The contemporaneity of voices

We have heard great voices: Gellert, Eichendorff, Storm and Thomas Mann; Kästner and Tucholsky; Ilse Aichinger, Peter Huchel and Heinrich Boll. Every text has its perspective on Christmas. Each embodies a voice, a melody in the symphony. And each of these voices is authentic in its own way, as literature or theology. Each text shows an indispensable dimension of the phenomenon of 'Christmas'. Joseph von Eichendorff and Peter Huchel – they truthfully wrote Christmas poems which could not be more contrary. Storm's 'Under the Christmas Tree' and Thomas Mann's Christmas scene in *Buddenbrooks* are worlds apart. But has Huchel made Eichendorff out of date? Is Storm's story falsified by Thomas Mann's novel?

Such categories do not fit into the sphere of great art, as I attempted to demonstrate in my discussion with George Steiner in the prologue to this book. In the natural sciences the laws of verification and falsification hold; in art the law of authenticity prevails in the harmony of content and form. Therefore Eichendorff's text is as true as that of Kästner and becomes an objective lie only if an author today still writes like Eichendorff or even Gellert. Then his text does not belong in the bookshops but in the rubbish bin.

But because this is the case, each of these voices has its right. For each of these voices conveys something of the theme of Christmas; what belongs there is indispensable. I would not want to be without any of these voices. Gellert's certainty of faith is just as legitimate ('Lord, you were born man') as Eichendorff's vision of a world permeated with wonder and grace. I cannot escape the magic of these particular strophes, which for me embody a bit of utopia from which our world is further removed than ever, but for which I sense a longing that almost brings tears to my eyes:

> Clear on high the stars are swinging,
> from the snow's bright, lonely face,
> rise the sounds of wondrous singing.
> O you time so full of grace!

At the same time we need Thomas Mann's view of the double ground of reality, of the scenes, settings and role plays in which we engage at Christmas so that our world does not collapse completely, so that Christmas does not degenerate into self-deception. At the same time we need Tucholsky's Christmas tree as a tree of freedom and Kästner's contrasts and sarcasm so that the utopia does not harden into a privatistic idyll. At the same time we need a political shake-up and active interventionist thinking with the slogan,

> Silent night and holy night.
> Stop your tears and laugh outright.

Yes, at the same time we need the constant tension between the great words about peace, the incarnation of God, joy and grace and the reality of people who are marginalized, exploited and afraid for their existence, as they have been described so grippingly and clear-sightedly by Ilse Aichinger. At the same time we need Huchel's radical confrontation of

the utopian cipher of Bethlehem with the anti-cipher of Stalingrad. And
to be able to bear all this we need Böll's vision of a Christmas as new
creation by the word; as the revival of dead hearts; as utopia and the
practice of incarnation. All these voices belong together when we talk
about Christmas; we cannot dispense with any of them. Only in the
polyphony of voices may I be a Christian, may I celebrate Christmas.

Think of the amazing series of young writers who have said farewell after a few extraordinary efforts. No outsiders and no weak pedants belong in this series, but the best: Hölderlin, who died mad; Georg Büchner, who died of a brain disease in exile; Karoline Günderode, who committed suicide; Kleist, who committed suicide; Lenz and Bürger, who went mad. Here in France that was the time of Stendhal and later Balzac. These German poets wrote hymns to their land, in whose social maw they met their deaths. Nevertheless they loved their land.[30]

'An overall poetic picture of society in our language' – that was the basic idea which increasingly began to dominate the author, now thirty-five. She wanted to write a big social novel, not least in order also to show her friends abroad that the Fascists had attacked their own people long before they set on others. In June 1935 she wrote in her diary:

> If it is a mistake for our French friends only rarely to present the foundations of our feelings, our ideas – often out of a simple lack of curiosity. This mistake is ours, for not having made ourselves sufficiently clear. Moreover a great deal of German literature has always been comprehensible only to Germans.[31]

The Civil War broke out in Spain in 1936, and a year later Seghers was also there when the Second International Congress of Writers met. She visited the International Brigade, and experienced bomb attacks and the heroism and solidarity of those who were ready to fall in the battle for the Spanish Republic. She spoke with numerous political refugees from Germany, including those who had escaped concentration camps; made drawings; engaged in research; and collected details about Fascist practices of persecution and the fate of prisoners who attempted to escape the Nazis.

Thus prepared, that same year, 1937, she began work on a new novel which was to become her greatest and was to be completed in the summer of 1938. It was entitled *The Seventh Cross*, and was dedicated 'To the anti-Fascists of Germany, dead and alive'. This novel was now to present an overall picture of the other Germany. But how? With what means and techniques? And what did all this have to do with Jesus, whose transfigurations we can trace here? Jesus, in the work of a Marxist author of Jewish origin?

A Communist in flight

Seven prisoners are escaping from Westhofen concentration camp. Six are recaptured and hung on 'crosses' on the parade ground of the camp; one gets away, the Communist Georg Heisler. His cross, the seventh, remains empty. That is the starting point for this novel, and it was this decisive literary device which enabled Anna Seghers to present a kaleido-scope of German reality. A Communist – hunted and pursued by the SS – seven days on the run through a part of Germany which can easily be recognized as the area of Rheinhessen from which the author herself came. In this way, with a single stroke she could enter the heart of Fascist society and lay it open. This was in fact a brilliantly simple piece of narrative technique. 'A Communist, who has escaped from a concentra-tion camp, runs for his life and compels all with whom he comes in contact to reveal what they are worth.'[32] This fugitive acts on them as a catalyst; he opens up relationships, modes of behaviour, releases inhibi-tions or obsessions, discloses what has been covered over, suppressed or hidden. People must take sides, for him or against him, and this decision 'judges' them. So this figure distorts the world and human being 'to the point of recognition' (as Ernst Bloch put it). And for no one involved in this confrontation will what was formerly familiar reality, apparently so sure, become what it once was.

What Seghers has succeeded in doing here is to write a novel of resistance. However, this resistance is not explained, but presented in a shy, restrained, indirect way. There is no description of great political actions, acts of heroic people helping the fugitive. Those given literary form here are the little people, the quiet people in the land, the ordinary people who do not understand much about politics and often do not see the connections, but who without political calculation do not refuse their help – out of an elementary feeling of humanity. This must be striking in the novel of a convinced Marxist. The Communist 'hero', feverishly sought by the SA and SS, does not live by the help of an organization or party, but by simple gestures of mercy from ordinary people: an old woman who gives him five pfennigs; the Jewish doctor who treats the injured man and asks no questions; a worker who puts himself and his family at risk with his solidarity. However, other figures reject the fugitive. But this rejection, too, is not a political action; it is more an understandable human protective reaction: the truck driver who takes the fugitive a little way and then suddenly drops him off when he sees what the game is; the former girl friend who shuts the door in his face out of fear. So this novel is not written in a tone of accusation and settling accounts; it is not a 'song of vengeance', but more an elegy, a book of gentleness and mercy. 'Grace instead of righteousness' – this formula, which appears in the novel itself, is the key to understanding the whole.

A night in the cathedral

To understand this better, let's look at a central scene of the novel, the 'cathedral scene' in *The Seventh Cross* which later became famous. The fugitive Georg Heisler manages to get shut in Mainz Cathedral on his first night of flight and thus to escape his pursuers. What now follows is a scene of recollection and identification, subtly worked out and skilfully shaped. It takes form round the Communist prisoner wandering in solitude around the cathedral by night:

> Georg held his breath. Right across the nave fell the reflection of a glass window which was perhaps illuminated by a light from one of the houses on the other side of the cathedral square, or by a street light: a tremendous carpet, glowing in all its colours, rolled out abruptly in the darkness, night by night, uselessly and to no purpose projected on the tiles of the empty cathedral, for there were guests like Georg only once in a thousand years. That external light, which perhaps comforted a sick child or lit a farewell, also poured out all the images of life as long as it shone. Yes, thought Georg, that must be the couple banished from paradise. Yes, those must be the heads of the cows looking into the manger where the child for whom there was no room anywhere else was lying. Yes, that must be the Last Supper when he already knew that he must be betrayed; yes, that must be the soldier who pierced him with a spear when he was hanging on the cross . . . For a long time now Georg had forgotten the pictures. He had never known many of them, since not all of them had been at home. Anything that brings out loneliness can comfort someone. Not only what is being endured by others at the same time but also what others suffered earlier.[33]

We learn that on his nocturnal wandering through the cathedral the prisoner comes upon a carpet of light and colour which is always rolled up there, night by night, as an extravagant luxury. This fugitive now discovers it, as though it had been laid there personally for him. Although long alienated from the religious tradition, he nevertheless begins to read the stories inscribed on this carpet of light, on the tiles of the cathedral, as his own story. In deciphering the biblical stories he reads the story of his own journeys. In an exciting act of rediscovery he discovers that his own biographical fate has already been outlined in primeval scenes from the Bible. Hasn't he been banished from paradise like the first couple? And isn't he like the child in the manger for whom similarly there is 'no room'? Isn't he like Jesus of Nazareth at the Last Supper, who was likewise 'betrayed', and to whom the soldiers tried to give the death blow? Isn't he on the way to being crucified, like the man from Nazareth, there in the concentration camp where the seventh cross is already awaiting him? Indeed, it is this deciphering of his own story as a passion story which gives the basic character in this novel his resemblance to Jesus. The one who is being persecuted and betrayed today makes links with the one who was persecuted and betrayed yesterday, especially the man from Nazareth who is the figure with whom all the persecuted feel that they are in solidarity. Wandering lonely and alienated in the cathedral, by referring to the great tradition of the persecuted he finds identity and comfort. Comfort – not consolation!

So this novel takes up primitive Christian symbolism, and here the Christian passion narrative is presented as the archetypal embodiment of all passion narratives, which is to give today's passion narrative sharp depth and symbolic significance. The crucified man from Nazareth casts a shadow which gives vividness and contours to the shadowless present. A reference to the great tradition of the history of suffering is needed to make it clear that a human theme also continues to be told in this current history of suffering: the fight of truth against the light, of justice against oppression, of humanity against barbarism.

And as this is a human theme, it is also understandable why a Marxist author should want to take up elements from the Jewish-Christian tradition. 1937 was the year of the International Communist Popular Front against the Nazi Terror. And active Christians could also be part of this anti-Fascist Popular Front. Anna Seghers' biographer Christiane Zehl Romero has therefore rightly emphasized that Seghers used 'features from myth, religion and fable to show the timeless human needs and hopes in what was happening at the time and to activate the power of old, powerful ideas for her message'. At the same time she added, misleadingly: 'In Segher's transformation of the Jewish-Christian tradition, however, the creator is not an all-powerful God but a plurality of threatened and apparently impotent people who only discover their power through action. This conversion of religious ideas into action and responsibility also affects the symbolism of the cross in the novel. The power of the seventh cross emerges precisely in the fact that through supreme human efforts it remains empty.'[34]

A cross as a sign of resistance

However, this is an ideologically coloured and one-sided interpretation of the cross. For Christians, too, the cross is more than a sign of failure and impotence. In the light of the resurrection of the crucified Christ it is a sign of resistance against death, and victory over the powers opposed to God. Therefore the interpretation of the cross in the novel must in no way be played off against the Christian tradition. Rather, structural analogies can be recognized between the faith of Christians and that of a Marxist like Anna Seghers. For, in this novel, for Anna Seghers as for Christians, the cross is ultimately a sign of triumph (against death and the powers of death).

Its point is that six prisoners were recaptured and bound to the 'crosses' dead or alive; six prisoners had hung again on these fearful gallows, as a visible triumph of Fascist power. But one cross remained empty. And it is this seventh still empty cross which now emanates hope for those in the camp and threat to those who guard it. It is this seventh empty cross which for the prisoners who still remain in the concentration camp becomes a sign that the total power of Fascism has been broken. It is this seventh empty cross which shows in a flash that the power of the powerful in this world can, after all, be broken. As one of the prisoners meditates: 'Yet it's a triumph, which suddenly makes one feel one's own power after a very long time, that power which had been rated for long enough, even by ourselves, as one of the many familiar powers on earth, which one assesses with measurements and numbers, whereas it is the only power which can suddenly become immeasurable, incalculable.'[35]

It is to this 'power', this human power which becomes immeasurable and incalculable, that this novel seeks to pay its respects. The empty seventh cross is its archetypal primeval symbol. So the novel ends, not with a hymn of triumph to the Communist party, but realistically, with the human hope that resistance is possible. The closing scene is typical. When the old commandant who failed so shamefully in the crisis over the prisoners is replaced by a new one, the new man immediately has the seven crosses taken down and burned as firewood. But the prisoners, forced witnesses to this burning, feel – as it is said – 'nearer to life than ever and also much nearer to it than all the others who seem alive'. Indeed, the prisoners know 'how deeply and fearfully external powers can reach into people, to their innermost depths', but at the same time they feel 'that there was something in their innermost depths which was unassailable and inviolable'.[36]

Therefore *The Seventh Cross* seeks to remind people that something unassailable and inviolable is hidden within them, something which can never be completely seized and fully destroyed either by the Fascist power or by any authorities and powers of the world.

In various portraits of Seghers, Marcel Reich-Ranick has kept pointing out: 'This novel does not canvass for any ideology and does not announce any political programme. The author of the passion narrative of the uncrucified Georg sets her hope on the honesty of the individual. Or should we say on love of neighbour? . . . Deep within people there is something "that was unassailable and indestructible". This is the value which Anna Seghers has celebrated in her finest books – and it is a value beyond Communism, the class struggle and revolution, beyond politics.'[37]

From a novel about flight to life on the run

'Often I saw her (Anna Seghers) in the Café de la Paix or a little café on Montparnasse among a chattering crowd of people. Her hair hung down over her face. But that didn't disturb her. She wrote and wrote. The pencil flew over the paper and the manuscript grew. Every week she brought me a bundle of sheets of which I made a fair copy,' noted a woman who had transcribed manuscripts for Anna Seghers in Paris.[38] When in 1937 the author began to work on a new novel, she could have had no inkling of what would personally await her, nor know that just as she had finished a novel about flight, she herself would soon be on the run. In June 1940 German troops were already outside Paris; links with the Soviet Union were cut after Stalin had made a non-aggression pact with Hitler. All at once the fate of the novel manuscript was quite uncertain. One copy was with a French friend who was to translate it, but he was now at the front and could not be contacted. A second had been lend to another friend, but had been destroyed in an air attack on her house. Shortly before German soldiers entered Paris, Seghers herself, in tears, had to burn a third manuscript so that it did not fall into the hands of the Fascists. Faint hopes were attached to just one copy which she had sent to a friend in New York.[39]

And now events caught up with her. With no certainty that her manuscript would survive and that the work of the last two years had been worthwhile, in 1940, after the German occupation of Paris, Anna

Seghers attempted to escape. When at first she did not succeed, she lived
– as she later once said – 'almost next to death' and slept – her children
were being lodged elsewhere – 'in a different place every night'. Then
with the help of friends she managed to travel to the south of France near
Le Vernet camp, in which her husband had been interned by the Vichy
authorities as an active German Communist. She spent a 'tormented winter' in the little town of Pamier near Le Vernet, fighting above all for exit
visas. She was lucky, since Mexico under its President, who was at that
time left-wing, was accepting Communists and those who had fought in
Spain. The North American Writers' Association also worked on her
behalf and paid the fares for the Seghers family.

They found a ship in Marseilles, but at first it sailed to Martinique.
And again they were interned – the Vichy government still had power
even in this last corner of French territory. After a month there was a
possibility of travelling on again, at first through Santo Domingo, where
pictures of the dictator Trujillo stared from all the walls, even from the
wall of the café in which the fugitive now sat writing a new novel. The
novel was to appear in 1944 under the title *Transit,* and used the author's
dramatic and traumatic experiences during her flight. Again another
detour was necessary. They had to travel by the USA to Mexico. In New
York, in June 1941, they were again detained, but learned of Hitler's
surprise attack on the Soviet Union, which gave them hope that the end
of Fascism had come. Then they travelled on and finally reached Mexico
in 1941. There they remained five more years, until Hitler's Germany
finally lay in the dust.

And what Seghers herself had hardly thought possible happened: the
manuscript of *The Seventh Cross* had reached New York. The book,
which had been written out of a love of Germany, first had to be
published in English (in 1942, by a Boston firm). It appeared in German
the same year from a Mexican publishing house in exile. In 1943 editions
appeared in three more languages, and before the end of the war in
Russian and French. Yet it is paradoxically this internationalization
which was to help this book by a German writer to become a world
success, not least because it was made into a film in Hollywood in 1944.
The dialectic of impotence and power, failure and victory could now also
been seen in the life of its author. Anna Seghers, driven out of Germany,
driven out of France, having fled to Mexico, all at once achieved what she
had originally wanted with this novel: she was able to make it clear also
to her friends abroad that there was another Germany, a Germany for
which these sentences had been written: 'We all felt how deeply and

fearfully outside powers could intervene, to its innermost, but we also felt that in the innermost there was something that was unassailable and inviolable.'

2. Violence can be conquered: William Faulkner

He had long been a distinguished author when in 1943 he had the idea of writing a new novel with the title *A Fable*. He had already written himself unmistakably into the literary history of the United States as an author of the South with novels like *The Sound and the Fury* (1929) and *Light in August* (1932). Born in New Albany, Mississippi, in 1897, he had his literary world shaped by the social conflicts in the southern states, shaken by race riots. The model for his writing is the area around the town of Oxford, Mississippi, where Faulkner's parents had gone as early as 1902 and where the author was to spend most of his life until his death in 1962.

This narrower background is given a poetic transformation in his writing. Faulkner chooses for it the Indian name Yoknapatawpha (a composite name made up of two Indian words: Yocnoa = river and Petopha = distributed land) and invents a separate capital for the area, Jefferson, Mississippi. Out of a love of this land and a close knowledge of its people Faulkner sketches out his own *comédie humaine*, a picture of human existence and destiny. Stories of individual families are linked together to form a whole saga. Faulkner tells of the splendour and decline of the Compson-Sartoris, of the clan of the Snopes, and of the McCaslins, the white and black descendants of the violent Carothers McCaslin. He writes a separate novel about the cotton-picking Sutpen family, its rise and fall. And like a dark ground bass there runs through these stories the question of the causes of all these tragi-comic destinies, of impulses, guilt and violence, especially where the races live together.

When the United States enters the world war after the Japanese attack on Pearl Harbor in 1942, Faulkner sees a great disaster coming. He cannot join the army on grounds of age and health. But at least he wants to make a contribution for a time which is to follow the conflagration. So – during his work for film production firms in Hollywood – in 1943 he has an idea:

(In the fable), in the middle of that war, Christ (some movement in mankind which wished to stop war forever) reappeared and was crucified again. We are repeating, we are in the midst of war again.

Suppose Christ gives us one more chance, will we crucify him again, perhaps for the last time? That's crudely put; I am not trying to preach at all. But that is the argument: We did this in 1918; in 1944 it not only MUST NOT happen again; it SHALL NOT HAPPEN again, i.e. ARE WE GOING TO LET IT HAPPEN AGAIN? Now that we are in another war, where the third and final chance might be offered us to save him.[40]

Christ comes again – in the midst of war

Faulkner's concern is to tell a Christ story which runs against the facts, about the forces which oppose violence, in the context of the war. And what is happening in the war makes it clear to him how urgent this work is. To avoid a long campaign, in 1945 the USA used a new, terrible weapon. 100,000 people died in the Japanese city of Hiroshima, 73,000 were wounded, many of them burned and mutilated by the radioactive heat wave; another 70,000 perished in the port of Nagasaki. And who can assess what effect the years of murder and brutality had had on the moral disposition of mankind? At any rate, with his 'legend' Faulkner wants to express the hope of spiritual resurrection, with a story of the second appearance of Christ in the midst of the war. He worked on his novel for more than ten years; it only appeared in 1954 and met with a divided response from the critics.[41] In the meantime, in 1950, he had been awarded the Nobel Prize for Literature for his already giant *oeuvre*, but Faulkner always felt that *A Fable*, when finally finished, was his best work.[42]

The main character in the novel is a corporal called Stephan, a French soldier in the First World War. His life is modelled in detail on that of Jesus. Even the individual chapters of the novel are the days of Holy Week from Monday to Sunday morning. Stephan is a simple, illiterate man of thirty-three. He had come with his half-sister Marya and Marthe, first to the coast of Asia Minor and from there to France, as a result of Marthe's marriage to a French colonial soldier. There the four together rent a farm at Saint Mihiel, until war breaks out and Stephan arrives at the front as a corporal, after an affair with a girl called Magdalena from a brothel in Marseilles. He stands out for his capacity for infinite patience, his endurance of suffering, and an unusually good and caring nature. He gathers twelve followers around him: one of them betrays him, another denies him, and a third, Paul, represents him during temporary absences.

His mutiny against the madness of killing inspires English and German soldiers equally. They too lay down their weapons and stop murdering. For a short time the war comes to a standstill on all fronts. But the generality of all the war parties join forces against the mutiny and agree to continue the war. Stephan is executed along with a murderer and a thief; he wears a crown of barbed wire and his body is looked after and buried by the three women Marya, Marthe and Magdalena.

The climax of the novel is a direct confrontation between the corporal and the supreme commander of the allied forces, who, as it proves, is Stephan's father. The father urgently attempts to convince his son to stop his quest for peace and save himself. He offers him 'the world'. But Stephen, steadfast and terse, rejects his father, as Jesus once rejected the diabolical tempter. In the end the old general has his son executed between two thieves. When the war flares up again, Stephan's corpse is blown from its grave by an artillery shell. By chance it lands in the catacombs under Fort Valaumont. The French authorities look after it without knowing whose corpse it is, for they need a soldier's body to lie under the Arc de Triomphe as France's 'Unknown Soldier'.

The closing scene of the novel is therefore extremely comical, since Faulkner has two people from the great game (a British runner, who out of sympathy for the mutineers brought on his degradation, and the French quartermaster-general, who was always the correct and eloquent helper of the ruling powers) in Paris to witness the interment of the old supreme commander. The commander's coffin is taken to the tomb of the 'Unknown Soldier'. The British runner had witnessed the events at the front; he had himself incited mutiny and had been severely wounded in the cross-fire. Now he hobbles on to the scene on crutches, supported by the quartermaster-general, and in the crowd he is so jostled that he falls into the gutter. Blood runs from his mouth:

> Then the man in the gutter opened his eyes and began to laugh, or tried to, choking at first, trying to turn his head as though to clear his mouth and throat of what he choked on, when another man thrust through the crowd and approached him – an old man, a gaunt giant of a man with a vast worn sick face with hungry and passionate eyes above a white military moustache, in a dingy black overcoat in the lapel of which were three tiny faded ribbons, who came and knelt beside him and slipped one arm under his head and shoulders and raised him and turned his head a little until he could spit out the blood and shattered teeth and speak. Or laugh rather, which is what he did first, lying in the

cradle of the old man's arm, laughing up at the ring of faces enclosing him, then speaking himself in French:

'That's right,' he said: 'Tremble. I'm not going to die. Never.'

'I am not laughing,' the old man bending over him said. 'What you see are tears.'[43]

So these two persons have the last word in Faulkner's novel: the eternal, nameless rebel and fighter, the man who can dispense with outward honour, who suffers terribly but is not afraid to give expression to his truth, blood in his mouth and a laugh in his throat – and the other, always aware of his duty, concerned and conscientious, as it were the eternal adjutant, who cannot laugh and never will laugh.

In his pioneering book on Faulkner, Heinrich Straumann has rightly interpreted this scene as follows: 'Here we have the two faces which appear once again quite emphatically at the decisive point: the fact that our being cannot be interpreted as a unity but only as a duality. There is always a power which wants order and a power which rebels against it; there is always a mass and an individual who risks being oppressed by it; there is always someone who fights and endures and someone who helps and compensates; there is always a weeping and a laughing, however hard they are to distinguish now and then – indeed sometimes one takes the place of the other, in that the one who endures knows how to laugh, and the one who helps weeps. And here, in this violent game which is never decisive, the irony also becomes visible, an irony which is to become conscious only to the reader, and remains hidden from those involved in the event. The corpse of the supreme commander is brought to the tomb of the unknown soldier, the model of bravery, self-sacrifice and national pride. But who lies in this tomb? None other than the corporal who was responsible for the mutiny of the French regiment and was executed on the orders of the very man whose body is now being buried alongside him as a last supreme honour. Should we laugh or cry?'[44]

Clumsy parallels?

Thus Faulkner's basic idea had been turned upside down: Christ returns in the middle of a murderous battle, and again he has been crucified. The urgent question is: what is the overall strategy of the novel? Does it consist above all in the fact that as a writer Faulkner wanted to invent a figure who echoed the Jesus figure of the Gospels as much as possible?

Did he want to show that as an author of the twentieth century he can invent a Jesus who is at least as interesting as the Gospels? That is suggested by the wealth of allegorical parallels with the people and events of Good Friday. And Faulkner has had to take a good deal of blame from literary critics for this overabundant allegory. The American specialist in German literature T.Ziolkowski speaks for many when he writes: 'It is precisely this sort of strained effort to introduce parallels – in this case the lance wound – even when they are totally irrelevant to the context that vitiates the power of Faulkner's narrative and reduces it to an often tedious allegory . . . In fact, in comparison with the finest fictional transfigurations it strikes us as a clumsy allegorical work. The author has strained our credulity, not to mention our aesthetic sensibilities, by imposing the Gospel parallels obtrusively from without.'[45]

But this criticism presupposes that Faulkner wanted to give his inter-pretation of Jesus above all the form of allegorical alienation. This is really unimaginable in an author who otherwise is so reflective in his work. For in fact it would be the expression of an almost childlike and naive drive to imitate were this author above all concerned to include as many parallels from the life of Jesus in his story as possible. That could only be clumsy and incredible. So this cannot have been the basic purpose of Faulkner, one of the greatest novelists of world literature. Such criticism already overlooks the simple fact that there are also consider-able differences between Faulkner's figure and the figure of Jesus. The similarities are essentially governed by the external circumstances. If we look closely, the life and person of the corporal are not at all imitations of Christ. Stephan may act like Christ in doing good, but he himself does not seem to know much of Christ. He does not call himself either Christ or a Christian, nor does he explicitly follow in Christ's footsteps. He is nothing but an individual who has had a good idea and acts accordingly. So by building up allegories of Christ and dissolving them at the same time, Faulkner shows that his concern in this novel is not to give a virtuoso demonstration of allegory.

But isn't this breaking through of allegory in particular an expression of the fact that Faulkner is using the 'symbolic myth of God and Jesus as a vehicle for completely un-Christian arguments'?[46] Doesn't this novel seek to be a single 'parody'[47] on the content of Christian faith? That seems to be supported by the fact that while Faulkner uses the Christian passion narrative as a foil to his novel, at the same time he strips it of any exclusive claim to salvation. Moreover the contradictions with a Christian salvation-historical interpretation of the passion of Christ are manifest. For here a 'Jesus' appears who with his revolts does not 'fulfil' the law but puts it in question; who does not act and endure on behalf of a loving father but in revolt against his hateful begetter; who does not descend to humankind but grows out of it.

Furthermore, it is the 'father' who attempts to persuade his son not to undergo his sacrificial death, to deny his faith and to betray his followers. This father knows that the sacrificial death of his son is much more dangerous for him than all that the mutiny has already done. Therefore the father who seems omnipotent fears for the ongoing existence of his rule. The one who has hitherto held people down in an iron grip is afraid of the force of their indignation. And it is the son, completely subordinate to him, who sees through the father, resists him and goes his way with an unshakeable fearlessness. What Faulkner had undertaken seems to have been resolved: Christ gave human beings another chance, but this chance has again been forfeited; he is buried as an unknown soldier. The drama of the crucified Christ appears in Faulkner as the primal image of the human tragedy. So doesn't the author after all want this novel to end in fatalism and resignation? With a radical renunciation of the Christian hope – paradoxically, precisely with the help of the Jesus material?

We should not speak here, in simple dualistic categories, of Christian and un-Christian. An early German review of the novel rightly stated: 'Faulkner is neither Christian nor anti-Christian. What a time so bent on cheap and easy antitheses finds it so difficult to understand is that he is Christian in a different way; perhaps he is not even Christian in a way which can be regarded as religious. Rather, he makes use of the symbols of Christian faith only to make an incomprehensible, a more than comprehensible, statement, and he has to veil it again, as if an eye used to a gentler light must be spared it.'[48] That is well said, and in fact the way in which Faulkner is Christian with a difference lies in his conviction that no redemption and no certainty of salvation emanates from the figure of Christ, but rather a spiritual force and an ineradicable hope, embedded in a tragic irony. And now we understand better why these Jesus allegories were necessary in the text: they are the feature which gives the story its tragic and ironic colouring.

The basic idea of the novel rests on the one notion of a man coming again who recalls Jesus in every respect; a 'Jesus' comes who could not be more clearly recognizable, and no one in today's Christian society notices him. Indeed, representatives of this Christian Western society do away with him as they did away with Jesus of Nazareth two thousand years previously. In short, the tragic irony consists in the fact that once again a

Christian society crucifies the Christ from whom it derives all the justification for its existence. But as though Faulkner wants to push his ironic
'game' with this society to extremes, he has the conscientious objector,
of all people, laid in the hero's grave for all soldiers. In this way Christian
society nevertheless honours 'Jesus' by its rituals without knowing that
it is doing so. It honours that mysterious 'counter-force' to the forces
of violence and destruction which had raged in the phenomenon of
war.

Passion for the unfact

Moreover in the key conversation between the supreme commander and
the corporal it becomes clear that this novel is about the shaping of two
basic forces which dominate the world, two basic ways of looking at the
'world'. Faulkner puts this insight ironically on the lips of the supreme
commander himself:

> I, champion of this mundane earth which, whether I like it or not, is,
> and to which I did not ask to come, yet, since I am here, not only must
> stop but intend to stop during my allotted while; you, champion of an
> esoteric realm of man's baseless hopes and his infinite capacity – no:
> passion – for unfact. No, they are not inimical really, there is no
> contest actually; they can even exist side by side together in this one
> restricted arena, and could and would, had yours not interfered with
> mine.[49]

It would be a misunderstanding to interpret this scene in simple dualistic
terms. Certainly there is no mistaking the allusion to the biblical story of
the tempting of Jesus by the devil. But it is not the principles of good and
evil, God and Satan, which stand over against each other here, but – if
you will – world and non-world. There is the world of fact, which presents itself cynically as the realism of the 'thus and not otherwise', and the
non-world of unfact, which in the simple gesture of refusal and dropping
out and the precious quality of the little life of the individual, defends
itself against the commander's global programme.

The way in which Faulkner shapes his 'Jesus' is unique in literature.
Nowhere in world literature is there a comparable attempt. On the one
hand Faulkner draws an abundance of parallels to the life of Jesus; on the
other he withdraws his 'Jesus' completely into the background. The
'Jesus-like' quality of the novel lies elsewhere: in the gripping simplicity

of the character, in the terseness of the dialogue, in the poverty of the action. This 'Jesus' is no one personified, nothing in person, the hollow form and emptiness incarnate. The philosopher Hans Blumenberg pointed this out in an early review of the novel: 'This corporal has no proclamation, no sense of mission, no claim to power. In doing what seems to him most obvious he so to speak discovers the other – what was obvious to him: to rise from the grave and make an end. The figure of the corporal is not a concentration of the good, the holy, the human and the superhuman; on the contrary, it is of terrifying poverty, without face, without soul. Precisely this inner emptiness, the stubborn lack of motive in this figure makes the step from the grave seem bare and elementary, the radically reduced form in which the person can become conscious of what he needs: 'to say "Enough" and no more'.[50]

How violence can be overcome

In fact, if we look at the way in which this decisive conversation is shaped, we will see these two basic forces being vividly worked out in their radical difference. Faulkner conveys the powerful potency and tremendous self-confidence of the general by making him speak without a pause: an overflowing flood of words cascades out of him. By contrast the corporal is very restrained; he is silent or limits himself to short, terse sentences. While his father, the general, threatens to choke him with language, the son retreats to the one decisive sentence which he keeps repeating like a refrain: 'And the other ten?' On more than fifteen pages of dialogue there is always only the one sentence: 'And the other ten?' The reference is to the 'disciple' comrades whom the corporal had to abandon when he saved himself. In an unmistakable allusion to Dostoievsky's parable of the Grand Inquisitor, for Faulkner too the 'power' of Jesus lies in the importance of silence; his presence in his withdrawal; his power in powerlessness; his fullness in emptiness. So in Faulkner what 'Jesus' is and embodies is not depicted through allegorical parallels but shines forth in the restraint of poverty, sparseness of words and silence. In this Jesus the counter-force can shine out against the powers which tend to rage in wars: a counter-force which can break the spell of the world power, because it does not join in the game.

So, like all Faulkner's work, this novel too is on the track of the secret of how to overcome violence. A critic has rightly remarked: 'Faulkner's true theme is not violence but its absolute negation. The old tragic question how despite its weakness the human can assert itself in the murderous wildness of living is here made particularly pointed.'[51] That means that in the end the novel is on the track of the question of the counter-force by which the world or the real, the world of facts, can be overcome. Here the big phrase of the general, Stephan's father, 'Take the earth' (he is speaking in sweeping global terms, thinking of armies and generations), is set against the 'little' counter-question of the son, the corporal, repeated like a refrain: 'And the other ten?' That is the ratio of the counter-ploy in the spirit of Jesus: the ten who have remained faithful against power over the earth; the small life against the administration of the centuries; the modest human against the world politics which inflame people. We can endorse the comment of Ursula Brumm, who has made an impressive study of 'religious typology in American thought', that here Christ is the 'hero of the unheroic, those without need and suffering. In setting these two parties over against each other, those who act and those who suffer as a result of those who act, he gives his novel a universal scope over and above its treatment of the World War. The World War is only one of the many historical catastrophes in which the ordinary person is "crucified".'[52]

The fact remains that Faulkner's own confidence, his boundless hope, does not come from the church's belief in Christ. His novel is therefore neither to be commandeered by Christians nor to be branded as un-Christian. Faulkner's faith does not stem from a certainty about salvation but – in precisely the same way as Anna Seghers – from trust in human beings, despite the way in which they can be led astray, despite the abysses in them. Moreover Faulkner kept referring to his basic conviction in what he said about the novel. In the novel it is put in this way: human beings have free will, and the will for freedom cannot be eradicated. Like Anna Seghers, Faulkner believes in the indestructible power in each human individual which in the end is stronger than any violence, any instinct, any destruction, any evil. In an address given on 28 May 1951, Faulkner could say:

It is not men in the mass who can and will save Man. It is Man himself, created in the image of God so that he shall have the power and the will to choose right from wrong, and so be able to save himself because he is worth saving; – Man, the individual, men and women, who will refuse always to be tricked or frightened or bribed into surrendering, not just the right but the duty too, to choose between justice and injustice, courage and cowardice, sacrifice and greed, pity and self; – who will believe always not only in the right of man to be free of injustice and rapacity and deception, but the duty and responsibility of man to see that justice and truth and pity and compassion are done.[53]

This text corresponds to another which is far better known: Faulkner's speech on being awarded the Nobel Prize in 1950. In this short address the writer makes clear that he is not prepared to believe in the end of humankind or to accept that human immortality consists in the mere ongoing existence of this living being:

I decline to accept the end of man. It is easy enough to say that man is immortal simply because he will endure . . . I refuse to accept this. I believe that man will not merely endure: he will prevail. He is immortal, not because he alone among creatures has an inexhaustible voice, but because he has a soul, a spirit capable of compassion and sacrifice and endurance. The poet's, the writer's duty, is to write about these things. It is his privilege to help man endure by lifting his heart, by reminding him of the courage and honour and hope and pride and compassion and pity and sacrifice which have been the glory of his past. The poet's voice need not merely be the record of man, it can be one of the props, the pillars to help him endure and prevail.[54]

3. Fighting the evil in the heart: Naguib Mahfouz

In a dimension which goes beyond culture, to grapple with Jesus is to grapple with the question of the basic forces with which people can control this world. And it is this question of power that also stands at the centre of probably the best-known novel by the Egyptian writer Naguib Mahfouz, *Children of our Alley* (completed in 1959 and first published in Beirut in 1967). The author, who was born in Cairo in 1912, became well-known to the world public at a stroke when in 1988 he was awarded the Nobel Prize for Literature – the first author in the Arabic-speaking world to gain this honour.[55] That was a remarkable event: according to the journalist Hassouna Mosbahi, the Arabic imagination had long been repressed by the prudery and the religious dogmatism of Islamic scribes. Between the fourteenth and the nineteenth century the Arabs had sought refuge in new forms of expression, above all an oral narrative culture. This oral literature had given rise to highly imaginative new myths and stories, stories which people told in the desert nights of Arabia, in the mountains of Yemen, in the depths of Egypt, on the roads of Tunisia and in the market places of Morocco – and still tell today.

A dangerous author

Here Naguib Mahfouz is very important as a modern 'classic', i.e. as by far the most popular Arabic writer, who is read from Yemen to Morocco. He is regarded as the father of the Arabic novel. He has 'liberated the Arab imagination from linguistic and religious confinement'. He has 'given the Arab imagination a capacity for literature, by incorporating the elements of oral literature – the art of popular story-telling – into his epic work . . . This gave classical Arabic a new living power of expression with which alone it could depict the reality of present-day Egyptian society in such a fascinating way.'[56]

However, the award of the Nobel Prize in 1988 also made the world public aware that already at the time of its first appearance in 1959 this novel had been surrounded by religious and political controversy, and this has dogged the person of Mahfouz to the present day. Fundamentalist Islamic circles stirred things up against this author at a very early age and made death threats, and not too long ago the author, by then eighty-five, narrowly escaped an attack in Cairo.[57]

Moreover the novel *Children of Our Alley* asks a great deal of trad-itional Islamic ears. It requires them to reflect on how the world is as it is when with the religions of Judaism, Christianity and Islam everything has been revealed which would serve the world's salvation. Had not the whole human world been given by God as a gift so that it might be distributed justly? Why then all the injustices, all the corruption and violence? Had people not understood the message? Had the religions possibly failed? Had the great founders, Moses, Jesus and Muhammad, perished in vain? The giant city of Cairo, where in a fascinating way beauty and dirt, splendour and misery, hope and despair exist side by side, could not provide a better setting for this question. Moreover, for Mahfouz the megalopolis with its old alleyways becomes a metaphor for the world.

The five long chapters of the book (it begins with a 'Preface') keeps – in an often witty, humorous and allegorical garb – to the 'salvation history' which Islam has long told. In the Preface we learn of an old landowner named Gabalawi, who lives in a big mansion at the end of an alleyway in the old city, on the edge of the desert. With his immense wealth he had set up an estate so that his sons and their descendants could benefit. However, he does not let anyone look at the foundation document which contains the detailed regulations and which he keeps in his house. And his estate achieves rather the opposite: instead of justice, corruption increasingly prevails among his descendants as a result of brutal stewards who terrorize the inhabitants of the alley with the help of a host of gangsters. There had already been a vigorous dispute among Gabalawi's sons, because he had preferred his youngest son Adham (= Adam) to the older one, Idris. The latter defends himself with an accusation against his father's act of capriciousness, is driven out of the house, and Adham takes over the administration of the estate.

For a long time all goes well. Adham falls in love with a young girl called Umaima; they marry and the wife becomes pregnant. That brings disaster on both of them: Idris, the rejected brother, one day joins the line of waiting tenants in order to be able to slip secretly into the great house. He urges Adham finally to take a look at their father's secret book. After initial hesitation Adham does this, together with Umaima. Then catastrophe comes, since the father returns early from his morning walk, discovers the couple and drives them out of the house. A life of toil, misery and poverty now begins outside the immense mansion. A world comes into being 'out there', and what could have been a history of salvation tuns into a history of doom. For after Adham's death, time and again individual stewards and their gangsters succeed in seizing power and, instead of administering the estate fairly, satisfy their greed. The great majority of the descendants of Gabalawi must vegetate in dirt and misery, exploited, scorned and terrorized by gangsters. And in all the following generations only three figures dare to put the dominant power structures in question. These are Moses, Jesus and Muhammad, in allegorical garb.

Gabal the snake-charmer (= Moses) is the first to rebel against the established authorities. He rages against the unjust conditions in the alley. But Gabal fights only for his own family; it alone profits from money from the estate. And Gabal himself rules with an iron hand. After his death the old conditions return: 'And who were these poor people? Men whose backs were swollen from beating, whose buttocks were inflamed from kicks. Their eyes were tormented with flies, and lice infected their heads . . . "Why has Gabalawi forgotten us?"'[58]

'Jesus' as the one who drives out the demons

Suddenly a strikingly good-looking young man named Rifaa (= Jesus) appears in the alley. His features radiate infinite peacefulness and goodness. His father intends him to become a carpenter, but he goes his own way. He prefers to go into the desert and round the mountain on solitary

walks. He has a heart tormented with dark passion, the depths of which
he himself does not yet know. In his unworldliness he even marries a
woman of doubtful reputation, Yasmina, simply because in the goodness
of his heart he wants to rescue her from a threatening situation. He does
not love her, or, rather, he loves he as he will love all human beings; later
she will betray him.

Rifaa loves one thing above all: listening to the stories of the age-old
estate of Gabalawi which the singers in the coffee houses continue to tell.
They make him aware of the decisive question in his life: how can peace
and love enter human hearts when people live in poverty, oppressed by
the scourges of the gangsters? In particular Rifaa takes in everything to
do with the mystery of driving out demons. He cannot hear enough from
a woman who has the art of exorcism; she conveys to him that every
human being has a demon which controls him. And at the same time that
not each of these demons need be an evil spirit which one must drive out.
Thus the young man learns the art of discerning the spirits and the
technique of controlling demons. Rifaa feels strengthened on his way by
the voice of Gabalawi, which he thinks he has heard at the great house,
adjoining the desert. What his parents regard as 'delusions' are for him
the great guiding force in his life. He tells his father:

> I would be the last to fight for the sake of the estate. The estate is noth-
> ing, father, and the happiness of a full life is everything. Nothing stands
> between us and happiness but the demons hiding within us, and it was
> not for nothing that I should love the treatment of demons and improve
> on it. Perhaps the will of the Lord of heaven has compelled me to it.[59]

Conquering evil in the heart

So that is Rifaa's determination: not to fight for the just distribution of
the resources of the estate, like Gabal-Moses before him and Qassem-
Muhammad after him, but to free every human being inwardly from the
demons of greed and hatred: they are what really causes distress and
poverty to human beings. To conquer evil by inward cleansing – that is
the approach which he carries through consistently, particularly among
the poor and sick. And as he takes no money from them, people love him
above all. Moreover Rifaa's successes are perplexing: someone who
used to suffer from nervous attacks is now a model of tranquillity and
equilibrium; someone who used to love quarrels and disputes is all at
once gentle and patient; someone who used to rob people as a pickpocket
now does honest work: someone who used to be a fault-finding

grumbler, a hopeless opium addict, a brute and an evil pimp has now been transformed.

And yet this non-violent man comes into conflict with the gangsters of the alley. The poor who have been freed from the demons make those in power uneasy, especially as Rifaa claims to speak in the name of Gabalawi, putting in question the steward's claim to be the sole representative. Rifaa's life is in danger; he must flee, but is betrayed by Yasmina. So the gangsters can seize him and kill him in the desert in a bestial way. On the journey there they had passed by the great mansion and Rifaa had vainly expected a sign from Gabalawi. He dies with a cry to Gabalawi.

But that is not the end of his story. For a long time a small community of followers had been gathering around Rifaa, and they now fight for his cause. A certain Ali (= Peter) puts himself at their head, and after fighting they manage to establish a separate community of Rifaaites in the quarter. This now has a share in the resources of the estate, so its worldly power is established. Mahfouz makes this chapter end ironically (the allusions to the history of Christianity are unmistakable):

Rifaa enjoyed respect, veneration and love in death that he had never dreamed of during his lifetime. There was even a wonderful story, retold by every tongue and recited to rebec tunes, particularly of how Gabalawi lifted up his body and buried it in his fabulous garden. All Rifaa's followers agreed on that and they were unanimously loyal and reverent to his parents, but they differed on everything else. Karim, Hussein and Zaki insisted that Rifaa's mission had been limited to healing the sick and despising power and majesty; they and their sympathizers in the alley did as he had done. Some went further and refrained from marriage, to imitate him and live their lives his way. Ali, however, retained his rights to the estate, married and called for the renewal of their community. Rifaa had not hated the estate itself, but only to prove that true happiness was achievable without it, and to condemn the vices inspired by covetousness. If the revenue was distributed justly, and put towards buildings and charity, then it was the greatest good.

In any case, the people were delighted with their good lives, and welcomed life with radiant faces; they said with confident security that today was better than yesterday, and that tomorrow would be better than today.

Why is forgetfulness the plague of our alley?[60]

It would be completely wrong to understand this novel as a disparagement of the religions. Rather – according to one of the great experts on Mahfouz in the German speaking world, Hartmut Fähndrich – it deals with the problem of power and repression. 'Essentially it is not so much about the relationship between religion and science, as is often claimed, as about the universal human problem of power and repression . . .For first of all *Children of the Alley* is not an attempt at a historical account of Moses, Jesus or Muhammad, in which facts are distorted or the content of faith is presented without respect; the author merely makes use of some traditions from the Bible, the Qur'an and popular religious tradition to make these bringers of salvation known as such. Secondly, these bringers of salvation are not put in a moral twilight, but rather their "disciples", those who distort or scorn the teaching after the death of the founders, so that the religions can no longer work in the world in the way that was originally intended. They cannot bring to bear their potential for liberation. People continue to be oppressed – and what remain are ultimately the songs and stories of the bards about a fine time and human hopes and dreams of a better future.'[61]

Hope of liberation is ineradicable

In fact, Mahfouz is not out to distort the content of Judaism, Christianity and Islam in a disrespectful way but to point to the discrepancy between the promise of salvation and unholy reality. A basic current of realistic scepticism runs through the novel, particular in connection with the achievements of the religions, but also in connection with the achievements of modern technology. The magician Arafa appears as the representative of this in a separate fifth chapter. With his art Arafa can not only heal the sick, cure impotence and protect spirits; he also works with a miracle weapon with the help of which he wants to free the inhabitants of the alley from the gangsters' reign of terror. So originally he is the one who brings to the masses great hopes of a final liberation from repression and an improvement of their circumstances.

But one day Arafa, too, is seized with curiosity finally to discover the secret of Gabalawi's legacy. By night he slips into the great mansion to get a look at the secret book – and is caught out in the same way as Adham once was. A servant is killed and Gabalawi himself also dies as a result of these events. Tortured with guilt-feelings, Arafa sells himself to the steward of the estate, but the steward uses him only for removing gangsters who have become troublesome and otherwise to establish his power still further. Here too is the old game: what began as an impulse for liberation becomes a means of oppression. Only when a servant of Gabalawi's brings Arafa Gabalawi's last message – he has forgiven him in the face of death – does Arafa find the strength to escape the alliance with power. Arafa perishes in his flight, but his brother Hanash is able to escape and he tries to hide the book in which the two of them had written down their scientific knowledge. It is left open whether he succeeds, but in this way the hope that things will get better can be kept alive among people. And according to Mahfouz's basic approach in this book, people live exclusively by hope – despite, indeed because of, the failure of all great prophets and projects. The author brings the novel to an end with his own melancholy humour:

> The alley endured a nightmarish atmosphere of fear, hatred and terrorism. Yet the people bore the outrages steadfastly, taking refuge in patience. They held fast to hope, and whenever they were persecuted they said, 'Injustice must have an end, as day must follow night. We will see the death of tyranny, and the dawn of light and miracles.'[62]

We cannot pursue further the complex history of the work of this unique writer. But however his giant novels will develop, the basic constant seems to lie in the author's conviction – and here he resembles Anna Seghers and William Faulkner – that it is the task of literature to fight evil in the form of violence, brutality and oppression and to commit oneself to the well-being especially of the underprivileged masses of people. And whereas in their persons and their work Anna Seghers and William Faulkner each combined two cultures (Jewish-German; American South and American North), Naguib Mahfouz embodies three cultures at the same time: the culture of the Pharaohs, the culture of Islam and the culture of the modern Western world. He described these influences in his Nobel Prize speech in 1988, and at the end he made his confession of faith:

> Despite everything that is happening around us, until the end of my life I shall remain an optimist, and I shall not say, like the philosopher Kant, that the good conquers only in the next world. No, it wins a victory every day, and perhaps evil is even weaker than we generally think. Our first ancestors, who were exposed without protection to the wild animals, the insects, the rigours of nature, plague, anxiety and selfishness, are the irrefutable proof of my assertion. Without the daily

victory of the good they would have no more survived than humankind would have been able to develop further, build cities, spread,
invent, conquer the cosmos and proclaim human rights. Yet evil is a
monster which strikes out around it with a roar, and as we know,
human beings feel what gives them pain more intensively than what
they enjoy. Therefore our poet Abu el-Ala Al-Maarri was right when
he said: the sorrow in the hour of death is far deeper than the feeling of
happiness that streams through one in the hour of birth.[63]

In the field of tension of the three contexts it is the achievement of this
great narrator that he advances the controversy with religion and science
to the point of the question how things are in creation, to the question of
the balance of power on earth, indeed to the question of God. For
Mahfouz, this description of conditions on earth is at the same time
bound up with the penetrating question of the spiritual forces in which
hope for a 'bright time of miracle' can be grounded. And this particular
question is also grappled with in a novel which is set in a quite different
context and yet tells of similar basic problems.

4. Hope for a people – Paraguay: Augusto Roa Bastos

Two people are talking on a train journey to the Paraguayan capital
Asunción:

The great guitar players of Paraguay are dead or they have all come to
grief. Or been driven to drink. In wretchedness and to forget. Gaspar
Mora has fled into the forest with his leprosy and has abandoned
Christ. Augustín Barros gave his last concert in a square and then left
in a hurry; no one knows where he is. It's the same with Ampelio
Villalba. They say that he plays and sings with a weak voice in the cafés
of Buenos Aires. Marcial Talavera shot himself. He sat on a camp bed
in his Sunday suit, looked at the sky through a vine arbour, shoved a
revolver into his mouth and pulled the trigger. I wrote an article about
the impossibility for our artists to live in their fatherland. I was
attacked for it.[64]

In this scene one of the most important Latin American writers,
Augustus Roa Bastos, has also portrayed his own life.[65] He was born in
the Paraguayan capital in 1917, grew up in modest circumstances,
learned Spanish from his father and the indigenous Guaraní from his

mother, and at the age of sixteen got involved in one of the most fearful wars in Latin America, the Chaco war between Paraguay and Bolivia. This was a frontier dispute with petroleum interests in the background which was fought between 1932 and 1935 and cost almost 100,000 victims. After the end of the war he began to work as a journalist and also worked as a radio reporter. When a civil war broke out in 1947, Roa Bastos emigrated to Argentina, where for the next thirty years he lived as a journalist, professor of literature, film-script writer and freelance author. He was a firm opponent of the dictator Alfredo Stroessner, who came to power in 1954 as a result of a military putsch and banned him from returning to his homeland. So when dictatorial repression also took hold in Argentina, Roa Bastos went into exile a second time, to France, where until 1982 he taught Latin American literature and Guaraní at the University of Toulouse. Only in 1989 – during the course of the political liberalization of his country – was it possible for him to return to Paraguay.

The fame of this writer, who in 1989 was awarded the Spanish Cervantes prize for his work,[66] is based above all on his novel *Son of Man*, published for the first time in Buenos Aires in 1960. It was revised and reworked at the beginning of the 1980s. Critics accord this book the same status as the Latin American *roman à clé One Hundred Years of Solitude*, by the Nobel Prizewinner Gabriel García Márquez, published in 1967. Purely formally, it is a chronological fresco of a century of Paraguayan political history displayed in a variety of loosely inter-connected scenes. The recollections of the figures go back to the time of the legendary dictatorship of de Francia (1814–1840), and through the war between Paraguay and Brazil, Argentina and Uruguay (1864–1870) and the great peasants' revolt of 1912 to the Chaco War against Bolivia, which has already been mentioned.

All these scenes are held together by the fictitious author of these notes, First Lieutenant Miguel Vera, who – in an ultimately incomprehensible distance from the event – reports in diary form partly what he has himself experienced, partly memories of his youth and what is experienced by third parties. After his death his notes are selectively edited by a doctor, Rosa Monzón, which produces an additional fragmentation of reality. The constantly changing scenes, written almost as reportage, which have both an attractive evocative language and a deep symbolism, centre on two places around which many of the events take place: the village of Itapé, in which there is an important figure of Christ, and the village of Sapukai, in which one of the greatest catastrophes of the peasant revolt of 1912 was to take place, when the explosion of a military train at the station caused thousands of deaths.

It is impossible to sum up even approximately a story which is described over ten chapters in dozens of scenes. Roa Bastos proves to be not only a highly thoughtful and complex narrator but also a virtuoso of the technique of narrative cutting. In a style comparable to film sequences, this emphasizes the many levels of an event all the more clearly by means of prism-like breaks. Precisely because the book is a rich collage of literary forms and thus offers only segments of reality (in Paraguay), it does justice to the complexity of this reality. And yet a few key scenes can be recognized which in the novel have the function of an in-depth interpretation; in them we sense that the author himself has presented his own creed – without ever becoming politically flat or ethically urgent. And these key scenes are directly or indirectly connected with the figure of the Son of Man, the figure of Jesus. Let's look at them more closely.

A 'Christ' as a sign of the people's resistance

The first key scene takes place right at the beginning of the book in the village of Itapé. The already almost mythical primeval story of all the people's hope for liberation is told: the story of a wood-carver called Gaspar Mora. It is told in the first person from the perspective of a very old beggar called Macario, who lives in the village, and is handed down by the narrator, First Lieutenant Miguel Vera, who himself comes from Itapé. Gaspar was a wood-carver and musician in the village; he was loved by all, and in addition to his artistic skill also showed a deep commitment to the poor. He paid the debts of fellow countrymen whose fields had been devastated by fire, hail or locusts; he provided clothing and food for widows and orphans; he built a small school, and in the evening he used to play his guitar so impressively that the people would sit on the grass to listen to him or came out from their ranchos. One day Gaspar disappeared, and only much later was the reason for this discovered in the village. Leprosy had broken out, and Gaspar had withdrawn into the forest in order to be able to die in peace. When the people of the village went out to look for him, he refused to meet them: 'The dead do not mix with the living,' he is said to have remarked, and also, 'I am already dead. And I can tell you that death is not as bad as people think.' This remark by Gaspar struck particularly deeply into the soul of Macario, who discloses Gaspar's whole 'secret':

It is good at least to know that one does not end, that one continues in another life, in another thing. For even in death one wants to live on. I know that now. Death has taught me to be patient. And so I allude to it a bit.[67]

Thus in this novel Gaspar Mora is the archetypal basic figure of selfless sacrifice for others. An analogy to the figure of Jesus can already be detected here, and Gaspar's story also ends with a dramatic point. When he is found dead in the wood and Macario and others enter his hut, at first they are deeply shocked. For on the wall is a figure in human form with arms stretched out wide. In uncanny silence it looks at anyone who comes in. Only when the men have got over their shock does it dawn on them that here is a life-size Christ made of wood, and that Gaspar carved this figure in his image. It is a life-sized Christ, carved in wood, with the hands of a leper. At Macario's request the wood body is not buried, but carried into the village: a strange procession sets out. A storm breaks and in 'rain, lightning and thunder' the Christ shines as 'though electrified'. But the plan to set up this Christ of the leper in the village church comes to grief on the pastor's opposition.

For the first time in this novel the element of criticism of the church appears. Here the popular religion of the original inhabitants of Paraguay (who speak Guaraní and largely live in the country) stands over against the official religion of a clerical elite which largely lives in the cities and speaks only Spanish. For the priest who comes into the village from outside, Gaspar Mora is nothing but a 'heretic, a man who has never entered the church, an unclean person who died where he should have died'.[68] To set up the work of such a heretic in the church is to commit 'blasphemy'. But when the pastor notes that opinions among the people are divided, he seeks to gain time. To calm people down he promises an investigation by the church authorities, but deceitful as he is, at the same time he orders his sacristan next door to burn this Christ. This plan is prevented by Macarios' attentiveness, and finally the Christ finds an appropriate place on a neighbouring hill.

From now on the Itapé hill of Calvary becomes a place of pilgrimage for the people. Granted, eventually the official church too gets hold of this rebellious Christ by integrating him into the official Good Friday liturgy, but before this the people celebrates with its Christ its own 'fresh, rebellious, earthy cult': every Good Friday its Christ is taken down from the cross by the people and taken to the church porch with the 'howling of songs of praise and lamentation'. After being promenaded round the excited crowd for a while, the Christ is taken back to his mountain. The official church has called this hill of Itapé 'the way of God'. But to the people of Itapé – not afraid of 'the reputation of being zealots and heretics' – it remains 'the way of man', the way not of the church's Son of God from above but of its Son of Man from below:

> I do not agree, Macario had already said at that time. The name should not have been changed. At any rate the hill of the leprous Christ should be called 'man's way' . . . For men, dear children, he said, almost repeating Gaspar's words, are born twice. Once at birth and once and death . . . They die, but live on in the others if they have dealt honestly with their neighbours. And if they learn to forget themselves during their lifetimes, while the earth swallows up their bodies, it does not swallow up their memories . . .[69]

This scene at the beginning cannot be overestimated as an archetype for the whole novel. For whatever is told in the following chapters of failed attempts at revolution, of peasants' revolts, of wars that swallow up people, of decades of dictatorship; whatever is unfolded as a history of constant exploitation and oppression of the indigenous population by a small class of landowners, the Christ of Itapé always confronts the reader as an expression of identification with the suffering of ordinary people and the overcoming of suffering. For the people of the village this Christ is 'their' Christ; he is as tattered they are; he is scorned, mocked and murdered as they are. Yet at the same time the hope of redemption clings to this figure with which they identify – according to the words of Macarios: 'As they were swept together by misfortune, the hope for redemption had to unite people.'[70] And this hope for redemption comes about in acts of selfless surrender for other people, who then live on 'immortally' in others.

This is also to be found in a second key scene in the novel. There is the figure of the 'doctor', a mysterious figure, who appears one day in the village of Sapukai. Initially this man is extremely alien to the villagers, terse and keeping himself to himself. Only through rumours do they discover that he must be a Russian emigrant. He lives as a recluse in his hut, wanders silently through the village, drinks his brandy in the bar without a word and later has no companion but a shaggy dog. However, one day he surprisingly goes into action, providing medicine to heal the gravedigger's daughter, Maria Regalada. From now on he gets the reputation of being a 'doctor'. In his basic attitude of complete unselfishness and unpretentious dedication to the most ordinary people this man, too, becomes a Christ figure, and moreover there are unmistakable allusions to Christ's healing actions:

Day by day the people began to swarm round his round-roofed hut in increasing numbers. From the remotest plantations, even from the neighbouring villages, sick people and cripples came on foot, on horseback and in carts to seek healing. Lepers also came. The doctor treated them all, one after the other, silently, patiently, without making any distinctions, unwilling to take any recompense from the poorest, who thereupon resolved to bring him something: some a chicken, others eggs and groceries or a bit of cotton so that he could replace the rags that he wore on his body.[71]

The doctor already has the reputation of being a mystic and increasingly becoming like a saint, so his strange behaviour of going to the bar at any time of day and drinking brandy to the point of getting drunk is striking. Moreover he treats only those who, carrying some old picture, knock on the door of his hut. He immediately snatches the picture from them and weighs it greedily in his hands, while his obsessed eyes trace the outlines of the work of art. And after he has spent a few months in this fashion, drunk, half-crazy, terser than ever, he suddenly vanishes. The inhabitants of the village discover that pictures of saints have been left behind in his hut, chopped to pieces with blows from an axe . . .

A man sacrifices himself for the people

And then there is the story of Casiano Jara and his wife Natividad. They are made an example – the third key scene – of one of the most blatant social problems of the Paraguay of the time, the terrifying practice of exploitation on the giant plantations. Casiano and Natividad, both from Sapukai, are lured to these plantations with money, not at first suspecting that they have fallen into a terrible trap. For on the Takurú-Purú plantation to which they are driven there is not only – as everywhere – a practice of merciless toil and exploitation. In addition it is impossible to escape this hell, since the plantation is surrounded by giant marshy primeval forest. With bitter sarcasm it is said in the notes:

All that had succeeded in escaping from Takurú-Purú were the verses of a 'composition' which with the strings of the guitar told of the

misery of Mensú, the day-labourer who was buried alive in the grave
of the tea plantations. The bilingual song by an unknown author told
of those men who every day of the year toiled under the lash and could
rest only on Good Friday; they too were relieved of their cross only for
a single day. However, it was without the boastful resurrection of the
other, solitary one, since these bare-footed, dark-skinned Christians in
truth died unredeemed and forgotten, not only on the tea plantations
of 'industrial Paraguay' but also on the other large estates. Festering
for three centuries like a curse on the forests of the Republic, they made
the former Jesuit rule seem like an idyllic patriarchal dream.[72]

Indeed, the times of the Jesuit state of Paraguay, a social experiment on
a religious basis for the Indios in the eighteenth century, were long past.
Now the indigenous population was shamelessly exploited by a thin
upper class, backed by foreign capital. When Casiano and Natividad
conceive a child, they are firmly resolved to attempt to break out,
especially when one of the overseers begins to make sexual advances to
the wife. However, the first attempt to escape has to be aborted when
Natividad has her child; Casiano has to pay for this with fourteen days of
the strictest incarceration. When they have recovered, they begin their
second attempt to escape, and the stations of their flight – marked by
guards and their dogs – through primal forest and marsh are among the
most exciting chapters of this book. The references to the Jesus story can
clearly be recognized. The three can be understood as a symbol of the
Holy Family on the flight to Egypt. The woman's name itself refers
literally to the 'birth of Christ', to Christmas. And the New Testament
flight scene in turn refers back to the Old Testament which has preserved
the great archetypal flight scene: the exodus of the people of Israel from
Egypt. So it is no coincidence that, in allusion to this, this chapter bears
the title 'Exodus'; here the happy ending is also taken over, since Casiano
and Natividad succeed in escaping from the hell of the primal forest.

Their son Cristóbal is probably the most significant 'christological'
figure in the whole novel; more than any other he embodies the three
qualities of brotherliness, readiness for sacrifice and rebellion. First, he
becomes the rebel leader in the Chaco war. Here, in a kind of suicide
squad, he manages to bring a water truck through the enemy lines to a
scattered band of troops. His mutilated arms tied to the steering wheel of
the truck, he sacrifices his life for his fellow soldiers. His cross is the
tanker with which he brings the life-giving water. And like Christ he must
accept death to bring life.

So he, too, becomes someone who is born twice: after birth, once again in death, for he, too, lives on 'immortally' in human memory for his act of selfless sacrifice. The novelist Gerda Schüler has rightly said of the three christological figures of the novel (Gaspar, Casiano and Cristóbal) that they 'are not symbols of Catholicism but symbols of oppression, the suffering of a whole people who are seen in analogy to the suffering of Christ. The three figures die a sacrificial death and through that bring hope and redemption, redemption of human beings by human beings. The religious symbols are exclusively related to this world, and in this way at the same time orientated on the future. A change of circumstances can be achieved only by those who are rooted in the people, through a return to mythical thought, and reflection on the ideas of value and faith in the pre-Columbian period and in primitive Christianity.'[73]

And finally – the fourth key scene – there is the story of the police chief of Itapé, Don Melitón Isasi, told from the perspective of a Franciscan sister. This story is set in a time when First Lieutenant Miguel Vera has become mayor of his village after the Chaco war. Hardly has he arrived there (his suffering wife named Doña Brígida de Isasi at his side) than this police officer begins to chase after the young girls of the village and make them sexually compliant. They include the young Felicitas Goiburú, whose twin brother is still in the army. Catastrophe happens when one day there is a rumour that she is pregnant by him. His own wife goes half-mad, an abortion is attempted, but it fails. Melitón leaves the village with Felicitas so that she can bring her child into the world in another place.

When the sister goes up to the leprous Christ days later on the mount of Calvary, she makes a gruesome discovery. She not only finds the bloodstained rosary of Dona Brígida; she also discovers that the Christ on the cross is all at once wearing boots:

> I raised my eyes rather higher, and saw that the Christ was wearing uniform, and that his garments were smeared with blood. Still kneeling, I finally recognized as in a ghostly appearance Melitón Isasi, tied to the black cross with the lasso bound round him several times, and half-beheaded.
>
> I got up to run away but stumbled over the wooden Christ which had been thrown into the undergrowth. It still glittered and sent out a thin cloud of incense. When I got up to run, on I saw in the depth of the hollow the body of Dona Brígida. I didn't learn more, for at that moment I lost consciousness and fell with my face in the glow . . .'[74]

An epic on the human power to resist

All three scenes are wild, cruel, archaic, and as readers we can now understand the significance of the narrative breaks better. Roa Bastos – a middle-class intellectual – is here reporting on an alien world the strangeness of which he cannot and will not tone down. He is not so naive as to think that he can simply identify his middle-class intellectual sphere with this popular world, a world full of wild beauty and cruel terror. So the detachment of the witness Miguel Vera is also his own.

But this distance in no way gets in the way of the author's solidarity with the hope of freedom which glimmers in the people. And as we read the apparently endless chain of violence, oppression, exploitation and annihilation, we become aware how important the key sentence at the beginning of this novel was: 'As they were swept together by misfortune, the hope of redemption had to unite people.' Therefore the two dimensions of this novel must be seen. As a literary critic wrote, it is first about 'the history of the fears and suffering of Paraguay'. But at the same time it is also 'a parable of its struggle, its hope, its efforts at redemption'.[75] Therefore this novel must be ultimately read as praise of the power of resistance of ordinary people, which has borne the permanent crucifixions with such infinite patience. As Augusto Roa Bastos himself writes:

> Being removed from my homeland has forced on me the theme of this novel. The long years of reflection on my country and its problems had damaged my sensitivity. When I wanted to remember the image of our people I came up against this will to resist and endure at any price, despite the unhappiness and misfortune in which our history was so rich. The initial motif which then became the thematic nucleus of *Son of Man* developed from this; its nine chapters are no more than variations on the human power to resist, in the face of not only physical extermination but also moral humiliation.[76]

Because this novel is ultimately a hymn of praise to the resistance and endurance of the people, its title needs to be interpreted carefully. That also becomes necessary because the author strategically puts some texts at the beginning of his book: three quotations from the book of Ezekiel and three verses from the Guaraní's 'Song of the Dead'. This provides a complex intertextual frame of reference for understanding the novel.

What does 'Son of Man' mean?

On the basis of the biblical tradition introduced here, the term 'Son of Man' is more than just a periphrasis for 'ordinary person', 'utterly human'. Certainly this dimension of understanding is constantly present in the novel. Indeed it is the ordinary person who is crucified day by day; in sum the 'Son of Man' is 'the oppressed, mocked, exiled, intimidated and buried people'[77] of Paraguay. But at least two further dimensions of meaning need to be taken into account.

Roa Bastos puts these sentences from the book of the prophet Ezekiel at the front of his book:

Son of man, you dwell in the midst of a rebellious house (12.2).

Eat your bread with quaking and drink water with trembling and fearfulness (12.18)

And I will set my face against that man, I will make him a sign and a byword and cut him off from the midst of my people (14.8).

As we know, the prophet Ezekiel was writing among the exiles of his people in Babylonia (in the years 593–571). His speeches and visions centre on one basic notion. The siege and destruction of Jerusalem and the deportation of the people is God's punishment of a rebellious people which has largely given itself over to idolatry and thus has sinned against Yahweh the God of the people of Israel. The prophet, addressed by Yahweh as 'son of man', dwells among this 'rebellious people' and speaks in vain against their blindness and deafness. It follows from this that Roa Bastos may have been signalling through the quotation of this saying that the 'Son of Man' is always on the one hand someone with a commission from God but on the other hand always resists the dominant conditions of his time.

This is emphasized once again by the other quotation from Ezekiel. The invitation for the son of man to eat his bread 'with quaking' and to drink his water with 'fear and dismay' is to be understood as an anticipatory symbolic action. In this way the prophet is to show what awaits the people as a whole in God's penal judgment. With this quotation Roa Bastos takes over the threats and warnings of the Jewish prophets. The 'quaking' and the 'fear and dismay' of the ordinary people is now merely an anticipation of what also awaits the rulers if they do not change the people's situation.

This threat to the rulers (who at the same time are the ungodly) is reinforced by the third Ezekiel quotation. The 'man' who is here made a warning sign and who is cut off from the midst of the people is the one who (as is clear from the context of Ezek. 14) attempts to justify himself before the prophets, although he has left idols in his heart. War is declared on him by God through his prophets: a warning sign is set up for him, he is made an example of, he belongs to death.

If the Old Testament son of man tradition which is taken over for the novel by the Ezekiel quotations thus contains elements of the prophetic resistance, the threats and the warnings, the New Testament Son of man tradition contains the perspective of the identification with suffering. As we know, Jesus of Nazareth is also addressed as Son of man in the New Testament (especially in the Gospels of Matthew, Mark and Luke), and here in the meantime the expression has become an 'honorific title'.[78] It denotes a heavenly figure who is chosen by God for a special role. Many New Testament Son of man sayings refer to the earthly Son of man who suffers and rises again. Already in the early strata of New Testament texts the Son of man is the poor man, the outcast, the homeless wanderer, misunderstood and scorned. Luke has handed down a Son of man saying to this effect:

The foxes have their holes and the birds their nests; but the son of man has nowhere to lay his head (9.58).

The same is true in the Gospel of Matthew:

For John came neither eating nor drinking, and they say, 'He has a demon'; the son of man came eating and drinking, and they say, 'Behold a glutton and a drunkard, a friend of tax collectors and sinners' (11.38f.).

This stratum of the New Testament Son of man sayings also appears in Roa Bastos. For his individual 'christological figures' (Gaspar, Casiano and Cristóbal) are figures 'from below': outsiders, homeless, needy, not to mention the people of Paraguay, for whom Roa Bastos created this unique epic. His novel is the resolution of that 'mystery' of life and death which Gaspar Mora addressed right at the beginning of the novel: the people lives on in the song of the poet; it can celebrate its resurrection in the medium of the epic, gain new life in the mode of poetic imagination. That is why these verses from the 'Death Song of the Guaranis', the fourth quotation at the beginning of the book are so telling:

I will make this voice flow again through the bones . . .
and I will make language flesh again . . .
When this time is past and a new time dawns . . .

So this novel is a modern passion novel and at the same time a modern resurrection novel which is not concerned with a world beyond, but with the beginning of a liberation movement in this world. Thus the title of the novel must be read as criticism of the church, in that it deliberately sets the people's Christ, the 'Son of man' below, over against the Christ of the official church, the Son of God above. In this way Roa Bastos draws the dynamic of transcendence into history and makes it a literary anticipation of what was later to be taken up and developed further by the programme of Latin American liberation theology.[79] The author makes the chief witness of all these notes, Miguel Vera, sum up this hope for liberation right at the end in these sentences:

> There must be a way out from the tremendous stubbornness of the man who was crucified by men. Otherwise one would have to believe that the human form is cursed for ever, that this is hell and we may hope for no redemption.
> There must be a way out, for otherwise . . . [80]

5. All human beings God's image: Cingiz Ajmatov

In 1986, in the Soviet Union, which still existed at that time, there appeared one of the boldest political novels, which then also attracted great attention internationally: *The Place of Execution*, by Cinghiz Ajjmatov, who was born in 1928.[81] The book was bold not least because more than any other Soviet author before him the author had dared openly to attack the social, economic and ecological problems of the USSR (alcoholism, drugs, organized crime, plundering of nature, deification of the military). It was also bold because in this novel basic questions of religion[82] are given a surprisingly central place: here the reader is present at a dialogue between Jesus and Pilate of a kind that no Russian-speaking writer had written since Dostoievsky's *The Brothers Karamazov* and Bulgakov's *The Master and Margarita*.[83]

A novel between the cultures

The author of this book is an inter-cultural phenomenon.[84] He is a Kirghizian, born in Seker in the Talas valley (in the region of Kirov), and at the same time, writing in Russian, the product of the former multi-cultural Soviet Union, to which he owes his schooling, his study of agriculture and later literature, indeed his whole career as newspaper editor, cultural official and author. His background is one of middle-class farmers, but he managed to gain high office in the cultural life of Moscow, and at the time of the reforms under Gorbachev which began in 1985 rose to be a member of the Presidential Council. He is a Muslim, but he is open to Russian Christianity and to the Bible, which he got to know for the first time at the end of 1980. By his own confession, reading it 'shed a new light on life'.[85]

Ajmatov's novel has been called a typical Perestroika novel, but it is far more than that. Already in its form it has an intercultural orientation, since it consists of an epic collage of different narrative sections and strands of action which are loosely linked together.

– It has a level of the animal world and natural religion, with animals as 'heroes' and critics. The story is told of the she-wolf Akbara and her family, the basis of whose life is being destroyed by constant brutal human excursions into nature. But we are also told of the fate of thousands of wild antelopes on the hitherto untouched steppes. Out of purely economic interests (to meet the Socialist Five Year Plan for meat production) they are driven together by helicopters and then slaughtered by guards and hunters in a terrible blood bath. So the steppes have become a place of execution.

– It has a Kirghizian level: the story of Boston, the shepherd, who seeks in vain in the confusions of Soviet officialdom to achieve a balance between nature and culture, the animal world and the human world, and on failing eventually chooses suicide in the Issyk-Kul lake.

– Finally, it has a Russian Orthodox level, at which the story is told of Avdi Kallistatov, the priest's son, who is expelled from the priests' seminary for heresy. He becomes a journalist and is sent by his paper to Central Asia to discover the background to the opium smuggling. Avdi finds out that the whole of the Soviet Union has long been covered by a net of producers, distributors, dealers and fixers. Disguised as an opium courier, he succeeds in getting to the boss of the drug Mafia, an ice-cold cynic who makes his money with this destructive drug. When Avdi begs the hemp-gatherers to stop what they are doing, they maltreat him and finally throw him from a moving train.

However, while Avdi is lying bloody and wounded on the track and losing consciousness, the author fits in an archetypal scene which is similarly about an 'eccentric', someone 'from Galilee'. In flashes, comparable to film cuts, the Jesus story (in its last phase with Pontius Pilate) is inserted into the text: this betrays the author's conviction from the beginning. His little story here and today is none other than the repetition of the great, unique history of Jesus of Nazareth in a new cultural constellation, in another age of space and time. Shortly after the publication of the novel, Ajmatov answered the question why this time he has not made a Muslim but a Christian his main hero:

> Of course that is no coincidence. Christianity gives a very powerful impulse with the figure of Christ. Islam, to which I belong by virtue of my origin, has no such figure. Muhammad was not a martyr. He had hard and tormenting days, but he was not crucified for an idea, and it is not said that he had been able to forgive people this for ever. Jesus gives me the opportunity to communicate something hidden to present-day men and women. Therefore I, an atheist, have encountered him on my creative course.[86]

Literary critics have criticized Ajmatov severely for his insertion of Jesus.[87] His Jesus story has been said to be a 'pale imitation' of the corresponding passage from Mikhail Bulgakov's novel *The Master and Margarita* (R. Schmitz); to seem 'like an alien body' (P. Wilke); to be of 'almost superfluous obtrusiveness' (A. Braun). Other critics have been more gracious and have emphasized the great continuity with a basic feature of Russian literature which Ajmatov probably intended: 'Avdi Kallistratov, son of a priest, thrown out of a priests' seminar, belongs among the fools in Christ in which old Russian literature is so rich. In particular, he is a descendant of the figures of Dostoievsky, for example the Idiot or Alyosha Karamazov.' And because a 'primitive Christianity with a Russian colouring' is expressed in Ajmatov, the Jesus passage in the novel is also taken seriously in quite a different way: 'How serious Ajmatov is about the name Avdi who takes the cross upon himself becomes clear in the insertion in which he portrays Christ himself, in the confrontation with Pontius Pilate, the steward of power.'[88] Let's look more closely at the literary technique of the insertion of Jesus.

Ways of making Jesus present

Anna Seghers uses the technique of vivid remembrance in the consciousness of her hero, a Communist prisoner fleeing from crucifixion by the Nazis, to tie this passion story to Jesus – in the interest of the solidarity of all who are persecuted for a just cause;

William Faulkner uses the age-old stylistic means of allegory and typology to depict his mutineer corporal Stephan as Jesus *redivivus* in the First World War, and at the same time, with the technique of withdrawing Jesus' principle of non-violence, critically illuminates all power that asserts itself and establish itself against him;

Naguib Mahfouz similarly depicts his exorcist Rifaa typologically as a Jesus who tries to overcome evil, greed and the lust for power by a spiritual cleansing of the inner person;

Augusto Roa Bastos uses the technique of the objective correlate (the carved wooden Jesus of Itapé) and the figurative encipherment (in the christological figures of the novel), to go on telling the story of Jesus as the story of the people;

Cinghiz Ajmatov chooses a whole set of different literary techniques to make Jesus present. First there is the technique of literary montage. In the second part of the novel, a chapter (Chapter 2) has been inserted which contains an extended dialogue between Pontius Pilate and Jesus – in Jerusalem among the marble pillars of Herod's terraced arcade.[89] Is this a dream, a vision of other images from within Avdi, who is lying wounded by the railway line?

Things are immediately different in the next section. For here the intensity of the references to Jesus is heightened: now with the technique of simultaneity the author deliberately inserts his hero into the story of Jesus.[90] Avdi is portrayed as someone who experiences the passion of Christ as an eye-witness – on his lips the burning question what he should do to save the Master from distress. Thus space and time are fused together – linked by the thought that the great stories are not things of the past, but live on and repeat themselves anew: 'From generation to generation good and evil are handed down in uninterrupted remembrance, endlessly through the time and space of the human world. So it is true to say that those of yesterday cannot know what is happening today, but those of today know what happened yesterday, and tomorrow those of today will be those of yesterday . . .'[91]

The third and last stage of the concentration of the references to Jesus is achieved by Ajmatov with the technique of typology. For the end of the Avdi story (among the guards and hunters) is a crucifixion – a deliberately cruel parody of the crucifixion of Jesus. The drunken drivers who had first attempted to force Avdi to deny his god, proceed to a lynching, which they stage as a mocking imitation of the execution of Jesus:

The rowdyism suddenly took an ominous turn. A malicious farce threatened to become a lynching: 'Only one thing is wrong, son of a bitch, in this wretched steppe we have no nails nor a cross. Pity, shithouse.' Mishash knocked the axle off. That would do. Crucify him. 'It doesn't matter, we'll tie him with ropes. He'll hang there just as well as with nails.'[92]

Demystifying power in the name of religion

So the steppe has becomes a place of execution, where human beings slaughter other human beings and also the animals. Thus the references to Jesus in this novel are far from being a 'foreign body' of 'superfluous obtrusiveness'. Rather, they give historical sharpness and depth to what is happening now. They make the reader (especially the atheistic Russian or the Muslim Kirghizian reader) aware that now, too – in the 'whole world' of the Socialist system – a drama is being continued in which humankind has always been involved. Strategically, the continuity with the Jesus story which Ajmatov wanted has this very purpose: against the ideology of the socialist revolution which has allegedly changed the world, it signifies that the old 'games' are still being played and that even after the October Revolution the world is an alienated one. Here recognition of the achievements of religion is relevant to Ajmatov in criticizing society. More than any Soviet author before him he dares – despite all the state ideology prevalent at that time – to give religion a force which enlightens people and gives them orientation.[93] Conversely, this post-Socialist, post-atheist revaluation of religion presupposes that the state socialist and materialist ideology has led to a horrifying alienation of human beings who are deceiving themselves. Instead of moral progress, scientific enlightenment and comprehensive humanism, it has furthered the 'religion of military superiority'.[94]

What Ajmatov is engaged in in this novel is thus a criticism of ideology in the name of true religion. The Soviet system had developed into a kind of substitute religion; new gods had arisen whose divinity fed on the availability of weapons of mass destruction. And the novel is written against this 'new, powerful religion', the 'religion of military superiority' – with reference to the alternative scheme for humankind embodied in Jesus of Nazareth. Thus the insertion of Jesus had a literally fundamental function in terms of the subject-matter: it demystifies the socialist state ideology, gives historical transparency and significance to the passions of the present, and introduces earliest Christianity as a spiritual counter-scheme. Recourse to the Jesus story serves to universalize the cause, which Ajmatov will later once again describe like this:

> Only if the artist emerges not simply as someone who depicts life but at the same time also as citizen, judge, prosecutor and prophet, who combines in his creative work both Jesus and Pontius Pilate, do persons and actions include the experience of time for the long term and for generations.[95]

Moreover, in the conversation between Jesus and Pilate, questions are discussed which have been at issue all down the centuries and still are: the question of power, of the violence of rulers, and the longing of men and women for 'happiness and equality for all'. Here Ajmatov takes the artistic liberty of developing the encounter between Pilate and Jesus into a dispute in political philosophy; and at this point one can in fact make aesthetic and theological objections. But in literary terms this is permissible, especially as here Ajmatov deliberately wanted to set counter-accents to Bulgakov's depiction of Jesus, in which Pilate as a tragic hero appears more credible and more vivid than Jesus.[96] For Ajmatov, by contrast, in Pilate and Jesus there is a confrontation of two basic attitudes which clash in argument. Here Pilate embodies the principle of the safeguarding of power and world order on the basis of military supremacy; supremacy of rule; the division of the world into the rulers and the ruled. He believes that the present world order is an unshakeable bulwark and that therefore any demand for a kingdom of 'righteousness for all' is a mental aberration. He believes that now the world must be ruled by the powerful and that the strong will dominate it for ever and ever. For him this order is as eternal as the stars in heaven. At the climax of the conversation he retorts to Jesus:

> I just ask myself: why did you kindle the fire in which you were the first to burn? The world cannot live without emperors; the power of the one involves the subject of the other, and you struggle vainly to compel another order which you have thought up as a new history. The emperors have their own gods; they do not worship your abstract Tomorrow-God who fuses somewhere into the infinite future and who belongs equally to all like the air, for anything that one can give in equal parts is nothing; it is inferior or empty; therefore the emperors are bound in their name to rule over each and all . . . Your concern for the human race is vain, and vain is the sacrifice of your life. Human beings cannot be given anything either by sermons in temples or voices

in heaven. They will always follow the emperors as shepherds follow sheep, and they will kneel before the strong and prosperous and honour the one who shows himself to be the most inexorable and powerful of all; they will praise the generals and their massacres where blood flows in streams, so that the one can rule and the other is subjected and humiliated.[97]

The analogies between Roman imperialism and Soviet imperialism are unmistakable, and are doubtless deliberately and consciously drawn by a Kirghizian author. Moreover Ajmatov portrays his Jesus as a radical counter scheme to a world in which the stronger has power and trusts in weapons more than in human hearts. Jesus embodies a 'higher authority', 'another truth', and as the truth cannot be shared, it must necessarily come into conflict with Pilate's truth. For a preacher like Jesus who promises 'happiness and equality for all and for ever', who proclaims 'one single God for all, for all lands and for the whole human race, and that for all times', who propagates 'a kingdom of righteousness for each and all' and thus 'wants to make all equal, from emperor to slave' in fact intensifies the differences and confuses the previous world order.

Jesus returns to humankind

But the deepest mystery of Ajmatov's Jesus is still not uncovered. It emerges in that question of which Pilate has heard rumours and which is the only one that really disturbs him. Will Jesus indeed come again as judge of the world? When will that be? It is understandable that Pilate wants to know this, since this return could be a factor causing unrest and instability in the imperial world order. For the novel, it is decisive that Ajmatov makes his Jesus correct this very idea: he will not come again as a person; rather, he will return to human beings 'in human beings'.[98] And he will do so when after an infinitely wearisome way of suffering human beings have struggled through to their innermost and truest determination: their determination 'to goodness and beauty'. Yes, Ajmatov's Jesus sees the meaning of his preaching as nothing other than awakening in human beings the awareness of their determination, their 'divine origin':

I was born into this world to serve as an eternal example for human beings. So that human beings may have hope in my name and come to me through suffering, through the daily battle with the evil in themselves, through the abhorrence of vice, violence and the shedding of blood which oppress souls so ominously, if they are not full of the love of God and consequently of their images, of human beings.[99]

But has this Jesus not identified human beings and God here? This is the answer to the question which is put in the mouth of Pilate:

> In a sense yes, and moreover all human beings together are God's image on earth. And the name is the God of that hypostasis – the Tomorrow-God, the God of Infinity, who has been given to the world by his creation . . . Thus hope lives in us inextinguishably as the light of God. Tomorrow-God is also the all-embracing spirit of infinity; in him the whole being, all actions and all human strivings are transcended; and whether this Tomorrow-God is beautiful or ugly, good-hearted or punitive, depends on human beings themselves. Such thought is fitting and is called for; God the Creator himself wants it from the thinking being, so human beings themselves should be concerned about the future on earth, for each is a part of the Tomorrow-God. Human beings themselves are the judges and creators of each of their days . . .[100]

Thus the mysteries of the image of God and human beings in Ajmatov's Jesus are laid open. And we understand both very much better if we do not measure and disqualify them with a dogmatic standard,[101] but hold them against the background of the socialist atheistic criticism of religion which was still prevalent at that time. For here Ajmatov arrives at a highly differentiated standpoint in matters of religion. He remains equidistant from the atheism of the socialist state and church orthodoxy, whose backward-looking nature and dogmatism (in the spirit of Leo Tolstoy) is subject to the most vigorous criticism in the chapter about the priests' seminary at the beginning of the novel.[102] In concrete terms this means that Ajmatov affirms talk of God against the official contempt for religion, but here religion – opposed to church orthodoxy – has no function for the other world, but exclusively for this world. Against the traditional criticism of religion, Ajmatov sets up the figure of Jesus; but here – and in opposition to church orthodoxy – not as a transcendent redeemer from whom human beings would expect all their salvation, but as an active liberator for a practice which brings change. Through Jesus – as an example – people should become aware of their divine origins, in order actively to take upon themselves 'the daily battle with evil'.

Talk of God in Ajmatov also has a clear function: it serves to give every individual a share in God's reality ('the spirit of infinity') in order to make them capable of feeling responsible for the whole of creation.

Ajmatov thinks it supremely important in the decisive passage that the religious metaphors which he uses should not encourage any belief in destiny. Talk of God should not make people passively expectant ('Last Judgment'), but liberate and motivate them from within, to 'be concerned themselves for the future on earth'. Where this happens, creation happens anew everyday; where this is refused, the Last Judgment takes place again every day.[103]

So it is only consistent that Ajmatov's Jesus refuses to elaborate transcendence in any way. For him the death of each individual is the end. In the transcendent world 'only the spirit glides noiselessly and unfathomable, like the shadows reflected on water', but no way leads there for the body. Accordingly this Jesus is concerned with 'immeasurable life, life on earth'. And therefore he tells Pilate – glad to be able to do so in the last hour before his death – of a tormenting vision which he had the previous night. It is the vision of an earth without human beings. It is the vision of an apocalypse which human beings have staged themselves, in which they have exterminated themselves. Nothing is more fearful for Ajmatov's Jesus than this scenario, since he has set all his hope on human beings. Without them he too cannot get anywhere; if human life is exterminated, then he too is finally dead, and hatred and enmity have won.

And because that is the case; because the Pilate principle is still fighting against the Jesus principle in a battle which has yet to be decided, the death of Jesus on the cross is also a consequence of this battle. So it is not surprising that Ajmatov's Jesus does not at any point defend himself against this death. He accepts it as predestined, as a clear consequence of his message. In a peaceful and relaxed way he goes to the Place of the Skull, his only concern to endure his 'destined fate' worthily and not to humiliate himself by 'howling like cattle'. Ajmatov does not let his Jesus think of bargaining with God; for in the end it is not up to him (he is only an 'example'), but up to human beings and how they behave in the battle between good and evil.

Overcoming evil for all times

That also explains the logic of the second Jesus insertion, which works with the technique of simultaneity. It is a piece of Christian passion mysticism, in which Avdi becomes the direct witness to the execution of Jesus, which he tries to prevent. This resistance to the crucifixion of Jesus has less to do with Ajmatov's Islamic origin[104] than with the logic of the novel. For in terms of narrative structure this piece of Jesus mysticism has an important double function. It is psychologically important, since it depicts the young idealist Avdi as someone who – to some degree all by himself – seeks to reverse the passion of Jesus. He is so affected by the fate of the Master that he is ready to do anything to stop this story, to make it not have happened. Thus Avdi is one of those passionate mystics who is ready once again to move mountains, to shift times, to do away with facts. After almost two thousand years of Christianity he cannot be content with the event on Golgotha: he wants to wind it back like a film. This young man in search of God thus to some degree rattles on the structures of time, knowing that two thousand years of Christianity have not made the world more saved nor human beings more redeemed.

But all these fictitious options are to no avail. World history will largely run contrary to the message of Jesus. The death of Jesus on the cross is in particular the expression of a story in which the outcome between salvation and doom is still undecided. Therefore this mystical insertion of Jesus into the novel also has an important function in terms of structure and content. It underlines the basic statement that the history of doom must repeat itself as long as Jesus' principle of goodness and beauty has not established itself. Therefore the passion narrative of Jesus must also reproduce itself in the twentieth century, because a large number of people do not act and do business in the spirit of Jesus of Nazareth but with the demonry of Pontius Pilate. No one embodies more cynically than the boss of the drug Mafia the principle that the stronger dominate the weaker.

But the decisive thing is that while the Jesus principle comes to grief in this novel, it remains as an image of hope for humankind. Indeed in this novel by a Muslim one can read astonishing reflections on the uniqueness of Jesus:

Since the day that He mounted the cross, the spirits have not let go of Him. Since those days, so much that came with the claim to immortality has long been forgotten and is in dust and ashes. Human life improves every day: what is new today is already old tomorrow; what seems better today pales tomorrow before something even more beautiful. Why then does the word of Jesus not grow old and lose its power? And was everything that happened from his birth to his execution, with all the consequences over time and generations, really so inaccessible and unavoidable for humankind? And where was the sense of this way into human history? What have they achieved? Where have they got to?[105]

This addresses two basic dimensions: the novel is sober and realistic to the point of scepticism (it knows the power of evil and accordingly makes both its heroes Avdi and Boston fail), and at the same time – hoping against hope – it establishes a goal which is identical with the all-embracing love of human beings and God that is uniquely embodied in Jesus of Nazareth. The crosses of world history are obviously unavoidable, but they are not strong enough to kill off this human longing for all-embracing love and beauty. Moreover a key passage in Avdi's mystical mediations on Jesus says ambiguously:

And you, master, prepare for the cruellest execution, so that human beings may become open to goodness and compassion, so that they may perceive the fundamental difference between the rational and the irrational, for laborious is the way of man on earth, and evil is deeply rooted in him. On the way do we achieve the absolute ideal – a mind winged with the freedom of thought? And the exalted personality which in itself overcomes evil for all times, just as an infectious illness can be conquered? Oh, if only this could be achieved! My God, what a burden you have laid on us to improve a world which cannot be improved?[106]

Cinghiz Ajmatov's novel, written in a completely different culture, is also a novel of resistance. It has been called a novel of warning, the writing on the wall. It brightly depicts the problems of a society in which the powers of evil seem to triumph. And yet it does not stop there. For all the 'hells' on earth cannot refute the real vision of humankind embodied in Jesus: that there may be a time in which human beings will have ceased to be one another's enemies, in which they will remember that 'all human beings together are God's image on earth'. The cross of Jesus Christ exerts its influence in an unculture of brutality, in a society in which human beings are wolves exterminating wolves, as the counter-force of impotence which goes against the facts.[107]

A question now almost demands to be asked of all these passion texts from Anna Seghers to Cinghiz Ajmatov: Jesus – the one who is near to us and yet wholly other, the primal symbol of passion and resistance, of utopia and failure? Christian tradition has always associated the confession of Jesus with the certainty that he is alive, through God and with God. He has been raised; God has not left him in death but made possible new life for him. We shall investigate in the next chapter the challenge this has posed to writers.

IV. Resurrection: a temptation for Christians who have become bourgeois

Those who like me were brought up in the Catholic Church will have had Easter hymns quite automatically stored in their memories. The melodies of these hymns, simple and yet so powerful, fell unresistingly on our ears, and when aroused, they still ring out in my head: 'Christ is risen from the tomb'; 'Empty the tomb, the hero raised', 'Praise be God in highest tone, with his well beloved Son, who the victory has won . . . ' And with these hymns, their theology also quite naturally rang out in our minds, without our having understood what we were singing.

1. Easter as the triumph of Christianity

All through my religious upbringing there was no question of a critical discussion of the 'content' of Easter. We were not invited to criticize; there was no dealing with the difficulties which the Easter texts in the New Testament already created. Why? We Catholics could joyfully sing:

> This is the day that God has made,
> his glory to the world displayed.
> With heart and soul let all rejoice
> proclaim his wonders with one voice (GL 220).

Easter hymns – sung joyfully and naively

We thus took the 'miracle' of Easter completely for granted. It was quite natural to us that this Christian event had a significance for the whole world: *all* the darkness of death had been 'lightened' by the resurrection of our Redeemer, *all* the 'suffering of the world' transfigured. On this festival it was quite automatic for us to think in universalistic terms and we did not suppose for a minute that this would be seen in quite a different light by billions of non-Christians: by Jews, Muslims, Buddhists, Hindus and Confucians. On the matter of Easter we were naïve universalists, intoning with great ardour:

> Be joyful here and everywhere
> for God the Lord is risen,
> for death itself he set death's snare
> broke open Hell's dark prison.
> The life of life now lives today
> o'er all the world he now holds sway
> and every power is broken (GL 226).

Yes, we believed uninterruptedly what the great Protestant baroque poet Paul Gerhardt had already written in the seventeenth century: Easter is the feast of the Christian triumph, the feast of Christ's victory. The images from the baroque period were still intact for us. And at Easter we loved to sing such battle songs and delighted in them: in the battle against hell and the fight against all the enemies of Christ. Christ was our victor, and with him we Christians were all victors. When it came to Easter we were naïve dualists, and intoxicated with a mystical-cosmic interpretation of the Easter event as it was presented to us by the great Catholic baroque poet Friedrich von Spee:

> Is that the body, Lord Jesus Christ,
> which in the tomb lay dead.
> Come, come you Christians, young and old,
> see it transfigured.
>
> The body is clear, as crystal clear,
> the wounds all ruby-bright.
> The soul shines through it light and pure
> a thousand rays of light.[108]

And so on. What this hymn suggested to us was that at Easter a transformation of cosmic extent came about. The body of Christ was changed in a miraculous way and shone out in unique beauty, unlike any other body. And this beauty of the body was to be transferred to all Christians, as is said in the last strophe of this hymn:

> That is the body, Lord Jesus Christ,
> which in the tomb lay dead.
> I live for you and die for you,
> give me a body transfigured.

Yes, when it came to Easter we were naively cosmic. And only later did it dawn on me that this triumphalistic, universalistic, dualistic and cosmic thought associated with Easter in the Reformation and the baroque period came to an unprecedented culmination. For there is one poet who like no other was able to stage the Christian resurrection as a cosmic-universal drama of salvation and battle. However, for him we must go back to the eighteenth century.

Resurrection as a cosmic drama: Friedrich Gottlieb Klopstock

Heavenly beings stand by the tomb of Jesus, angels, archangels; the 'fathers' from the old covenant awake from their sleep of death and gather round the place of the dead man: Abraham, David, Joseph, Ezekiel, Daniel and Isaiah, delighted at the opportunity of a new life. Around the tomb – a storm flash, the surge of prayers and songs which penetrate the cosmos. Among them ring out the cries of command of the Roman legionaries, pagans who believe in another God, one who has now come under suspicion. Abaddon the angel of death hastens to the Dead Sea, whither the adversaries of God have been banished, and gives them the choice: they can finally go to hell or partake in the resurrection of Christ to their own scorn. Indeed the hour of the resurrection has come; primal hurricanes rage through the heavens, giant forests bend their crown before the tomb, the mountains shake, rivers and floods dance, the trumpets of the archangels ring out . . .

And suddenly all see him, Christ, the Son of the Eternal One, risen in heavenly glory: all the archangels and patriarchs, the prophets and pagans, but also Satan, the hater and destroyer who is now finally banished to his hell. A Roman soldier brings the Pharisees the news of the empty tomb, and one of the Pharisees, Philo, who had previously joined in the violent death of Jesus. takes the soldier's sword and kills himself – the laugh of a madman on his lips..

1768: when this thirteenth song of Friedrich Gottlieb Klopstock's *Messiah* appeared, the author was forty-four and at the height of his literary career. The first songs of his monumental epic had appeared twenty years previously and it was to be another five years before all twenty songs, of around 20,000 lines, were completed.[109] Endowed with a princely pension by the king of Denmark, Klopstock had been able to work on his giant epic. He may be called the first professional German writer who could live not only on princely money but also on his own royalties and profits from his publishing house. Klopstock was 'a radical new type of citizen and literary producer', a 'self-producer powerfully over-compensating for his lowly social position'.[110]

Not only was the poetic-dramatic language which Klopstock used for his epic *Messiah* unprecedented; so too in literary wealth and depth was the way in which he gave literary form to the resurrection of Christ in the thirteenth song. For the first – and last – time a German author of literary stature can make it possible to experience the resurrection of Christ directly as a universal, cosmic and salvation-historical drama, by taking up the scant biblical reports and at the same time overtrumping them in literary terms. Adam and Eve beside the patriarchs and prophets of the old covenant at the tomb of Jesus! Convinced that the Christian revelation in part only provides 'outlines' which the poets have to elaborate in keeping with the main features; obsessed with the idea that it is the task of 'holy poetry to raise us above our short-sighted way of thinking, to snatch us from the current by which we are drawn on',[111] Klopstock is concerned to create a universal picture of the resurrection scene which truly fuses space and time. In his literary work of art the reader is as it were the contemporary and eye-witness of Christ's resurrection; suggestively, contemporaneity is produced between past and present, between once and now. Here literature still puts itself completely at the service of the Christian revelation. Moreover Klopstock loyally keeps to the facts of the church's doctrine, from which he dares to deviate only in the case of the dogma of the eternity of punishment in hell.

In other words, it was still possible for this poet to make angels and devils come and go in his resurrection story; it was possible to describe the patriarchs of Israel as longingly waiting for the Christian redemption; it was possible to make the cosmos, nature and history function for a drama of history conceived of exclusively in Christian terms, and to make the resurrection of Christ the final triumph of Christianity over Judaism and paganism. Here the poet is still exclusively understood as a holy seer, as an inspired interpreter of the biblical documents – carried away, intoxicated, emphatically reflecting on the eternal thoughts of God himself and elaborating them aesthetically with creative imagination. Indeed in the middle of the eighteenth century there was still a unity of Christianity and literature, church and poetry, and already in Klopstock's time countless Christians celebrated Holy Week and Easter with *The Messiah* in their hands. Their motto could have been: 'I hear the message and I have the faith.' And I am aware that we Catholics, with our hearty singing of Easter hymns, found ourselves in consciousness and poetry in the seventeenth and eighteenth centuries.

2. All I lack is faith: Johann Wolfgang Goethe

Change of scene. We shall look at probably the most famous Easter scene in the history of German literature and attempt to understand it step by step. A man in the search of the truth despairs. He has had more than his fill of all the superficialities of everyday life and the pursuit of knowledge. All this torment over knowledge – where in the end does it lead him but to the insight that really one cannot know anything? All the efforts to discover the basic forces of reality, to understand what holds the word together inwardly – are they a lost labour of love? All the loneliness of the questing scholar, all the renunciation of possessions and recognition – what is this if not a dog's life? But in his heart there is still a gaping hole. What was at the beginning of all beginnings? On what regularities is our world built? What holds the microcosm and the macrocosm together? Should one not conjure up the 'Great Spirit' with the help of magic? The spirit which rules in 'floods of life' and 'storms of action', which rules over birth and tomb, death and life?

A man seeks truth on his own initiative

And yet, when the great spirit appears, the scholar cannot bear it and turns away in fear like a worm. The one who wanted to treat the Great Spirit as an equal is told: 'You are like the spirit which you understand, not like me.' The man is resolved to put an end to his life. It is Easter Eve, the night between cross and resurrection, between life and death. But a remarkable thing happens: with the poison flask at his lips, he suddenly hears from a neighbouring church the message of the resurrection of Christ:

> Christ is arisen!
> Joy to the mortal
> freed from the baneful,
> insidious ills
> that man is heir to (lines 737–741).

He hesitates, puts it down – and this moment is enough to restore him to life:

> What depth of resonance, what clarity of tone,
> can drag the goblet from my lips?
> Do you announce so soon, you muffled bells,
> the first solemnities of Eastertide?
> Do you sing now, you choirs, the hymn of consolation

that by the darkened tomb, from angels' lips,
proclaimed the certainty of a new covenant? (lines 742–748)

When this scene from Goethe's *Faust* was written at the end of the eighteenth century, Klopstock's literary and religious world was already col-
lapsing.[112] Like a ghost, Klopstock's Easter scenery has disappeared from
German literature. For in *Faust* no poet intoxicated with religion puts
himself in the situation by Jesus' tomb – on a familiar literary footing
with prophets and patriarchs, angels and devils. Here, rather, at the most
'Christian' part of the whole drama, an author creates for himself an
unmistakably ironic distance from the church's Easter faith, which could
not be more sobering precisely because this scene takes place on Easter
Eve. If Faust's first reaction was to listen to the 'comforting song' of the
Easter message in happy spontaneity, the second more conscious reaction
of this intellectual thinker is essentially more critical and detached. As
if he has already granted the Easter message too much, in his second
reaction Faust must at the same time unmask it critically:

Celestial tones, so gently strong,
why do you seek me here amid the dust?
Be heard where tender mortals dwell!
I hear the message, all I lack is faith,
a faith whose dearest child is the miraculous.
I do not dare aspire to the spheres
from which your word of grace peals forth,
and yet these sounds, familiar since my youth,
summon me now again to life.
There was a time when in the sabbath's solemn quiet
the kiss of heaven's love would overcome me,
when there were portents in the choiring chimes,
and when a prayer was fervent pleasure;
some strange sweet longing would compel me to
rove through wood and meadow,
and to a flood of ardent tears
I'd feel a world arise within me.
This hymn announced the lively games of youth,
the happy freedom of spring celebrations;
the memory of childlike feelings now
keeps me from taking the last, solemn step.
O sweet celestial songs, sound on –
my tears well forth, and I am earth's again! (lines 762–84)

It is clear that in this great document of literature, Easter is no longer present as a triumphalistic saving drama about Judaism and paganism, but as a quotation from a submerged world. Only fragments of Klopstock's scenery are left, taken up in the antiphon of the 'women', 'angels' and 'young men', which are introduced into the world of Doctor Faust as substitutes from the Easter Eve liturgy. That is no coincidence, but a calculated symbolic act. On this most Christian of all Christian nights, Goethe's Faust is deliberately no longer at worship, but in his study – as someone seeking on his own initiative the truth which he manifestly does not find there in the church. While the congregation celebrates the 'new life;' in Christ with the Easter liturgy, Faust remains outside the walls of the church, indeed plays with his own life in a way which even in Goethe's time was offensive and wicked.

Ironical breaks in Easter

Thus if one looks closely, evidently Goethe can speak of Easter only in a threefold break.

First, the evocative presentation of a cosmic drama of salvation is no longer possible. The perspective is reduced to a figure of the present in whom the effects of the church's feast of Easter are critically reflected.

Secondly, an intellectual identification with the Christian Easter faith is no longer possible. This is seen through as a 'miracle' which psychologically serves to fulfil wishes and therefore is sheer illusion. The allusion to 'tender mortals' in whom these 'heavenly tones' of the resurrection could still ring out points to the same pattern of criticism of religion ('medicine') which Mephistopheles will use later in the drama to his pupil (I already went into this passage in the prologue to the present book): religion is at best something for 'tender', i.e. weak, possibly sick people, who need it as much as a medicine. That calls for the opposite conclusion: 'hard', 'healthy' people like Doctor Faust clearly no longer need this strengthening. Here the indication that he, Faust, does not want to 'dare' to strive for those spheres, i.e. for that realm which is covered by the Christian mystery of salvation, is full of irony. Doctor Faust leaves this boldness to those for whose faith miracle is its 'dearest child'.

Thirdly, the content of Christian faith is open to parody. This alienation in parody can be heard above all in the choirs of women, angels and young men which are blended into this scene. Commentators have rightly pointed out that with these choruses Goethe is alluding to the tradition of the church's Easter liturgy, in which since the Middle Ages there have been responses from a three-part choir of women, angels and young men. But at the same time they have made it clear that with his choirs Goethe has removed himself both from the liturgical tradition and from the New Testament models. In fact, in *Faust* all that is left is the three choruses and the repeated resurrection cry 'Christ is arisen'. Otherwise the text of the choruses alludes to such a 'painfully overloaded play on sounds' (as A.Schöne put it) that the ironic detachment of their author is impossible to miss. For example Goethe makes the 'choir of angels' say (or sing):

> Christ is arisen
> from the womb of corruption.
> Be of good cheer
> and get rid of your bonds!
> You whose deeds praise Him,
> who demonstrate charity,
> nourish your brethren,
> wander and teach them,
> promise them bliss –
> to you is your Master near
> for you He is here.

We may therefore agree with the literary critic Hans Arens, to whom we are indebted for extensive commentaries on Goethe's *Faust* poems: 'But where the angels are to say something essentially Christian, the formally artificial nature gets in the way of their power of conviction; for if half of the six syllables of a verse are dominated by the rhyme, and this is repeated three to five times, that is an excess which turns art into artifice. For what does not come from a poet's heart cannot – in his own words – go to the heart, and where faith is lacking – as also in Faust himself, none can be communicated by poetry . . . It seems to me that Goethe is allowing himself a joke, probably aware that by the exaggerated play on sounds he can drown out the dogmatic, homiletic content . . . If we ask why Goethe decided for these failed responses . . . after an objective and aesthetic consideration of the text we come to the conclusion that it is because here he does not give the church's hymns their objective other-worldly validity, as he does in the cathedral scene, but wanted to veil his own inner detachment and criticism ironically in a pseudo-archaic, worthy form; here the mixture which has gone off the rails at the same time explained Faust's lack of faith.'[113]

In addition, an observation on the structure of the text: the placing of the two choirs of young men and angels at the end of the scene. As a result, the message of the resurrection is repeated once again after Faust has already rejected it sarcastically as a desire for miracle. After this scepticism, affirmed once more, it sounds as if it is spoken into the void, which heightens its character as illusion. That Christ is near to the active, loving and merciful through their doing works of charity, as the choir of angels sing, no longer has any meaning for Faust. He does not see himself as a practising Christian who through the resurrection of Christ allows himself to be detached 'from bonds' (what is probably meant is bonds of transitoriness, limitation, despair). He is a seeker and acts on his own initiative.

Reminiscences of childhood

Certainly in this drama the message of Easter serves to keep Goethe's hero from committing suicide. However, this is not because he believes in the resurrection as such, but because the festival of Easter awakens in him memories of his childhood and thus arouses a will to live which he had stifled in his intellectual musings. To be specific, it is not the content of faith that saves Faust's life, but musical sounds which echo in his study and evoke sentimental memories of the past. In these few lines of the second reaction of his Faust, Goethe has used something of a 'sentimental journey'. Here intellectual words are less important than the 'sweetest heavenly tones' from the world of unburdened childhood. 'Easter' no longer points to a transcendence but biographically back to a time of 'lively games', the free happiness of 'spring celebrations'. So for Goethe's Faust, 'Easter' is no longer an objective reality, but nothing but 'a subjective memory', a 'sound from youth'.

Furthermore, in this uniquely dense text, Christian faith in the resurrection of Christ is clearly distinguished from the general religious feeling of Doctor Faust. For Faust does not want to strive for 'those spheres' which are identical with the Christian mystery of salvation, but just for 'those spheres'. Before he took the cup of poison in despair at knowledge, Faust had in fact wanted to be transported into the mysteries of reality with the help of magic. He wanted to penetrate the innermost depths of the world and was put in his place by the Earth Spirit. At any rate in this scene, Faust remembers that in his childhood, religion (and thus probably also the faith of the Christian church) had been the basis for his efforts. What has now broken through in this meditative scholar, resolved for anything, thus has its roots in the religion of his childhood. The allusion to the 'sabbath stillness' points to the repose of contemplation which he had experienced earlier; in the sound of the church bell an intimation already made itself audible; a prayer led to 'ardent enjoyment' and it was driven on by a longing that was not yet understood, which drove the young Faust not into the church but into the solitude of nature, and so stirred him that he felt 'a world' arise in him – still before the level of language, unconscious, more intimated than thought, more felt than expressed. So what he now does programmatically as a scientific researcher (penetrate the inner depths of the world), has its foundations in the religious experience of his childhood.

But because Faust recalls this 'world' in his breast with the theme of 'Easter', because he make himself aware that this has all been instilled in him at an early stage, he gives up his plan of suicide. And as if he could not get enough of these 'sweet celestial songs', which act as a catalyst releasing such memories in him, he ends with the words:

> sweet celestial songs, sound on –
> my tears well forth, and I am earth's again!

It follows from this that in literary terms, at the latest after Goethe, the time is past when a writer of some stature could still depict the miracle of the resurrection enthusiastically and give it dramatic form. Literature is now no longer at the service of revelation but in tension with it and at a distance. In the process of Enlightenment the miracle of the resurrection is also seen through as the 'dearest child' of faith, and no literature can raise it to life again. Literature follows its own laws. Certainly, for Faust religion remains present – as part of a world of childhood which can also evoke 'childlike feelings', a 'holy longing' in the adult. However, for the world of the adult the new slogan of an enlightened time holds: 'I hear the message, all I lack is faith'. To offer intellectual comfort about the abysses of earthly existence with the help of belief in another world is not allowed. For the generation of poets after Klopstock, the Easter faith seems already to be intellectually finished, aesthetically unproductive, at best useful for parody. And Goethe himself was capable of this parody, as we can infer from one of his Venetian Epigrams, which he wisely did not have published during his lifetime. In a satirical way this takes up the criticism (as disseminated by Samuel Reimarus in the time of Goethe) that the 'resurrection' of Jesus was nothing but a deception on the part of the disciples:

The tomb stands open! What a glorious wonder! The Lord is
risen – Who believes it? Rogues, you took him away.[114]

Another change of scene.

3. Resurrection in the midst of life: Leo Tolstoy

A man is a member of the jury at a Moscow trial. The twenty-seven-year-
old prostitute Yekaterina Maslova is accused of murder by poisoning.
And while this woman's story is unfolded before the court, the member
of the jury recognizes that this is the woman whom eight years previously
he had seduced in his aunt's estate, made pregnant and then abandoned.
This woman was then driven away in shame and thus in practice condemned to the life of a prostitute. That is one thing that the man, Prince
Nekhlyudov, has to recognize. The other is that through a mistake by the
court this woman is now also condemned to four years forced labour in
Siberia, although the Prince is convinced that she is innocent.

A man atones for his guilt

Affected by these experiences, Nekhlyudov resolves to atone for his guilt
over this woman and offer to marry her. He breaks with his previous
surroundings and gives a large part of his estate to his peasants. And
when all his efforts to have the sentence lifted by the higher authorities in
Petersburg fail, he also follows this woman into her exile. At any rate the
prince manages to get a pardon for Katerina shortly before the beginning
of forced labour on the settlement in Siberia. So nothing more seem to
stand in the way of a marriage. But although Katerina knows what she
recently owes to the prince, she rejects the well-meant arrangement and
marries not Nekhlyudov but another man, Vladimir Ivanovich
Simonson.

   However, this is not out of bitterness. On the contrary, affected by the
readiness of the man who once raped her to sacrifice himself for her,
slowly Katerina's hatred had also changed to affection. At the end of the
novel there is a gripping farewell scene in which, while Katerina refuses
to marry the prince, at the same time she gives him the feeling that this
refusal takes place out of love:

   'Forgive me', she said, so low that he could hardly hear her. Their eyes
   met, and Nekhlyudov knew by the strange look of her squinting eyes
   and the pathetic smile with which she said not 'Goodbye', but 'Forgive

me', that of the two reasons that might have led to her resolution the second was the real one. She loved him, and thought that by uniting herself to him she would be spoiling his life. By going with Simonson she thought she would be setting Nekhlyudov free, and she felt glad that she had done what she meant to do, and yet suffered at parting from him. She pressed his hand, turned quickly, and left the room.[115]

That is one dimension of the novel: it tells a story in which 'resurrection' takes place in the midst of life. For the remarkable thing about this book of Tolstoy's with the programmatic title *Resurrection* (1899) is that nowhere in it is there mention of a resurrection of Christ in the dogmatic sense. It appears neither, as in Klopstock, in the form of a direct literary representation of the Christian drama of the resurrection nor, as in Goethe, in the detached ironical quotation of the church's resurrection liturgy. But that is no coincidence. For this Russian writer at the end of the nineteenth century can no more cope with the resurrection as mere 'miracle' than could the German poet at its beginning. Rather, for him 'resurrection' has become an inner spiritual event. It stands for the decisive spiritual changes in the midst of a human life.

Moreover that is the point of the novel: Tolstoy has his Prince Nekhlyudov and the young Maslova experience resurrection in a quite personal way. He makes them rise from their old life to a new one. Nekhlyudov above all does something unheard of, something that Goethe's Heinrich Faust is already no longer capable of in his urge for self-realization: he voluntarily accepts guilt and actively expiates it. It is unthinkable that Faust should offer to marry Gretchen! But in Tolstoy precisely the opposite of the Faust-Gretchen story takes place: whereas Goethe's 'hero' drives the pregnant Gretchen to misery and madness, only at the end plagued with guilt feelings to start the attempt to free his former beloved from prison, Tolstoy's Nekhlyudov seizes the opportunity to bring about the rescue of betrayed and deceived woman even before the final catastrophe. And whereas Gretchen is only 'saved' at the end of *Faust* I (as it were by an act of divine intervention), for her Russian sister Katerina, resurrection takes place in the midst of life – in the spirit of the merciful Jesus of the Sermon on the Mount.

Total confrontation with the church

Moreover there is also an allusion to Jesus' Sermon on the Mount in the very last chapter of the novel. Indeed, on the last pages of the novel this text, which is said always to have 'touched' Nekhlyudov,[116] becomes the moral manifesto against the prevailing state-church relations in Tolstoy's Russia. That addresses the second dimension of the novel: the criticism of state and church. For after detailed research Tolstoy wanted with great moral passion to attack the Russian prison and camp system of the time. The conditions which he found here were literally offensive to him. Thousands upon thousands of people lived in abominable conditions: brutality, corruption, mercilessness, caprice prevailed everywhere. And it was also abominable to Tolstoy that the Russian Orthodox Church had made itself an accomplice of the state in maintaining this camp system.

Moreover the novel contains one of the most bitter accusations against religion of which the author was capable, where Tolstoy describes in detail a service which this church used to hold within the prisons:

> And none of those present, from the inspector down to Maslova, seemed conscious of the fact that this Jesus, whose name the priest repeated such a great number of times, whom he praised with all these curious expressions, had forbidden the very things that were being done there: that he had not only prohibited this meaningless much speaking and the blasphemous incantation over the bread and wine, but had also, in the clearest words, forbidden men to call other men their master or to pray in temples; had taught that every one should pray in solitude; had forbidden to erect temples, saying that he had come to destroy them and that one should worship, not in a temple, but in spirit and in truth; and, above all, that not only had he forbidden to judge, to imprison, to torment, to execute men, as was done here, but had even prohibited any kind of violence, saying that he had come to give freedom to the captives.[117]

That was unmistakably a frontal attack on the existing state-church system and the 'symphony' of church and state engaged in for centuries and preserved in Greek and Russian Orthodoxy. This attack was all the more severe since here Tolstoy confronted the church directly with the gospel of Christ, which he sees expressed in a unique way in the Sermon on the Mount. Moreover at the end of the novel – literally in the last chapter – Tolstoy makes his prince reflect on his life once again in the room of an inn and then take up the New Testament. Not by chance, he opens the eighteenth chapter of the Gospel of Matthew and here comes upon the parable of the unmerciful creditor (Matt. 8.21–35). Its theme is that a servant who is himself forgiven acts mercifully towards a fellow servant. The conclusion drawn is that in following Jesus people are to forgive 'not seven times, but seventy-times seven'; God's forgiveness is to be handed on to fellow human beings. In a flash it becomes clear to Nekhlyudov that the key to the solution of the problem of guilt and atonement lies here:

> The answer he had been unable to find was the same that Christ gave to Peter. It was to forgive always, everyone; to forgive an infinite number of times, because there are none who are not themselves guilty, and therefore none who can punish or reform. 'But surely it cannot be so simple,' thought Nekhlyudov; and yet he saw with certainty, strange as it had seemed at first, that it was not only a theoretical but also a practical solution of the question.[118]

It is a solution which is then made more specific by the 'five commandments' of the Sermon on the Mount. For as Nekhlyudov now begins to read the same Gospel from the beginning, the significance of the Sermon on the Mount dawns on him in a completely new way. For the first time he sees in these texts not abstract thoughts, not exaggerated demands which cannot be fulfilled, but 'simple, clear, practical laws, which if carried out in practice (and this is quite possible) would establish perfectly new and surprising conditions of social life, in which the violence that filled Nekhlyudov with such indignation would not only cease of itself, but the greatest blessing attainable by men – the kingdom of heaven on earth – would be reached'.[119]

A writer is excommunicated

However, the reaction to this novel was anything but non-violent. On the contrary. For Tolstoy personally this novel had decisive consequences. For almost twenty years his life as a writer had been dogged by bans and censorship, without the Orthodox Church of Russia taking the extreme step. But now evidently it had had enough. Two years after the publication of the novel, the Russian Orthodox hierarchy communicated to the 'loyal children of the Orthodox Russian-Greek Church', in a document dated 11 February 1901, that Count Leo Tolstoy had been excommunicated:

> In his writings and letters which have been disseminated everywhere in large numbers by him and his disciples, but particularly with the limits of our dear Fatherland, he (Tolstoy) has preached with the zeal of a fanatic the downfall of all dogmas of the Orthodox Church and of the essence of the Christian faith. He denies the personal living God who

is praised in the holy Church, the Creator and Sustainer of the world; he denies the Lord Jesus Christ, the God Man, the Redeemer of the world, who for our sake has suffered and for our salvation has risen from the dead; he denies the conception of the Lord Christ without seed and the virginity of the holy Mother of God, Mary; he does not recognize the future life and retribution, denies all the sacraments of the church and the work of the Holy Spirit in bringing salvation in the same, and mocks the greatest of all sacraments, the holy eucharist . . . In thus making known his apostasy from the church, we pray to God to help him to repent.[120]

And Tolstoy? In a statement in February 1901 he concedes with all the clarity one could wish that he has in fact dissociated himself from this form of church. He is convinced that the doctrine of the church is in theory 'a deceitful and harmful lie', but in practice a 'collection of the crudest superstitious notions and witchcrafts' which have completely concealed the meaning of the teaching of Christ.[121] But equally resolutely Tolstoy defends himself again having denied or betrayed the 'essence of Christian faith', the 'living God', the 'Lord Jesus Christ'. On the contrary, he had another view of the nature of this God, another image of Christ. Were Christ to 'come now' and see what was happening in the church in his name, he would – Tolstoy was convinced – 'with even greater and legal wrath throw out all these fearful spears, vessels, containers, candles, pictures of the saints and all the means of magic by which God and his teaching are hidden from people'. Then follows his own confession of faith:

> I believe in the following. I believe in God, whom I understand as God, as love, as primal source. I believe that he is in me and I am in him.

> I believe that the will of God is expressed most clearly and most comprehensibly in the man Christ, and therefore regard it as the utmost witchcraft to regard him as God and pray to him.

> I believe that true human salvation consists in the fulfilment of the will of God, but that his will is for human beings to love one another and therefore to act towards one another as they would want others to act towards them; as it also says in the Gospel, that this is the whole meaning of the Law and the Prophets.

> I believe that the meaning of the life of each individual consists merely in the intensification of love in itself, that these intensifications of love

lead the individual to ever greater salvation in this life, and that life brings all the greater salvation, the more love there is in a person, and at the same time contributes most to the bringing about of the kingdom of God in the world, i.e. an order of life under which the now prevalent division, treachery and violence will be replaced among human beings by the former harmony, truth and brotherly love.

I believe that there is only one means towards furthering love among men, prayer – not as public prayer in the temple, which is directly forbidden by Christ (Matt. 6.5–13), but prayer after the pattern of Christ, solitary prayer, which consists in the restoration and strengthening of the meaning of life in awareness of and dependence on the will of God.[122]

There was no reconciliation between Tolstoy and the Orthodox Church. But his case is a model one to the utmost degree. For, around a century after Klopstock and Goethe, here literature had finally come into conflict with the church. This had already happened in Germany with the authors of *Vormärz* and *Junges Deutschland* (Heine on the Index, blasphemy proceedings against Gutzkow). If Klopstock had still been painfully concerned not to allow himself too great deviations in matters of orthodoxy, and Goethe, Privy Councillor and 'Culture' Minister of his principality, could skilfully avoid a conflict between church and art as a master of masks and disguises also in matters of religion, at the end of the nineteenth century the conflict between church and literature had burst into flame. It would also be tangible in Germany, where after the turn of the century there were again blasphemy proceedings against writers, Oskar Panizza and Carl Einstein.

'Resurrection' as spiritual change

But seen in the perspective of the history of motifs, Tolstoy's novel means more than a first climax in a fatal tradition of condemnation in the relationship between literature and the church. Tolstoy's novel above all means a resurrection of the topic of resurrection in world literature. To be specific, like Goethe, Tolstoy too rejects faith in the 'miracle of resurrection' and refuses to make literature the illustration of a dogmatic model of Easter. But against Goethe and with Klopstock, the Russian maintains the spiritual substance of the Christian message – and does so also in literary terms.

In other words, Tolstoy restores to the topic of resurrection its great anthropological depth-symbolism: resurrections do not take place miraculously at the end of life, but in the midst of life, whenever human beings bring about spiritual transformations in themselves. Thus fifty years before Bultmann's demythologizing programme, Tolstoy becomes an existential translator of the Christian theme of resurrection into secular worldly language. He can dispense with the miraculous story for the sake of the anthropological content. His novel could have been written from the slogan: 'I have faith. What need do I have of such stories?'

It has become clear to me that in matters of resurrection Tolstoy gives literature the function which it alone can still fulfil – under the conditions of the modern critique of religion. Literature can no longer be about the fantastic elaboration of biblical scenes to confirm or heighten traditional truths of faith; nor, however, can it be about the illustration of a rationalistic denial of a belief in miracles understood in a miraculous way (which would also settle the matter). It can only be concerned with the literary reflection of the transforming power of the spirit which makes people capable of 'resurrections': of surrendering old roles dominated by power and instinct, of giving up cemented modes of behaviour, of exploding armoured identities. That is what literature can describe: what happens to people – no more and no less. So if modern literature can make a contribution to shaping the theme of resurrection, it is manifestly here, with Leo Tolstoy. I asked myself: can this be heightened even further in literature? Can literature express even more with the means at its disposal? I came across a play by Friedrich Dürrenmatt the title of which already promised surprises. It is called *The Meteor*, and was performed for the first time in the Zurich Theatre in 1966.[123]

4. What if a dead man rises? Friedrich Dürrenmatt

At the level of pure action this is a macabre and crazy play which rests on the one basic idea: a man rises from the dead and cannot believe in his resurrection. 'Risen! Me! From the dead! What a joke!' We are presented with a brief extract from the last phase of the life of a winner of the Nobel Prize for Literature by the name of Wolfgang Schwitter. In a clinic he has conclusively been declared dead by the medical authorities. But while the mourning ceremonies are being held and the radio programme has already switched over to classical music, he wakes up, creeps out from under the wreaths sent by the government and the Nobel Prize committee and goes to the dwelling were he once began forty years previously as an artist without means. Here he wants finally 'to die honestly without fiction and without literature'. The apartment has meanwhile been lived in by the mediocre painter Nyffenschwander and his attractive wife Auguste by whom Schwitter, a drunk and noisy man of the senses, is immediately attracted erotically: 'Were I not on my deathbed I would make you my lover . . .'

A *grotesque, crazy piece:* Meteor

But the grotesque happens: whereas Schwitter attempts scene by scene to die, without succeeding, his constantly new resurrections from the bier cause one death after another in his surroundings.

The hospital chaplain, Pastor Lutz, who follows Schwitter to his old abode and is overwhelmed by the physical 'miracle' of the resurrection, dies;

Nyffenschwander, who is thrown down the steps by the householder and building giant Muheim, dies;

Old Muheim himself, carried off by the police for murdering the painter, dies;

Professor Schlatter, who has twice failed grievously as a medical authority in diagnosing death and who does not want to survive this humiliation, dies;

Schwitter's fourth and last wife, the former call-girl Olga, dies. She had already been dressed by Nicki, her couturier, as 'widow of the year' and had been effectively promoted by the media; she turns up in the apartment and is again sent packing by Schwitter ('You are the gift that I bequeath to the public; Caesar bequeathed his gardens; I bequeathe a tart').

The businesslike and profiteering abortionist Wilhelmine Nomsen, mother of Olga and Schwitter's mother-in-law, dies. She sees Olga's death as an inappropriate mixture of business and feeling (a whore who marries has allowed herself 'feelings'; but these don't belong in the business).

Schwitter's son Jochen dies. He is out for nothing but his father's money and therefore can't wait for his death – according to the slogan: 'Do me a favour. For the first time in your life, be kind, old man, and die!'

And finally the Salvation Army leader Major Friedli, whom Schwitter strangles with his own hands at the end of the play because of his triumphant song of joy . . ., dies.

So a macabre dance of death is staged around a man who not only cannot die but has to keep rising again and rebels against the incursion of an unasked-for grace into his life. Like a meteor, Schwitter's resurrections break into life and leave behind fearful, terrible things.

They leave behind above all the truth in all the figures who come under the spell of death and resurrection. On the level of theatre, Dürrenmatt's play is a play about disillusionment and the breakthrough of truth – in the face of the sheerly incomprehensible fact that a man returns from death. If we look closely, the different figures come from four spheres of life: business, the arts, science and religion. In the fiery tail of the invading meteor they are confronted with their lives, and they do not survive this confrontation. In detail, this is what it looks like:

Business – a sphere of justice? For Mulheim, the eighty-year-old 'vital building contractor and houseowner', it is the opposite. From small beginnings he has fought his way upwards and his credo now runs: 'Life is power, battle, victory, humiliation and crime.' And in accordance with his motto he behaves all his life as 'the meanest' among the mean in the competitive struggle. He had excluded only his private life from this game; he had remained faithful to his wife and had mourned for her when she died fifteen years previously. Now the last remnant of illusion collapses when Schwitter tells him that when he had been living in Mulheim's home he had cheated the great businessman with his own wife, a piece of information which is withdrawn again later but which destroys Mulheim once for all. The schizophrenia of *homo economicus* (business life must be a mean competitive struggle; only private life is an exception) will ultimately take his life.

Art – a sphere of the spirit? As little as the economy is a sphere of fairness. For in several refractions the play makes clear that art is an utterly frivolous matter. Schwitter's literature already lived by the shameless aestheticizing of extreme situations in life, the exploitation of life for the purpose of self-assertion on the market ('I invented stories and nothing more. I occupied the imagination of those who bought my stories, and for that had the right to make money, and did'). Moreover Schwitter first tells the painter Nyffenschwander that death is 'crazy': 'You should experience it! The thoughts that come to one, the inhibitions which fall, the insights which dawn on one. Simply great.' And Schwitter happily tells Lutz the hospital chaplain that the very night after the suicide of his second wife he had gone to his room – after the eighth cognac – and written a story of 'how an village school class beat their idealistic teacher to death and a farmer with a tractor rolled over the teacher and hushed up the case'. That had been the 'best piece of prose' he had ever written.

Moreover Schwitter had long since seen through his whole literary career:

> I was unconcerned when I began to write. I had nothing in my head but my ideas; I was a drunkard and antisocial. Then came the successes, the prizes, the honours, the money and the luxury. My manners got better and better; I filed my finger nails and refined my style.. The Nobel Prize gave me the rest. A writer whom our present-day society takes to its bosom is corrupt for all time.[124]

Science – a store of truth? If we look at the scientific 'capacity' of the play, Professor Schlatter, it is above all a store of vanities. For this doctor, the Schwitter case is above all a personal disaster, a humiliation which cannot be borne, indeed the 'greatest setback of the century'. Moreover, how does a scientifically trained doctor stand? Two unobjectionable diagnoses of death, but the patient lives:

> It's terrible. The thinking world is convinced that I am ridiculous and the believers, my child, are convinced of your resurrection. That's the catastrophe. For some I've gone gaga and for others I've been teased by God; either way I get the blame. Sit down. That a Nobel prizewinner of all people has to rise! The health minister telephoned me, and I could only calm the culture minister down by promising him that you would certainly be dead by tomorrow afternoon. Now he's standing there with his speech and his state funeral. The scandal is gigantic. It all falls on me. And I gave the world Schlatter's forceps and relief for arthritis![125]

Religion – a sphere of bold hope against all hope? Quite the opposite. Both of its representatives in this play, Pastor Lutz and Salvation Army Major Friedl, are weak figures. Their religion is an expression of either their anxiety about life or their naïve alienation from the world. A pastor like Emanuel Lutz is introduced as a kind of 'infantile phenomenon'. Already pitiful in stature, he is afflicted not only in his health, powerless and unspeakably weary, but also in his faith. He finds it difficult, but by his own confession he no longer lives in a time when God is accustomed to do miracle after miracle. Today it has become difficult 'to proclaim the miracle of Christ's sacrificial death and resurrection and have no other proof than faith'. But with Schwitter's resurrection, hope has returned to the pastor's troubled heart. Now he can revive:

The miracle, the excitement, the immediate presence of the Almighty. I'm quite beside myself. It is as if the heavens had opened, as if his glory were around us . . . God chose you, Herr Schwitter, so that the blind could see and the godless believe in him.[126]

And to create a grotesque conclusion to the comedy, at the end of the play Dürrenmatt introduces a Salvation Army choir under Major Friedli, who similarly regards Schwitter's resurrection as a confirmation of his belief in miracle. And as this completely disconcerts Schwitter, his wild blasphemies at creation ring out against the Hallelujah of the believers:

I am Major Friedli of the Salvation Army. Hallelujah.
Get out. Immediately.
You are welcome whom Jesus Christ hallowed! Hallelujah.
You're in the wrong place. People don't preach here, they die.
Hail, you Risen One. Hallelujah! It has happened to you in accordance with your faith. You are called to eternal life.
I am called to die, only death is eternal. Life is an unparalleled cheat of nature, an obscene mistake of carbon, a malignant growth on the earth's surface, a scab that will not heal. Composed of the dead, we decay to death. Tear me apart, you heavenly drummer.
Hallelujah! Hallelujah!
Stamp on me, you barrel organ brothers.
Hallelujah, Hallelujah.
Trample me under the steps, you psalm-yodellers.
Hallelujah, Hallelujah.
Be gracious, you Christians.
Hallelujah, Hallelujah.
(*Schwitter goes to Friedli and strangles him.*) Strike me dead with your guitars and trombones!
Hallelujah (Friedli collapses).
When will I finally kick the bucket? (*he turns round*). When will I finally kick the bucket? (*he runs down the staircase*) When will I finally kick the bucket? When will I finally kick the bucket?
(*The choir intones monumentally*)
Drive out through your might
Blackout
Our night
Curtain.[127]

The abolition and transcending of all positions

As an aesthetic whole this is an artistically constructed and at the same a remarkably sensual and grotesque play on many levels. When set over against the reality of death and resurrection, the modes of reaction from the different spheres of life are unmasked as the expression of a pseudo-security. The death and resurrection of Schwitter function as a catalyst. They show that the security of the world is not authentic but rests on crude projection, is a function of the way of coping with anxiety. All in their own way need this phenomenon of death and resurrection: the religious for their anxieties about faith; the writer for his literature; the publisher for his business; the doctor for his reputation. In this way they rob the phenomenon of death and resurrection of the dark secret which evades all interpretation. Instead of asking what this incursion does to their picture of the world, the various ideologies remain unshaken. Nowhere can an awareness of deeper perplexity about the fact of the world be recognized . . .

So we can follow the Catholic theologian Dietmar Mieth, who has subjected Dürrenmatt's play to a precise structural analysis, in defining the basic aesthetic strategy of the play as the abolition and transcending of the different positions in life. Here there is the same crisis for all ideologies which interpret the world, whether economic, aesthetic, scientific or religious. So the aesthetic strategy of the piece can be described like this: 'The poetic "statement" about life and death must always free itself from ideological assertions. Nothing would be more inappropriate than an ideological controversy. Nevertheless the issue is not "pure" negation, pure critique of ideology. But the position is not static or theoretical; it is in permanent flux and still not at an end. Therefore while the play has an end, the idea does not. One cannot protect oneself from ideology with the ideology of having no ideology – Schwitter's "nihilism" – but only with movement. The play is one single oxymoron. It constantly produces itself as something new; it is not the depiction of a theory; it does not know itself precisely in advance any more than it knows its topic, reality – it cannot catch itself up precisely afterwards, but only make itself visible.'[128]

Moreover it is here that the difference from all the previous works that we have considered in connection with resurrection lies. For Klopstock, Goethe and Tolstoy, art was identical with positions. For Dürrenmatt art is pure form, mere play, a suspension of possibilities and options. In the face of death and resurrection Dürrenmatt no longer indicates any

position at the level of art. He stages a transcending and abolition of all
positions – in the medium of comedy. Thus for the first time Dürrenmatt
does not define a literary position in the discussion of the topic of resurrection but puts all options in question. He is post-Enlightenment in the
best sense of the word. But in this way Dürrenmatt gains freedom for
extra-aesthetic, extra-dramatical, existential discourse.

However, this existential discourse only comes about the moment the
viewer or reader makes Dürrenmatt's primal question his or her own:
What if someone really rises from the dead? How would one react?
Moreover in non-literary explanations of his play Dürrenmatt has
constantly insisted on the factuality of the resurrection. That is why he
gave his drama the programmatic title a 'wild play', an 'extreme play', in
which tragedy and comedy stand in abrupt contrast.[129] Dürrenmatt did
not want any symbolism in matters of resurrection (in the style of
Tolstoy) but wild realism: his Schwitter was not merely to seem dead but
really to be dead. And only because he had really been dead could he also
really rise. The whole thing is enigmatic, uncanny, but a fact. To this
degree Dürrenmatt's play is not just a play about dying, death and the
consequences for those around, but a play about sheer impossibility and
total paradox: a resurrection in which the risen person does not, cannot,
believe. In interpreting himself Dürrenmatt emphasized:

> *The Meteor* is not about dying but about resurrection. Indeed,
> Schwitter is the Lazarus of our time. Usually the dead rise in the theatre
> only when the curtain has fallen; Schwitter rises with the curtain. That
> is the decisive idea, and I believe an eminently theatrical one . . . The
> situation may be improbable, but what develops from it is not: like any
> 'miracle' it causes perplexity.[130]

This 'perplexity' is not made concrete in the aesthetic discourse of
the play in that the positions abolish themselves; clearly it is meant to
communicate itself also to the extra-aesthetic discourse of the readers or
the audience. Here perplexity first of all means a lack of answers, not
knowing what to make of things. The play is obviously first of all meant
to deprive the audience or the readers of their familiar language and
ready-made patterns of thought. As author, Dürrenmatt by no means
excludes himself here:

> Schwitter's resurrection is an event which challenges us; and I do not
> know how I would behave in his situation or in the situation of those
> whom he confronts. Perhaps not better. I cannot and will not exclude
> myself.[131]

This perplexity also relates to the fact that with Schwitter's resurrection what happens is not comforting and edifying, but 'fearful' and terrible. Here Dürrenmatt links up with traditions which he had already used in his early story 'The Tunnel' (which we considered in detail in part B of this book); the dimension of the offensive, the invasive, the disturbing. He explicitly emphasizes:

> I want to say that in my play the resurrection is taken for what it really is, a scandal, an offensive story, which in the New Testament too is told as an offensive story; indeed in the Luther Bible it is said very directly that Lazarus already stinks. That means that Christ is not pleased to perform the miracle; he is 'angry', and when he has performed it the Pharisees resolve, 'This man must die.' Thus what we relate as edification is intrinsically an offensive event. And now this story today. The question arises: is there any possibility of our believing this story if we encountered it? That means that Schwitter cannot believe in his own resurrection. Now the whole event develops in this fiction, in this theatrical fiction.[132]

A man rises and does not believe in it

Here in fact is the decisive insight of Dürrenmatt as an author of the second half of the twentieth century – seventy years after Tolstoy and one hundred and seventy years after Goethe's *Faust*. For with his Schwitter, Dürrenmatt creates a figure of the kind that is possible only in the second half of that century: after Nietzsche, Freud and Sartre. In it he has included the spiritual gaps that the century has to offer: in the sphere of the erotic and sexual just as in the sphere of the aesthetic, the material and the existential. With Schwitter we have a figure who seems to be synthesized from Faust's self-realization, Nietzsche's nihilism, Freud's lifting of sexual taboos and Sartre's existentialism.

Thus in the sphere of the erotic Schwitter has uninhibited drives and a cynical delight in the senses. He had spent his life with four women. The first had been 'robust, sensual, red-haired and uneducated', and had deceived him first with a milkman and later with a tailor. The next two wives? 'Increasingly refined women', since they organized Schwitter's literary fame while he 'worked himself to death', finally to become a 'classic'. His second wife, the daughter of a great industrialist, finally took her life; in this marriage Schwitter had experienced nothing but 'torture'. In general (he thought) 'all the wives' were one mistake after another. Finally Schwitter marries a call-girl (she was 'the best') and this is symptomatic of his image of women and marriage generally. Sexual libertinism everywhere. Schwitter had just slept with the wife of Mulheim the building giant – 'lover of art' as she was – just as he now takes Auguste, the wife of the painter Nyffenschwander, into his deathbed . . .

And as it was with Schwitter in life, sensual and cynical, so too it is in death: instead of departing with a 'certain human greatness', Schwitter drinks a whole bottle of Cognac, and then has another, with the motto: 'Drinking is healthy for pushing off'. All this points to Schwitter's basic materialist and existentialist attitude. In love with death as he is, he can therefore throw away his life like his 1.5 million marks, which he burns in the fireplace of the apartment, since in any case his view is that life dissolves 'into its ingredients', into 'water, fat and minerals'. Schwitter doesn't recognize the slightest moral justification for his action – since he is of the cut of Nietzsche. When he learns from Frau Nomsen of Olga's death by poisoning, this is his reaction:

> The little one is dead. I will neither justify nor excuse myself; don't expect such lack of taste from me. Guilt, expiation, justice, freedom, grace, love, I renounce the exalted talk and reasons which people use for their regulations and plundering expeditions. Life is cruel, blind and transitory. It depends on chance. An indisposition at the right time, and I would never have met Olga. We both had bad luck, that's all – [133]

No wonder that Schwitter – grown old and sick – has been seized with disgust at life. He is overcome with dismay at his old, fat, gangrenous body. And this disgust at life is matched by the drive towards death, the love of death, the longing for death. For since nothing in life is important, valuable or meaningful for Schwitter any longer, now death is the only thing that is real for him, the only thing that is not transitory, the only experience that remains.

> Death rushes to one like a locomotive, eternity whistles around one's ears, creations cry out, clash together, a giant accident , the whole – [134]

Note that Dürrenmatt makes such a 'product' from Faust, Nietzsche, Freud and Sartre, such an unscrupulous, lecherous and cynical contemporary of the late twentieth century, rise again. Of all people he makes an aesthetic, erotic man of the senses with a nihilistic and existentialist attitude come upon the only thing that can still shake this man who has experienced everything: a 'religious' miracle. Dürrenmatt makes this man in particular run into the 'metaphysical trap', a man who has long since seen through and dismissed all metaphysics as consolation. This man in particular, who is disillusioned to the depths: calculating, shameless, blasphemous, addicted to death. But precisely because after Goethe and Tolstoy the Enlightenment with its criticism of miracle has established itself as something that intellectuals take for granted, Dürrenmatt can play with it again as a comedian. For him the breaking of anti-religious taboos is aesthetically as productive as the breaking of religious taboos was in the time of Goethe and Tolstoy.

In other words, in the second half of the twentieth century – in the face of all the ideological options that are played through – once again a writer tests reality as a whole, with the apparently archaic language of the resurrection of a dead man. This strikes a secure world, interpreted to the end, literally like a meteorite. and destroys a society which – one hundred and fifty years after Goethe's scepticism about resurrection – reacts to such invasions with either rationalistic suppression or existentialist indignation. *The Meteor* is the announcement of an end of elements in culture which can be taken for granted and one long attack on 'well-established surprises' which are practised by society.

Against the toning down by bourgeois Christianity

First, representatives of Christianity come under radical criticism in this play – in the name of 'religion'. For these Christians become ridiculous figures not because they react in a religious way, but because their religious way is not radical enough. The 'resurrection' of a dead man does not disturb them but merely confirms what they firmly believe anyway. However, Dürrenmatt accentuates what he means by religion (in Kierkegaard's sense) further like this:

> I simply want to show that the religious in itself is something terrible and not 'nice'. We have made this religion a kind of comforting picture and in reality it is an unpleasant and scandalous affair . . . Comedy is the transformation of things, the things that we really take on trust, for example Easter: we go to church and we speak of resurrection. These are such fine symbols. The transformation of these symbols into reality is very disturbing.[135]

Already in his comedy Dürrenmatt therefore unmasks the resurrection faith of particular Christians as an expression of weakness in life and a blindness to reality. In testimonies, over and above this he keeps attack-

ing a 'middle-class Christianity' which has toned down the offence of the
resurrection of all flesh. Here Dürrenmatt does not allow the objection
that it is really 'the cross' that is the offence in Christianity:

> In itself the cross has long ceased to be a scandal, compared with the
> monstrosities of barbarism which have been committed often enough
> on humanity in the name of the cross. The inhumanity of the Crusades,
> the Wars of Religion, the Inquisition, the wars between individual
> nations and races, and also Auschwitz, are greater scandals than the
> cross. The cross becomes a scandal and a folly not only to the Jews
> or the Greeks but also to modern men and women through the resur-
> rection. Merely as a result of that, 'from a Christian perspective' the
> terrible takes on meaning. Therefore to see the cross alone as a scandal
> is an attempt to install a Christianity without faith, to make Christian-
> ity a world-view. *The Meteor* becomes dialectically impossible within
> this attempt because it is impossible for a dead person to rise. Thus *The
> Meteor* is a scandal for Christians who have become middle-class; a
> pastor even told me that I should not claim that God would have
> forgiven an adulterer and drunkard like Schwitter, as if grace depended
> on a blameless middle-class attitude; but also a scandal for those who
> are not Christians, but only aesthetes.[136]

So this play is meant to be an offence – above all for 'Christians
who have become middle-class' and have blunted the offence of faith.
Durrenmatt already emphatically emphasized this character of offence in
his 'Twenty Points on *The Meteor*', written for a discussion of his play in
1966. The idea of his play represents 'no damping down in favour of a
moralized cultured Christianity'; indeed, Dürrenmatt goes so far as to see
'present-day Christianity' also symbolized in Schwitter's denial of the
resurrection:

> Originally Christianity was aware that it was a scandal for Jews and
> folly for the Greeks. Today it is offended that it is to be a folly for
> non-Christians. Present-day Christianity has become a scandal to
> itself. In this perspective the one who has risen and does not believe in
> his resurrection is a figure which symbolizes present-day Christianity.
> In so far as we count ourselves part of it we laugh, are offended,
> whistle about ourselves.'[137]

Against the 'mere aesthetes'

Just as radical is Dürrenmatt's attack on the mere 'aesthetes'. His theatre
as a sphere of disturbing counter-reality touches on this particular world
at its most sensitive point: its closed regularities. For with the element of
'intervention', as it depicts the resurrection of a dead person, Dürrenmatt
confuses the regularity of a world which does not want to experience any
more surprises and tends to denounce ideas of this kind. The slogan for
his play could have been: after a long time someone has risen from the
dead again, but no one understands what this means. All already have
their way of copying with this event. Thus the author makes talk of
'resurrection of the dead' an attempt at a last attack on a world which has
made itself so free of surprises and has sealed itself off deterministically.[138]
Seen in this way, Dürrenmatt's play is the reversal of Faust's critique of
religion. If Faust unmasked the resurrection as the favourite child of
faith, Dürrenmatt makes the resurrection the ultimate weapon of a
critique of the world.

Therefore the literary critic Jan Knopf is right in observing on *The
Meteor*: 'It is the anti-Enlightenment tradition, a lack of belief in a
completely furnished world, or rather a world which can be completely
furnished by human beings, that is articulated here. It turns Lessing's
statement from *Emilia Galotti*, that chance is blasphemy, that nothing
under the sun is chance, into the statement that blasphemy lies
specifically in that which is not chance, in total order, total reasonable-
ness with its stringent logic . . . Lessing, the man of the Enlightenment,
accepts miracle into the world . . . In Dürrenmatt, however, the anti-
Enlightenment man, who has said good-bye to any belief that human and
divine reason correspond, the miracle breaks into the everyday world,
unmasks and destroys it, because human beings no longer believe in
miracles and chance happenings that could put their accustomed life in
question (as unbelieving offspring of the Enlightenment); they see the
meaning of the world and life only in its total order. Dürrenmatt explicitly sets chance as an alternative over against the world, as a possibility
of destroying its order, as an alternative, as a counter-reality to the
everyday, unconscious existence of men and women.'[139]

The contemporaneity of voices

Klopstock – Goethe – Tolstoy – Dürrenmatt, four voices. What are we to
think of them? The presupposition must be that a theological reflection
on the theme of the resurrection of Christ will have to start from the fact

that there are irrefutable elements of truth in all four positions. What was true of the topic of Christmas is also true here: each of the positions is not simply made obsolete by the next one to come along. The voices can be heard simultaneously. Faith has a polyphonic structure:

– Who as a Christian can deny that by bringing out the cosmic and salvation-historical dimension of the resurrection of Christ, Klopstock has taken up and strengthened the bedrock of the New Testament message of the resurrection? According to the New Testament the resurrection of Christ is indeed the dawn of a new age, a change of rule over the world in the spirit of love. But we who have been born after Auschwitz have said farewell to Klopstock's confrontational triumphalism against Gentiles and Jews. The resurrection of Christ is no victor's myth.

– Who as a contemporary Christian of the post-Enlightenment twentieth century may deny that we have Faust's scepticism in us: I hear the message, all I lack is faith. But it is this doubt which first makes faith faith. And faith in the resurrection of Christ in particular cannot be had without tribulation, without being suspected of illusion and consolation. Here there is not only faithfulness to one's own faith but also faithfulness to one's own doubts. But Faustian scepticism (coupled with a moral recklessness) must not become a general scepticism which knows only the encapsulation of human beings in the contradictions of their existence.

– Who as a Christian could deny that talk of the resurrection of Christ has an existential dimension for each individual Christian – in the sense of Leo Tolstoy, for whom the Sermon on the Mount becomes a central ethical manifestation. If we look at the New Testament, new creation in the spirit is the consequence of belief in the resurrection of Christ. Christians are therefore spiritually 'a new creation'. So resurrection in fact takes place anew every day, whenever the spirit of love triumphs over cowardice or wickedness of heart. But why should this resurrection in the midst of life be played off against a resurrection after life? Don't the two belong together? Those who live here and now in the spirit of love will not want this love broken off when they have passed through the earthly sphere.

– Who as a Christian may overlook the fact that Dürrenmatt has made a decisive point in the debate: the possibility of resurrection as a shattering of apparent certainties, as an intervention of God in a world which imprisons itself in one dimension. Dürrenmatt confronts a post-Christian world which is accustomed to treating everything ironically in the tradition of Goethe or interpreting it symbolically in the tradition of Tolstoy with a possibility with which this society has long ceased to reckon: the incursion of the 'wholly other' – not the triumphalistic demonstration of the truth of Christianity (from Klopstock to Dürrenmatt's Pastor Lutz), but rather the paradoxical questioning of a reality which is believed to be so certain.

Theological discussion of Dürrenmatt's play must preserve this transcending of positionality in the face of the riddle of death and resurrection. Otherwise it risks lapsing into Salvation Army lyrics. A theological reception which reduces the play to a simple message (in accordance with the pastoral motto: we all ought really to believe in the resurrection again) incurs the ridicule hurled at the positions of Pastor Lutz and Salvation Army officers like Friedli. So an appropriate view of the play can hardly be identical with positions which are already parodied in the play. On the contrary, an adequate basic theological attitude on the question of the resurrection of all flesh would be to endure what Dürrenmatt's Pastor Lutz could not endure for anxiety, so that he replaced it with his desire for miracle: the inner crisis, indeed the dark night of faith which has nothing but the saying about 'hoping against hope'.

But this hope goes far beyond resurrections of the kind that Schwitter experienced on the stage. According to the New Testament there are indeed resurrections in the style of Lazarus to which Dürrenmatt refers. But the resurrection of Christ is decisive and not at all to be compared with that. It does not mean a return to the former life, but entry into a new life with God. The risen Christ does not illustrate the continuation of previous life but the transformation of life, of one's own body in the spirit and to the spirit. Schwitter's resurrection is again threatened with death, as is that of Lazarus; Christ lives as a witness to and guarantor of the resurrection of all Christians. Schwitter's body will decay; the spiritual resurrection body is incorruptible.

So the voices can still be heard in this polyphonic conversation: the voice of Klopstock (Christ has broken the power of the world and its death), the voice of Faust (miracle is the favourite child of faith), the voice of Tolstoy (arise in the spirit of love), and the voice of Dürrenmatt (what if a dead man really rises?). They all accompany the voice of one who similarly did not stand at the tomb of Christ. but who must have had a quite personal experience with the risen Christ, which fundamentally changed his life and transformed him from Saul to Paul:

Behold, I tell you a mystery: We shall not all sleep, but we shall all be changed, in a moment, in the twinkling of an eye, at the last trumpet. For the trumpet shall sound, and the dead shall be raised incorruptible, and we shall be changed . . . Then will be fulfilled the word which is written: 'Death is swallowed up in victory. Death, where is your victory? Death, where is your sting?' (I Cor. 15.51f., 54).

V. Sketches of a christopoetics

We began from the theme of the sparing of Jesus: in all the criticism of the church and religion, which is often so bitter, Jesus himself is usually spared criticism and treated gently; indeed he himself often becomes the sharpest critic of a church and society which is all too sure of its legitimation from him. For writers of the twentieth century this man from Nazareth is an archetype of unadapted, rebellious, provocative humanity, an authority to appeal to with whom they unsparingly show up the discrepancy between utopian ideal and miserable reality, and attack the treachery practised to the cause of Jesus.

At the same time we should note *how* Jesus is depicted. An evaluation of the literary evidence purely in terms of content suppresses the aesthetic dimension and has no eye for the literary form. But this needs separate consideration. Reflection on how to describe a figure like Jesus in literary form, the manner of the evocation of his mystery, is the task of poetics, a christopoetics.

1. The familiar stranger

On the basis of the material I have presented so far, a first basic insight of christopoetics makes itself felt: the figure of Jesus of Nazareth cannot be 'grasped' directly, as if it were 'tangible'; as if a writer (a human being) knew his secret; as if it could be deciphered, indeed demystified, with the help of literature. Jesus escapes any direct description; he slips through the fingers of those who try to grasp him; those who think that they have him have lost him. And as the mystery of this figure escapes all comprehension, we can understand why even the great figures among the poets could only depict him indirectly, for example in representative figures. Great literature also shows the unfathomable depth of a figure like Jesus precisely in evoking him in many forms, reflecting him in many faces, and making him live among us under different names – as the known unknown, the one who is near and yet far, as familiar and yet a stranger to us.

At the same time literature can make this ultimate remoteness of Jesus a special theme: how it is possible to describe one who cannot be described. Christopoetics can become part of poetry; as an act of writer's self-certainty that in the last resort literature too only founders on the complete portrayal of a figure like Jesus, and that this failure of description can be productive in literary terms. Max Frisch is an example of this.

2. A trace of christopoetics: Max Frisch

Max Frisch opens his first Diary (1946) with a story about the puppeteer Marion from the land of Andorra. This Marion stands on a street in some town, an open box beside him, a large crowd around him, and takes a puppet from the box. When a policeman – unsettled at the disturbance – comes up, Marion holds out the puppet to him: 'Jesus Christ'.[140] As is well known, for Frisch Andorra is the cipher for a social and political sphere which functions according to particular social, political and psychological rules. And in this Marion story, a representative of the ruling class of Andorra is the art patron Cesario.

Why does Frisch tell this story with which he introduces the Andorra material into his work, and put it right at the beginning of his first Diary, which is so fundamental? He tells it to show from the start the basic tension between art and social power: the problem of the position of the artist in society. In this story Marion is the type of the innocent, pure, cheerful, playful, almost childishly naïve man who can hardly be distinguished from the one whom he likes to play best, Jesus, the pure and innocent. The powerful in society, above all Cesario, attempt to domesticate the artists and poets, to bribe them with parties, to accord them a niche in the activities of society called culture. That also happens to the puppeteer Marion, who has the whole dramatic personal arsenal of the Jesus stories among his puppets: Moses, the three kings, Pilate. There is only one puppet that he does not have: Judas, the traitor. But a surprising thing happens: the longer the story of Marion goes on and the more this puppeteer sees himself commandeered for the purposes of the powerful, the more the poet of the puppets himself becomes the puppet of the rulers, the more Marcion feels that he has grown into this role of Judas. He himself, initially the figure who plays the innocent and pure Jesus, increasingly becomes the Judas of his own innocence, a traitor to himself who – at the end looking in horror at his face in the mirror – like

Jesus hangs himself. It is clear that in this Christ-Judas drama Frisch is making himself aware of the role of art in society generally.

Furthermore – as the Tübingen Germanist Jürgen Schröder showed as early as 1965 in a brilliant analysis – here Frisch has given up 'the innermost secret of his understanding and experience of writing'.[141] According to Schröder, it rests 'on the poetic of a secularized Gospel of John', which in concrete terms means that writing, too, lives from the 'miracle of the word', but that with every story people betray themselves in an irresolvable ambiguity:

> Every story speaks of self-knowledge and a failure to know oneself, of love of self and hatred of self; every human story repeats the encounter of Christ and Judas. The history of literature tells a single *Ecce homo* story: Christ before Pontius Pilate.. Frisch meant Andorra as a model. We are all Andorrans who in the 'Jew' Andri betray people, sonship and brotherhood. But by writing our Judas life, literature spares our betrayed Christ-life as an unwritten role.[142]

That is the one aspect which is important in Max Frisch's Christ parable: Christ and Judas are roles which each plays in himself: the role play of innocence and guilt, of not suspecting and betrayal. And writers of our time repeatedly play these roles as representatives of others. However, the betrayal, the loss of innocence, is unavoidable for writers if they still want to surrender themselves in the word. Walter Jens once pointedly described this irresolvable conflict of the writer with reference to Frisch: 'The poet is the man from Iscariot who sets out to betray; a Judas *redivivus* who ensures that what can only be disclosed through a surrender amounting to self-humiliation is brought to light.'[143]

Secondly, the traces of a poetological reflection on the possibilities of describing Christ in any literary form run through Frisch's diary. It was the puppet metaphor which would not let Frisch go. And when later in the diary he reports on a visit to a puppet theatre, he returns in an associative yet calculated way to the puppeteer Marion, who had depicted Jesus Christ as a puppet. It struck Frisch that puppets seem to succeed far more easily than human actors in also depicting beings which are not human, 'an earth spirit, a spectre, monsters and fairies, dragons, the spirit of the air and the heart's desire'. Human actors who attempted to embody such roles (say an earth spirit) on the stage could hardly make 'an ultimate horror or an unearthly delight' credible. But the puppet can. For it remains only 'an image, a sign', which *a priori* points beyond itself and does not play what it is not. From this Frisch concludes:

And thus the scene, however admirably it is played, *a priori* is played on two different levels which are not credible in the same way. But they are in the puppet theatre. And also in ancient theatre with its masks: if Athene and Odysseus wear a mask in the same way, if they remain equally improbable and symbolic, we can also believe in the goddess.[144]

In addition, in the puppet theatre the word with which the role of the puppet must be brought to life is 'always out of date', so that it cannot be confused with our everyday language. It is 'supernatural', simply because it is separated from the puppet; it as it were lives and weaves over the puppet; it is greater than it would ever correspond to its wooden chest. It is more than the noisy accompaniment which comes to us daily from the mouth:

It is the word that was in the beginning, the word that creates all things. It is language. The puppet theatre cannot for a moment be confused with nature. For it only one thing is possible, namely poetry: that remains its sole sphere of language.[145]

Then Frisch transfers this option to 'Christ as puppet'. The author suddenly recalls that as a student he once saw a last supper of Jesus as a puppet play. He was 'shaken'. It was 'holy to a degree that would never have been possible for a human presenter who wanted to offer us a Christ':

A Christ from limewood like the one Marion made:; one thinks of a crucifix, and there too it is not felt to be blasphemy. The puppet, as opposed to the bodily actor, encounters us *a priori* as a figure, as an image, as a creation of the spirit, which alone can present the holy. The human being still remains flesh and blood, even when playing an image. The puppet is wood, an honourable and good wood which never makes the seductive claim to present the real Christ, and we should not think that it does; it is only a sign, a formula, a writing which means that it wants to be what is meant. It is a game, not a deception; it is spiritual as only a game can be – .[146]

Here we have come upon a trace of christopoetics. It flashes out in the reflection of the artists on how a figure like Jesus can be depicted in art in such a way that through it 'more' appears than can be made visible; that something that belongs to the 'supernatural' flashes out on the level of the natural. In this way, a 'transcendent background' can still be experienced in the foreground of what is depicted. The analogy which Frisch draws here is of the utmost importance for our context. Just as in an ancient play with masks a goddess still becomes credible as a goddess even today (in contrast to the role of a goddess played by a person), so in a puppet play it is possible through the puppet (which *a priori* does not claim to present the real Christ) to point to another reality. The 'spiritual', 'mysterious' character of this figure (in theological terms the divine in it) can only appear on this way – through the puppet as a mere sign which does not set out to be what is meant. In this way the onlooker is made aware that Christ is always more mysterious, spiritual, 'divine'. It follows from this that art withdraws and itself breaks through the illusion that Christ can be depicted adequately in its sphere. By withdrawing itself into the purely symbolic realm, art does not peddle the mystery of Christ, but opens it up, makes it possible to intimate. Such art points away from itself to this mystery.

What significance does this literary finding have for Christian theological reflection about Jesus of Nazareth? It opens our eyes to the way in which Jesus can already be depicted in the Christian foundation documents, the New Testament. If literature in its depiction of Jesus is more christopoetic than is thought, then in its belief in Christ, its christology, is the foundation document of primitive Christianity, the New Testament, possibly more literary than people are generally aware of? It might be worth making a separate investigation of the technique of the evangelists as writers – with the aim of asking whether analogies can be discovered between the literati of the first century and the twentieth.

3. The evangelist as a poet of Christ

With what techniques and stylistic means do the foundation documents of Christianity themselves speak of Jesus as 'the Christ'? How, purely in terms of literary techniques, is it stated that Jesus of Nazareth is not just one of the many prophets and teachers, but can be understood at the deepest level only if one sees that he stands for God, that God himself has acted in him and so has made himself known to us?[147]

Let me make a first thing clear: as we know, Jesus did not speak of himself as Christ, as Messiah and Son of God, as an incarnate God-man. Jesus did not speak 'christologically' about himself, and did not proclaim a christology about himself. Rather, he pointed away from himself: to

God himself, the kingdom of God, the will of God. It follows from this that the person of Jesus himself stands at the beginning of Christianity and not an explicit christology. This allows the reverse conclusion: any critique of christology is not alien to theology but immanent in it.

Let me make a second thing clear: it is typical that Jesus did not reflect theologically about himself, but *narrated* in concrete terms what he wanted to convey. Jesus illustrated his message and made it specific with the help of parables and similes which he invented; he told stories about the kingdom of God. He was certainly not a writer, but he was a story-teller through and through, and always a poet. To put it in a pointed way: he was the arch-poet of his cause, who expressed his way and his message (the dawn of the kingdom of God) in mirror stories, explained and expounded himself through narrative, invented fictitious figures in order to make his concern clear indirectly, illuminating it by representative figures or objective correlates. The Good Samaritan is one such fictitious figure, as is the father of the 'prodigal son'. So too is the king who arranges a marriage feast for his son, the owner of the vineyard who sent his son to the murderous tenants . . . But concrete details, too, like the fig tree, the mustard seed, the leaven, can become objective correlates of the kingdom of God. It follows from this that at the beginning of Christianity we do not have a theologian but a storyteller, who interprets himself in literary forms. This allows the reverse conclusion: the literary garb of the message must not be artificially painted over by Christian theology, but is given with it from the beginning.

Let me make a third thing clear: after his violent death and under the impact of his new life with God, Jesus, the story-teller, himself becomes the object of stories by his followers, indeed the object of songs and hymns which were sung, say, during worship. After Easter, on the basis of the experience of the resurrection, there is a new way of making Jesus literary, which now increasingly is the setting down of the Jesus tradition in writing. If Jesus was still the archpoet of his cause, the evangelists who initially collected and structured Jesus material which had been told orally present themselves to us as writers. With recognizable literary means, i.e. with particular literary structural characteristics and techniques, they attempt to make clear what significance and depth this man from Nazareth has for them and is to have for all men and women. Conversely, this means that the 'christological' does not present itself in the Gospels at the level of intellectualized teaching and speculative reflection but indirectly through a particular form of narration, a literary technique.

To be specific: with well-calculated literary means it is to be made clear to the readers and hearers of the Gospels that the one who is spoken of here evades all categories with which people attempt to understand him. The one who is told of here can certainly be grasped in word and deed, but ultimately he is incomprehensible; in his preaching he certainly takes up familiar details from everyday life and tradition, yet he usually breaks through all expectations: through his appearance and his preaching he certainly arouses particular expectations (Son of Man, Son of God, Messiah, political liberation hero), yet he transcends all these expectations either by surprisingly withdrawing into mystery and silence (the 'messianic secret' in Mark) or by a surprising change of perspective from above downwards, from power to impotence, from exaltation to lowliness, from familiarity to strangers: 'The foxes have holes and the birds of the air have nests, but the son of man has nowhere to lay his head' (Matt. 8.20). Certainly he is illuminated in numerous mirror figures: by his disciples or his mother, by disputes with Pharisees and scribes, by numerous encounters with the sick, to whom he gives new life. And yet no matter how many the figures in which his image also breaks through, he himself is identical with none of them. He is not explained by any interpretation of him by someone else; indeed he is often more enigmatic and crazy to his own followers than to his initial opponents. The New Testament has answers about who he was in his innermost depths and in the last resort, but the peculiarity of these answers is that they do not silence the questions. On the contrary, as writers the evangelists show that this Jesus ultimately evades all who want to grasp and domesticate him.

The way in which the evangelists tell of Jesus allows me to draw only one conclusion: by the technique of breaking expectations, by the form of dialogical disputes, by a change of perspective in pointed parabolic stories, by reflections and breaks in subordinate figures, it is to be made clear to the readers and hearers that here someone has appeared who was 'different' from usual, who was more than the familiar. He was different from the powerful apocalyptic son of man expected from heaven, different from a royal son of God entering his rule, different from the longed-for messiah of royal, prophetic or priestly origin. And here was someone who was more: more than Jonah, more than Solomon, more than Moses, more than the prophets, kings and teachers of the law put together. Only in the light of this presentation of Jesus as different and more can we understand that the New Testament saw the basis for these qualities in Jesus' mysterious relationship with God, indeed that after Easter it confessed that he stood guarantor for this wholly other God.

From that I draw the conclusion that the New Testament itself already has a christopoetics that we can recognize, i.e. a particular literary way of presenting Jesus to the people of the time as God's Christ. Certainly christopoetics is not christology. Reflection on the way in which the figure of Jesus Christ can be depicted in literature is not yet a confession of Christ, far less a doctrine of Christ. But if we look closely in the New Testament, the 'christological' as the confession of the one who was crucified and raised is always communicated through a particular mode of literary description. The foundation of this christopoetics of the New Testament is the recognition that Jesus is always 'different' and 'more' than people can say and understand.

4. The otherness and incomprehensibility of Jesus

No one from the guild of literary criticism or theology has seen this more clearly or described it more impressively than Walter Jens in his 1976 essay 'The Evangelists as Writers'. Jens makes the surprising discovery that if we look at the Gospels more closely in the light of this question, consider the details in the description of geography, people, actions; if we have an eye for the particle of reality, the structure of the scenes, the characteristics, the objects, we cannot avoid saying: 'There is little trace of hagiographical stylization here, and even less of Rilke's gold leaf. The tenor of the narrative is sobering: precision dominates; we learn more – far more – than we, who have long confused the Gospel reports with a sum of pious substitutes, had ever imagined.'[148] And for the description of Jesus of Nazareth in particular, according to Walter Jens the evangelists adopt a characteristic procedure:

> In striving to describe adequately that man who for them was at the same time both human (and utterly human) and God (and again utterly God), the evangelists have staged in connection with Jesus of Nazareth an interplay of realism and stylization, of brutal reality and abstraction, because they saw that only in this way was it possible to portray the contact of a man with a world to which he fell victim – being handed over to it – and yet which could not touch him. That means that, in order to show in the one under threat the one who, as it is said in Luke, passes through the midst of people in order to make visible the features of the risen one behind the image of the one who was flogged and – literally – torn (and also to show in the risen one the one who was tortured), the four writers have used a technique of alternation. This makes it possible for them to realize nearness and distance, the

'exposed' and the 'elevated', earthly nearness and heavenly distance, one immediately after the other, indeed sometimes with one another.[149]

So already in the New Testament we encounter a literary depiction of Jesus in the awareness of the dialectic of grasp and withdrawal; in the awareness of the familiarity and alien nature of Jesus; in the awareness of the explosion of customary schemes, the breaking of traditional images. And what about present-day literature? In principle it, too, knows no other techniques when it comes to depicting Jesus. Certainly, for many writers in the modern, post-Enlightenment period the spiritual horizon is a radically different one. What the evangelists took for granted (unbroken faith in the God of Abraham, Isaac and Jacob) can only rarely be followed by writers today. And yet in their poetic texts they, too, grapple with Jesus in such a way that it is still possible to trace something of the otherness and incomprehensibility of this figure.

Certainly this christopoetics of present-day literature differs fundamentally from that of the evangelists in that its aim is not the confession of Jesus as God's Christ. The New Testament christopoetics is grounded and ends in a belief in Christ, a christology; in extreme cases, that of contemporary writers arrives at an openness to the figure, its otherness, incomprehensibility. But both are aware that Jesus is always 'more' and 'different'. The poets of the first and twentieth centuries know the discrepancy between what is real and what can be told: the discrepancy between the depth and the truth of Jesus and the impossibility of giving it adequate linguistic and formal expression. But the poets today articulate more radically and directly that the failure to depict Jesus in literature can be aesthetically productive. Max Frisch showed it. His notes show a christopoetic awareness: at the level of art it is possible only to set down signs which do not mean what is meant.

5. Expression of culture – resistance to culture

Theology needs intercultural competence. I therefore chose key novels of world literature from different cultural spheres: Germany, the United States, Egypt, Paraguay, Russia. Here two basic insights emerge:

1. In different cultural contexts Jesus appears under different names, with different faces. Each time his story is told anew:
– as the story of a political prisoner fleeing from crucifixion, who learns to read the story of the flight and suffering of Jesus anew for his own comfort;

– as the story of a simple corporal who in a simple act of refusal is able for a short time to stop the murderous machinery of a war and is executed by the authorities for his 'threat';
– as the story of a gentle, unskilled exorcist who seeks to free people from the inner causes of their alienation, greed for life and lust for power, and in so doing clashes with those in power who rule life;
– as the story of an exploited, oppressed and despised people among whom, despite everything, the longing for redemption and liberation glimmers through;
– as the story of a journalist who tackles the cynical power cartel of a drug Mafia and nevertheless cannot let go of the vision that 'all human beings taken together are the image of God on earth'.

So the cultural context, the names and the faces under which Jesus re-emerges in the context of the twentieth century and lives out his story again could not be more different:

– his face is that of Georg Heisler, a Communist, who is hunted by Germany;
– his face is that of Stephan, the corporal who manages for a moment to silence the weapons;
– his face is that of Gaspar Mora, the carver and guitar player; of Casiano, Cristobál and many of the people of Paraguay;
– his face is that of the theologian and journalist Avdi Kallistratov, who wages a crazy war against the drug Mafia;
– his face is that of the gentle and unskilled exorcist Rifaa from Cairo, who attempts to turn peoples' hearts;
– his face shines out where Jewish children are afraid for their lives (as in Ilse Aichinger's Christmas play narrative) or a stammering husband is given a word (as in Heinrich Böll's Christmas story). His face shines out where the utopia of Bethlehem threatens to be quenched by the cynicism of Stalingrad (as in Peter Huchel's unique poem), where transformation of the heart in the spirit of goodness, forgiveness and mercy takes place (as in Tolstoy's novel about Prince Nekhlyudov and Yekaterina Maslova) and where a world that has encapsulated itself in one dimension has rid itself of surprises and totally encapsulated itself is put in question (F.Dürrenmatt). New contexts filter the story of Jesus afresh, select it, accentuate it and in this way discover dimensions which the tradition of interpretation in theology and the church has rejected, suppressed or forced to the periphery.

2. These stories of Jesus are not simply to be commandeered 'christo-logically' and thus put to the credit of Christian faith. They have their own aesthetic and autonomous claim to truth. Here Jesus of Nazareth does not stand in isolation as a figure of faith, but joins the totality of great universal figures of world literature. There are only a few such great archetypal figures in world literature, i.e. figures which are universal in space and time: Don Juan is among them, as are Hamlet, Job, Odysseus, Oedipus and also Antigone and Cassandra. They all interpret basic situations of the human condition and tell something of how human beings can be led astray; their dependence on love and hope; their incessant quest for meaning; their restless striving for home; the tragedy of their quest for truth; their readiness to resist, which does not shrink from self-sacrifice; their intimation of catastrophes. Jesus, too, stands in this series. He too is such a universal figure of humankind.

Jesus has his unmistakable profile in the circle of these great archetypal figures, whose fate can always be retold 'mythically'. His story is a unique combination of utopia, disaster and new utopia; of a message of love, execution and restoration; of hope, extermination and hope that cannot be exterminated. This triad constitutes the distinctive basic structure of the drama of Jesus. No one in world literature embodies as he does the dialectic of impotence and power, failure and victory, defeat and greatness. No one is as he is ' the matchless example of suffering and sacrifice and the promise of hope' – to use a phrase of William Faulkner's. No one embodies as he does the fact that one is crucified for an idea and forgives people this for ever (to use words of Ajmatov). The figures among whom he reappears in our century therefore all have something in common. They show the might of unfact: that despite all the failure, the idea of humankind embodied in Jesus has not been intrinsically refuted:
– that (to speak with Anna Seghers) there is something in human beings 'which was unassailable and inviolable', and the power of the weak will prove stronger than the power of those ruling for a while;
– that (to speak with William Faulkner) the recognition that the impossibility to change suffering is bound up with the conviction that human beings have the power to endure and sustain everything – in the conviction that the human being has a soul, a spirit, capable of compassion, sacrifice and endurance;
– that (to speak with Naguib Mahfouz) goodness establishes itself every day against evil;
– that (to speak with Augusto Roa Bastos) there must be a way out of the tremendous madness in which one human being is crucified by others;

– that (to speak with Cinghiz Ajmatov), evil can be overcome for all time.

Literature is a critical conversation of the cultural contexts with themselves. If it is aesthetic and creative, it succeeds in denouncing the plausibility of traditional contexts, i.e. in countering standardized perspectives and exploding established patterns of interpretation. Therefore great works of art always display a paradoxical structure: they interpret Jesus as part of culture, but at the same time they make people aware that no cultural context can really 'absorb' the figure of the man from Nazareth. They show Jesus as an authentic expression of culture, but at the same time demonstrate that no culture can level down his person to the point of triviality. Overlayings of context, overlappings of context and conflicts of context crystallize in this figure. Completely an ingredient of culture, Jesus can at the same time explode contexts.

This power of contextualization and at the same time of resistance against levelling down to the prevailing contexts is of the utmost theological relevance. For this simultaneity of immanence in culture and transcendence of culture is characteristic of Jesus and the message of him as the Messiah of Israel and Kyrios of the world from the beginning. But this power of transcendence is an expression of the hope that the cultural context can always be changed – in the spirit of Christ. Thus more than almost any other figure in world literature, Jesus is indispensable as a court of appeal, as someone with whom to identify, to show solidarity with, and to pin hope on for all whose faces are still distorted and who wait for the incarnation of humanity.

A Personal Note

This book has a long history. In 1991, studies of mine were published under the title 'Vielleicht hält Gott sich einige Dichter . . .' Literarisch-theologische Porträts. Here I had already expressed the hope that one day I would write a theopoetics, a systematic theology in dialogue with the literature of the twentieth century. The portraits in that book of Heinrich Heine, Franz Kafka, Rainer Maria Rilke, Joseph Roth, Hermann Hesse, Reinhold Schneider, Paul Celan, Nelly Sachs, Heinrich Böll and Rolf Hochhuth were intended as a first step 'towards a theopoetics'.

The second step is now being taken with this book. It is not the destination, but now it finally indicates the direction in which I shall be moving in the future. It says something about character, style, preliminary decisions for the future. Here I am presenting a kind of blueprint which – though there may be a wealth of changes – suggests what it will all look like at the end. My final goal is a comprehensive anthropology, theology and christology in dialogue with the great writers – beyond German-speaking culture. I am aiming at an a intercultural theology. I attempt it in this book with the inclusion of writers from North America, Russia, Egypt and Latin America.

Again I have abundant thanks to give in connection with this book. First of all to my closest collaborators here in Tübingen. Hans-Peter Buppus read through the whole manuscript critically, gave me valuable suggestions and in addition was very helpful in getting books and reading proofs. Frau Ute Netuschil was a model of competence, efficiency, reliability and charm in putting the countless versions of the manuscript on to the computer. I am also grateful to my former colleague Dr Georg Langenhorst, now Academic Adviser for Catholic Theology and Religious Education at the College of Education in Weingarten, who despite his other professional burdens took a good deal of trouble to read through the manuscript and offer suggestions.

Not least, I want to thank my friend and colleague Heinz-Dieter Assmann, Professor in the Faculty of Law in our University. He read parts of the manuscript, and his judgment has been particularly important to me. With him I share, among other things, a love of literature. We have had many conversations about his adventures in reading. An acute legal mind, at the same time he has preserved a passion for existential questions on the frontier of literature and religion. We have held successful interdisciplinary seminars with students from the faculties of theology and law on 'The Problem of Guilt Today from a Legal, Theological and Literary Perspective' (Winter Semester 1992/3) and 'Global Economy and Global Ethic' (Summer Semester 1995), and plan one on the problem of law and justice in the work of Friedrich Dürrenmatt (Summer Semester 1998). I am grateful for this collaboration, but above all for my friendship with Heinz-Dieter and Stephanie Assmann.

I have dedicated this book to the Theological Faculty of the University of Lund, Sweden. It awarded me an honorary doctorate in theology on 30 May 1997 and thus honoured in particular my efforts for a dialogue between the cultures, the world of theology and the world of literature. This token of honour by a Swedish university which is so rich in tradition is a reason for joy and gratitude, and encouragement on my way. With my dedication I want to endorse the link which has now been established and which I hope will be developed in the future.

Karl-Josef Kuschel   Tübingen, July 1997

Books by Karl-Josef Kuschel according to Subject Area

Systematic and ecumenical theology

Lust an der Erkenntnis. Die Theologie des 20. Jahrhunderts. Ein Lesebuch, Munich 1986, new edition Munich 1994

Wörterbuch des Christentums (edited with V. Drehsen, H. Häring and H. Siemer), Gütersloh 1988

Gegenentwürfe. 24 Lebensläufe für eine andere Theologie (edited with H. Häring), Munich 1988

Born Before All Time? The Dispute over Christ's Origin (1990), London and New York 1992

Leben in ökumeñischem Geist. Ein Plädoyer wider die Resignation, Ostfildern 1991

'Ich schaffe Finsternis und Unheil.' Ist Gott verantwörtlich für das Übel? (with W. Gross), Mainz 1992, ²1995

Hans Küng: Denkwege. Ein Lesebuch, Munich 1992

Hans Küng. New Horizons of Faith and Thought (edited with Hermann Häring), London and New York 1993

Laughter. A Theological Reflection, London and New York 1994

On the theology of inter-religious dialogue

Weltfrieden durch Religionsfrieden. Antworten aus den Weltreligionen (edited with H. Küng), Munich 1993

A Global Ethic. The Declaration of the Parliament of the World's Religions (edited with H. Küng), London and New York 1993

Christentum und nichtchristliche Religionen. Theologische Modelle im 20. Jahrhundert, Darmstadt 1994

Abraham. A Symbol of Hope for Jews, Christians and Muslims, London and New York 1995

Vom Streit zum Wettstreit der Religionen. Lessing und die Herausforderung des Islam, Düsseldorf 1998

Intolerant im Namen Gottes? Grundriss einer Theologie der Religionen (in preparation)

On the theology of culture

Jesus in der deutschsprachigen Gegenwartsliteratur (with a Foreword by Walter Jens), Zurich and Gütersloh 1978, reissued Munich 1987

Stellvertreter Christi? Der Papst in der zeitgenössischen Literatur, Zurich and Gütersloh 1980

Der andere Jesus. Ein Lesebuch moderner literarischer Texte, Zurich and Gütersloh 1983, Munich ²1991

Weil wir uns auf dieser Erde nicht ganz zu Hause fühlen. 12 Schriftsteller über Religion und Literatur, Munich 1985

Theologie und Literatur. Zum Stand des Dialogs (edited with W. Jens and H. Küng), Munich 1986

Und Maria trat aus ihren Bildern. Literarische Texte, Freiburg im Breisgau 1990

Wie kann denn ein Mensch schuldig werden? Literarische und theologische Perspektiven von Schuld (with U. Baumann), Munich 1990

'Vielleicht hält Gott sich einige Dichter.' Literarisch-theologische Porträts, Mainz 1991, ²1996

'Ich glaube nicht, dass ich Atheist bin.' Neue Gespräche über Religion und Literatur, Munich 1992

The Poet as Mirror. Human Nature, God and Jesus in Twentieth-Century Literature, London 1999

Jesus im Spiegel der Weltliteratur. Eine Jahrhundertbilanz in Texten und Einführungen, Düsseldorf 1999

Notes

Prologue

1. This book is based partly on my studies and investigations (see the bibliography on pp. 349f.) and partly on the following of my more programmatic articles:

- 'Theologen und ihre Dichter. Analysen zur Funktion der Literatur bei Rudolf Bultmann und Hans Urs von Balthasar', *Theologische Quartalschrift* 172, 1992, 98–116
- 'Ästhetik ohne Ethik? Analysen zur Gegenwartsliteratur', in W. Wolbert (ed.), *Moral in einer Kultur der Massmedien*, Freiburg and Vienna 1994, 51–70
- 'Gegenwart Gottes? Zur Möglichkeit theologischer Ästhetik in Auseinandersetzung mit George Steiner', in W. Lesch (ed.), *Theologie und Ästhetische Erfahrung. Beiträge zur Begegnung von Religion und Kunst*, Darmstadt 1994, 115–65
- 'Christopoetik. Spurensuche in der Literatur der Gegenwart', *Theologie und Glaube* 85, 1995, 499–517
- 'Theopoetik. Auf dem Weg zu einer Stillehre des Redens von Gott, Christus und dem Menschen', in P. Reifenberg (ed.), *Gott – das bleibende Geheimnis. FS W. Seidel*, Würzburg 1996, 227–54
- 'Ist es so schwer, den falschen Weg zu meiden? Über die Unverzichtbarkeit der Theologie in den geistigen Auseinandersetzungen der Zeit', in J. P. Wils (ed.), *Warum denn Theologie? Versuche wider die Resignation*, Tübingen 1996, 51–88.

2. Fundamental works on the aesthetics of reception are: W. Iser, The *Implicit Reader*, Baltimore 1974; id., *The Act of Reading*, Baltimore and London 1979. Also above all H. R. Jauss, *Ästhetische Erfahrung und literarische Hermeneutik*, Frankfurt am Main 1982; id., *Die Theorie der Rezeption. Rückschau auf ihre unerkannte Vorgeschichte*, Konstanz 1987; id., *Studien zum Epochenwandel der ästhetischen Moderne*, Frankfurt am Main 1989. P. V. Zima, *Literarische Ästhetik. Methoden und Modelle der Literaturwissenschaft*, Tübingen 1991, Chapter VI, 'Die Rezeptionsethik zwischen Hermeneutik und Phänomenologie', gives a good survey of the debate. Cf. also H. Steinmetz, 'Sinnfestlegung und Auslegungsvielfalt', in *Literaturwissenschaft. Ein Grundkurs*, ed. H. Brackert and J. Stückrath, Hamburg 1992, 475–90.

3. There are good surveys of various anthropological, theological and christological aspects of contemporary literature in the more recent works of distinguished authors who have made a name for themselves as pioneers of a theological investiga-

tion of modern literature in the German-speaking world: P. K. Kurz, *Gott in der modernen Literatur*, Munich 1995; F. Frühwald, 'Religion und Literatur am Ende des 20.Jahrhunderts', in K. Lehmann and H. Maier (eds.) *Autonomie und Verantwortung. Religion und Künste am Ende des 20.Jahrhunderts*, Regensburg 1995, 23–37; cf. also 38–51. M. Motté, *Auf der Suche nach dem verlorenen Gott. Religion in der Literatur der Gegenwart*, Theologie und Literatur VI, ed. K.-J. Kuschel, Mainz 1997.

4. J. G. Goethe, *Faust* I, lines 1984–1987, in Volume 2 of the Collected Works, edited and translated by Stuart Atkins, Princeton 1994. Cf. the extremely instructive article by D. Breuer, 'Mephisto als Theologe', in *Goethe-Jahrbuch* 109, 1992, 91–100. Here I think gratefully of my former German teacher Dr Helmut Enninghorst, who sadly died all too early. He made a great impression on me as a schoolboy with his humanity and his ability to communicate, his great objectivity and competence.

5. A. Camus, *The Outsider*, translated by Stuart Gilbert, Harmondsworth 1961, 118.

6. E. Wiesel, 'Die politisch-moralische Aufgabe des Schriftstellers heute. Nach Auschwitz haben die Worte ihre Unschuld verloren', in *Erinnerung als Gegenwart. Elie Wiesel in Loccum*, Loccum Protokolle 25, 1986, 117. I am also thinking of something that Elie Wiesel wrote in his autobiography: 'Nothing justifies Auschwitz. Were the Lord himself to offer me a justification, I think I would reject it. Treblinka erased all justifications and all answers. The barbed-wire kingdoms will forever remain an immense question mark on the scale of both humanity and its Creator. Faced with such unprecedented suffering and agony, He should have intervened, or at least expressed Himself. I would like to assume that in His perpetual compassion He allowed Himself to be overwhelmed by our pain, which He further intensified in His own way. Which side was He on? Only on that of the victims? Isn't He the Father of us all? It is in this capacity that He shatters our shell and moves us. How can we fail to pity a father who witnesses the massacre of his children by his other children? Is there a suffering more devastating, a remorse more bitter?' (*All Rivers Run to the Sea*, New York 1996, 105).

7. For my discussion with F. Stier see K.-J. Kuschel, 'Fridolin Stier als Theologe und Sprachkünstler. Zur Bedeutung einer neuen Übersetzung des Neuen Testaments', *Stimmen der Zeit* 208, 1990, 687–702.

8. F. Stier, *Vielleicht ist irgendwo Tag. Aufzeichnungen*, Freiburg im Breisgau 1981, 19f.

9. G. Benn, 'Altern als Problem der Künstler', *Gesammelte Werke* IV, ed. D. Wellerhoff, Wiesbaden 1968, 1116–46: 1143.

10. Stier, *Vielleicht ist irgendwo Tag* (n.8), 25.

11. Ibid., 247f.

12. Ibid., 347.

13. D. Sölle, *Das Eis der Seele spalten. Theologie und Literatur in sprachloser Zeit*, Mainz 1996, 76. This book, which appeared as volume V of the series Theologie und Literatur which I edited, contains all Dorothee Sölle's important texts on literature.

14. G. Steiner, *Real Presences*, London 1989.

15. Cf. K.-J. Kuschel, 'Gegenwart Gottes? Zur Möglichkeit theologischer Ästhetik in Auseinandersetzung mit Georg Steiner' (n.1).

16. Steiner, *Real Presences* (n.14), 227.

17. K. Barth, 'Church and Culture' (1926), in id., *Theology and Church. Shorter Writings 1920–1928*, London and New York 1962, 337.

18. Ibid., 339.

19. Cf. the comprehensive study by T. Kucharz, *Theologen und ihre Dichter. Literatur, Kultur und Kunst bei Karl Barth, Rudolf Bultmann and Paul Tillich*, Theologie und Literatur IV, Mainz 1995. Similarly K.-J. Kuschel, 'Theologen und ihre Dichter' (n.1).

20. K. Barth, 'Wolfgang Amadeus Mozart' (1956), in *Religion and Culture. Tillich Festschrift*, New York and London 1958, 67f.

21. Ibid., 68.

22. Ibid., 77.

23. C. Zuckmayer and K. Barth, *Späte Freundschaft in Briefen*, Zurich 1977, 17.

24. Ibid.

25. Ibid.

26. Ibid.

27. Ibid.

28. Steiner, *Real Presences* (n.14), 216.

29. Ibid.

30. This and the preceding quotation in the text, ibid., 218f.

31. Ibid., 220.

32. Ibid., 224.

33. Ibid., 225.

34. Ibid., 7.

35. Ibid. , 218.

36. Ibid.

37. Ibid.

38. Ibid.

39. Ibid., 226.

40. Ibid.

41. P. Tillich, 'Religiöser Stil und religiöser Stoff in der bildenden Kunst', in id., *Die religiöse Substanz der Kultur. Schriften zur Theologie der Kultur*, Gesammelte Werke IX, Stuttgart 1967, 320.

42. R. Guardini, *Über das Wesen des Kunstwerks*, Stuttgart-Tübingen 1948, 49.

43. The category of 'suspension' is the central feature of the great history of aesthetics by the Tübingen philosopher W. Schulz, *Metaphysik des Schwebens. Untersuchungen zur Geschichte des Ästhetik*, Pfullingen 1985.

44. Cf. E. Jüngel, ' "Auch das Schöne muss sterben." Schönheit im Lichte der Wahrheit. Theologische Bemerkungen zum ästhetischen Verhältnis', in id., *Wertlose Wahrheit. Zur Identität und Relevanz des christlichen Glaubens*, Munich 1990, 378–96.

45. Steiner, *Real Presences* (n.14), 231f.

46. Cf. the informative article 'Inculturation', *Lexikon für Theologie und Kirche* V, Freiburg im Breisgau 1996, 504–10.

47. G. Schulze, *Die Erlebnisgesellschaft. Kultursoziologie der Gegenwart*, Frankfurt am Main and New York 1993, 542.

48. German Conference of Catholic Bishops, *Kunst und Kultur in der theologischen Aus- und Fortbildung*, Arbeitshilfen 115, 5 Oktober 1993.

49. The most extensive catalogue of works so far is F. G. Zehnder, *Herbert Falken. Aus der Dunkelheit für das Licht,* Cologne 1993. M. Ostermann, *Herbert Falken. Werkprinzipien,* Münster dissertation 1989, has made a thorough historical classification.

50. Extracts from the dialogue between K.-J. Kuschel and H. Falken were published under the title 'Gedanken zu Christusbildern von Herbert Falken', *Theologische Quartalschrift* 175, 1995, 279–93 (Vol 4: *Theologie und die Bilder der Kunst*).

51. This text from the Tübingen dialogue lectures has not yet been published. I have quoted from the manuscript in my possession.

A. The Riddle of Human Nature

1. K. Tucholsky, 'Der Mann am Spiegel (1928)', in *Gedichte*, ed. M. Gerold-Tucholsky, Hamburg 1983, 579–82.
2. The biblical texts are usually taken from the Revised Standard Version.
3. The conversation with Günter Kunert has been published in K. J. Kuschel, *'Ich glaube nicht, dass ich Atheist bin.' Neue Gespräche über Religion und Literatur,* Munich 1992, 26–44.
4. Ibid., 34.
5. G. Kunert (ed.), *Dichter predigen. Reden aus der Wirklichkeit,* Stuttgart 1989, 7.
6. G. Kunert, *Stillleben. Gedichte,* Munich and Vienna 1983, 91.
7. Ibid., 53.
8. Kunert, *Dichter predigen* (n.5), 8.
9. Kuschel, *'Ich glaube nicht, dass ich Atheist bin'* (n.3), 44.
10. G. Kunert, 'Erstes Buch Mose. Die Schlange und die Vertreibung', in id., *Die letzten Indianer Europas. Kommentar zum Traum, der Leben heisst,* Munich 1991, 36.
11. Ibid., 40f.
12. K. Dunne, *Der Sündenfall. A parabolic key to the image of human existence in the work of G. Kunert 1960–1990,* Frankfurt am Main 1995, 18f.
13. G. Kunert, *Fremd daheim. Gedichte,* Munich 1990, 76.
14. The conversation with W. Hildesheimer has been published in Kuschel, *'Ich glaube nicht, dass ich Atheist bin'* (n.3), 79–97.
15. I have discussed the work of Wolfgang Hildesheimer in W. Gross and K.-J. Kuschel, *'Ich schaffe Finsternis und Unheil!' Ist Gott verantwortlich für das Übel?,* Mainz ²1995, 121–35, C II, on 'Talk of "God's guilt" as the Fatigue of Theodicy: Wolfgang Hildesheimer's *Tynset*.'
16. Cf. W. Hildesheimer, 'Mein Judentum' (1978), in id., *Gesammelte Werke* VII, Frankfurt am Main 1991, 159–69.
17. W. Hildesheimer, 'Über das absurde Theater', in id., *Gesammelte Werke* VII, Frankfurt am Main 1991, 17.
18. W. Jens, 'Ein Ausgelieferter übertönt die Nacht', in *Über Wolfgang Hildesheimer*, ed. D. Rodewald, Frankfurt am Main 1971, 121–7: 124.
19. W. Hildesheimer, *Tynset*, in id., *Gesammelte Werke* II, Frankfurt am Main 1991, 138.

20. Ibid., 64f.

21. The text of 'Herr, gibt ihnen die ewige Ruhe nicht. Gedanken über Leben und Tod – und über Mozart' (1986), is in W. Hildesheimer, *Gesammelte Werke* VII, Frankfurt am Main 1991, 723–33. His commentary on it is in the same volume, 806–10. See also the conversation with K.-J. Kuschel (n.14), esp.93–7.

22. W. Jens, 'Spiel und Vernichtung. Eine Erinnerung an Wolfgang Hildesheimer, den melancholische Dichter der Hoffnung', *Die Zeit*, 20 December 1996.

23. Hildesheimer, 'Herr, gibt ihnen die ewige Ruhe nicht' (n.21), 729.

24. Ibid., 807.

25. Ibid., 726f.

26. Jens, 'Spiel und Vernichtung' (n.22).

27. Hildesheimer, 'Herr, gibt ihnen die ewige Ruhe nicht' (n.21), 725.

28. For the topic of apocalypse in literature see K.-J. Kuschel, 'Vor uns die Sintflut? Spuren der Apokalypse in der Gegenwartsliteratur', in *Weltgericht und Weltvollendung. Zukunftsbilder im Neuen Testament*, ed. H.-J. Klauck, Freiburg im Breisgau 1994, 232–60 (with bibliography). There are also important contributions in K. Stierle and R. Warning (eds.), *Das Ende. Figuren einer Denkform*, Poetik und Hermeneutik XVI, Munich 1996.

29. W. Hildesheimer, 'Der Künstler und die Endzeit' (1986), in *Gesammelte Werke* VII, Frankfurt am Main 736–8: 736f.

30. For the history and influence of the apocalypse see D. Dormeyer and L. Hauser, *Weltuntergang und Gottesherrschaft*, Mainz 1990.

31. J. van Hoddis, *Gedichte*, ed R. Nörtemann, Frankfurt am Main 1990, 13.

32. H. Hornbogen, *Jakob van Hoddis. Die Odysse eines Verschollenen*, Munich and Vienna 1986, 71. K. Vondung, *Die Apokalypse in Deutschland*, Munich 1988, also contains a wealth of contemporary material.

33. G. Heym, 'Die Menschen stehen', in *Lyrik des Expressionismus*, edited with an introduction by S. Vietta, Munich and Tübingen 1976, 101f.

34. W. Jens, *Das A und das O. Die Offenbarung des Johannes*, Stuttgart 1987, 31.

35. G. Kunert, 'Zur Apokalypse. Eine Strafpredigt', *Neue Rundschau* 101, 1990, 19f.

36. G. Anders, 'Über die Bombe und die Wurzeln unserer Apokalypse-Blindheit', in id., *Die Antiquiertheit des Menschen. Über die Seele im Zeitalter der zweiten industriellen Revolution*, Munich 1956, 233–324.

37. For the work of C. Amery see the conversation in K.-J. Kuschel, *'Ich glaube nicht, dass ich Atheist bin.' Neue Gespräche über Religion und Literatur*, Munich 1982, 45–60.

38. C. Wolf, *Voraussetzungen einer Erzählung: Kassandra, Frankfurter Poetik-Vorlesung*, Darmstadt and Neuwied 1983, 86.

39. Ibid., 97.

40. K. H. Götze, 'Die friedliche Nutzung eines Störfalls. Christa Wolfs Bericht über ihren Tschernobyl-Tag', *Frankfurter Rundschau*, 16 May 1987.

41. W. Lepenies, 'Die Wissenschaft und die Angst. Über die Wiederkehr der Furcht im technischen Zeitalter', *Frankfurter Allgemeine Zeitung*, 1 August 1987.

42. Günter Grass, *The Rat*, translated by Ralph Manheim, London 1987, 132.

43. Ibid., 161f.

44. Ibid., 3.

45. G. Grass, 'Mir träumte, ich müsste Abschied nehmen. Gespräch mit B. Pinkerneil', in *Werkausgabe X, Gespräche*, Darmstadt and Neuwied 1987, 342–58: 350.

46. Grass, *The Rat* (n. 42), 79f.

47. G. Grass, 'Der Vernichtung der Menschheit hat begonnen. Rede zur Verleihung des Internationalen Antonio-Feltrinelli-Preises für erzählende Prosa in Rom (November 1982)', in *Werkausgabe IX, Essays, Reden, Briefe, Kommentare*, Darmstadt and Neuwied 1987, 830–3: 831f.

48. Ibid., 833.

49. Grass, *The Rat* (n. 42), 356f.

50. Ibid., 358.

51. The following quotations are taken from the conversation between G. Grass and B. Pinkerneil (n.45).

52. Grass, 'Mir träumte' (n. 45), 350.

53. K. Marti, *Mein barfüssig Lob*, Darmstadt 1987. The following poems are quoted from this slim volume.

54. Cf. K.-J. Kuschel, *Laughter*, London 1994.

55. For the work of Max Frisch see K.-J. Kuschel, *Jesus in der deutsch-sprächigen Gegenwartsliteratur. Mit einem Vorwort von Walter Jens*, Zurich and Cologne 1978, 115–23; id., 'Max Frisch und die Frage der Schuld', in *Grenzfall Literatur. Die Sinnfrage in der modernen Literatur der viersprachigen Schweiz*, ed. J. Bättig and S. Leimgruber, Fribourg CH 1993, 209–23.

56. M. Frisch, 'Stimmen eines anderen Deutschland? Zu den Zeugnissen von Wiechert und Bergengruen', in *Gesammelte Werke in zeitlicher Folge* II. 1, Frankfurt am Main 1976, 297–311: 304.

57. M. Frisch, 'Nun singen sie wieder. Versuch eines Requiem', in *Gesammelte Werke* II/1, 104.

58. M. Frisch, 'Verdammen oder verzeihen? Briefe an BI, der Verfasser des Leitartikels in der NZZ vom 23 Mai 1945', in *Gesammelte Werke* II/1, 292–6: 293f.

59. Ibid., 294.

60. Ibid., 295.

61. W. Schmitz, *Max Frisch Homo Faber. Materialien, Kommentar*, Munich and Vienna 1977; F. A. Lubich, *Max Frisch: 'Stiller', 'Homo Faber' und 'Meine Name sei Gantenbein'*, Munich 1990, are key to the interpretation of *Homo Faber*.

62. Max Frisch, *Homo Faber*, Harmondsworth 1974, 180f.

63. Ibid., 144.

64. Ibid., 127.

65. Max Frisch himself once said this about the figure of Walter Faber: 'This man falls short of himself because he imitates an image which is generally on offer, that of "technology". Basically the "Homo Faber", this man, is not a technician, but he is a handicapped man who has made a picture of himself, who has let himself make a picture which prevents him coming to himself' (in W. Schmitz, *Max Frisch* [n.61], 16).

66. M. Frisch, '"Wem wird man schon fehlen?", Gespräch mit Volker Schlöndorff', *Der Spiegel* 12, 1991, 241.

67. Ibid., 238.

68. M. Frisch, *Bluebeard*, translated by Geoffrey Skelton, London 1983, 8.

69. Ibid., 34, cf. also 85.

70. W. Schmitz, *Max Frisch. Das Spätwerk (1962–1982). Eine Einführung*, Tübingen 1985, 149.

71. For Kafka's understanding of guilt cf. K.-J. Kuschel, *'Vielleicht hält Gott sich einige Dichter . . .' Literarisch-theologische Porträts*, Mainz ² 1986, Chapter III: 'Kafka und die Unheimlichkeit der Welt'.

72. Frisch, *Bluebeard* (n.68), 61.

73. Ibid., 81.

74. 'Blaubart', in *Kindlers Neues Literaturlexikon*, ed. W. Jens, V, Munich 1989, 850.

75. J. Kaiser, *Erlebte Literatur. Vom 'Doktor Faustus' zum 'Fettfleck'. Deutsche Schriftsteller in unserer Zeit*, Munich and Zurich 1988, 169f.

76. G. Steiner, *Language and Silence*, New York 1967, German edition *Sprache und Schweigen. Essays über Sprache, Literatur und das Unmenschliche*, Frankfurt am Main 1969, 7–10: 8f.

77. P. Weiss, 'Die Ermittlung' (1965), in id., *Stücke I*, Frankfurt am Main 1980. The following quotations are on pp.445f., 448f.

78. I have discussed Rolf Hochhuth's work in detail in K.-J. Kuschel, *Stellvertreter Christi? Der Papst in der zeitgenössischen Literatur*, Zurich and Gütersloh 1980, III/3, and in *'Vielleicht hält Gott sich einige Dichter . . .' Literarisch-theologische Porträts*, Mainz 1991, ²1996, X: 'Rolf Hochhuth und die Gottesfrage nach Auschwitz'.

79. I gave the Laudatio for Rolf Hochhuth on 29 January 1991 in Elisabeth Langgässer's birthplace, Alzey. The chapter 'Rolf Hochhuth und Die Gottesfrage nach Auschwitz' mentioned in n.78 is a considerably expanded and revised version of this lecture.

80. D. Goldhagen, *Hitler's Willing Executioners*, New York and London 1996, 387.

81. R. Hochhuth, *The Representative. A Christian Tragedy*, translated by Robert David McDonald, London 1963 reissued 1998, 254–6.

82. Ibid., 263f.

83. Ibid., 259.

84. *The Spiritual Exercises of Saint Ignatius*, translated by Anthony Mottola, New York 1964, 59: First Week, Fifth Exercise.

85. Hochhuth, *The Representative* (n.81), 290

86. Ibid., 261.

87. R. Hochhuth, 'Der Mensch sollte so leben als gäbe es Gott. Gespräch', in K. J. Kuschel, *'Ich Glaube nicht, dass ich Atheist bin.' Neue Gespräche über Religion und Literatur*, Munich 1993, 168–93: 182.

88. A. Solzhenitsyn, *The First Circle*, London 1968, 14.

89. Ibid., 581.

90. Cf. K.-J. Kuschel, 'Die Erfahrung des Höllischen und Teuflischen in der Literatur des 20.Jahrhunderts', in A. Biesinger and M. Kessler (eds), *Himmel – Hölle – Fegefeuer*, Tübingen and Basel 1996, 31–54.

91. K. Korn, 'Mawrino. Allegorie der Hölle', *Frankfurter Allgemeine Zeitung*, 21 September 1968.

92. I. Winogradow, 'Solshenizyn. Die Paradoxien seines Moralismus', *Frankfurter Allgemeine Zeitung*, 12 May 1990.

93. T. W. Adorno, *Negative Dialectics,* London 1973, 361f. A similar notion occurs in his key work on moral philosophy, *Minima Moralia. Reflections on a Damaged Life*, London 1979: 'But even if things have always been so, although neither Timur nor Genghis Khan nor the English colonial administration in India systematically burst the lungs of millions of people with gas, the eternity of horror nevertheless manifests itself in the fact that each of its new forms outdoes the old. What is constant is not an invariable quantity of suffering, but its progress towards hell: that is the meaning of the intensification of antagonisms. Any other would be innocuous and would give way to conciliatory phrases, abandoning the qualitative leap. He who registers the death-camps as a technical mishap in civilization's triumphal procession, the martyrdom of the Jews as world-historically irrelevant, not only falls short of the dialectical vision but perverts the meaning of his own politics: to hold ultimate calamity in check' (233f.).

94. T. Mann, 'An die gesittete Welt' (1983), in E V, 28–35: 31f. (wherever possible I have quoted the essays of Thomas Mann from the best edited edition, with a masterful commentary by H. Kurzke and S. Stachorski, E – volume – page, Frankfurt am Main 1993–1997).

95. T. Mann, E V, 29.

96. T. Mann, 'Kultur und Politik' (1939), in id., *An die gesittete Welt. Politische Schriften und Reden im Exil,* Frankfurt am Main 1986, 291–9: 297. The quotation here is from the Frankfurt Edition (= FE).

97. Ibid., 299. Cf. also 324 (FE).

98. T. Mann, 'Ansprache anlässlich der Aufnahme in den Phi-Beta-Kappa Orden der Berkeley University' (1941), ibid., 410–14: 414, see also 492, 642, 643 (FE).

99. T. Mann, 'Deutschland' (1941), in id., *An die gesittete Welt* (n.96), 426–36: 433 (FE).

100. T. Mann , 'Lob Amerikas' (1942), ibid, 458–61: 460 (FE).

101. T. Mann, 'Ansprache an die amerikaner deutscher Herkunft' (1942), ibid., 461–4: 464 (FE).

102. T. Mann, 'Deutschland und die Deutschen' (1945), in EV 250–81: 264.

103. T. Mann, E V, 265.

104. Cf. M. Maar, 'Der kalte Schatten grosser Männer. Über den Teufel in Thomas Mann's "Doktor Faustus"', *Frankfurter Allgemeine Zeitung*, 13 June 1992.

105. T. Mann, 'Die Entstehung der Doktor Faustus' (1949), in id., *Doktor Faustus/Die Enstehung des Doktor Faustus*, Frankfurt am Main 1981, 723.

106. Ibid., 727f.

107. T. Mann, *Doctor Faustus*, London 1949, 249.

108. Ibid., 245f. For graphic reasons I have made new paragraphs.

109. Ibid., 503.

110. Ibid., 634.

111. Ibid.

112. Ibid., 502.

113. Ibid.

114. These two theological and philosophical positions over evil from the classical tradition cannot be interpreted further here. In the novel they are developed in the narrative of chapters 12 and 13, during Adrian Leverkühn's theological studies in Halle. Here the hero meets the Protestant theologian Ehrenfried Kumpf (who calls for evil to be fought in a cheerful Christian way) and the Protestant theologian Eberhard Schleppfuss (for whom evil is a necessary outflow of the good). Both positions are left as they are in the composition of the novel without a key to the 'essence' of evil being offered.

115. H. Koopmann, 'Doktor Faustus – Schwierigkeiten mit dem Bösen und das Ende des "strengen Satzes"', in id., *Der schwierige Deutsche. Studien zum Werk Thomas Manns*, Tübingen 1988, 125–44: 138f.

116. T. Mann, *Entstehung des Doktor Faustus* (n.105), 830.

117. T. Mann, *Doctor Faustus* (n.107), 490f.

118. T. Mann, *Entstehung des Doktor Faustus* (n.105), 723.

119. T. Mann, *Doctor Faustus* (n.107), 510. Cf. Also T. Mann, 'Deutschland und die Deutschen' (1945), in E V, 281: 'Finally the German misfortune is simply the paradigm of the human tragedy generally. We all need the grace which Germany needs so urgently.' The same notion occurs again often, as in a letter from Thomas Mann to Walter von Molow dated 7 September 1945: 'The pact with the devil is a deeply Old German temptation, and a German novel which was concerned with the suffering of the last years, the suffering over Germany, would have to be about this grim promise. But even over Faust's individual soul, in our greatest poem, the greatest is finally deceived, and far be it from us to imagine that Germany has now finally banished the devil. Grace is higher than any letter in blood. I believe in it and I believe in the future of Germany, however desperate its present may seem, however hopeless the destruction' (*Letters* II, ed. E. Mann, Frankfurt am Main 1979, 446)

120. T. Mann, 'Vom künftigen Sieg der Demokratie' (1938), in E IV, 214–24: 222f.

121. R. Safranski, *Schopenhauer und die wilden Jahre der Philosophie*, Munich 1987; id., *Ein Meister aus Deutschland. Heidegger und seine Zeit*, Munich 1994.

122. Cf. R. Safranski, 'Auf dem Rücken des Tigers. Gespräch über Geschichte und Aktualität des Böse', *Der Spiegel* 52, 1996; id., *Das Böse oder Das Drama der Freiheit*, Munich and Vienna 1997.

123. R. Safranski, 'Destruktion und Lust. Über die Wiederkehr des Bösen', in H. Schwilk and U. Schacht (eds)., *Die selbstbewusste Nation. 'Anschwellender Bocksgesang' und weiter Beiträge zu einer deutschen Debatte*, Frankfurt am Main and Berlin 1994, 237–48, esp. 237–40.

124. Ibid., 241f.

125. See the fine essay by J. P. Wils, 'Handeln in der Spur Gottes', in id. (ed.), *Warum denn Theologie? Versuche wider die Resignation*, Tübingen 1996, 149–84: 175.

126. Thomas Mann, 'Letter to Else Vielhaber of 30 March 1955', in *Briefe III* (1948–1955 and posthumous), ed. E. Mann, Frankfurt am Main 1979, 390.

B. God the Abyss

1. This text can be found in EGB under no.278. It comes from the highly impressive, personal notes by T. Haecker (1879–1945), *Tag- und Nachtbücher 1939–1945*, ed. H. Siefken, Innsbruck 1989, 143 (no.675), first published posthumuously in 1947. Cf. also no.682: 'Never let God rest when you are in danger. Simply give him no rest and then he will not let you rest, and that is your salvation.'

2. The following is developed at more length in W. Gross and K.-J. Kuschel, *'Ich schaffe Finsternis und Unheil!' Ist Gott verantworlich für das Übel?*, Mainz ²1995, B. Theologiegeschichtliche Perspektiven. In the present book I once again sum up the problems briefly (B I) and then take them further in dialogue with literature (B II-IV). The abbreviation DH used in the following church texts refers to the new edition of Denziger (= D) edited by P. Hünermann (= H), Heinrich Denzinger, *Kompendium der Glaubensbekenntnisse und kirchlichen Lehrentscheidungen*, Freiburg im Breisgau ³⁷1991.

3. G. Büchner, 'Briefe an die Braut', in *Werke und Briefe,* Munich 1965, 162. The following quotations come from pp.33, 60, 39f.

4. W. Kasper, *The God of Jesus Christ*, London 1984, 197.

5. G. Greshake, *Wenn Leid mein Leben lähmt. Leiden – Preis der Liebe?*, Freiburg im Breisgau 1978, reissued 1982, 30.

6. C. Westermann, *Die Klagelieder. Forschungsgeschichte und Auslegung*, Neukirchen-Vluyn 1990, 78. It should be pointed out here that a major interdisciplinary study on a 'theology of lamentation and complaint' is currently in preparation in Tübingen. Here the questions which arise for exegesis, the history of theology and systematic theology will be discussed at length.

7. F. Dürrenmatt, *Der Hund/Der Tunnel/Die Panne. Erzählungen*, Zurich, Werkausgabe Vol.20, 1980, 97–8. There are surveys of the work in E. Brock-Sulzer, *Friedrich Dürrenmatt. Stationen seines Werkes*, Zurich 1973; J. Knopf, *Friedrich Dürrenmatt*, autorenbücher 611, Munich ⁴1988; G. P. Knapp, *Friedrich Dürrenmatt.*, Sammlung Metzler 196, Stuttgart and Weimar ²1993.

8. Brock-Sulzer, *Friedrich Dürrenmatt* (n.7), 339.

9. Knapp, *Friedrich Dürrenmatt* (n.7), 37.

10. Examples in E. Weber, *Friedrich Dürrenmatt und die Frage nach Gott. Zur theologischen Relevanz der frühen Prosa eines merkwürdigen Protestanten*, Zurich 1980, 208.

11. Examples in ibid., 210, and in J. Bark, 'Dürrenmatt's Pilatus und das Etikett des christlichen Dichters', in G. P. Knapp, *Friedrich Dürrenmatt. Studien zu seinem Werk,* Heidelberg 1976, 54f.

12. F. Dürrenmatt, *Der Winterkrieg im Tibet, Stoffe I*, Diogenes Taschenbuch ed., Zurich 1984, 43; id., *Die Entdeckung des Erzählens. Gespräche 1971–1980*, Vol. II, Zurich 1996, 119.

13. F. Dürrenmatt, *Mondfinsternis/Der Rebell. Stoffe II/III*, Diogenes Taschenbuch ed., Zurich 1984, 19f.

14. For the significance of Kierkegaard for Dürrenmatt see Weber, *Friedrich Dürrenmatt und die Frage nach Gott* (n.10). In 1977, on the occasion of the award of the Buber-Rosenzweig Medal, in his lecture 'On Tolerance' Dürrenmatt confessed: 'In the last year of my studies a lecturer appeared who sought to befriend us with

Heidegger's existentialism. My animosity towards Heidegger, which has remained with me, must date from this time. I had intended to write a dissertation on "Kierkegaard and the Tragic". But I didn't. However, Kierkegaard continued to disturb me. My father had already been interested in Kierkegaard. For a long time I was preoccupied with his *Unscientific Postscript*, which I regard as Kierkegaard's most important work', in F. Dürrenmatt, *Philosophie und Naturwissenschaft. Essays und Reden*, Werkausgabe XXVII, Zurich 1980, 125f.

15. For the significance of Karl Barth for Dürrenmatt see Weber, *Friedrich Dürrenmatt und die Frage nach Gott* (n.10), 50–7. The speech 'On Tolerance' contains the remark: 'My relations with theology have been burdened with the fact that as a pastor's son I am stamped with a natural antipathy to everything theological. The best reason for being interested in it. I owe much to theology, though in its contrary impulses. Karl Barth's *Romans* was a revolutionary book for me; his *Dogmatics*, in which I often read, a mathematical masterpiece. The passages on Judaism are taken from it, Volumes I/2 and II/3' (127f.).

16. Dürrenmatt, *Mondfinsternis/Der Rebell* (n.13), 128, 129.

17. Dürrenmatt, *Die Entdeckung des Erzählens* (n.12), 83.

18. D. von Gersdoff, *Marie Luise Kaschnitz. Eine Biographie*, Frankfurt am Main and Leipzig 1992, 196.

19. M. L. Kaschnitz, *Neue Gedichte* (1957), in *Gesammelte Werke V, Die Gedichte*, Frankfurt am Main 1985, 245–265 ('Tutzinger Gedichtkreis'). Henceforth abbreviated as GW – volume – page. For a discussion of religion in the author's work see the helpful study by U. Suhr, *Poesie als Sprache des Glaubens. Eine theologische Untersuchung des literarischen Werkes von Marie Luise Kaschnitz*, Stuttgart, Berlin and Cologne 1992. There are also surveys of research in U. Schweikert (ed.), *Marie Luise Kaschnitz*, Frankfurt am Main 1984; E. Pulver, *Marie Luise Kaschnitz*, Autorenbücher 40, Munich 1984.

20. M. L. Kaschnitz, *Gedichte zur Zeit* (1947), in GW V, 159f.

21. Ibid., 163f.

22. M. L. Kaschnitz, *Von der Gotteserfahrung* (1945), GW VII, 3–38.

23. Ibid., 37f.

24. E. Fried, 'Manchmal grosse Lyrik', *Die Zeit*, 5 December 1957.

25. H. E. Bahr, *Poiesis, Theologische Untersuchungen der Kunst*, Munich and Hamburg 1965, 164.

26. Quoted in von Gersdoff, *Marie Luise Kaschnitz* (n.18), 198f.

27. M. L. Kaschitz, 'Vom Wortschatz der Poesie' (1949), in GW VII, 536–42: 540f.

28. M. L. Kaschnitz, *Engelsbrücke. Römische Betrachtungen* (1955), in GW II, 135f.

29. Ibid., 136.

30. M. L. Kaschnitz, *Wohin denn ich* (1963), GW II, 551.

31. Quoted in von Gersdoff, *Marie Luise Kaschnitz* (n.18), 273.

32. M. L. Kaschnitz, *Tage, Tage, Jahre. Aufzeichnungen* (1968), in GW III, 166.

33. Ibid., 309f.

34. Quoted in von Gersdoff, *Marise Luise Kaschnitz* (n.18), 197.

35. Pulver, *Marie Luise Kaschnitz* (n.19), 67.

36. I have discussed Heine in more detail in K. J. Kuschel, '*Vielleicht hält Gott*

sich einige Dichter.' *Literarisch-theologische Porträts,* Mainz ²1996: Chapter II, 'Heinrich Heine und die Doppelgesichtigkeit aller Religion'. The following books are important for interpreting the late work: J. Brummack (ed.), *Heinrich Heine. Epoche – Werk – Wirkung,* Munich 1980, esp.275–86; W. Preisendanz, *Heinrich Heine. Werkstructuren und Epochenbezüge,* Munich 1973, ²1983 (especially the sections on 'Heine's poetry' and 'The poems from the mattress tomb'). S. Prawer, *Heine's Jewish Comedy,* Oxford 1983, is a basic study of religion in Heine. For the figure of Jesus see B. Wirth-Othmann, *Heinrich Heines Christusbild. Grundzüge seines religiösen Selbstverständnisses,* Paderborn 1994 (with bibliography).

37. H. Heine, *Deutschland. A Winter's Tale* (1844), translated with an introduction and notes by T. J. Reed, London 1986, 31.

38. H. Heine, letter to H. Laube of 7 February 1850, in *Briefe,* ed. F. Hirth, Vol.III, Mainz and Berlin 1950 (no.1027).

39. G. Lukács, 'Heine als nationale Dichter (1935)', in id., *Deutsche Realisten des 19.Jahrhunderts,* Berlin 1951, 89–146: 121.

40. H. Heine, postscript to 'Romanzero' (1851), in *Sämtliche Schriften in 12 Bänden,* ed. K. Briegleb, Vol.XI, Munich and Vienna 1976, 182f. Henceforth abbreviated as SW – volume – page. Cf. similarly the letter to H. Laube of 25 January 1850: 'To make things clear to you in a word, I have given up the Hegelian God or rather the Hegelian godlesssness and replaced it with the dogma of a real, personal God who is outside nature and the human disposition. This dogma, which can be carried through as well as our Hegelian synthesis, was already depicted most profoundly, according to the testimonies of the Neoplatonic fragments, by the old magi. Later, in the foundation documents of Moses, it emerges with an enthusaism for truth and an eloquence which truly cannot be found in our more recent dialecticians. Hegel has come down in my estimation; the old Moses flourishes' (in SW XII, 220). Similarly, to H. Laube, 12 October 1850: 'I lie huddled, in pain day and night, and though I believe in a God, sometimes I do not believe in a good God. The hand of this great animal tormenter lies heavy on me. What a generous and lovable God I was in my youth, when through Hegel's grace I swung up to this high position' (in SW XII, 221).

41. H. Heine, 'Geständnisse' (1854), in SW XI, 501. For understanding these 'Confessions' see the detailed commentary by K. Briegleb in SW XII, 201–27. He makes the convincing observation: 'Already in the first answer to this misunderstanding (withdrawal of the earlier utopias of perfection), in the Preface of 1852 Heine rejected the notion of conversion and intensified the figurative biblical symbolism of his reflections: being cast down from the height of darkness means a correction of the standpoint of political theology and popular poetry, not its abandonment. The challenge posed by a newly exposed reality to the author's capacity for interpretation shows itself with inexorable harshness in the basic structure of his literary treatment of reality. The "Job messages" do not prompt him to any repentance, for his efforts in the days of happiness were "just", but rather to reflection to the point of despair about this new objection from reality' (218).

42. H. Heine, Draft Testament of 13 November 1851, in SW XI, 548f.

43. H. Heine, 'Spätere Note' (March 1854), in SW IX, 190. Immediately afterwards Heine continues (and these sentences are worth documenting): 'How is it that on the return from Babylon the pious Temple Archive Commission, whose president

Ezra was, accepted that book into the canon of holy scripture? I have often asked myself this question. My conjecture is that those God-enlightened men did not do it out of ignorance but because in their high wisdom they knew that doubt is deeply grounded in human nature. It is justified, and one must not completely suppress it in a clumsy way, but must only heal. They acted in a very homeopathic way in this cure, using like on like, but they did not give homoeopathically small doses; rather, they increased these tremendously, and the book of Job is such an over-strong dose of doubt. However, this poison must not be absent from the Bible, the great domestic pharmacy of humankind. Indeed, just as people when they suffer must cry out, so they must express their doubts if they feel grievously insulted in their claims to happiness; and as through the loudest weeping, so too through the highest degree of doubt which the Germans so rightly call despair, comes the crisis of moral healing. – But probably for those who are healthy and need no physician!' (190f.)

44. H. Heine, 'Zum Lazarus' , in SW XI, 201f. The English translation is by Alistair Elliot, H. Heine, *The Lazarus Poems*, London 1979, 55.

45. H. Heine, *Miserere*, SW XI, 332f.

46. H. Heine, *Götterdämmerung* (1824), in SW I, 151.

47. H. Heine, *Ideen, Das Buch Le Grand* (1826), in SW III, 253.

48. H. Heine, *Aufzeichnungen*, in SW XI, 625.

49. H. Heine, *Geständisse,* in SW XI, 499. A remark in a letter dated 21 August 1851 to Heine's Hamburg publisher Campe makes clear how much Heine's images of God deliberately change in the different statements, from the 'great tormentor of animals' through the mocking God to the God who is ironically called 'dear God'. 'My state of health, or rather my state of sickness, is still the same. I suffer a tremendous amount, I endure truly Promethean pains, through rancour of the gods, who growl at me because I gave people some nightlights, some penny lights. I say the gods, because I do not want to talk about the good God. I now know his vultures and have every respect for them' (quotation from SW XII, 222f.).

50. H. Heine, 'Ruhelechzend', in SW XI, 489.

51. Preisendanz, *Heinrich Heines Dichtertum* (n.36), 20.

52. I have written at length on the work of Elie Wiesel and especially on *The Schamgorod Trial* in W. Gross and K.-J. Kuschel, *'Ich schaffe Finsternis und Unheil!' Ist Gott verantwortlich für das Übel?*, Mainz ²1995, C III, on talk of 'God's guilt' as a rejection of theodicy. See R. Boschki, *Der Schrei. Gott und Mensch im Werk von Elie Wiesel*, Theologie und Literatur III, ed. K. J. Kuschel, Mainz 1994. There are also important studies of theological reception in D. Mensink and R. Boschki (eds.), *Das Gegenteil von Gleichgültigkeit ist Erinnerung. Versuche zu Elie Wiesel*, Mainz 1995. The American Jewish theologian, D. Blumenthal, *Facing the Abusing God. A Theology of Protest*, Louisville, Ky 1993, has taken up and radicalized Wiesel's theology of protest. I can only refer to this important work here; a thorough evaluation and critical discussion will follow in the study announced in n.6.

53. E. Wiesel, *All Rivers Run to the Sea*, New York 1996, 85.

54. E. Wiesel, *Der Prozess von Schamgorod. Ein Stück in drei Akten*, Freiburg 1987.

55. Thus the author himself at a conference of the Protestant Academy at Loccum in May 1986. This is documented in E. Wiesel, 'Die politisch-moralische Aufgabe des

Schriftstellers heute. Nach Auschwitz haben die Worte ihre Unschuld verloren', in *Erinnerung als Gegenwart. Elie Wiesel in Loccum*, Loccumer Protokolle 25, 1986, 118–19.

56. Wiesel, *Der Prozess* (n.54), 41, 42.

57. Ibid., 90.

58. Ibid., 98.

59. Ibid., 117.

60. Ibid., 117f.

61. Thus in *Erinnerung als Gegenwart* (n.55), 118.

62. See n.6.

63. For more recent debate on the relationship between the Old Testament and the New cf. E. Zenger, *Das Erste Testament. Die jüdische Bibel und die Christen*, Düsseldorf 1991; id. (ed.), *Der Neue Bund im Alten. Studien zur Bundestheologie der beiden Testamente*, Freiburg im Breisgau 1993. There is a thematic volume *Alter Bund – Neuer Bund* in the *Tübinger Theologische Quartalschrift* 176, 1996, Vol.4 (see especially the contributions by W. Gross and M. Theobald).

64. Cf. the comprehensive study by G. Langenhorst, *Hiob unser Zeitgenosse. Die literarische Hiob-Rezeption im 20.Jahrhundert als theologische Herausforderung*, Theologie und Literatur I, ed. K.-J. Kuschel, Mainz 1994.

65. Thus, in his very precise analysis of this psalm, W. Gross, 'Ein Schwerkranker betet. Psalm 88 als Paradigma', in G. Fuchs (ed.), *Angesichts des Leids an Gott glauben? Zur Theologie der Klage*, Frankfurt am Main 1996, 101–18: 112.

66. E. Wiesel, *Célébration talmudique. Portraits et légendes*, 1991, German *Die Weisheit des Talmud, Geschichten und Portraits*, Freiburg im Breisgau 1992, 182.

67. Ibid., 184.

68. Ibid., 183.

69. Ibid., 193.

70. E. Wiesel, *Célébration hassidique* II, 1981, German (selection), *Geschichten gegen die Melancholie. Die Weisheit der chassidischen Meister*, Freiburg im Breisgau 1984, 78f.

71. Ibid., 80.

72. Ibid., 80f.

73. Ibid., 74.

74. Wiesel, *Célébration hassidique* I, 1972, German *Chassidische Feier*, Vienna 1974, 104.

75. Ibid., 106.

76. Ibid., 105.

77. Ibid., 106.

78. Z. Kolitz, *Jossel Rakovers Wendung zu Gott*, Möhlin-Villingen 1994 (translated from the Yiddish by B. Badde). For the history of this story see the thoroughly researched introduction by B. Badde (11–39). The Jewish philosopher E. Lévinas, who also comes from Lithuania, describes this story as a 'beautiful and true' text in 'Die Thora mehr lieben als Gott', in id., *Schwierige Freiheit. Versuch über das Judentum*, Frankfurt am Main 1992, 109–13.

79. Kolitz, *Jossel Rakovers Wendung zu Gott* (n.78), 52f.

80. Ibid., 62f.

81. Ibid., 54.

82. Ibid., 66f.

83. Ibid., 63f.

84. Lévinas, 'Die Thora mehr lieben als Gott' (n.78), 110f.

85. Ibid., 112f.

86. Kolitz, *Jossel Rakovers Wendung zu Gott* (n.78), 71f.

87. K. Rahner, 'Erfahrungen eines katholischen Theologen', in K. Lehmann (ed.), *Vor dem Geheimnis Gottes den Menschen verstehen. Karl Rahner zum 80.Geburtstag*, Munich and Zurich 1984, 105–16: 106f.

88. Ibid., 108f.

89. M. Frisch, *Tagebuch 1946–1949*, in GW II/2 (1944–1949), Frankfurt am Main 1976, 378f.

90. F. Stier, *Vielleicht ist irgendwo Tag. Aufzeichnungen*, Freiburg im Bresigau 1981, 82.

91. Cf. the article 'Abgrund', in *Historisches Wörterbuch der Philosophie* I, ed. J. Ritter, Darmstadt 1971, 5.

92. Meister Eckhart, Predigt 13, in id., *Deutsche Predigten und Traktate*, edited and translated by J. Quint, Munich ³1969, 213f.

93. *Die Predigten Taulers*, ed. F. Vetter, Berlin 1910, Predigt 67 (p.368, line 14); Predigt 52 (239 line 4); Predigt 45 (201, lines 4–6).

94. K. Rahner, 'Gott ist keine mathematische Formel', in id., *Gnade als Freiheit. Kleine theologische Beiträge*, Freiburg im Breisgau 1968, 19–23: 20.

95. E. Jüngel, 'Die Offenbarung der Verborgenheit Gottes. Ein Beitrag zum evangelischen Verständnis der Verborgenheit des göttlichen Wirkens', in Lehmann (ed.), *Vor dem Geheimnis Gottes* (n.87), 79–104: 85f. Also in id., *Wertlose Wahrheit. Zur Identität und Relevanz des christlichen Glaubens*, Munich 1990, 163–82: 168f. Jüngel's early article, '*Quae supra nos, nihil ad nos*. Eine Kurzformel der Lehre vom verborgenen Gott – in Anschluss an Luther interpretiert', in id., *Entsprechungen: Gott – Wahrheit – Mensch*, Munich 1980, 202–51, moves in the same direction.

96. K. Rahner, 'Sorge der Kirche für das Leben des Glaubens heute', in *Handbuch der Pastoraltheologie. Praktische Theologie der Kirche in ihrer Gegenwart*, III, ed. F. X. Arnold et al., Freiburg im Bresigau 1968, 521. This element of doubt as the legitimate downside of faith has recently been worked out well again by the young Tübingen theologian D. Steinfort, 'Dank an Pfarrer Matull. Ein Gespräch uber Glaube und Zweifel zwischen Günter Grass, D. Bonhoeffer und Karl Rahner', *Geist und Leben* 86, 1996, 327–37. A very early writing, *Von der Not und Segen des Gebetes*, Freiburg im Breisgau 1958, ⁷1965, especially the chapter on 'The Prayer of Need', documents that Karl Rahner was one of the first Catholic theologians of this century who dared to allow elements of complaint and accusation as legitimate elements in the relationship to God.

97. Rahner, 'Sorge der Kirche' (n.97), 522.

98. Ibid., 525.

99. J. B. Metz, 'Gotteskrise. Versuch zur "geistigen Situation der Zeit"', in id. et al. (eds), *Diagnosen zur Zeit*, Düsseldorf 1994, 84f.

100. G. Janosch, *Gespräche mit Kafka. Aufzeichnungen und Erinnerungen*, Fischer TB 5093, Frankfurt am Main 1968, 184. The sentence in italics is my addition.

C. Faces of Jesus

1. H. Heine, *Deutschland. A Winter's Tale* (1844), translated with an introduction and notes by T. J. Reed, London 1986, 57f.

2. H. Heine. 'Zur Geschichte der Religion und Philosophie in Deutschland', in *Sämtliche Schriften in 12 Bänden*, ed. K. Breigleb, V, Munich 1976, 562.

3. H. Heine, *Ludwig Börne. Eine Denkschrift*, SW VII, 41.

4. Heine, 'Zur Geschichte der Religion' (n.2), 516.

5. Ibid.

6. Ibid., 517.

7. W. Schnurre, 'Gott im Termitengehirn? Fragen an einen Atheisten', in K.-J. Kuschel, *Weil wir uns auf dier Erde nicht ganz zu Hause fühlen. Zwölf Schriftsteller über Religion und Literatur*, Munich 1985, 96.

8. K. Strick, 'Jesus, die Ketzer und das Rufen nach Gott. Über Religion, Liebe und die Erfahrung von Frauen von heute', in Kuschel, *Weil wir uns auf die Erde . . .* (n.7), 58f.

9. I. Drewitz, 'Prometheus, Jesus und der Mut zum Leben. Über Hoffnung, Zuversicht und Religion', in Kuschel, *Weil wir uns auf die Erde . . .* (n.7), 84.

10. A. Muschg, 'Podiumsdiskussion: Ist "Gott" heute literarisch darstellbar?', in *Theologie und Literatur. Zum Stand des Dialogs*, ed. W. Jens, H. Küng and K.-J. Kuschel, Munich 1986, 250.

11. The most comprehensive collection of Christmas texts has been made by W. Jens (ed.), *Es begibt sich aber zu den Zeit. Texte zur Weihnachtsgeschichte*, Stuttgart 1988.

12. C. F. Gellert, 'Weihnachtslied' (1757), in *Werke*, ed G. Honnefelder, I, Frankfurt am Main 1979, 258f.

13. J. von Eichendorff, 'Weihnachten' (1837), in *Werke in sechs Banden, I (Gedichte – Versepen)*, ed. H. Schulz, Bibliothek deutscher Klassiker 21, Frankfurt am Main 1987.

14. The most thorough study has been made by W. Mezger, *Sankt Nikolaus. Zwischen Kult und Klamauk*, Ostfildern 1993.

15. T. Storm, 'Unter dem Tannenbaum' (1862), in *Sämtliche Werke in zwei Bänden*, Munich 1967, I, 326–49.

16. Ibid., 339.

17. Ibid.

18. T. Mann, *Buddenbrooks*, London 1924.The Christmas scene, described in Part 8 Chapter 8, is here on pp. 426–43.

19. K. Tucholsky, 'Weihnachten' (1918), in *Gedichte*, ed. M. Gerold-Tucholsky, Hamburg 1983, 147.

20. E. Kästner, 'Weihnachtslied, chemisch gereinigt' (1928), in *Gesammelte Schriften für Erwachsene I (Gedichte)*, Zurich 1969, 94f.

21. I Aichinger, *Die grössere Hoffnung* (1948), Frankfurt am Main 1974. For interpretation cf. K.-J. Kuschel, *Jesus in der deutschsprachigen Gegenwartsliteratur*, Zurich and Gütersloh 1978, 273–6; D. C. G. Lorenz, *Ilse Aichinger*, Königstein im Taunus 1981, 60–76; S. Moser (ed.), *Ilse Aichinger. Materialien zu Leben und Werk*, Frankfurt am Main 1990 (with a documentation of important reviews of *Die grössere Hoffnung*, 129–49).

22. Aichinger, *Die grössere Hoffnung* (n.21), 108.

23. Ibid.,135.

24. P. Huchel, 'Dezember 1942', in id., *Chausseen, Chausseen. Gedichte,* Frankfurt am Main 1963, 64. For interpretation cf. K-J. Kuschel, *Jesus in der deutschsprachigen Gegenwartsliteratur,* XIII-XV (Foreword by W. Jens) and 268–73.

25. H. Böll, 'So ward Abend und Morgen' (1954), in id., *Als der Krieg ausbrach. Erzählungen,* Munich 1965, 95–103.

26. Ibid., 97.

27. Ibid., 102f.

28. It will not escape the attentive reader that the Jesus novels which follow represent the type of indirect portrayal of Jesus which transfigures him: Jesus, reflected in representative figures from the contemporary context. Great literature, indeed world literature, has produced only this literary type in our century. However, another literary type of less aesthetic importance is still popular: the direct or indirect depiction of Jesus in the historicizing and psychologizing novel. Here Jesus is described either directly (as a literary 'hero'), or indirectly (from the perspective of mirror figures) in the context of *his* time. The archetype of this genre is Ernest Renan's *Life of Jesus* (1862). It is also present in a way which transcends cultures in novels from Italy (G. Papini, *Life of Christ,* 1924), Sweden (P. Lagerquist, *Barabbas,* 1950), Poland (J. Dobraczynski, *Gib mir deine Sorgen,* 1954), Greece (N. Kazantzakis, *The Last Temptation*) and Portugal (J. Saramago, *The Gospel of Jesus Christ,* 1993) as well as Germany (M. Brod, *Der Meister,* 1952; G. Fussenegger, *Sie waren Zeitgenossen,* 1983; L. Rinser, *Mirjam,* 1983). For a literary and theological discussion of these novels cf. T. Ziolkowski, *Fictional Transfigurations of Jesus,* Princeton 1972; K.-J. Kuschel, *Jesus in der deuschsprachigen Gegenwartsliteartur,* Zurich and Gütersloh 1978 (pocket book edition with a postscript by the author, Munich 1987); G. Langenhorst, 'Die literarische Wiederentdecking Jesu in Romanen der achtziger Jahre', *Stimmen der Zeit* 210, 1992, 751–60; 819–30.

29. J. Stern, 'Das Floss der Anna Seghers', in S. Hilzinger (ed.), *Das siebte Kreuz von Anna Seghers. Texte, Daten, Bilder,* Frankfurt am Main 1990, 10–14. More recent biographical and bibliographical introductions are: K. Sauer, *Anna Seghers,* Autorenbücher 9, Munich 1978; C. Zehl Romero, *Anna Seghers mit Selbstzeugnissen und Bilddokumenten,* Hamburg 1993.

30. A. Seghers, 'Rede auf dem Ersten Internationalen Schriftstellerkongress' (1935), in Hitzinger (ed.), *Das siebte Kreuz* (n.29), 52.

31. A. Seghers, 'Sechs Tage, sechs Jahre! Tagebuchseiten', in ibid., 58.

32. C. Wolf, 'Glauben an Irdisches' (1968), in ead, *Die Dimension des Autors. Essays und Aufsätze, Reden und Gespräche 1958–1985,* Darmstadt and Neuwied 1987, 300. The other essays on Anna Seghers in this volume, 255–377, are also worth noting.

33. A. Seghers, *Das siebte Kreuz,* Darmstadt and Neuwied 1973, 57f. (pocket book edition). I have given a first interpretation in Kuschel, *Jesus in der deutschsprachigen Gegenwartsliteratur* (n.28), 136–44.

34. Zehl Romero, *Anna Seghers* (n.29), 66.

35. Seghers, *Das siebte Kreuz* (n.33), 7.

36. Ibid., 288.

37. M. Reich-Ranicki, 'Die Kraft der Schwachen. Zum 80. Geburtstag von Anna Seghers', *Frankfurter Allgemeine Zeitung*, 15 November 1980. After the 'change', the same critic once again wrote on Anna Seghers and her novel *The Seventh Cross*, 'from the present situation'. Though critical of Anna Seghers' passive role in the political trials in the German Democratic Republic in the 1950s, Reich-Ranicki nevertheles comes to the conclusion: 'In the meantime *The Seventh Cross* has lost little of its evocativeness. Certainly the book is no longer as exciting as it used to be, but one still marvels at the sovereignty and also the undoubted virtuosity of a narrative which combines the traditional means of expression and modern techniques of composition in a most happy way. Whatever we feel about Anna Seghers in the future will not affect our gratitude for her best books' (*Frankfurter Allgemeine Zeitung*, 21 July 1990).

38. L. Wolf, 'Sie schrieb und schrieb', in Hilzinger (ed.), *Das siebte Kreuz* (n.29), 107.

39. Cf. C. Wolf, 'Ein Gespräch mit Anna Segers', in ead., *Die Dimension des Autors* (n.32), 285; cf. also 306–8.

40. W. Faulkner, letter to Robert K. Haas of 15 January 1944, in *Selected Letters of William Faulkner*, ed. J. Blottner, New York 1977, 180.

41. For the reception see S. B. Oates, *William Faulkner, His Life and Work* Similarly S. Opfermann, *Der Mythos der Neuen Welt im Amerikanischen Europa-Roman*, Erlangen 1985, 127–217 (with bibliography).

42. Cf. Opfermann, *Der Mythos der Neuen Welt* (n.42), 135–42.

43. W. Faulkner, *A Fable*, New York 1954, 370.

44. H. Straumann, *William Faulkner*, Frankfurt am Main and Bonn 1968, 263f.

45. T. Ziolkowski, *Fictional Transfigurations of Jesus*, Princeton 1972, 179.

46. Ibid., 177.

47. W. Grenzmann, 'Nobelpreisträger William Faulkner. Sein Weg und seine Dichtung', *Universitas* 14, 1959, 909–20: 918.

48. W. von Einsiedel, 'Revolte des Menschensohnes. Zu W. Faulkners Eine Legend', *Merkur* 10, 1956, 282–90: 287. D. Sölle, 'Ein Beispiel für Realisation: William Faulkner, A Fable', in ead., *Das Eis der Seele spalten. Theologie und Literatur in sprachloser Zeit*, Mainz 1996, 22–34, has interpreted this novel from a more recent theological perspective (originally this chapter was part of the book *Realisation*, Darmstadt 1973).

49. Faulkner, *A Fable* (n.43), 294.

50. H. Blumenberg, 'Mythos und Ethos Amerkas im Werk William Faulkners', *Hochland* 50, 157/58, 234–50: 248.

51. E. Franzen, 'William Faulkners puritanischer Mythus', *Merkur* 5, 1951, 629–41: 638.

52. U. Brumm, *Die religiöse Typologie im amerikanischen Denken. Ihre Bedeutung für die amerikanische Literatur- und Geistesgeschichte*, Leiden 1963, 178.

53. W. Faulkner, 'Address to the Graduation Class of the University High School in Oxford, Mississippi' (28 May 1951), in *Essays, Speeches, Public Letters by William Faulkner*, ed. J. B. Meriwether, New York 1965, 122–4: 123.

54. W. Faulkner, 'Address upon Receiving the Nobel Prize for Literature' (Stockholm, December 10, 1950), in ibid., 119–21: 120.

55. For the interpretation of the work of N. Mahfouz, cf. M. Peled, *Religion, My*

Own. The Literary Works of N. Mahfous, New Brunswick and London 1983; H. Fähndrich, 'Ein erzählerisches Werk aus Kairos Quartieren', *Neue Züricher Zeitung*, 7/8 January 1989; id., *Nagib Machfus*, Munich 1991 (with bibliography); M. Beard and A. Haydar (eds.), *N. Mahfouz: From Regional Fame to Global Recognition*, Syracuse 1993. For the novel *Children of Our Alley* cf. especially H. Kiesel, 'Brudermord, Streit. Machfus' Roman über die Religionen', *Frankfurter Allegemeine Zeitung*, 2 October 1990; H. Fähndrich, 'Politisches und Religiöses bei N. Machfus', *Neue Züricher Zeitung*, 3 December 1990; J. C. Bürgel, 'Gott ist tot auf ägyptisch. N. Machfus' Roman *Die Kinder unseres Viertels*', in id., *Allmacht und Machtigkeit. Religion und Welt im Islam*, Munich 1991, 351–3; S. G. Smith, 'Abraham's Family in "Children of Gebelaawi"', *Literature and Theology* 11, 1997, 168–84.

56. Thus the journalist H. Mosbahi, who comes from Tunisia and lives in Germany: 'Die Kunst ist Phantasie und Vorstellung. Die Welt des Nagib Machfus', *Frankfurter Alegmeine Zeitung*, 19 November 1988.

57. Cf. H. Fähndrich, 'Die Beunruhigung des Nobelpreisträgers', *Neue Züricher Zeitung*, 28 April 1998. Similarly D. Kilias, postscript to N. Machfus, *Die Kinder unseres Viertels*, Zurich 1990, 563–72.

58. N. Mahfouz, *Awlad Haratina* (1959), English translation *Children of the Alley*, by Peter Theroux, New York 1996, 178.

59. Ibid., 204.

60. Ibid.,249f.

61. Fähndrich, *Nagib Machfus* (n.55), 104.

62. Mahfouz, *Children of the Alley* (n.58), 448. Granted, in some passages in this last decisive Chapter 114 the prospects of the religions are depicted in the darkest colours ('To see the estate, its conditions and the words of Gabal, Rifaa and Qassem as wasted dreams, good only to accompany poets' melodies, not for anything else in this life', 445), and the preference is apparently given to science and technology ('And if we had to choose between Gabalawi and magic, we'd choose magic', 448: or, 'They lifted up his [Arafa's] name even above the names of Gabal, Rifaa and Qassem', 560), but this must not in any way be confused with the view of the narrator of the novel or even the author. A clumsy criticism that Mahfouz wrote this novel because he wanted to replace the religions by science and technology suppresses the different narrative perspectives. (In the otherwise good book by N. Peled [n.55], this problem is discussed, but too little attention is paid to the literary and aesthetic dimension of the narrative structure of the last chapter in particular, cf. 170–83, 184–96). All the statements in the last chapter are explicitly given as people's opinions, as ways in which people react in the alley, of which there are many. Here Mahfouz proves not to be a simple propagandist for science, but a subtle expert in human nature who knows the hopes on which people rely and the promises they follow. So the closing sentences of the novel are not to be read cynically but humorously and ironically. They show that people need little, indeed that they even trust a rumour (the rumour that the book of science was rescued from Hanash's rubbish heap), to maintain their hope.

63. N. Machfus, 'Rede anlässlich der Verleihung des Nobelpreises für Literatur' (1988), in H. Fähndrich, *Nagib Machfus*, Munich 1991, 150–4: 154.

64. A. Roa Bastos, *Hijo de Hombre* (1960), German *Menschensohn*, translated from the Paraguayan Spanish by C. Meyer-Clason, Munich and Vienna 1991, Fischer TB 11600, Frankfurt am Main 194, 84.

65. Surveys of the work are offered by R. Bariero Saguier, 'Augusto Roa Bastos und die zeitgenössische Erzählkunst Paraguays', in *Lateinamerikanische Literatur*, ed. M. Strausfeld, Frankfurt am Main 1989, 167–83. For the novel *Son of Man* in particular see L. Pollmann, 'Die Sprache des Mythos. Zur "musikalischen" Komposition von Roa Bastos' Hijo de Hombre', in G. Ernst and A. Stefenelli (eds.), *Sprache und Mensch in der Romania. H. Kuen zum 80.Geburtstag*, Wiesbaden 1979, 117–26; W. Lustig, *Christliche Symbolik und Christentum im spanischsprachigen Roman des 20.Jahrhunderts*, Frankfurt am Main 1989, Chapter 9, 'Hijo de Hombre: Die Prophetie eines lateinamerikanischen Christentums' (416–91). Here there is also a discussion with criticism in the Spanish language; G. Schüler, 'Religion und Mythos in "Hijo de Hombre" of Augusto Roa Bastos', in C. Wentzlaff Eggebert (ed.), *Realität und Mythos in der lateinamerikanischen Literatur*, Cologne and Vienna 1989, 265–76. German reviews worth noting were published in the *Frankfurter Allgemeine Zeitung*, 21 October 1991 (H. Brode); *Frankfurter Rundschau*, 16 November 1991 (W. Matz); and *Süddeutsche Zeitung* 6 May 1992 (H.-J. Schmitt).

66. Lustig, *Christliche Symbolik* (n.65), 422–3, puts the novel in the context of its work, time and the history of its reception.

67. Roa Bastos, *Menschensohn* (n.64), 26.

68. Ibid., 33.

69. Ibid., 41.

70. Ibid.

71. Ibid., 63.

72. Ibid., 96.

73. Thus G. Schüler, 'Religion und Mythos' (n.65), 272f.; cf. also Lustig, *Christliche Symbolik* (n.65), 441.

74. Roa Bastos, *Menschensohn* (n.64), 331.

75. Thus Bariero Saguier, *Augusto Roa Bastos* (n.65), 174.

76. Quoted from ibid.

77. Thus again ibid.

78. For the New Testament Son of Man tradition in the context of contemporary research cf. K.-J. Kuschel, *Born Before all Time? The Dispute over Christ's Origin*, London 1992, 228–36.

79. W. Lustig has convincingly interpreted this novel as an artistic anticipation of the later programme of Latin American liberation theology and said of the theology of this book which was written before the council (!): 'To sum up, one can say that the "theology of *The Son of Man*" remains relatively true to its Christian roots. It merely places some accents which at the end of the 1950s inevitably seemed revolutionary and heretical. Conceptually, Roa maintains the central Christian statements of faith. His reinterpretation differs radically from the perspective normally to be found in the popular church of Latin America. Nevertheless there is in no way an *inversión de la fe*, but a *reorientación de la fe*, in the direction of the historical and social existence of human beings. At any rate, the orientation on this world is not heretical – one can understand it as an anticipation of *aggiornamento*' (*Christliche Symbolik* [n.65], 483).

80. Roa Bastos, *Menschensohn*, 362.

81. C. Ajmatov, *Plakha* (1986), German *Der Richtplatz*, translated from the Russian by F. Hitzer, Zurich 1987. There are surveys of the work in J. Gutschke,

Menschheitsfragen, Märchen, Mythen. Zum Schaffen C. Ajmatovs, Halle and Leipzig ²1986; O. Schwenke (ed.), *Richtplatz Literatur. Ajmatov in Loccum*, Loccumer Protokolle 16, 1988; B. Clebnikov and N. Franz, *Cingiz Ajmatov*, Munich 1993; J. P. Mozur, Jr, *Parables from the Past. The Prose Fiction of Cinghiz Ajmatov*, Pittsburgh and London 1995 (with bibliography). For the novel *The Place of Execution* in particular see C. Ajmatov, 'Der Widerhall unseres Wortes, Gespräch mit N. Anastasjew' (1987), in id., *Karawane des Gewissens. Autobiographie, Literatur, Politik*, ed. F. Hitzer, translated from the Russian by F. Hitzer and C. Kossuth, 224–64; S. Kleinmichel, 'Annäherung an das Wesen der heutigen Welt. Ajmatovs Roman "Die Richtstatt"', *Weimarer Beiträge* 34, 1988, 615–25; A. Latchinian, 'Der Mensch als Richter und Schöpfer. Ajmatovs Roman "Die Richtstatt"', *Weimarer Beiträge* 34, 1988, 626–40; J. P. Mozur, Jr, 'C. Ajmatov's *Plakha*: A New Religion for Soviet Man?', in *Studies in Comparative Communism* 21, 1988, 263–73; A. Olcott, 'What Faith the God-Contemporary? C. Ajmatov's *Plakha*', *Slavic Review* 49, 1990, 213–26; N. Kolesnikoff, 'The Polyphony of Narrative Voices in *Plakha*', *Russian Literature* 28, 1990, 33–44; N. Franz, 'Vom Logos zum Mythos. Die Christusfigur in C. Ajmatovs Roman "Plakha"', in *Neueste Tendenzen in der Entwicklung der russischen Literatur und Sprache*, ed E. Wedel, Hamburg 1992, 23–38.

82. The social and religious-political significance of the novel in the context of Perestroika is well illustrated by Mozur, 'Ajmatov's "Plakha"' (n.82), Chapter 7, 'Soviet Society at the Crossroads: "New Thinking" and "The Place of the Skull".

83. Mikhail Bulgakov's (1891–1940) novel *The Master and Margarita* (written between 1928 and 1940) is a milestone in the history of Russian literature; indeed it is a piece of world literature. This novel caused a literary sensation when it was first published posthumously in 1966/1967. There is an English translation by M. Glenny, London 1967. Cf. Chapter 2, devoted to Jesus and Pilate ('Pontius Pilate'), Chapter 16 ('The Execution') and Chapter 25 ('How the Procurator attempted to Rescue Judas from Kiriath').

84. Cf. the different autobiographical testimonies: C. Ajmatov, *Karawane des Gewissens*, Zurich 1988. Similarly id., *Friedrich Rückert – Vorläufer einer neuen Zeit*, ceremonial lecture for the tenth award of the Friedrich Rückert Prize of the city of Schweinfurt, ed. W. Fischer, Würzburg 1994.

85. Quoted from Clebnikov and Franz, *Cinghiz Ajmatov* (n.81), 135.

86. Quoted from Franz, 'Vom Logos zum Mythos' (n.81), 23. Originally as an answer to questions in an interview with I. Risia, *Literatrunaja gazeta* 33 (13 August), 1986, 4.

87. Cf. R. Schmitz, 'Das Kreuz in der Savanne Mujun-Kum', *Die Welt*, 20 November 1987; A. Braun, 'Vom Wolf im Menschen', *Stuttgarter Zeitung* 16 January 1988; P. Wilke, 'Sie wollen alle nur das Beste', *Unsere Zeit* (literature magazine), Düsseldorf, October 1987.

88. S. Brandt, 'Ein Narr unter Wölfen', *Frankfurter Allgemeine Zeitung*, 17 November 1987.

89. Ajmatov, *Der Richtplatz*, 197–328.

90. Ibid., 239–51.

91. Ibid., 240.

92. Ibid., 298f.

93. Cf. the critical discussion about the role of religion in the novel in the context of the Soviet society of the time in Mozur, *Parables from the Past* (n.81), 240–52.

94. Ajmatov, *Der Richtplatz*, 244.

95. Quoted in Clebnikov and Franz, *Cinghiz Ajmatov* (n.81), 136.

96. Ajmatov made this comment on his relationship to Bulgakov in a conversation with N. Anastasjev: 'Of course I understood that; I saw very well how risky it is to take the way which was once taken by so revered a writer as Mikhail Bulgakov, whom I respect so highly. Nevertheless I could not give up what I in particular needed. Moreover I wanted to arrange the figures differently. It is for others to judge whether I have succeeded. In the case of Bulgakov it is uncertain who is portrayed in the stronger terms, Jeshua or Pontius Pilate.' *Anastasjev*: 'Who should be the stronger? Both are depicted strongly.' *Ajmatov*: 'But it seems to me that in *The Master and Margarita* Pilate puts Jesus somewhat in the shade; Jesus is somewhat monotone against the background of the personality of the procurator with its inner tensions. Moreover, perhaps that is what Bulgakov wanted. However, I have had to bring Jesus to the centre and make him the central figure' (in *Karawane de Gewissens* [n.84], 235f.)

97. C. Ajmatov, *Der Richtplatz*, 228, 229f.

98. Ibid., 225.

99. Ibid., 225f.

100. Ibid., 226.

101. Franz, 'Vom Logos zum Mythos' (n.81), succumbs to this danger when he dismisses Ajmatov's picture of Jesus too coolly with references to dogmatics: 'In such a view of history Jesus Christ merely has the function of an example who serves people as a task. Thus the historic significance of the incarnation, to which the Western church and others attempted to do justice by attaching the zero point in history to him, falls away. The central concern of Christianity, the doctrine of redemption *in* – not *from* – history remains in the conception developed in the *Plakha*. The same thing happens with the reformulation of the picture of God by Jesus Christ and the question of the Spirit and the church. Here too the Jesus of the novel is not the Christ believed in by Christians. The Jesus figure lacks all basic features of a theology of history, as if the Jesus chapter is incoporated into the stories in the novel. Thus the divine Logos becomes a voluntary myth' (32). Virtually everything is wrong in this criticism – in both literary and theological terms. As I have shown, the Jesus chapters are incorporated into the novel, and Ajmatov's understanding of Jesus – for all the difference from an Orthodox soteriology – in no way rests on an unhistorical myth. In this novel Ajmatov thinks completely in terms of a theology of history, indeed eschatologically, when he understands the liberation of human beings for goodness and beauty as a process immanent in history which has its goal in Jesus Christ, and which at the same time is driven forward by the Spirit of Christ from within people. Expressed in theological terminology, in this novel Ajmatov does not put forward a christology 'from above' but a christology 'from within', not so much a christology in the spirit of dogma as a christology in the spirit of spirituality and mysticism.

102. Cf. Ajmatov, *Der Richtplatz*, 59–126. In the argument with the Father Co-ordinator the dogmatism of the Russian Orthodox Church is vigorously criticized – very much in line with Tolstoy's criticism of the church – and the way is prepared for Avdi Kallistratov's picture of God and human beings later.

103. J. P. Mozur, 'Cingiz Ajmatovs "Plakha"' (n.81), 263–73, has drawn parallels with the thought-world of the famous Russian philosopher of religion N. Berdyaev.

104. A. Olcott, 'What Faith the God-Contemporary?' (n.81), has attempted to demonstrate influences of Islam on Ajmatov's depiction of Jesus. In view of a weak religious socialization in Islam which Ajmatov himself concedes, and the influence of the Bible at the time of the composition of the novel, I think this reconstruction improbable. At any rate it is not attested anywhere.

105. Ajmatov, *Der Richtplatz*, 243.

106. Ibid., 247.

107. Ajmatov's perspectives on world politics and world religion have been developed further above all in the impressive book of conversations, C. Ajmatov and D. Ikeda, *Begegnung am Fudschijama. Ein Dialog*, German translation from the Russian by F. Hitzer, Zurich 1992. Cf also Ajmatov's speech on receiving the Friedrich Rückert Prize (n.84).

108. No. 823 in the diocesan appendix to *Gotteslob* for the diocese of Rottenburg-Stuttgart.

109. F. G. Klopstock, *Der Messias*, in *Ausgewählte Werke* I, ed. K. A. Schleiden, Munich and Vienna 1991, 195–770.

110. P. Rühmkorf, 'Friedrich Gottlieb Klopstock. Ein empfindsamer Revolutionär', in id., *Walther von der Vogelweide, Klopstock und ich*, Hamburg 1975, 79–119: 86.

111. F. G. Klopstock, 'Von der heiligen Poesie', in *Ausgewählte Werke* II, ed. K. A. Schleiden, Munich and Vienna 1981, 997–1009: 998, 1001.

112. Quotations are from Goethe, *Faust I & II*, Volume 2 of the Collected Works, edited and translated by Stuart Atkins, Princeton 1994. Cf. the commentaries by E. Trunz, *in Goethes Faust. Der Tragödie erster und zweiter Teil. Urfaust*, Hamburg 1968, 504–6; A. Schöne, in *Johann Wolfgang Goethe, Faust. Kommentare*, Bibliothek deutscher Klassiker 114, Frankfurt am Main 1994, 226–9; H. Arens, *Kommentar zu Goethes Faust* I, Heidelberg 1982.

113. Arens, *Kommentar zu Goethes Faust* I (n.112), 117f., 120.

114. J. W. Goethe, 'Venezianische Epigramme' (posthumous), in *Sämtliche Werke in 40 Bänden, I,I (Gedichte 1756–1799)*, ed. E. Eibl, Bibliothek deutscher Klassiker Frankfurt am Main 1987, 467.

115. Leo Tolstoy, *Voskresnie (1899)*, English translation by Louise Maude, *Resurrection*, Oxford 1916 reissued Oxford 1994, 473.

116. Ibid., 481.

117. Ibid., 149.

118. Ibid., 481.

119. Ibid.

120. *Graf Leo Tolstoj und der Heilige Synod*, German text by N. Syrkin, Berlin 1902, 13f.

121. Ibid., 30.

122. Ibid., 40f.

123. For the text of *The Meteor* I have kept to the 1978 'Vienna Version' which Dürrenmatt declared in 1980 to be 'valid as literature'.

124. Dürrenmatt, *Der Meteor* (n.123), 46.

125. Ibid., 8of.

126. Ibid., 23f.

127. Ibid., 94f. The layout is mine, for pragmatic reasons: italics, Friedli; normal type, Schwitter.

128. Mieth, 'Friedrich Dürrenmatts "Der Meteor"' (n.123), 134.

129. F. Dürrenmatt, '20 Punkte zum "Meteor"', in the appendix to the 1985 edition (n.123), 159–62.

130. F. Dürrenmatt, *Der Klassiker auf der Bühne (Gespräche 1961–1970)*, ed. H. L. Arnold, Zurich 1996, 202. Henceforth abbreviated as *Gespräche* I + page.

131. *Gespräche* I, 203.

132. Ibid., 105

133. Dürrenmatt, *Der Meteor*, 9of.

134. Ibid., 62.

135. *Gespräche* I, 212f.

136. F. Dürrenmatt, 'Sätze über das Theater' (1970), in *Theater. Essays und Reden, Werkausgabe in 30 Bänden*, XXIV, Zurich 1980, 176–211: 196f.

137. Dürrenmatt, '20 Punkte zum "Meteor"' (n.129), 161.

138. For a philosophical discussion of the problem of a deterministic or causal picture of the world cf. F. Dürrenmatt, 'Albert Einstein. Ein Vortrag' (1979), in id., *Philosophie und Naturwissenschaft. Essays und Reden, Werkausgabe XXVII*, Zurich 1980, 150–72; similarly the appendix, 175–201.

139. J. Kopf, *Friedrich Dürrenmatt*, Munich [4]1998·, 118f.

140. M. Frisch, *Tagebuch 1946–1949*, in *Gesammelte Weke in zeitlicher Folge* II,2, Frankfurt am Main 1976, 351.

141. J. Schröder, 'Spiel mit dem Lebenslauf. Das Drama Max Frischs', in W. Schmitz (ed.), *Über Max Frisch*, II, Frankfurt am Main 1976, 60.

142. Ibid., 65

143. W. Jens, 'Der Poet als Verräter', *Frankfurter Allgemeine Zeitung*, 9 May 1961.

144. M. Frisch, *Tagebuch 1946–1949* (n.140), 478.

145. Ibid.

146. Ibid., 469.

147. For a deeper treatment see K.-J. Kuschel, *Born Before All Time? The Dispute over Christ's Origin*, London and New York 1992.

148. W. Jens, 'Die Evangelisten als Schriftsteller', in id., *Republikanische Reden*, Munich 1976, 30.

149. Ibid., 33f.

Index

Passages where an author or work is discussed at length are indicated in **bold**.